Oxford University Press, Walton Street, Oxford OX2 6DP
Oxford New York Toronto
Delhi Bombay Calcutta Madras Karachi
Petaling Jaya Singapore Hong Kong Tokyo
Nairobi Dar es Salaam Cape Town
Melbourne Auckland
and associated companies in
Beirut Berlin Ibadan Nicosia

Oxford is a trade mark of Oxford University Press

Published in the United States
by Oxford University Press, New York

British Library Cataloguing in Publication Data
Regional problems, problem regions and public
policy in the UK.
1. Regional planning—Great Britain
2. Great Britain—Economic conditions
—1945- —Regional disparities
I. Damesick, P. J. II. Wood, P. A. (Peter A)
330.941'0858 HC256.6
ISBN 0–19–823257–8
ISBN 0–19–823256–X Pbk

Library of Congress Cataloging in Publication Data
Regional problems, problem regions, and public policy
in the UK.
Includes index.
1. Regional planning—Great Britain. 2. Urban
policy—Great Britain. 3. Great Britain—Economic
conditions—1945- . I. Damesick, P. II. Wood,
Peter Anthony
HT395.G7R444 1987 361.6'0941 86–31187
ISBN 0–19–823257–8
ISBN 0–19–823256–X (pbk.)

Set by Spire Print Services Limited
Printed and bound in Great Britain by
Biddles Ltd, Guildford and King's Lynn

CONTENTS

PREFACE

The period since the early 1970s has seen major changes in policy responses to problems of regional and urban development in the United Kingdom. In particular, the role of conventional regional policy has been called into question, with progressive reductions in both emphasis and expenditure on this form of intervention. At the same time, a variety of new area-based initiatives for economic development have been introduced by both central and local government. These shifts occurred in a period of rapid economic change during which the geography of growth and decline became more complex. Different parts of the country, including some which formerly had been regarded as relatively prosperous, experienced radical changes in their economic fortunes, leading to altered and more diverse views of the nature of 'regional problems and problem regions'. The last decade has also seen a transformation of the political climate within which questions about regional development and inequality are framed and debated.

Against this background, we believe that a volume which examines the present character of regional development problems in the UK and related public policy issues is both useful and timely. Most of the contributors to this volume were involved in an earlier inquiry into regional problems in the UK, carried out under the auspices of the Regional Studies Association. The report of that inquiry was published in 1983 as a contribution to the debate then taking place on the future direction of spatial policy. Events have since moved on, of course. As well as taking account of more recent developments and thinking, however, this volume has a different and wider purpose than that of the 1983 report. In particular, it aims to give expression to one of the most striking features of the evidence assembled during the RSA Inquiry, but inadequately reflected in the 1983 report: the wide diversity not only in the regional experience of economic change and policy impacts, but also in attitudes towards how central and local government should respond to regional and local economic problems. Any consensus which underlay thinking up to the mid-1970s had been dissipated by the 1980s.

This volume therefore combines discussion of regional development trends and policy changes at the national level with detailed evaluations of specific types of problems and policy approaches within particular regions. The first three chapters review the changing economic context for regional development since the 1960s, the main features of regional industrial and employment change, and the evolution of national spatial policy. There follows a series of chapters which consider the distinctive economic, environmental, and spatial planning problems in different regions of the UK, linked to discussion of the policy approaches that have been or might be adopted to tackle such problems. These regionally focused chapters do not follow a standard format or approach.

Contributors were encouraged to address the particular themes and issues that they found most pertinent to the region under consideration, thus highlighting the diversity of views which characterizes the debate over policy options. In the final chapter, the editors attempt to draw together a number of strands regarding regional problems and policies which emerge from the earlier contributions.

Our coverage of the UK regions is not comprehensive. The absence of contributions dealing specifically with the South West, East Midlands, or East Anglia is largely a function of the book's emphasis on 'regional problems and problem regions'. This is not to suggest that the problems of Devon and Cornwall, for example, are unimportant, or that the omitted regions do not offer interesting contrasts to certain 'problem regions' in containing areas of more favourable development trends, such as the Bristol and Cambridge subregions. It was decided, however, that the volume would focus on problems associated with decline in the country's major urban–industrial areas and with unbalanced intraregional development. These have been most prominent in recent policy debates, and have received more sustained research attention.

As editors, we should like to thank our contributors for their co-operation in this venture, for their positive responses to our suggestions for revisions, and in some cases for actually meeting the deadlines which we tried to set. We wish also to thank Simone Gatsky for drawing the maps and figures.

P. J. Damesick
P. A. Wood

LIST OF FIGURES

LIST OF TABLES

LIST OF CONTRIBUTORS

M. R. Bristow: School of Geography, University of Manchester.
P. J. Bull: Department of Geography, The Queen's University of Belfast.
R. J. Buswell: School of Geography and Environmental Studies, Newcastle upon Tyne Polytechnic.
A. G. Champion: Department of Geography, University of Newcastle upon Tyne.
P. N. Cooke: Department of Town Planning, University of Wales Institute of Science and Technology.
P. J. Damesick: Formerly Department of Geography, Birkbeck College, University of London. Coopers and Lybrand Associates Ltd.
P. Foley: Department of Town and Regional Planning, University of Sheffield.
D. H. Green: Department of Town Planning, Leeds Polytechnic.
M. Hart: Department of Environmental Studies, University of Ulster at Jordanstown.
M. Marshall: Formerly Economist, West Midlands County Council.
J. Mawson: Formerly Director of Economic Development, West Midlands County Council.
J. N. Randall: Formerly Economic Adviser, Industry Department for Scotland.
A. R. Townsend: Department of Geography, University of Durham.
P. A. Wood: Department of Geography, University College London.

CHAPTER 1

The Changing Economic Context for Regional Development in the United Kingdom

P. J. Damesick

Socially and spatially, the United Kingdom in the 1980s seems increasingly as if it might be more aptly named the Disunited Kingdom. Between the urban riots of 1981 and the bitter year-long miners' strike of 1984–5, the 'Falklands spirit' evaporated as quickly as it had materialized. With the number of unemployed at an all-time record, class divisions and inequalites in welfare and opportunity appear in sharper relief. There are glaring disparities in the health of different sectors of the economy—the buoyancy of the financial services sector, some branches of high-technology industry, and the tourist trade, for example, contrasts starkly with the recent devastation of much of the country's traditional manufacturing base and the beleaguered state of many public services. On both right and left of the political spectrum, attitudes have tended to polarize around positions outside the consensual 'middle ground' occupied by an earlier generation of governments and opposition parties. Central–local government relations are generally strained, reaching open conflict in several of the country's major cities.

The UK has also become more divided in geographical terms. Other aspects of disunity are both reflected in and partly shaped by the differences between such places as Hackney and Harrow, Cambridge and Consett, or Swindon and Strabane. Maps of change based upon the Censuses of Population and Employment 1971–81 highlight the crescent of growth in population and jobs from Norfolk to Hampshire and Dorset. Elsewhere in the country, the maps show some mainly rural outliers of expansion, and localized oil-based growth, of questionable durability, in north east Scotland. The differential regional impact of recession and job loss has been 'a tale of two nations'—North and South (Martin 1982). Hall (1981: 537) has gone so far as to assert that 'Britain's future, if it has one, is in that broad belt that runs through Oxford and Winchester through Milton Keynes to Cambridge'. Some among the high proportion (40 per cent or more) of the unemployed in the northern conurbations who have been out of work for over twelve months might readily agree that the future does not lie in their area.

Geographical disparities in economic health within the UK are not, of course, new; nor is government intervention ostensibly to promote a more balanced pattern of regional development. If the ultimate purpose of such intervention is to help keep the United Kingdom united, however, then it is perhaps at first sight surprising that, in terms of its level of funding and the absence of location controls on employment, regional policy in the mid-1980s is at its weakest for over twenty years.

Throughout its fifty-year history in the UK, the fortunes of regional policy have waxed and waned with changing political perceptions of its role and value, notably the degree to which it has been seen by governments as consistent with their macroeconomic objectives. Such perceptions are themselves, of course, strongly influenced by the broader economic context in which policy must operate, and it is clear that this context has changed markedly over time. The 1970s saw the emergence of a growing challenge to the regional policy approach inspired originally by the Barlow Commission's Report of 1940 and fashioned into its most active form in the 1960s. By the 1970s it was widely perceived that the circumstances confronting this policy had changed in certain fundamental respects, including the nature of spatial economic problems. Against this background, considerable debate took place over the appropriate form of regional policy to meet these changed circumstances. This first chapter examines the context of that debate in the UK since the 1960s.

After the long boom: industrial decline and mass unemployment

Unemployment has always been central to the rationale for regional policy. A critical change in the 1970s was the emergence of a generalized unemployment problem, which tended to overshadow regional imbalances in job opportunities, as labour shortages disappeared even in the more prosperous regions formerly considered to be experiencing excess pressure of demand. For some twenty years after the Second World War, the national unemployment rate ranged between 1 and 2.5 per cent. Against this background, the National Economic Development Council argued in 1963 that the 'social' problem of above average levels of unemployment in certain regions could also be interpreted as a valuable national resource in the shape of labour reserves. The use of such reserves, by diverting labour demand from regions of 'overfull' employment, could thus help in the achievement of faster growth in national output without unacceptable inflation. The persuasiveness of this argument must be seen in the light of governments' general concern in the early to mid-1960s with labour supply constraints on national growth, and particularly the view that one reason for Britain's relatively slow postwar growth, compared with other West European countries, was the lack of a significant labour reserve in agriculture capable of absorption into the higher-productivity manufacturing sector (Kaldor 1966). This view underlay the Labour Government's introduction in 1966 of a Selective Employment Tax (SET), intended to induce a 'shake-out' of labour from low-productivity service industries and to increase its availability for manufacturing.

As it happened, the year which saw the introduction of SET, and a major intensification of regional policy measures and extension of their spatial coverage, also saw manufacturing employment in the UK reach its absolute peak. After 1966, manufacturing employment in the UK exhibited a declining trend, with significant accelerations in the rate of job loss during the 1970s and especially after 1979 (see Figure 1.1). Between June 1971 and June 1983 the number of employees in Britain's manufacturing industries (Standard Industrial Classification (SIC) 1980) declined from 7.9 to 5.5 million, a relative loss of 30 per cent. Two-thirds of this decrease, 1.6 million jobs, occurred after June 1979 and coincided with a 15.6 per cent fall in manufacturing output.

The period since 1966 has also been one of consistently higher unemployment than the previous twenty years. Moreover, the long-term trend in unemployment has been strongly upwards, with the jobless total reaching successively higher cyclical peaks and tending to remain at progressively higher levels in any subsequent economic upturn (see Figure 1.2). The fastest and largest increase in unemployment occurred after 1979, with the number claiming unemployment benefit doubling to reach over three million in 1982. Demographic factors added their influence to that of recession in the increases in unemployment of the late 1970s and early 1980s in the UK. A high level of young entrants to the labour market, in consequence of the rising birth-rate between 1955 and 1964, coincided with a relatively reduced proportion of workers reaching retirement age as a result of the low birth-rate during the First World War. Despite a recovery of national output from the trough of recession in 1981 and the evidence for an upturn in employment from mid-1983, unemployment was still rising in the first three quarters of 1985, although at a slower rate than in 1979–82.

The impact of recession and demographic trends on the growth in unemployment were in turn superimposed onto the effects of longer-term structural changes in manufacturing labour demand in the UK, reflected in the fact that the decline in manufacturing employment after 1970 affected every major industry grouping. In the simplest, but not necessarily the most helpful, use of the term, this trend has been labelled 'de-industrialization' (Thirlwall 1982). The term has also been defined in ways which attempt to signify the process underlying the contraction of manufacturing employment. Thus, for example, in the view of the so-called 'Cambridge school', de-industrialization means a progressive failure to achieve a sufficient surplus of manufactured exports over imports to maintain the economy in external balance at full employment. Blackaby (1979) suggests that this meaning of de-industrialization, with its emphasis on the relative competitive weakness of British industry, is simply a new name for an old problem.

While the scale of its recent industrial decline distinguishes the UK among the advanced market economies, the country has also suffered from trends affecting these economies generally. They experienced severe dislocation after 1973, when sluggish or no growth and rising unemployment contrasted sharply with the buoyant conditions sustained throughout the earlier part of the post-war period. The slowdown in growth and related economic problems of the post-1973 period were most obviously associated with the impact of the oil-price rises of 1973–4 and 1979–80. Many commentators, however, have argued that these price shocks exacerbated the effects of longer-term adverse changes in the Western industrialized economies, whose origins predate 1973.

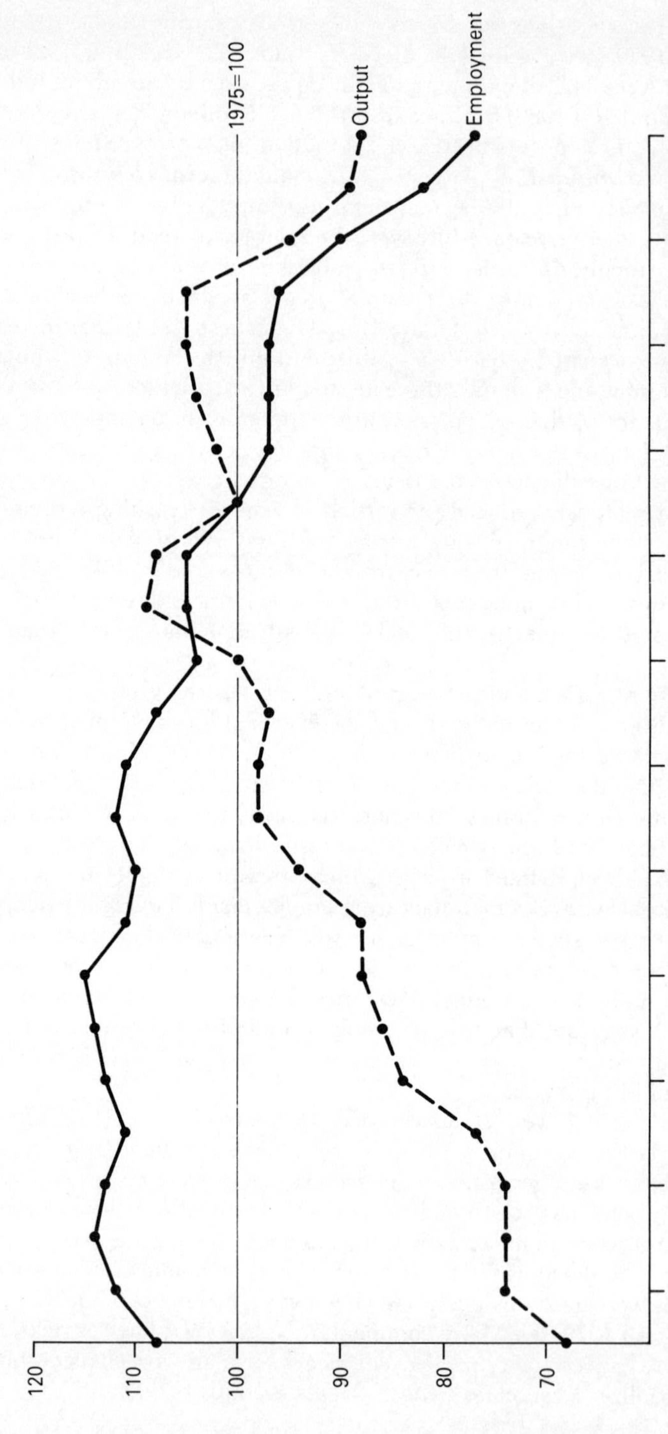

Figure 1.1. Indices of manufacturing employment and output (at constant factor cost) in the UK, 1959–82 (1968 SIC), 1975 = 100

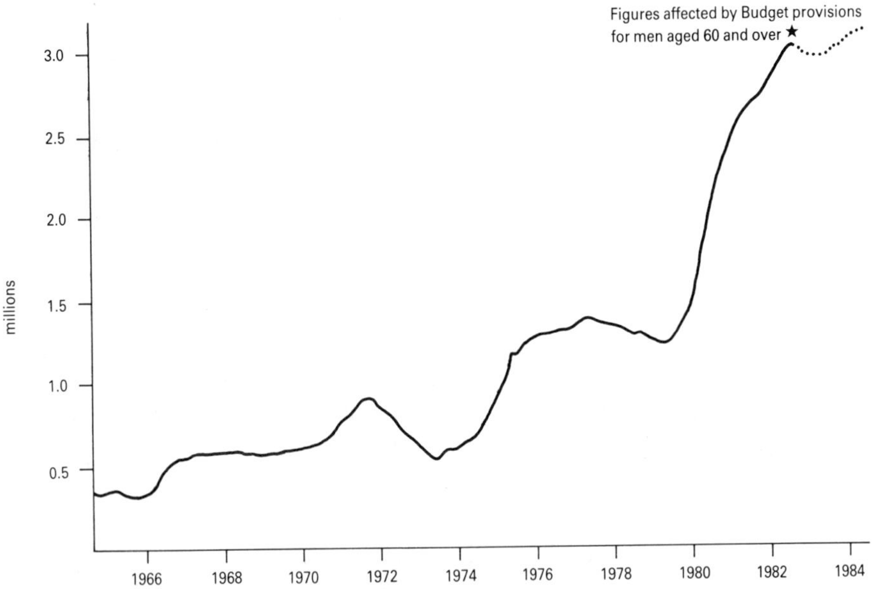

Figure 1.2. Unemployment: UK, 1965–84

Long-wave theories of economic development

Several competing perspectives may be adopted on the nature of these changes. One view is that capitalist economic development is subject to 'long waves' of around fifty to sixty years' duration, in which a phase of sustained expansion is followed by one of stagnation and recession. The post-1973 period is seen as marking the downswing phase of the most recent cycle, following the 'long boom' from the 1940s to the 1960s. In the previous cycle, the interwar slump was in turn preceded by a phase of rapid growth in the 1890s and the early years of the present century up to the First World War. An earlier long cycle is perceived to have covered the phase of vigorous expansion from the late 1840s to the early 1870s, followed by the 'Great Depression' from then to the early 1890s. Going back further, the development of the British economy in the period from around 1780 to the so-called 'Hungry Forties', when the country was the only major industrial power, has also been interpreted in long-wave terms.

The Russian economist Kondratieff is usually credited with the initial elaboration of the notion of long waves in economic development in the 1920s, although earlier references have been noted (van Duijn 1983). The concept was subsequently embraced by Schumpeter (1939), and more recently has received renewed attention from a number of both Marxist and non-Marxist writers (Mandel 1980; Mensch 1979; Freeman *et al.* 1982; Van Duijn 1983; Rostow 1985). The identification of long waves, their precise phasing, and the underlying causes of long-term cyclical movements in economic growth are matters of considerable debate and speculation. Much controversy centres around the impetus to the initial upswing into an extended phase of economic expansion. One group of long-wave theorists, inspired principally by Schumpeter's ideas, emphasize the growth-generating capability of 'basic' innovations, those which create new industries and new markets. Much recent political and academic interest in the potential of new technologies as agents of industrial regeneration and employment creation can be related to this line of thought on the mechanics of the long cycle.

In the Schumpeterian model, long-wave growth is explicable in terms of the impact over time of such basic innovations as railways, electricity, and motorized transport. Historically, such innovations have been associated with the growth of new leading industries which, by their 'demonstration' effect of successful innovation and input–output linkages, were capable of pulling the rest of the economy into a phase of sustained growth. Conversely, stagnation sets in when the possibilities of growth from an older batch of innovations are exhausted as their markets become saturated. In the depression which follows, Mensch (1979) argued, firms turn to new possibilities for transforming technical knowledge into basic innovations: such innovations thus tend to occur in bunches during long-wave depressions. Mensch sought empirical verification for this theory by plotting the dates of the introduction of each of a list of 'basic' innovations and identifying a tendency for temporal clustering, for example in the late 1930s.

According to Freeman *et al.* (1982), however, considerable ambiguities surround the definition and timing of 'basic' innovations as identified by Mensch. Their own attempt to develop an improved data set on 'radical' innovations in the UK 1920–80 supports the idea that innovative activity shows temporal discontinuities, with a peak in the 1930s and a decline in major innovations in both the 1920s and the 1970s. Equally, however, Freeman *et al.* identify a continuing flow of radical innovations in the 1950s and 1960s, although with process innovations outnumbering product innovations by the latter decade. Van Duijn (1983) argues that the relative propensity for innovation is in fact likely to vary by type and by industrial sector over the long cycle. In some cases innovation is more likely when market conditions are generally favourable, i.e. during expansion rather than depression. One alternative long-wave model ascribes a dominant cycle-forming role to the inherent time-lags in the supply response of capital goods industries to changes in demand. Since the capital goods sector has initially to re-equip with part of its own output in order to meet increased demand from the consumer goods sector, an initial growth stimulus is likely to be amplified and prolonged. The resulting capital investment will embody new technological developments, and hence, in this model, innovation is seen as a consequence, rather than a cause, of growth.

Freeman *et al.* (1982), however, reject a purely demand-led theory of innovation, preferring the Schumpeterian view of at least some autonomous impetus for growth emanating from technological advance and its use by imaginative entrepreneurship. Also following Schumpeter, they argue that, once innovation-led growth is under way in certain branches of industry, important secondary demand-led innovations may take place which serve to sustain and accelerate growth. The temporal 'swarming' of innovations that is of key importance is not just a clustering of disparate developments, but the diffusion of a set of inter-related innovations of wide applicability which tend to engender further innovations, social and economic as well as purely technical. The diffusion of such constellations of interconnected innovations, which Freeman *et al.* label 'new-technology systems', provides the main explanation for the upswings in the long wave. Two new-technology systems which they see as having had pervasive growth-generating effects in the postwar boom involved innovations in synthetic materials and electronics.

From Mandel's (1980) Marxist viewpoint, this is not an adequate explanation of the postwar expansionary phase. He argues that the distinctive feature of a long-wave expansion is that it is a phase of more intensive capital accumulation, characterized by improved profitability compared with other periods and thus by a strengthening of the countervailing forces within capitalism which oppose the inherent downward pressure on the rate of profit. What must be explained is how the improvement comes about, i.e. what conditions facilitate faster capital accumulation. Explanations relying upon an autonomous technological push into growth are deemed unsatisfactory, a point that would probably be accepted by many non-Marxists. The effects of depression itself may contribute to the conditions necessary, but not sufficient, for renewed growth; but in Mandel's view the turning-points from stagnation to recovery are typically associated with radical changes in the external environment of capitalism. Thus, key factors which he sees as inducing the postwar boom include the war itself, fascism's earlier defeat of working-class movements in several European countries, falls in the prices of raw materials, and major improvements in transport and communications systems. Mandel agrees that, once an expansionary wave is under way, technological developments may help to sustain its momentum, particularly in terms of the opportunities for innovative firms to obtain technological 'rents' which can help to drive up the average rate of profit.

There seems no reason to dispute the likely significance of exogeneous, and partially extra-economic, factors as the precursors of postwar economic growth. Equally, it seems widely accepted among long-wave theorists that the emergence of constraints on profitability was the key to the eventual waning of the boom. As innovations became more widely diffused, and products and processes more standardized, technological 'rents' were eroded. The growth of demand for the products of the boom's leading industries slackened as markets began to approach saturation. The length of the boom itself led to upward pressure on wage costs, as labour reserves were depleted and workers acquired greater bargaining power with full employment. Against the background of these forces exerting a squeeze on profits by the mid- to late 1960s, the sharp rise in primary commodity prices in the early 1970s, culminating in the 1973 oil shock, provided the final ingredient needed to turn a faltering boom into a generalized slump in the Western economies.

Industrial restructuring since the 1960s

The transition from expansion to recession was marked by a failure to sustain a flow of market-creating innovations comparable in their impact to those which fuelled the growth of the 1950s and 1960s. Equally, industry in the advanced economies did not remain passive as profits were squeezed and the boom waned. Firms sought in various ways to maintain or increase their market shares and/or to penetrate new sectors of demand. Helped by the relaxation of trade restrictions, international competition in manufactured goods intensified in the 1960s and 1970s. There was also an increase in the level of company mergers and acquisitions, as firms sought a competitive edge through scale economies and diversification into new areas of activity. Increased pressure to raise labour productivity resulted in growth in both capital stock and industrial floor-space per worker and reductions in the volume and (in some cases) the skill content of labour inputs to production processes. There was thus a shift in emphasis, from investment to increase productive capacity towards investment to improve competitiveness through the exploitation of scale economies and labour-saving process innovations in existing industries.

These trends were accompanied by shifts in the location of investment and production at both national and international levels. The more widespread exploitation of scale economies, frequently associated with the standardization of products and components, and the increasing prevalence of routinized assembly-type production processes, provided a growing range of manufacturing activities with greater locational flexibility. Competitive pressures prompted firms to use such flexibility to seek out new, less costly, and less organized reserves of labour. Areas which had escaped large-scale industrialization in earlier phases of economic development assumed increased attractiveness for certain branches of manufacturing. The result, reinforced by the increasing space-intensity of modern industry, was a general trend towards the spatial deconcentration of manufacturing employment within the industrialized economies. At the same time, an international shift in the location of production towards low-wage countries, for example in South East Asia, was also apparent.

Well before the final collapse of the postwar expansionary wave, therefore, important structural changes were taking place in the advanced economies, affecting the location and character of industrial investment and its impact on jobs. Freeman *et al.* (1982) note a change in the relationship between manufacturing output and employment in the UK and other Western European economies from the mid-1960s. In nine EEC countries in combination, both manufacturing output and employment grew steadily between 1951 and 1966. From 1966 to 1974, while output continued to grow, employment (with some year-to-year fluctuations) remained stable. Between 1974 and 1980, manufacturing output grew only slowly, while employment showed a sharp decline. In the USA, on the other hand, no clear break in trends is apparent in the 1960s, while in Japan, where manufacturing output expanded much faster than in the rest of the OECD throughout the 1960s and 1970s, the phenomenon of jobless growth in manufacturing did not appear until the mid-1970s.

The UK's economic problems

The experience of recent economic change has thus been far from uniform among the advanced economies, a point to be borne firmly in mind alongside attempts to employ long-wave models of postwar economic development. This is especially true with regard to the UK. During the 1950s and 1960s, the country recorded a rate of economic growth which was exceptional by its own historical standards. It was, however, plagued by persistent balance-of-payments problems and, by comparison with the growth rates achieved in most other leading industrial countries, the UK was a distinct laggard. The comparative performance of UK industry was thus a source of concern well before the harsher economic climate of the 1970s. Successive governments failed to break an adverse circle of causation—weak competitiveness leading to poor profitability and relatively slow growth, which in turn underlay lower rates of productivity increase compared with other countries.

The origins of the deep-seated problems of the UK economy have been extensively debated. Some commentators have located them in the final quarter of the last century, when the UK failed to embrace, as fully as its new international competitors like Germany and the USA, the opportunities for growth and diversification provided by the technological advances of the third 'Kondratieff wave'. The reasons for this, in Hobsbawm's view (1968), arose from characteristics of economic behaviour and economic structure acquired during the UK's long and pioneering role as the first industrial nation, largely in the absence of international competition. The result was a complacent and precarious over-commitment to a narrow range of industries, relying upon markets in the formal and informal British Empire. The origin of the 'depressed area problem' lay with the differential regional impact of the interwar collapse of these markets (see Chapter 2).

Once lost, industrial leadership was never regained. Before 1940 the UK lagged behind the USA in the adoption of new mass production techniques and the mass consumption patterns that were to be a major foundation of postwar growth. So too did the UK's main European competitors and Japan; but by the 1960s and 1970s these countries' industries had proved more successful in the 'catching up' process. Their superior competitiveness, born of faster growth and greater productivity gains, created serious problems for British industry in both its domestic and its export markets. The growth of import penetration in the UK consumer durables market, for example, was, by the mid-1970s, one of the most obvious symbols of the country's 'de-industrialization'. In 1983 the UK's trade in manufactured goods went into deficit, following a trend of almost continuous decline in the surplus of manufactured exports over imports since the 1950s.

In certain fundamental respects, the problems of the UK industrial economy in the mid-1980s are not dissimilar to those noted by many commentators in the mid-1960s. The critical difference is that, in the intervening period, as the apparently endemic competitive weakness persisted, the problems were very much more starkly exposed by the fading of the postwar boom. As a result, the country now has three million fewer manufacturing jobs, and a level of unemployment that would have been thought unacceptable twenty years ago.

There have, of course, been other important changes affecting the UK industrial economy since the mid-1960s. As already indicated, one of these is a significant increase in the average capital-intensity of manufacturing production. Another is the growth in the size and international character of industrial enterprises. Entry to the EEC has affected, among other things, the nature of the UK's trading links. The exploitation of North Sea oil and natural gas resources has transformed the country's energy supply position since the 1960s. From a situation of reliance upon petroleum imports for over 40 per cent of the country's energy needs at the start of the 1970s, the UK by 1983 had become the world's sixth largest oil producer and a net exporter. This development appears to have been something of a mixed blessing. In so far as it contributed to the sharp appreciation in the value of sterling in 1980–1, it compounded the competitive problems of UK industries at a time of international recession and when the UK government was seeking to reduce inflation through monetary restraint policies. The severity of the post-1979 recession in the UK must be viewed against the background of this particular combination of forces. In addition, the scale of job loss in manufacturing has given added significance to a further important change in the pattern of labour demand in the UK, namely the pronounced shift towards service sector employment.

The shift into services

In all advanced economies, the proportion of the labour force directly engaged in the production of commodities has been declining over recent decades. In Britain, the number of employees in the officially defined service industries rose by 2 million (18 per cent) between 1971 and 1984, growing as a proportion of total employees from 53 to 65 per cent. The service industries have so far been the sole source of net job creation in the upturn in employment since the first half of 1983, with increases in retailing, hotels and catering, and financial and business services. As in the expansion of service employment in the 1970s, this most recent growth has shown a very strong bias towards jobs for females and a high proportion of part-time work. Female part-time employment in services (SIC 1968) grew by 1.1 million jobs in 1971–81, equivalent to 63 per cent of the total gain in service industry jobs over this period, when the proportion of all employees in part-time jobs rose from 15 to 20 per cent. Part-time female employees accounted for nearly 80 per cent of the total increase in the numbers in work in the year to June 1984 (Department of Employment 1985). This largely explains why the recent upturn in employment has so far failed to make any impact on the numbers claiming unemployment benefit.

When account is taken of the growth in part-time jobs, the overall increase in service sector employment appears somewhat less impressive than at first sight. Nonetheless, within the totality of employment, non-production workers now constitute a substantial majority. That said, however, although more people are now involved in work which does not directly produce a physical output, much activity undertaken in 'service industries' is complementary to production, and may be no different in kind from that undertaken within manufacturing firms which internalize the provision of certain services—for example, catering, road haulage, accountancy, or market research. The proportion of the workforce in manufacturing engaged in service-type jobs has also been growing. By 1975, almost three out of every ten workers in manufacturing industry in Britain were in administrative, technical, or clerical jobs (Gudgin *et al*. 1979).

The distinction drawn between manufacturing and service sector employment in official statistics is thus to some extent an arbitrary one. Moreover, the service sector itself is very heterogeneous, and generalizations about service employment in aggregate are not particularly helpful. Not all service industries have been growing in employment; the transport sector, for example, contains some notable examples of decline since the 1960s—railways, road passenger transport, and seaport services—in consequence of a combination of declining demand and labour productivity growth. It is useful, therefore, to look at the dynamics of service employment growth in more detail. Initially, the factors underlying the overall shift into services in the distribution of the labour force are considered, since this may help to shed some light on the forces affecting different categories of service employment.

Three possible reasons for the growing share of services in total employment can be suggested:

(*a*) faster growth in final demand for services compared with goods as consumer incomes rise—in other words, households spend a greater proportion of their income on services;
(*b*) above-average growth in intermediate demand for services with increased specialization and division of labour within and between firms—in other words, over time a given level of national output requires a growing level of intermediate service inputs;
(*c*) slower labour productivity growth in services compared with manufacturing, inducing a shift of labour into services with increasing aggregate demand but without demand for services growing any faster than average.

The relative importance of these three factors is a matter of some uncertainty. Traditionally, (*a*) was often the most favoured explanation—based upon Engels' Law which describes the tendency, as societies become richer, for consumers to spend successively more of their income on manufactured as opposed to primary goods, such as food, and then, on services. Fuchs (1968) concluded from a study of services in the USA, however, that differential rates of labour productivity growth were the most important reason for the shift into services. Gershuny (1978) threw further doubt on (*a*) by showing that, although cross-sectional studies of consumer expenditure indicated that the rich spent more of their income on services than did the poor, there was less evidence that, over time, services accounted for a growing proportion of aggregate consumer expenditure. Gershuny and Miles (1983) argue that the reason for this is that the tendency for people to spend proportionately more on services as they become better-off was offset by the effects of slower labour productivity growth in service industries on the relative prices of services compared with consumer goods. Households thus tended to substitute goods (and their own labour resources) with which they could provide service functions for themselves (cars, washing machines, vacuum cleaners, televisions) for externally supplied services such as public transport, laundries, domestic servants, and cinema and theatre tickets. With the growth of the 'self-service' economy, based on increasing ownership and use of consumer durable goods, demand for and employment in some services declined. Thus, in Gershuny and Miles's view, growth in final demand for services has been more important as a cause of growth in consumer goods production than as an explanation for the employment shift towards services.

This conclusion requires qualification on several counts. First, some consumer services appear to have escaped the goods-substitution effect. These include a group of recreational and leisure services in which jobs have been growing since the late 1960s and early 1970s, helped in part by the growth of international tourism. One million people were employed in hotels and catering in Britain in 1984, a rise of over 300,000 since 1971 (see Table 1.1) although once again the growth was in part-time employment to a significant degree. Civil aviation has been another area of service expansion which in part reflects the growth of tourist travel with increasing affluence. Second, the increasing use of consumer goods to provide services within households has itself stimulated growth of service activities needed to sell, maintain, and repair these goods—what Gershuny and Miles (1983) call 'intermediate consumer services'.

Table 1.1. Great Britain: service employment changes, 1971–84

	1971–7		1977–84		1971–84	
	000	%	000	%	000	%
All services (SIC 1980)	1,318	11.6	684	5.4	2,002	17.6
Wholesale and repairs	70	7.3	119	11.5	189	19.6
Retail distribution	99	5.1	46	2.2	145	7.4
Hotels and catering	176	25.4	133	15.3	309	44.7
Transport	−75	−6.9	−152	−14.9	−227	−20.8
Postal services and telecommunications	−24	−5.5	7	1.7	−17	−3.9
Banking, finance, insurance, business services	178	13.5	359	24.0	537	40.7
Public administration	205	11.8	−122	−6.3	83	4.8
Education	288	22.8	−18	−1.2	270	21.4
Medical and health services	207	22.0	144	12.6	351	27.4
Other services	193	19.7	176	15.0	369	37.7

Source: *Employment Gazette, Historical Supplement no. 1*, April 1985.

DIY shops and garage services are obvious examples. The production of television programmes or video films may also be counted in this category; the service provided by television or video equipment relies upon these 'intermediate' inputs.

Third, account must be taken of public sector services, which were among the most important job generators in the economy in the 1960s and 1970s. In the period 1971–7, employment growth in medical services, education, and public administration accounted for half the total net increase in service industry jobs (see Table 1.1; the share would be higher if allowance were made for the proportion of part-time jobs in different services). Public services can be seen as meeting final demand in large part, but the fact that they are non-marketed means that the effect of slower labour productivity growth on their 'relative prices' was not felt directly by the consumer, and hence was not reflected in contracting demand. Their growth depended upon political decisions on the rechannelling of aggregate demand through public expenditure and taxation policies, thus increasing the so-called 'social wage' faster than personal disposable incomes (Bacon and Eltis 1976). The supposed negative effects of this transfer upon the economy as a whole, through rising tax burdens and increased government borrowing, played an important part in the shift in policy emphasis which began in 1976 and became even more prominent after 1979, towards the restraint of public expenditure. As a consequence, overall employment growth in public services virtually ceased after 1976, with job losses in some services (see Table 1.1). This was the principal reason for the marked slowdown in the growth of total service employment in the late 1970s.

The growth of producer services

Table 1.1 indicates that three broad groups of services were primarily responsible for the overall growth of employment in the sector in the period 1971–84. Two of these have been mentioned: first, a group of services related to the growth of recreation and leisure, represented most clearly by hotels and catering, and second, public services such as education, in which growth was strongest in the first half of the period. The third group was composed of private services which, in whole or in part, meet intermediate rather than consumer demand, paralleling the growing importance of non-production functions within manufacturing organizations. In contrast to public services, employment in private services, after a mild downturn during the worst of the post-1979 recession, continued to grow in the 1980s; the largest absolute and relative growth in jobs during 1977–84 occurred in banking, finance, insurance, and business services. Financial and business services are also distinguished by an occupational structure dominated by white-collar jobs, and by their major contribution to the growth of full-time jobs in private services. In the period 1971–81, the Insurance, Banking, Finance, and Business Services Order of the 1968 SIC accounted for 87 per cent of the total growth of full-time employment in private services.

Alongside the growing share of white-collar employment within manufacturing, the increase in employment in financial and business services reflects the expansion of intermediate demand for 'producer' services in the modern economy (see (*b*) above). Gershuny and Miles (1983) show that the level of intermediate service inputs needed for a given level of primary and manufacturing industry output in the UK increased in the period 1963–73. The usual explanation for this trend is that the pace and complexity of economic and technical change necessitate greater utilization by the production sector of more specialist and sophisticated services, e.g. in research, design, marketing, technical training, the financing and planning of investments, and in corporate management and administration generally. Essentially, competition in the modern industrial system requires firms to be adaptive and responsive, dependent upon elaborate intelligence gathering and the ability to process and act upon specialized information effectively (Schon 1972). Hence Marquand's comment: 'In an age of rapid technological change, what is particularly important about certain producer services is that these provide the source and mediators of that change' (1983: 128).

The growth of financial, business, and some professional services employment can thus in part be explained by the changing input requirements of manufacturing industry. However, some of this expansion seems much less directly related to production—if indeed it is related at all. A substantial part of the total demand for business services comes from within the service sector, from central and government, and from the construction industry. Studies of business service linkages (for example Marshall 1983) suggest that some of the key relationships in the dynamics of these services are intrasectoral rather than with manufacturing. This points also to the importance of the growth of intermediate service demand, and increased specialization and refinement of the division of labour, within the service sector itself, as a factor in the development of producer services.

It is also worth noting that some commentators on the UK economy (for example, Glyn and Sutcliffe 1972) have stressed the distinction between, if not the actual divergence of, the dynamics and interests of industrial capital, deriving profits from commodity production, and finance capital—companies whose business is owning and trading stocks and shares, property, government bonds and currencies, and providing such services as insurance, pensions, credit card facilities, hire purchase, and mortgage finance. Clearly, the activities of the latter should not be interpreted simply as the development of a supporting framework for manufacturing, and certainly not UK manufacturing. Financial institutions are as likely to invest in commercial property abroad as in domestic industry, and imported goods are just as easily bought by credit card or hire purchase as the home-produced item. On the other hand, financial and business services do make an important contribution to the UK's export earnings, and, as Robertson *et al.* (1982) point out, increases in such earnings, evident between 1968 and 1978 for example, will have been a further stimulus to their employment growth. Moreover, the role of London as a major world financial centre has recently been associated with an influx and expansion of foreign banking operations. The number of foreign banks directly represented in London increased from 163 to 390 between 1970 and 1983, and employment in foreign banks and securities houses in London rose from just under 12,000 to 38,000 over the same period (Thrift 1985). To an extent, therefore, the development of producer services in Britain, especially those associated with the City of London, is subject to trends and forces which are independent of and indifferent to the fortunes of the country's manufacturing industry.

Structural change in the UK economy: de-industrialization or post-industrial development?

The foregoing sections have focused upon two pre-eminent changes in the UK's economy and employment structure over the last two decades: the decline of manufacturing employment and the growth of service jobs. While the former trend has led to the UK being described as an economy experiencing 'de-industrialization', the latter has been identified as a hallmark of the evolution of a 'post-industrial' society. Both terms lack unequivocal definition, but they tend to have significantly different connotations, and imply differing views of the process of structural change in the national economy.

Of the two terms, 'post-industrial' has the more positive connotations. At its simplest, a post-industrial economy is one in which a majority of the labour force are engaged in service work; but in Bell's (1974) use it implies something more—a natural and progressive development of an economy and society, with fewer workers needed for production because of increased productivity and the prominence of professional and technical employment. Some uses of the term imply a society characterized by an expansion of recreation and leisure activities, sustained by the increased efficiency of production and a higher income elasticity of consumer demand for services compared with goods.

At least two different models of structural change underlie these views. The first focuses on the producer side, and on the changing pattern of labour inputs to production (of both goods and services). Specialist knowledge and skills of various kinds are seen as key resources, education and research are leading sectors, and there is increased 'professionalization' of work. In Bell's view:

> A post-industrial society is based on services. . . . What counts is not raw muscle-power, or energy, but information. The central person is the professional, for he is equipped by his education and training to provide the kind of skills that are increasingly demanded in post-industrial society. (Bell 1974: 127)

However, Kumar (1978), amongst others, has questioned the criteria which Bell uses to define post-industrial society, pointing out that many of these—rationality and the increased importance of specialist knowledge in business decisions, professionalization of work, the growth of bureaucracy, etc.—represent the fuller development of earlier identified traits of industrial society rather than the emergence of distinctive new structural characteristics. Bell's post-industrial society is in fact an advanced industrial society developing along the path outlined by Weber and others. The primacy of production has not been usurped by services, even if, partly as a result of a further stage of internationalization, it appears to have a reduced employment role in the advanced economies themselves. Orwell's observation, from the imperial period of this country's history, that the British often forgot that a substantial proportion of their working class live in Asia and Africa, still has relevance. Another of Bell's diagnostics of post-industrial development, the growth of research effort, is, in the UK and USA at least, to a large extent a defence-related phenomenon rather than a harbinger of a new type of economy.

The second, and older, view of structural change in post-industrial development is basically an extension of the Clark–Fisher model of the changing sectoral distribution of employment. This focuses on the pattern of consumption in terms of the Engels' Law proposition that consumers spend proportionately more of their incomes on services as they become richer. This is usually seen as a feature of individual consumption patterns; but equally the trend, until recently, of rising public expenditure on, and jobs in, health, education, and welfare services could be interpreted as a collective, society-wide expression of Engels' Law.

This is the model of structural change which Gershuny (1978) and Gershuny and Miles (1983) seek to overturn by stressing the substitution of consumer goods for consumer services, and by giving greater emphasis to the growth of intermediate demand for services. But in aggregate terms, Gershuny and Miles argue that the growing share of services in total employment is largely a consequence of their slower labour productivity growth compared with manufacturing. The dominance of services in employment thus emerges almost by default—it simply reflects the greater efficiency of manufacturing, and the economy is no less dependent on production. In this case, too, therefore, the term 'post-industrial' is a misnomer.

'De-industrialization' is also a problematic term. It can mean simply an absolute reduction of manufacturing employment, or a fall in its share of total employment; but frequently it has been used with the negative connotation, in the UK case, of a competitive weakness in manufacturing, and an associated failure to maintain a sufficient surplus of manufactured exports over imports (Singh 1977). This has implications for the demand for services, which may be constrained by weak manufacturing competitiveness; but in so far as services are increasing their share of employment, this may be simply because they are less exposed to international competition and, so far, to labour-saving automation. In constrast with 'post-industrial' perspectives, the growth of services is not a positive or progressive development. Indeed, it may be irrelevant to the main processes of change, which remain firmly centred around the competitive fortunes of manufacturing industry.

The picture is complicated by the possibility of a divergence of interests between industrial and finance capital in the UK—that is to say, the development of services connected with the latter may be partially independent of, or even detrimental to, the former. Thus it has been argued that through, for example, the terms and conditions on which finance is made available to industry, the export of capital abroad, and the diversion of investment funds into property development, the UK's financial services have failed to support the country's manufacturing sector and have contributed to its loss of employment.

The terms 'de-industrialization' and 'post-industrial development' should perhaps be seen as no more than labels for different aspects of recent structural change in the UK economy, reflecting the fact that some positive, as well as negative, trends can be observed. As such, they may also be helpful in understanding the differential regional experience of economic change within the UK over the last two decades, which is discussed in general terms in Chapter 2, and in more detail in the regionally focused chapters of this book. In the context of the national changes already outlined, the balance between positive and negative trends over the last two decades has shown wide spatial variations, producing a transformation of the country's economic geography. In particular, the spatial pattern of manufacturing employment change has been such as to overturn previously accepted definitions of the 'regional problem'. As with the country's economic history, however, recent geographical changes do not mark a clean break with the past; as we shall see, elements of an older pattern of regional inequality are to be found within the new map of economic health.

References

Bacon, R. and Eltis, W. (1976), *Britain's Economic Problem: Too Few Producers*, London, Macmillan.

Bell, D. (1974), *The Coming of Post-Industrial Society*, Harmondsworth, Penguin.

Blackaby, F. ed. (1979), *De-industrialization*, London, Heinnemann.

Department of Employment (1985), *Employment. The Challenge for the Nation*, Cmnd. 9474, London, HMSO.

Freeman, C., Clark, J., and Soete, L. (1982), *Unemployment and Technical Innovation. A Study of Long Waves and Economic Development*, London, Francis Pinter.

Fuchs, V. R. (1968), *The Service Economy*, National Bureau of Economic and Social Research, New York, Columbia University Press.

Gershuny, J. (1978), *After Industrial Society? The Emerging Self-Service Economy*, London, Macmillan.

Gershuny, J. I. and Miles, I. D. (1983), *The New Service Economy*, London, Francis Pinter.

Glyn, A. and Sutcliffe, R. B. (1972), *British Workers, Capitalism and the Profits Squeeze*, Harmondsworth, Penguin.

Gudgin, G., Crum, R., and Bailey, S. (1979), 'White Collar Employment in UK Manufacturing', in P. W. Daniels, ed., *Spatial Patterns of Office Growth and Location*, Chichester: Wiley.

Hall, P. (1981), 'The Geography of the Fifth Kondratieff Cycle', *New Society* 55, 535–7.

Hobsbawm, E. J. (1968), *Industry and Empire*, Harmondsworth, Penguin.

Kaldor, N. (1966), *Causes of the Slow Rate of Economic Growth in the United Kingdom*, Cambridge, Cambridge University Press.

Kumar, K. (1978), *Prophecy and Progress*, Harmondsworth, Penguin.

Mandel, E. (1980), *Long Waves of Capitalist Development*, Cambridge, Cambridge University Press.

Marquand, J. (1983), 'The Changing Distribution of Service Employment', in J. B.

Goddard and A. G. Champion, eds., *The Urban and Regional Transformation of Britain*, London, Methuen.

Marshall, J. N. (1983), 'Business service activities in British provincial conurbations', *Environment and Planning A* 15, 1343–59.

Martin, R. L. (1982), 'Britain's Slump: The Regional Anatomy of Job Loss', *Area* 14, 257–64.

Mensch, G. (1979), *Stalemate in Technology*, Cambridge, Mass., Ballinger.

National Economic Development Council (1963), *Conditions Favourable to Faster Growth*, London, HMSO.

Robertson, J. A. S., Briggs, J. M., and Goodchild, A. (1982), *Structure and Employment Prospects of the Service Industries*, Research Paper no. 30, London, Department of Employment.

Rostow, W. W. (1985), 'The World Economy Since 1945: A Stylized Historical Analysis', *Economic History Review*, 2nd series, XXXVIII, 252–75.

Schon, D. (1972), *Beyond the Stable State*, Harmondsworth, Penguin.

Schumpeter, J. (1939), *Business Cycles*, New York, McGraw-Hill.

Singh, A. (1977). 'UK Industry and the World Economy: A Case of De-industrialisation?' *Cambridge Journal of Economics* 1, 113–36.

Thirlwall, A. P. (1982), 'De-industrialisation in the United Kingdom', *Lloyds Bank Review* (April), 22–37.

Thrift, N. J. (1985), 'Research Policy and Review I. Taking the Rest of the World Seriously. The State of British Urban and Regional Research in a Time of Economic Crisis', *Environment and Planning A* 17, 7–24.

van Duijn, J. J. (1983), *The Long Wave in Economic Life*, London, Allen & Unwin.

CHAPTER 2
Regional Economic Change Since the 1960s

P. J. Damesick

Introduction: the genesis of the regional problem

The origins of a 'regional problem' in the UK lay with the interwar collapse of the Victorian industrial economy and associated changes in the geography of industrial growth. Spatially, earlier expansionary phases had been dominated first by Lancashire, the West Riding, and the Black Country, later joined by the coalfield-based heavy industrial regions such as South Wales and North East England, producing the nineteenth-century pattern of regional specialization in a limited range of export industries. The newer industries of the twentieth century, such as motor vehicles and electrical goods, were more orientated towards domestic markets and much less dependent on primary fuel and raw material supplies. Market access and agglomeration economies were key locational factors in their early development, so that the London region and the West Midlands came to dominate the new pattern of industrial growth.

The interwar economic buoyancy of these areas, however, was probably a function not simply of relative location, but also of industrial traditions and a business environment that were more conducive to new manufacturing activities. Elsewhere, regional specialization in the leading industries of earlier expansionary waves not only meant vulnerability to structural decline when markets were lost, but also inhibited diversification into new sectors. Thus, while parts of the West Midlands successfully developed new industries in the late nineteenth and early twentieth centuries, partly by building upon and adapting existing strengths and traditions, Clydeside remained predominantly specialized in shipbuilding and heavy engineering. This specialization has been likened by Checkland to an 'upas tree' which 'killed or discouraged the growth of other industries of a more modern kind beneath its massive and intertwined branches' (1981: 48). In time, arguably, the motor industry and its attendant growths were to impose a similar burden upon the West Midlands' capacity for adjustment. Research comparing the formation of new manufacturing establishments in the Clydeside and West Midlands conurbations 1963–72 (Firn and Swales 1978) found that the birthrate of new independent enterprises in the latter was in fact lower than in the former and, the researchers concluded, well below the rates of new firm formation achieved in the West Midlands in the interwar period (Beesley 1955).

The older, peripheral industrial regions did receive an infusion of new industries during and immediately after the Second World War, but conscious efforts to diversify their economies and employment structures then lapsed for a decade. The problem of their over-commitment to structurally declining industries remained, but was obscured during the 1950s by the prevailing boom conditions, and, for a time, by the relatively buoyant demand for certain of their staple industries. Coalmining, for example, increased its output to a postwar peak in 1956. Cotton textiles fared less well, but the real crisis of overcapacity in the industry was fully acknowledged only at the end of the 1950s. In general, however, throughout the 1950s the old industrial regions recorded a relative deterioration in their employment performance compared to the country as a whole. Mackay (1979), on the basis of a subsequent shift-share analysis, has suggested that the changes in the Development Area regions were in fact more adverse than would have been expected on the basis of their regional industrial structures (see also Moore *et al.* 1977). At the same time there was a continuation of the interwar trend in favour of new industrial growth in areas of high market potential. Thus Keeble notes: 'Various evidence agrees that the 1950s witnessed massive absolute and relative manufacturing growth in and around the central industrial conurbations of London and Birmingham' (1976: 14).

The changing geography of manufacturing employment since 1960

After about 1960, location trends in manufacturing employment underwent a marked change from the patterns of the previous decades. There was a strong shift of manufacturing jobs away from the country's major cities, with the rate of job loss being particularly rapid in the Greater London area, and towards smaller towns and more rural areas. Associated with this trend was an upsurge in manufacturing growth in several traditionally non-industrial and less urbanized areas such as East Anglia and parts of the South West. In addition, from about 1963, it is possible to identify a marked improvement in the employment performance of the problem regions of the North, Scotland, Wales, and Northern Ireland (Moore and Rhodes 1974; Mackay 1979). The improvement in the last of these regions was cut short by the onset of the 'troubles' at the end of the 1960s (see Chapter 11), but in the other main assisted regions it persisted until the recession in the mid-1970s. By then these changes, together with the impact of massive industrial job loss in London upon overall employment trends in the South East, and the erosion of the advantage of a favourable manufacturing structure in the West Midlands (due largely to the changed job prospects in the car industry), were prompting the identification of a new trend of regional convergence (Keeble 1977). The apparent narrowing of regional differences in prosperity up to the mid-1970s was a factor in growing calls for spatial policy to confront the new problem of urban, rather than regional, economic decline, which was manifest in London and Birmingham as well as the northern conurbations.

The temporal coincidence of more favourable employment trends in the assisted regions with the reactivation of regional policy in the early 1960s suggests an obvious causal connection. However, the intensified and, from the mid-1960s, more spatially extensive regional policy was operating at a time when, as we have already seen, other factors were encouraging greater dispersion in industrial location at all spatial scales—international, interregional, and from larger to smaller urban centres and rural areas. The nationwide contraction of urban manufacturing which began in the 1960s must also be viewed in this context. We may note, of course, a list of adverse conditions held to affect manufacturing in large urban centres such as cramped sites, obsolescent premises, inadequate road access, high land costs, and greater unionization and labour militancy, and compare these with more favourable conditions outside the cities. However, this does not explain why these factors should have come into play so strongly during the 1960s to produce such a rapid decline of manufacturing employment in the cities. Urban land costs, for example, had been higher than those elsewhere for a long time.

An important difference in the forces affecting the location of manufacturing jobs in the 1960s was that, under the pressures of international competition and the squeeze on profitability, industry in the UK experienced more rapid growth in capital intensity and an increase in the floor-space required per worker. Thus, Fothergill and Gudgin (1982) argue that displacement of labour by machinery on existing floor-space was the main cause of the loss of manufacturing jobs in cities, which could not be offset by job gains in new factories and extensions because of the physical constraints on floor-space growth in built-up urban areas. The expansion of industrial floor-space, and associated gains in jobs, took place outside the largest cities (Fothergill *et al.* 1985).

In some branches of manufacturing, changes in the amounts of capital stock and factory space per worker were associated with changes in production methods, in the scale of operations, and in skilled labour requirements (Massey and Meegan 1979; 1982). Massey and Meegan (1978) see this industrial restructuring of the 1960s and 1970s as having a strongly adverse effect on jobs in the cities, not simply through a change in the physical space requirements of manufacturing, but because of altered relations between capital and labour in the production process. In this context, the major industrial conurbations suffered from having a preponderance of the skilled labour-intensive production activities, often using older plant in older premises, which corporate reorganizations were typically designed to eliminate so as to improve competitiveness and restore profitability. At the same time, the increasing dominance of larger firms meant that the economies of scale which smaller separate firms traditionally sought through agglomeration in a major industrial centre were often internalized within single organizations. Thus, aided also by less reliance upon the skilled labour found in the old industrial cities, large companies were able to organize production in more dispersed spatial patterns; in the process they could take advantage of cheaper and more spacious sites, possibly more tractable labour, and, where available, regional policy incentives.

The particular combination of forces which led to an increasing share of national manufacturing jobs being located in the peripheral assisted regions, albeit within a declining total after 1966, while at the same time inducing massive job loss in the largest cities, operated to greatest effect in the decade

Table 2.1. Regional manufacturing employment (SIC 1968) in Great Britain: percentage changes 1966–74, 1974–8, and 1978–82

	Per cent change: employees in employment		
	1966–74	1974–8	1978–82
South East	−14.5	−7.9	−15.3
Greater London (included in SE)	−27.0*	−14.7	−18.9
East Anglia	18.5	−2.0	−13.4
South West	4.4	−4.7	−16.0
West Midlands	−9.7	−8.5	−26.0
East Midlands	−2.2	−2.7	−17.0
Yorkshire and Humberside	−11.2	−7.4	−23.9
North West	−12.9	−8.4	−23.0
North	1.3	−10.4	−22.9
Wales	5.7	−7.2	−28.2
Scotland	−6.9	−10.7	−23.3
Great Britain	−8.4	−7.6	−20.5

Sources: *Employment Gazette*; *estimate from Dennis (1978).

Note: Employment figures for 1982 are provisional. The change in the SIC (1980) means that estimates of employees in employment for the regions for years after 1982 are not available on a basis comparable to the years before 1971.

leading up to the mid-1970s recession. Dennis's (1978) estimate suggests that, between 1966 and 1974, manufacturing employment in Greater London declined at around three times the national rate of loss, while the manufacturing workforce in Wales and Northern England actually expanded, and Scotland managed a rate of loss below the national figure (see Table 2.1). Employment also increased in the South West and East Anglia, very rapidly in the case of the latter, while North West England's above-average rate of decline reflects an urban structure dominated by two conurbations.

After 1974, however, the pattern changed again as new economic conditions had their effect. In recession, job losses arising from actual declines in output became more important, while new investment was less likely to have any job generation effect, being concentrated upon the replacement and modernization of existing productive capacity. Investment was also decreasingly likely to produce mobile employment. The number of jobs generated by inter-regional industrial movement in 1972–5 was barely above the level achieved in the 1950s, when regional policy was in abeyance; it fell very much further in the second half of the 1970s (Department of Trade and Industry 1983). Moreover, the average employment associated with each move had declined from the mid-1960s, reflecting manufacturing's increasing capital intensity. These trends had serious implications for the effectiveness of a regional policy which sought to reduce regional unemployment disparities principally through subsidies to manufacturing investment in the assisted areas.

While recession in the 1970s and the changing character of industrial investment reduced the supply of mobile employment for the peripheral assisted regions, the same trends can also be seen as to some extent reducing the urban–rural differential in manufacturing employment change. The cities' lack of space for physical expansion was less of a disadvantage compared with other areas in a period of slow or no growth in manufacturing output. Although in absolute terms Greater London's rate of industrial job loss accelerated during 1974–8 as compared with 1966–74, its decline appears to have slowed somewhat in relation to the national trend (see Table 2.1). In the period 1978–82, covering the much deeper post-1979 recession, the rate of employment decline in manufacturing in Greater London was actually marginally below the national average. This still meant a massive absolute and relative job loss, of course; but it marked an improvement over earlier trends, which was in sharp contrast to the fortunes of the peripheral assisted regions and the West Midlands when compared with the country as a whole.

The 1960s upturn in the manufacturing employment performance of the peripheral assisted regions proved short-lived as the economic crises of the 1970s and early 1980s deepened. Between 1974 and 1982, Wales, the North, and, to a lesser extent, Scotland all recorded a sharp reversal of earlier favourable trends in manufacturing employment relative to national changes (see Table 2.1). Wales was particularly badly hit by steel closures from 1978, but the second fastest rate of manufacturing job loss in 1978–82 occurred in the West Midlands, with a major contraction of employment in the region's vehicles, engineering, and metal goods industries.

Recession thus re-established and accentuated the longstanding North–South disparity in economic health, with the important difference that the 'North' now moved south to embrace the West Midlands, and the dividing line between more and less favoured Britain lay roughly between the Severn and the Wash. Shift-share analysis of regional manufacturing employment changes between 1978–81 suggests, however, that the larger proportionate job losses in northern and western regions cannot be attributed solely to an unfavourable industrial structure compared with the country as a whole in this period (see Table 2.2). Townsend (1982) and Martin (1982b) found that the regions with the highest levels of manufacturing redundancies in the recession, both in the periphery and in the former industrial heartland of the country, recorded more job losses through redundancies than would be expected from their industrial structures. The converse was true in the three southern English regions and the East Midlands. Fothergill and Gudgin (1982) argue that industrial structure has been of decreasing significance as an explanation of differential regional employment change since the mid-1960s, mainly because of the reduction in inter-industry rates of employment change as overall decline in manufacturing jobs set in after 1966. Other reasons for the uneven regional toll taken by the recession must therefore be sought.

Table 2.2. Shift-share analysis of regional manufacturing employment changes, June 1978–September 1981

Region	Total employment change		Components					
			National		Structural		Differential	
	'000	(%)	'000	(%)	'000	(%)	'000	(%)
Gtr. London	−119	(−15.5)	−129	(−16.8)	24	(3.1)	−13	(−1.7)
Rest of SE	−101	(−9.2)	−183	(−16.8)	25	(2.3)	58	(5.3)
E. Anglia	−18	(−9.0)	−34	(−16.8)	5	(2.6)	10	(5.2)
South West	−56	(−13.1)	−72	(−16.8)	6	(1.5)	9	(2.2)
West Midlands	−216	(−21.8)	−166	(−16.8)	−16	(−1.6)	−34	(−3.4)
East Midlands	−84	(−14.0)	−101	(−16.8)	−17	(−2.9)	34	(5.7)
Yorks. and Humb.	−139	(−19.6)	−119	(−16.8)	−17	(−2.4)	−3	(−0.4)
North West	−182	(−18.2)	−168	(−16.8)	1	(0.1)	−15	(−1.5)
North	−80	(−19.1)	−70	(−16.8)	0	(0.0)	−10	(−2.3)
Wales	−77	(−24.7)	−52	(−16.8)	−10	(−3.2)	−15	(−4.8)
Scotland	−119	(−19.7)	−101	(−16.8)	1	(0.2)	−19	(−3.1)
Gt. Britain	−1,193	(−16.8)						

Source: *Employment Gazette*.

The new geography of industrial growth

In this search, and with an eye to the differing regional prospects for recovery from the recession, it is important to consider not just possible causes of greater vulnerability to decline, but also factors preventing the northern and western regions benefiting from offsetting sources of growth, such as product innovation and new enterprise formation. The greater resilience to the impact of recession in southern Britain must in part reflect a superior capacity to attract such growth. In contrast, the legacy of older industrial structures in the less prosperous regions, especially if combined with unfavourable plant size characteristics, can still exert a depressing influence upon new local growth, even where the potential job losses in such industries are now less than in the past. The 'upas tree' effect of specialization in heavy industry (Checkland 1981) has obvious parallels with the findings of other researchers on the detrimental impact of large plant dominance in local economies on the rate of new firm formation (Fothergill and Gudgin 1982). Areas of heavy industry and/or large plant dominance of employment such as Tyneside and Teesside in the North East, parts of South Wales, and West Central Scotland thus contribute strongly to regional differences in 'entrepreneurship potential' as measured, for example, by Storey (1982). The West Midlands conurbation, traditionally viewed as a major centre of small firm activity, in fact had, as did the adjacent Coventry area, a much greater dependence upon manufacturing employment in large plants (i.e. over 1,000 workers) by the early 1970s than Greater London, Manchester, or West Yorkshire (Regional Studies Association 1983: 52–3). Merseyside also had a high proportion of its manufacturing jobs in large plants, partly as a function of the type and size of establishments, including motor industry projects, induced to locate there by regional policy from the early 1960s. Buswell *et al.* (Chapter 8) note a similar bias towards large plants among postwar in-migrant industry in the Northern region.

It is also necessary to take account of changes in the spatial structure of employment which accompanied the trend towards dispersion of manufacturing activities from the early 1960s. In particular, with the increasing tendency towards the geographical separation of functions within large enterprises, regional differentiation based upon sectoral specialization (for example, steel, textiles, or shipbuilding) was joined by a new geographical division of labour based upon specialization by corporate function (management, research and development, or assembly-line production, for example). In this new division of labour, the more peripheral regions of the UK came to be characterized by relative dependence upon more standardized branch plant manufacturing, often of products in a mature stage of their life-cycle. In contrast, the South East tended to retain the higher-order corporate planning and control functions, and research and development activities. The under-representation of managerial, marketing, and research functions in the peripheral regions contributes to a relative shortage of the skills needed for successful entrepreneurship and innovation. Research has demonstrated a link between the on-site presence of a research and development capability in industrial establishments and successful product innovation (Oakey *et al.* 1982; Thwaites 1982). New product development is much more likely to be a source of job generation compared with the job-displacing propensity of process innovations (Thwaites 1983). The marked concentration of industrial research and development in the south of the country—South East England had 57 per cent of all research and development services jobs in 1976 (Howells 1984)—is thus likely to be one factor behind the area's superior performance in industrial innovation compared with the peripheral regions.

Two other factors can be identified as contributing to the relative dynamism and prosperity of Southern Britain, especially in the so-called English 'Sunbelt' stretching between the Severn estuary and the Solent north east to Cambridgeshire. These factors are urban structure, allied to high quality environmental amenities, and the pattern of government spending. Much of Southern England outside Greater London has a settlement pattern of smaller and often traditionally non-industrial centres, set in extensive and attractive open countryside. These areas offer the type of residential and working locations which the more affluent and mobile sections of the workforce have long found most congenial—as of course would most of the rest of the population if given the chance. One thing which distinguishes the managerial, professional, and technical workforce, however, is that the demand for their skills has meant that the location of those branches of industry dependent upon qualified personnel has increasingly responded to their preferences as to where they would like to live and work. Towns and villages in suitably 'rural' areas of Southern England have been the main beneficiaries. No matter that the regions of the north and west contain most of Britain's National Parks and many other areas of scenic beauty; these assets are offset, it would seem, by the negative images projected by the urban–industrial areas within the same regions. In addition, the concentration of the more highly qualified workers in the south is a cumulative and self reinforcing process. Employers there find it easier to recruit such personnel from each other. The individual's prospects for career advancement without long-distance residential movement are enhanced by the geographical concentration of higher-grade job opportunies. In turn, the spatial concentration of white-collar employment within manufacturing means that Southern England benefits from a large pool of potential entrepreneurs with managerial and technical expertise, who are more likely than their less well-qualified counterparts to be the founders of successful, growing new firms (Fothergill and Gudgin 1982; Lloyd and Mason 1984).

The effects of public intervention on the country's industrial geography are often considered solely in terms of the impact of regional policy and planned overspill arrangements. As shown in other chapters of this book, this is an unfortunately compartmentalized view of the impact of public policy upon regional development, and one likely to miss the important spatial implications of other non-spatial policies. Government spending has played a part in the development of the new growth areas of Southern England, just as policies of disinvestment and rationalization in nationalized industries have had powerful impacts upon coalmining, shipbuilding, and steelmaking areas elsewhere in the country (Hudson, 1984). Government support for the aerospace industry and defence contracts have underpinned key high-technology sectors in the Bristol subregion's economy (Boddy and Lovering 1986). In 1977–8 the South West and South East regions together accounted for 56 per cent of Ministry of Defence procurement of equipment (Short 1981), compared with their combined share of net manufacturing output of 34 per cent. In the Thames valley growth corridor west of London, the juxtaposition of public investments in the M4 motorway, high-speed rail links, and Heathrow airport, together with the presence of government research and defence establishments, must be seen as crucial ingredients in the area's growth. At least part of the 'Cambridge Phenomenon' (Segal Quince Wicksteed 1985)—the burgeoning and interwoven development of new high-technology firms in and around the town over the last two decades—can be attributed to public-sector support for its university and research institutes as centres of excellence.

Overall, then, many less urbanized areas of Southern England—the 'Greater South East'—have benefited from a particular conjunction of attributes and influences which have helped them to develop new sources of growth, especially in the more technologically advanced sectors of industry. If national industrial regeneration and employment creation are, in line with current government hopes (Department of Employment 1985), to be strongly based on the exploitation of new technologies and the expansion of new and small businesses, then this will tend to favour areas where conditions have already proved to be most conducive to innovation and new firm formation and growth. Present indications are that these areas are predominantly located south and east of a Severn–Wash divide. Elsewhere in the country, there are outliers which appear to be able to offer a similar environment such as parts of Cheshire or East Central Scotland; but they do not compare in scale with South East England, and their positive features tend to be overshadowed by severe problems of decline in adjacent areas. Equally, South East England should not be regarded as a uniform honeypot of growth (see Chapter 4). At the core of the region, Greater London's manufacturing workforce has shrunk to around half its size at the start of the 1960s. The earlier postwar specialization in manufacturing in some of London's New Towns has proved a weakness in their employment structure, while in the Medway Towns the closure of the naval dockyards has produced local economic problems reminiscent of those of northern industrial centres. The map of relative economic health has become more complicated in recent years.

There is also cause for caution over the direct employment-creation effects of both new technologies and new firms within the conventionally defined manufacturing sector. As already noted, many technological advances in manufacturing in recent years, rather than creating new products and new markets, have taken the form of labour-saving process innovations. There is no reason to see an early end to this trend. Differences in rates of new enterprise formation are likely to have a substantial effect only in the longer term. As Wood (Chapter 4 below) notes, the principal means by which parts of the outer South East gained manufacturing jobs in the late 1970s was through *in situ* expansion of existing medium-sized plants, rather than by new openings exceeding closures. In East Anglia, Gould and Keeble's (1984) finding that new manufacturing firms established since 1971 accounted for approximately 5 per cent of the region's total manufacturing employees in 1981 led them to conclude:

> If this is all that can be achieved in a region with one of the highest levels of manufacturing firm formation in Britain, national-level new firm policies seem likely to be of only strictly limited significance, at least in the short term, for industrial restructuring and job generation. (Gould and Keeble 1984: 199).

The same research also indicated that the tendency to associate new manufacturing firms with new technology is ill-founded. Only 10 per cent of the East Anglian new firms were in 'high-technology' industries. It is worth noting that a high proportion of the new high-technology enterprises contributing to the 'Cambridge Phenomenon' have not been manufacturing concerns as such, but firms involved, for example, in research, design, and development (Segal Quince Wicksteed 1985). With regard to the contribution of high-technology industry in general to employment growth, research from both Bristol (Boddy and Lovering 1986) and Berkshire (Breheny *et al*. 1983) indicates that even in these prominent centres of high-tech development, more job gains in the 1970s came from the expansion of office-based financial and business services (see also Chapter 4 below).

Recent studies of the regional anatomy of job loss have understandably concentrated on manufacturing industry. The above observations suggest, however, that this concentration is less helpful when considering the anatomy of job generation. Greater attention must here be given to service-sector employment.

Regional patterns of service employment change

The conventional view of services in regional development is as a largely 'dependent' sector which responds to changes in the pattern of demand generated directly and indirectly by the 'basic' sector of manufacturing. We should, however, beware of assuming that the pattern of service employment change can be fully accounted for by change in the manufacturing sector. The impact of the latter upon demand for consumer services is in any case largely indirect—that is, it depends upon the influence of manufacturing (and other 'basic' sector) employment change upon population and income levels. Moreover, as noted earlier, demand for producer services does not emanate only from manufacturing.

While it may be assumed that many consumer services will be distributed broadly in relation to population, some producer services must be regarded as less dependent upon meeting a purely local or even regional demand. This is true whether the demand for producer services is generated by manufacturing or by other sectors of the economy. Probably more important in determining how far the location of supply is determined by that of demand is the nature of the service product itself. A broad distinction between goods-handling and

Table 2.3. Great Britain: regional service employment changes, 1971–81 (SIC 1968)

	% employment change		
	1971–6	1976–81	1971–81
South East	7.8	3.5	11.6
Greater London	2.1	−1.1	1.0
Rest of South East	15.8	9.3	26.5
East Anglia	19.4	6.9	27.6
South West	13.0	7.6	21.6
West Midlands	11.9	3.7	16.2
East Midlands	20.9	6.1	28.3
Yorkshire and Humberside	13.4	2.3	16.1
North West	8.6	2.7	11.6
North	13.6	1.3	15.0
Wales	14.0	4.1	18.7
Scotland	12.2	4.4	17.1
Great Britain	11.0	3.9	15.3

Source: *Employment Gazette*, Continuous Estimates of Employees in Employment and Annual Census of Employment.

information-handling activities in producer services is helpful in this respect. Thus, as a simple instance, the location of service workers involved in the physical movement of goods or the repair and maintenance of equipment may be more closely tied to the geography of demand than the location of those who advertise the goods or insure the equipment. Some business services are thus capable of contributing to a region's export base.

In contrast to the location of consumer services, therefore, the geography of some producer services is, like other 'basic' industries, likely to reflect differences in regional comparative advantages in terms of supply factors, including skilled labour availability and scale and agglomeration economies. This is illustrated in the distinctive concentration of employment in insurance, banking, finance, and business services, which serve both producer and consumer markets, in South East England, and especially in Greater London. A Department of Industry study of the rapidly growing computer services sector in the UK found that the South East contained 69 per cent of company head offices, 56 per cent of all offices, and 71 per cent of employment in this sector, with 44 per cent of jobs being located in Greater London alone (Green 1983). South East England outside London is the leading area for employment in research and development services in Britain, with 45 per cent of the total in 1981.

Classical export base theory's treatment of services thus requires some qualification. Nevertheless, as the theory would predict, the trend towards interregional dispersion in the location of manufacturing jobs in the decade up to the mid-1970s was to some extent mirrored in the changing regional distri-

Table 2.4. Great Britain: regional changes in distribution and miscellaneous service employment, 1971–81

	% employment change		
	1971–6	1976–81	1971–81
South East	6.2	6.5	13.1
Greater London	−2.2	1.3	−0.9
Rest of South East	17.1	12.1	31.3
East Anglia	18.9	10.8	31.8
South West	14.6	8.4	24.2
West Midlands	10.1	5.3	16.0
East Midlands	16.9	13.0	32.1
Yorkshire and Humberside	15.7	3.3	19.6
North West	9.4	6.6	16.6
North	13.6	2.6	16.6
Wales	14.9	7.1	23.0
Scotland	9.7	6.7	17.0
Great Britain	10.4	6.6	17.6

Source: *Employment Gazette*, Continuous Estimates of Employees in Employment and Annual Census of Employment.

bution of total service employment in the period 1971–6 (see Table 2.3), with a declining share of national service employment in the South East and North West, and relative gains in all other regions. This period, in contrast to the previous five years, was one of strong service employment growth nationally. There was a rapid expansion of public service jobs, accompanied by a revival of workforce growth, largely in part-time jobs, in distribution and miscellaneous services (Harris and Taylor 1978) which can plausibly be related to the abolition of Selective Employment Tax and the expansionary economic policies of 1971–3.

The evidence suggests that the peripheral assisted regions benefited, to varying degrees, from both of these trends. Growth in both total service employment and in the predominantly consumer-orientated distribution and miscellaneous services (see Table 2.4) was above the national average in the North, Yorkshire and Humberside, and Wales. In Scotland, above-average job growth appears to have owed more to public rather than private services, while in North West England, positive national trends in services were partly offset by structural weaknesses in Merseyside's port-orientated service economy (Lloyd and Reeve 1982). The fastest growth of service jobs occurred in East Anglia and the East Midlands.

In the subsequent period 1976–81, total service employment growth was much more modest, largely because of aggregate job loss in public services. Relative dependence on publice service jobs (i.e. employment in education, health, and public administration as a proportion of all service employment)

Table 2.5. Great Britain: regional changes in public and private service employment, 1976–81

	% service employment in public services* 1976	% employment change 1976–81	
		Public services*	Private services
South East	34.0	−3.3	7.0
Greater London	30.8	−8.4	2.1
Rest of South East	38.0	1.8	13.9
East Anglia	36.0	−4.4	13.3
South West	37.3	5.3	10.7
West Midlands	39.0	−2.3	7.5
East Midlands	41.5	−4.5	13.7
Yorkshire and Humberside	37.9	−1.1	4.4
North West	37.2	−0.9	4.9
North	40.1	−2.0	3.4
Wales	44.5	0.8	6.7
Scotland	38.9	3.5	5.0
Great Britain	37.0	−1.5	7.0

Source: *Employment Gazette*.

**Note*: Public services are defined here as Minimum List Headings 872, Education, 874, Medical and dental services, and Order XXVII, Public administration of the 1968 SIC. As these groups contain privately supplied educational and medical services, they are a slight approximation. They do not include public service employees in the transport sectors.

varied between regions in 1976, being lowest (34 per cent) in the South East and highest (40 per cent or more) in the North, East Midlands, and Wales. Comparison of regional changes in public and private service employment 1976–81 (Table 2.5) indicates that relative dependence upon the former in the North and East Midlands served to depress total service employment growth as a result of above-average losses of public service jobs. In Wales, conversely, with the highest proportion of service jobs in the public sector, and in Scotland, changes in public sector services went against the national trend of marginal decline, thus helping to maintain service job growth in these regions above the national average. Arguably, this reflects the distinctive administrative status of Scotland and Wales, with their own territorially based ministers and government departments, and their above-average levels of public expenditure per capita in this period.

In terms of private service employment growth, a clear North–South disparity emerged in the period 1976–81, with percentage increases in all three northern English regions, and Scotland and Wales falling below the national average. A sharp reversal of trends from the first half of the 1970s can be seen in the reduction in employment growth in the predominantly consumer-orientated distribution and miscellaneous services in the North, Yorkshire and Humberside, and Wales (see Table 2.4). The rate of employment growth in these services in the first two of these regions was actually exceeded by that in the South East 1976–81, a situation contrasting sharply with that over the previous five years, when the South East had the lowest growth rate in distribution and miscellaneous services, as a result of job losses, in the context of rapid population decline, in Greater London. Total private service employment in the South East as a whole increased at the national rate during 1976–81, and at nearly twice that rate in the region outside London. Growth in the East Midlands, South West, and East Anglia was also well above the national average.

In insurance, banking, finance, and business services, in contrast to the service sector as a whole, the growth in employment was larger and more rapid in 1976–81 than in the previous five years. The growth rate in the South East was below the national average in both 1971–6 and 1976–81 (see Table 2.6). This was a result of small proportionate increases in Greater London, with over 30 per cent of national employment in this SIC Order, in contrast to rapid growth in the rest of the region. However, in the North West, with the second largest regional concentration of jobs in financial and business services, there was no growth in employment during 1971–6, and an increase only marginally above the national average during 1976–81. The implication is that the regional business centres of Manchester and Liverpool were declining in importance in the 1970s. The contraction of Liverpool's port-based service economy must be one contributory element here, while in Manchester's case large-scale industrial decline and increased external control of manufacturing in the city's hinterland both tended to reduce the market for regionally based business services. Mergers and rationalizations in banking and insurance also adversely affected employment in the city's financial services in the early 1970s (Roger Tym and Partners 1982). Scotland, with the third largest total of employment in financial and business services, showed above average growth in 1971–6, but then a markedly slower expansion in 1976–81. In the earlier period, Scotland benefited from having its own banking industry at a time of rapid expansion nationally in this sector (Morris 1982). In the later 1970s, however, constraints on growth in the Scottish banking market and some rationalization of activities limited further job growth, while building societies were relatively slow to expand their operations in Scotland, where levels of owner-occupation have traditionally been lower than in England. Scotland, like North West England, was also traditionally an important centre of the insurance industry; both regions lost employment during the 1970s, with locally based companies being absorbed by South East-based institutions and a shift away from the types of insurance business concentrated there (Morris 1982).

Elsewhere, the fastest growth in financial and business service jobs was recorded in East Anglia and the South West. The high growth rate in the former region is partyly due to a low base level of employment, but the even more rapid expansion in the South West reflects the importance of Bristol, Swindon, and Cheltenham, along with other locations in the favoured western axis, as

Table 2.6. Great Britain: regional changes in insurance, banking, finance, and business service employment, 1971–81

	% employment change		
	1971–6	1976–81	1971–81
South East	10.8	16.0	28.9
Greater London	5.4	8.5	14.6
Rest of South East	27.8	36.0	73.8
East Anglia	35.0	25.9	70.0
South West	39.0	29.7	87.0
West Midlands	18.0	38.0	60.1
East Midlands	20.6	26.8	52.9
Yorkshire and Humberside	15.1	26.2	45.3
North West	0.0	21.2	21.2
North	14.8	25.8	44.4
Wales	8.7	32.0	50.0
Scotland	16.9	13.2	32.3
Great Britain	12.9	20.4	35.9

Source: *Employment Gazette*, Continuous Estimates of Employees in Employment and Annual Census of Employment.

destinations for offices moving from London in the 1970s. Interestingly, the West Midlands also emerged as a relatively fast-growing region in financial and business jobs, especially in 1976–81, in some contrast to its growth in service employment overall. This region traditionally was relatively poorly endowed with employment in financial and business services, compared, for example, with the North West and Scotland. Paradoxically perhaps, this may have been an advantage; the region could benefit from the overall expansion of financial services but did not suffer to the same extent as the North West and Scotland from the impact of merger and rationalization on locally based institutions.

Service employment change in local labour market areas

Owen and Green (1984) have examined total service employment changes in 1971–81 at the level of local labour market areas, defined according to the functional urban region classification developed in the Centre for Urban and Regional Development Studies at Newcastle University (Coombes *et al*. 1982). At this spatial scale the patterns of change appear more complex. The strong growth of service employment in the South East outside London and in adjacent regions was not spatially uniform. The areas with the greatest relative increases in service sector jobs lay in a broad belt to the north and west of London (see also Chapter 4 below). Elsewhere in the country, there was rapid growth in the Grampian and Highland regions in northern Scotland, presumably oil-related, and in several so-called 'conurbation subdominant towns', i.e. smaller urban centres within the hinterlands of the provincial conurbations. Arguably, the latter type of growth reflects the response of service industries to the dispersal of population within large urban regions. The lowest growth rates were in general recorded in the conurbations, including London. However, outside the largest urban areas, the strong inverse relationship between employment growth and urban size which has been observed for the manufacturing sector (Fothergill and Gudgin 1982; Fothergill *et al.* 1985) was somewhat less evident with services. In particular, when considered in aggregate, several categories of (mainly southern) small- to medium-sized urban labour market areas gained service jobs faster than either northern or southern rural areas during 1971–81, which suggests that some services maintained a stronger affinity for urban locations than manufacturing activities (Owen and Green 1984).

Regional trends in the 1980s

Owen and Green's examination of service employment changes in the shorter period 1978–81 largely confirms the impression given by the regional-level data that trends in service sector growth in recession moved against northern and western areas of the country. The regional data suggest that, in Scotland and Wales (and also in Northern Ireland: see Chapter 11 below), the trends were moderated somewhat by relative stability or continued gains in public service employment.

Consideration of trends in service employment beyond 1981 is hampered by a change in the industrial classification of employment used in official figures, and by reliance upon estimates until the results of the 1984 Census of Employment are available. Current estimates indicate a trend of marginal decline in service jobs from 1981 to early 1983, followed by renewed growth, producing an overall gain of 1.5 per cent between June 1981 and June 1984; the bulk of the net increase was in part-time jobs for women.

Regional estimates for 1981–4 suggest some modification of the spatial contrasts in service employment change noted for 1976–81 (see Table 2.7). The South East gained service jobs faster than the country as a whole, as did East Anglia and the South West, but the East Midlands appeared to lose some of its earlier dynamism. Growth in the North, Yorkshire and Humberside, and now also the West Midlands was below average. Above-average growth in the North West in 1981–4 was largely due to an estimated job gain of 4.8 per cent in public administration, compared with a national loss of 2.2 per cent. Scotland and Wales, where services again performed slightly better than average, also recorded smaller job losses in this category than most other regions. The way in which public service employment changes can offset the effects of other forces is worth noting. The other side of the coin is that the reversal of public service employment growth from the late 1970s had notably adverse implications for many of the country's inner urban labour markets with a high dependence upon

Table 2.7. Great Britain: regional changes in total service employment (SIC 1980) and employment in public administration, 1981–4 (June); percentage of total regional employment in services, 1984

	% employment change 1981–4		% total employment in services 1984
	All services	Public administration	
South East	2.0	−2.3	71.5
East Anglia	5.9	−5.7	62.6
South West	2.6	−4.1	66.4
West Midlands	0.3	−0.6	55.2
East Midlands	1.5	−11.1	53.6
Yorkshire and Humberside	0.5	0.0	59.0
North West	2.3	4.8	63.3
North	0.0	−7.7	60.8
Wales	1.8	−1.8	63.7
Scotland	1.7	−1.7	65.0
Great Britain	1.5	−2.2	64.6

Source: *Employment Gazette.*

public service jobs, compounding the effect of employment decline in other sectors.

Overall, therefore, while there is some evidence for an 'export base effect' on the changing distribution of service jobs, this is clearly not the whole story. Examination of changes at a disaggregated service industry level, or at a finer spatial scale than the regions, reveals both greater complexity and weaker links with manufacturing. It is evident, however, that, in so far as trends in the 1970s reduced the dominance, in employment terms, of Greater London in the distribution of financial and business services, the main beneficiaries were areas elsewhere within the 'Greater South East' (Regional Studies Association 1983), while some leading regional business centres like Manchester were shrinking in importance.

Producer services and regional development

In view of the proportion of total employment now concentrated in services in Britain, regional disparities in the development of this sector are clearly critical to the pattern of job generation. They may also be seen as having wider significance to problems of regional imbalance. In particular, disparities in producer service endowments affect the size and diversity of the export base in different regions, and also have a significant impact upon regional occupational structures, and thus upon the range and quality, as well as the volume, of employment opportunities in different areas. This in turn may have implications for differences in regional 'entrepreneurship potential' (Storey 1982).

A further line of argument which has recently gained ground is that the availability, range, and quality of producer services in a region can have a significant effect upon competitiveness, and upon the capacity for successful adjustment to change in that region's manufacturing sector. This argument in part relies upon drawing parallels at the regional level with relationships established between national economic performance and relative specialization and investment in 'human capital-intensive' activities (Marquand 1983). 'Human capital intensity' in this context is often associated with increased inputs of higher-order producer services in manufacturing, whether internally or externally supplied. The argument is also seen as supported by some evidence that firms which use certain business services—management consultants, for example—record marked improvements in performance (Johnson 1963; Marshall 1982). If, so the argument runs, access to such business services is a significant influence upon their cost and likely use, then the spatial pattern of supply is crucial to the prospects for successful adaptation and self-reliant growth in particular regions.

At present we have only 'some tantalizing incomplete pieces of evidence' (Marquand 1983: 134) for these postulated links between business service inputs, access to supply and manufacturing performance at the regional level. Here, the argument has to rely on inference from spatial correlation. For example, the demonstrated link between the on-site presence of R & D and establishments' innovation records (Thwaites 1982) leads to the suggestion that the regional distribution of R & D helps to explain regional differences in rates of industrial innovation. Oakey *et al.* (1980) have also shown a statistical association between regional differences in innovation rates and variations in the proportion of non-production workers within regional manufacturing.

In the Northern region, a low level of business service use among locally based firms, with little emphasis on marketing or research (Marshall 1979), has been seen as a result of the problem of access to business services and specialised information sources, and in turn as a factor in the poor performance of indigenous enterprise in the region. Equally, of course, the poorly developed state of the business service sector in a region like the North may be viewed more as a result of weak local demand than as a constraint on indigenous growth. The observed tendency for externally owned branch plants in peripheral regions like the North to generate relatively few local business service demands may thus represent a rational response to the supply situation there—which tends, as noted by the Department of Trade and Industry (1983), to reinforce the under-representation of business services in these regions. This also provides a strong argument for reducing the traditional regional policy emphasis on subsidies to capital investment in manufacturing, since this is likely to have accentuated the bias in the assisted regions towards investments with low service input requirements, and thus limited multiplier effects on the local economy, while more service-intensive functions have remained concentrated in the South East.

Conclusion

This chapter has shown that the impact of economic restructuring and recession since the early 1970s has been sharply differentiated between areas—reinforcing but also partly reshaping the pattern of spatial inequality in job opportunities in both quantitative and qualitative terms. In the mid- to late 1970s, both academic and policy attention to such inequality shifted away from concern with broad regional disparities towards differentials associated with urban status—inner cities versus outer suburbs, conurbations versus non-conurbation areas, and 'urban–rural' contrasts in general. The recession which followed, however, brought regional differences back into focus. Thus, by 1982, Martin could observe: 'the economic collapse of the past three years has re-established with a vengeance, and with addition of the West Midlands, the North–South unemployment disparity that for four decades regional policy has sought to narrow' (Martin 1982: 262). Owen *et al.* (1984), from a detailed analysis of the components of change in labour supply and demand in local labour market areas over the period 1971–81, also emphasize broad regional differences:

> Across a range of labour market change components—employment, participation rates, net migration and unemployment—local labour markets to the north and west of the Severn–Wash line are performing considerably worse than their southern and eastern counterparts. (Owen *et al.* 1984: 486).

The highly uneven toll taken by the post-1979 recession thus lends support to the notion that a basic regional dualism can be identified within the UK between an area comprising much of South East England together with adjacent parts of East Anglia, the East Midlands, and the South West, on the one hand, and most of the rest of the country, on the other. This dualism is not simply a product of the recent recession, but reflects the differential regional experience of longer-term structural changes in the UK economy which have systematically tended to favour some areas while disfavouring others. To use the terminology introduced in Chapter 1, it can be argued that this dualism essentially reflects the difference between 'de-industrialization' and 'post-industrial' development as alternative perspectives on the nature of structural change in the UK economy.

A 'post-industrial' perspective appears most relevant to an understanding of the relative prosperity and economic buoyancy of the 'Greater South East'. The positive and dynamic aspects of service activity development are most in evidence here—London's role as a 'world city' and the internationalization of its financial and business service activities; the concentration of corporate control functions and associated producer services, including R & D; the growth of services catering for international business and private tourism; the development of recreational and leisure services based upon the higher incomes generated by the region's other service functions. These are all prominent features of the evolving specialization of the South East's economy and employment structure, contrasting with its much-diminished role as a base for volume consumer goods manufacture.

It should of course be noted that the emerging trajectory of 'post-industrial' development in the South East is not without its problems. Most obviously, the decline of London's manufacturing base has not only reduced the total job stock there, but has also eroded the 'middle ground' of the local employment structure, in terms of jobs for skilled and semi-skilled manual workers, thus tending to produce a polarized labour market. Less skilled and unskilled workers are increasingly concentrated into lower-grade service jobs, if they have jobs at all, while the capital's large clerical workforce faces depletion through the wider deployment of new information technologies. Outside London, there are serious imbalances in growth and development between the west and east of the surrounding region (see Chapter 4).

In very general terms, a different trajectory of development to that in the Greater South East can be discerned in northern and western regions of the UK, in which the negative aspects of structural change, 'de-industrialization', are more evident. Here the decline of production employment has been most pronounced, outside London itself, and there have not been offsetting gains in producer services and higher-order corporate functions. Service job growth in these regions has relied heavily upon the public sector and private consumer services; the latter, however, have been affected by the impact of industrial decline and rising unemployment, while the former has operated within a more stringent public expenditure regime since the late 1970s.

Again we must beware of over-generalization: the regions of the north and west should not be viewed a homogeneous group of relatively disadvantaged areas. While high unemployment is a common attribute, there are important differences between the less favoured areas in terms of their history of economic development, and their industrial, corporate, and plant size structures. As shown in subsequent chapters, for example, the West Midlands, Merseyside, and South Wales should not be treated as having the same characteristics and problems. There are also signs that Scotland saw some improvement in its relative position among the UK regions in the 1970s (see Chapter 10).

This division between 'post-industrial' and 'de-industrialized' regions of the UK, opposite faces of the same coin, is thus only a starting-point in considering the relationships between structural change in the national economy and evolving spatial differentiation. It should not lead to the diagnosis of a single 'regional problem' solely in these terms. Instead, we should recognize that, within the process of uneven spatial development, problems of decline and economic adjustment are widely distributed, but that these have different impacts in different contexts, and are more concentrated and severe in some regions than in others. While certain broad spatial distinctions in relative prosperity can still be made, more detailed inspection reveals a complicated mosaic of development experiences and problems. This growing complexity in regional and local problems was, of course, one important factor which undermined confidence in conventional regional policy from the mid-1970s.

References

Beesley, M. (1955), 'The Birth and Death of Industrial Establishments: Experience in the West Midlands Conurbation', *Journal of Industrial Economics* 4, 45–61.

Boddy, M. and Lovering, J. (1986), 'High Technology Industry in the Bristol Sub-region: The Aerospace/Defence Nexus', *Regional Studies* 20.

Breheny, M., Cheshire, P., and Langridge, R. (1983), 'The Anatomy of Job Generation? Industrial Change in Britain's M4 Corridor', *Built Environment* 9, 61–71.

Checkland, S. G. (1981), *The Upas Tree: Glasgow 1875–1975 . . . and after 1975–1980*, 2nd edn., Glasgow, University of Glasgow Press.

Coombes, M. G., Dixon, J. S., Goddard, J. B., Openshaw, S., and Taylor, P. (1982), 'Functional Regions for the Population Census of Great Britain', in D. J. Herbert and R. J. Johnston, eds., *Geography and the Urban Environment: Progress in Research and Applications*, Vol V., Chichester, Wiley.

Dennis, R. D. (1978), 'The Decline of Manufacturing Employment in Greater London: 1966–74, *Urban Studies* 15, 63–73.

Department of Employment (1985), *Employment. The Challenge for the Nation*, Cmnd. 9474, London, HMSO.

Department of Trade and Industry (1983), *Regional Industrial Policy. Some Economic Issues*, London, Department of Trade and Industry.

Firn, J. R. and Swales, J. K. (1978), 'The Formation of New Manufacturing Establishments in the Central Clydeside and West Midlands Conurbations, 1963–73', *Regional Studies* 12, 199–213.

Fothergill, S. and Gudgin, G. (1982), *Unequal Growth. Urban and Regional Employment Change in the UK*, London, Heinnemann.

Fothergill, S., Kitson, M., and Monk, S. (1985), *Urban Industrial Change. The Causes of the Urban–Rural Contrast in Manufacturing Employment Trends*, Inner Cities Research Programme 11, London, HMSO.

Gould, A. and Keeble, D. (1984), 'New firms and rural industrialization in East Anglia', *Regional Studies* 18, 189–201.

Green, S. (1983), 'The Location, Mobility and Financing of the Computer Services Sector in the UK', London, Department of Industry: South East Regional Office.

Harris, D. F. and Taylor, F. J. (1978), *The Service Sector: Its Changing Role as a Source of Employment*, Research Series 25, London, Centre for Environmental Studies.

Howells, J. R. L. (1984), 'The Location of Research and Development: Some Observations and Evidence from Britain', *Regional Studies* 18, 13–29.

Hudson, R. (1984), 'The Paradoxes of State Intervention: The Impact of Nationalized Industry Policies and Regional Policy in the Northern Region in the Post-war Period', in R. Chapman, ed., *Public Policy Studies: North East England*, Edinburgh, Edinburgh University Press.

Johnson, J. (1963), 'The Productivity of Management Consultants', *Journal of the Royal Statistical Society*, Series A, 237–249.

Keeble, D. (1976), *Industrial Location and Planning in the United Kingdom*, London, Methuen.

——, (1977), 'Spatial Policy in Britain: Regional or Urban?' *Area* 9, 3–8.

Lloyd, P. E. and Mason, C. M. (1984), 'Spatial Variations in New Firm Formation in the United Kingdom: Comparative Evidence from Merseyside, Greater Manchester and South Hampshire', *Regional Studies* 18, 207–20.

—— and Reeve, D. E. (1982), 'North West England 1971–77: A Study in Industrial Decline and Economic Restructuring', *Regional Studies* 16, 345–60.

Mackay, R. (1979), 'The Death of Regional Policy—or Resurrection Squared', *Regional Studies* 13, 281–8.

Marquand, J. (1983), 'The Changing Distribution of Service Employment', in J. B. Goddard and A. G. Champion, eds., *The Urban and Regional Transformation of Britain*, London, Methuen.

Marshall, J. N. (1979), 'Ownership, Organization and Industrial Linkage: A Case Study in the Northern Region of England', *Regional Studies* 13, 531–57.

——, (1982), 'Linkages Between Manufacturing Industry and Business Services', *Environment and Planning A* 14, 1523–40.

Martin, R. L. (1982*a*), 'Britain's Slump: The Regional Anatomy of Job Loss', *Area* 14, 257–63.

——, (1982*b*), 'Job Loss and the Regional Incidence of Redundancies in the Current Recession', *Cambridge Journal of Economics* 6, 365–75.

Massey, D. B. and Meegan, R. A. (1978), 'Industrial Restructuring Versus the Cities', *Urban Studies* 15, 273–88.

—— and —— (1979), 'The Geography of Industrial Reorganization: The Spatial Effects of the Restructuring of the Electrical Engineering Sector under the Industrial Reorganization Corporation', *Progress in Planning* 10, 155–237.

—— and —— (1982), *The Anatomy of Job Loss*. London, Methuen.

Moore, B. and Rhodes, J. (1974), 'The Effects of Regional Economic Policy in the United Kingdom', in M. Sant, ed., *Regional Policy and Planning for Europe*, Farnborough, Saxon House.

——, ——, and Tyler, P. (1977), 'The Impact of Regional Policy in the 1970s', *CES Review* 1, 67–77.

Morris, D. (1982), 'An Inquiry into Changes in the Insurance, Banking and Finance Sector and their Influence on the Location of its Activities', Interim Report to the Department of Industry, University College London, Department of Geography (mimeo).

Oakey, R. P., Thwaites, A. T., and Nash, P. A. (1980), 'The Regional Distribution of Innovative Manufacturing Establishments in Britain', *Regional Studies* 14, 235–53.

——, ——, and —— (1982), 'Technological Changes and Regional Development: Some Evidence on Regional Variations in Product and Process Innovation', *Environment and Planning A* 14, 1073–86.

Owen, D. W., Gillespie, A. E., and Coombes, M. G. (1984), 'Job Shortfalls', in 'British Local Labour Market Areas: A Classification of Labour Supply and Demand Trends 1971–81', *Regional Studies* 18, 469–88.

—— and Green, A. E. (1984), 'Modelling Population and Sectoral Employment Change in British Local Labour Market Areas, 1971–81', Discussion Paper 11, University of Newcastle upon Tyne, Centre for Urban and Regional Development Studies.

Regional Studies Association (1983), *Report of an Inquiry into Regional Problems in the United Kingdom*, Norwich, Geo Books.

Roger Tym and Partners (1981), *Capital of the North. The Business Service Sector in Inner Manchester/Salford*, Report to the Inner Manchester/Salford Partnership, London, Roger Tym and Partners.

Segal Quince Wicksteed (1985), *The Cambridge Phenomenon: The Growth of High Technology Industry in a University Town*, Cambridge, Segal Quince Wicksteed.

Short, J. (1981), 'Defence Spending in the UK Regions', *Regional Studies* 15, 101–10

Storey, D. (1982), *Entrepreneurship and the New Firm*, Beckenham, Kent, Croom Helm.

Thwaites, A. T. (1982), 'Some Evidence on Regional Variations in the Introduction and Diffusion of Industrial Products and Processes within British Manufacturing Industry', *Regional Studies* 16, 371–81.

—— (1983), 'The Employment Implications of Technological Change in a Regional Context', in A. Gillespie, ed., *Technological Change and Regional Development*, London, Pion.

Townsend, A. R. (1982), *The Impact of Recession*, Beckenham, Kent, Croom Helm.

CHAPTER 3

The Evolution of Spatial Economic Policy

P. J. Damesick

Introduction

The American researcher Sundquist, reviewing regional development policies in several European countries in the early 1970s, noted: 'With the Industry Act of 1972, Britain after nearly half a century of experimentation with regional policy was very near consensus' (1975: 64). The 1972 Act was part of the Heath Government's rapid reversal of an initial drive to reduce intervention in the economy, and marked a return to a vigorous anti-disparity regional policy initiated a decade earlier. The incoming Labour government in 1974 retained the 1972 Act as the basis of regional policy, but also restored the value of the Regional Employment Premium (a direct labour subsidy to manufacturing firms in Assisted Areas), which had been eroded by inflation since its introduction in 1967. Some Assisted Area designations were upgraded and expanded, with Special Development Area Status for Merseyside; and the Hardman report proposals on Civil Service dispersal were amended to send more jobs to the assisted regions. In the context of a quickening debate over devolution and a parliament in which Scottish nationalist MPs were helping to keep a minority Labour government in power, there was a further strengthening of regional policy in the winter of 1975–6 with the establishment of the Scottish and Welsh Development Agencies.

After a brief interlude of weaker policy, the early to mid-1970s thus saw an intensification of regional measures and increasing expenditure. By the end of the 1970s, however, the situation had changed markedly. McCallum (1979: 38) could write: 'Enough of the traditional interpretations and prescriptions have been shaken to make the future of British regional policy fundamentally uncertain. A consensus, nearly fifty years in the making, is probably collapsing.' A substantial part of the background to that collapse has already been outlined in the previous two chapters. This chapter considers the form of the collapse and consequent developments in spatial policy.

The retreat from regional policy

Three features of the context and nature of the renewed boom in regional policy in 1972–6 are worth noting; in retrospect, they provide clear signposts to the subsequent direction of policy development. First, and most obviously, the return to an active regional policy was closely followed by the onset of the longest and deepest recession since the 1930s, marked by a combination of high inflation and rising unemployment. Control of the former took priority in government policy, which was generally deflationary and involved the reduction of public expenditure's share of GDP as a key element in the counter-inflation strategy.

Second, an important difference in the implementation of regional policy in the 1970s compared with the 1960s was the far more relaxed application of Industrial Development Certificate control, which research has suggested was one of the most powerful policy instruments in the earlier period. The volume of industrial movement was much lower in the 1970s and increasing concern over national industrial decline and the performance of the London and West Midland economies militated against controls on the location of new investment.

Third, whatever the broad consensus about the need for regional policy in the early to mid-1970s, even at this time there was considerable disquiet in some quarters over whether the particular means adopted were cost-effective in terms of the policy's objectives. As the 1972 Industry Act reached the statute book, a lengthy and detailed review of regional incentives by a House of Commons Expenditure Subcommittee began. Its 1973 report was very critical of the frequent changes made in regional policy, and of the failure to evaluate properly the cost-effectiveness of policy measures—hence its now famous conclusion: 'Much has been spent and much may well have been wasted. Regional policy has been empiricism run mad, a game of hit-and-miss played with more enthusiasm than success' (House of Commons Expenditure Committee 1973: 73).

Thus, a combination of factors—changing national economic circumstances, government reluctance and/or inability to enforce controls on industrial location in favour of the Assisted Areas, and nagging doubts about the cost of the policy and effectiveness of the measures—points towards the shaky foundations of the strengthened regional policy after 1972. Sundquist noted the belief of some supporters of regional policy at this time that 'the one thing that could eventually destroy the national consensus in favour of that policy is its cost'. In his version of a senior official's view: 'The consensus could vanish fast when some future government feels itself under compulsion to cut back spending and is looking for somewhere to get a big chunk of money quickly' (Sundquist 1975: 74).

And so it came to pass. In December 1976, in a 'mini-Budget' crisis package, the immediate abolition of the Regional Employment Premium was announced, effectively reducing regional aid by a third. Ostensibly the end of the REP was necessitated by EEC competition policy rules against this type of labour subsidy. The lack of warning and the wider policy context of growing pressure on public expenditure suggest, however, that this was an excuse to reduce the cost of regional policy substantially and quickly.

The incoming Conservative Government in 1979 acted promptly to reduce the cost of regional policy further as part of a general attempt to cut public spending. In June of that year the Industry Secretary announced the Govern-

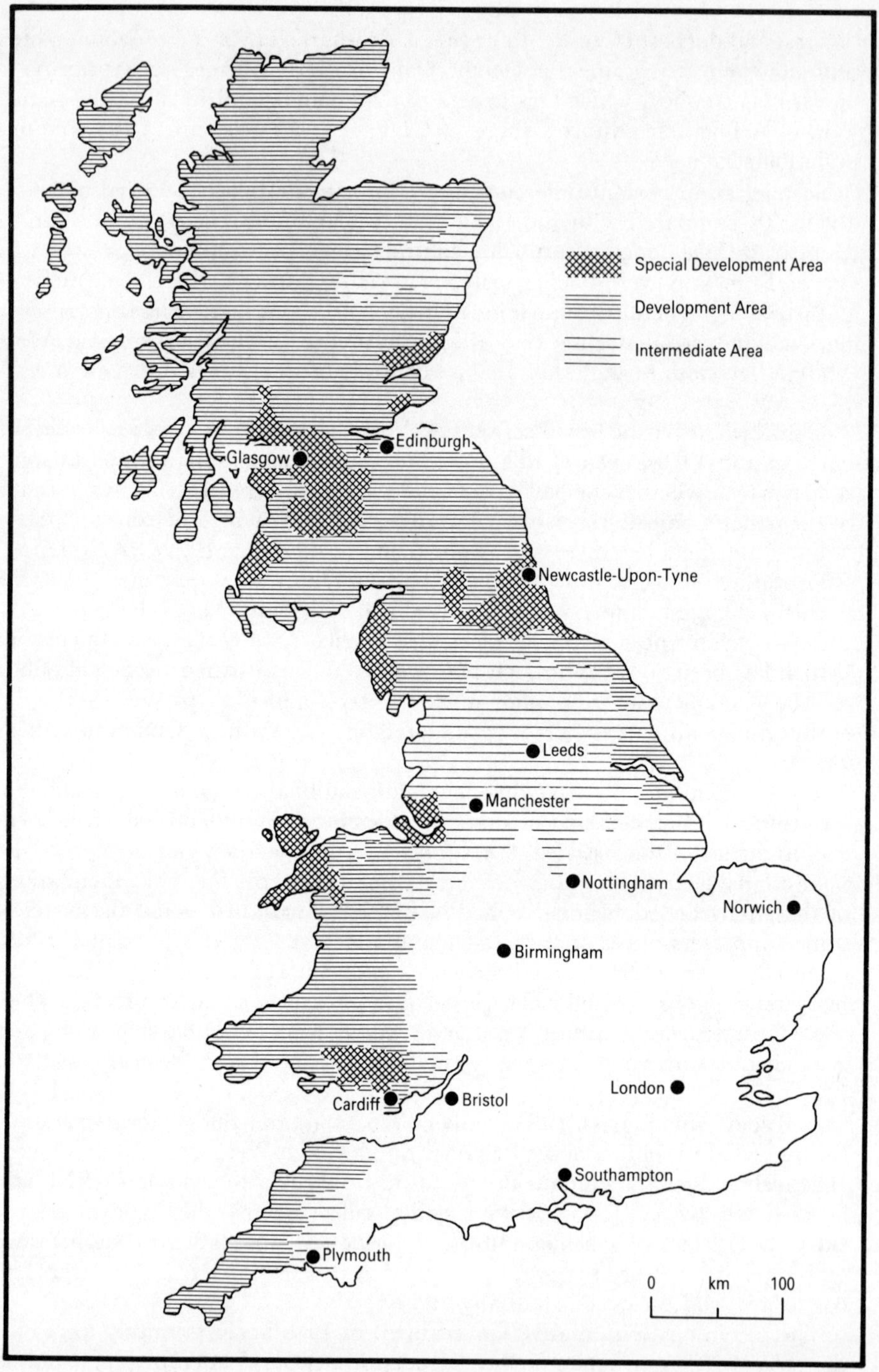

Figure 3.1. Assisted Areas, 1979

ment's intention of reducing projected expenditure on regional aid by 38 per cent by 1982. There was to be a progressive reduction, over a three-year period, in the coverage of Assisted Areas, which fell from over 40 per cent of the working population to 27.5 per cent in 1982 (see Figures 3.1 and 3.2), and a cut in the rate of Regional Development Grant in Development Areas from 20 to 15 per cent. The government also imposed a four-month delay in the payment of RDGs.

Aid was now to be concentrated on the 'areas of greatest need', measured in terms of unemployment rates; but increasingly the rationale for regional policy began to be questioned. On the one hand, there was a body of opinion, most prominent among the West Midlands business community, in favour of the complete abolition of regional aid and the redirection of resources to schemes of sectoral industrial support. A shift of this kind did take place to some extent and the West Midlands had also benefited, of course, from the massive injection of public funds in the British Leyland rescue operation, initiated in the mid-1970s.

The Government's view was that, however socially desirable it might be to help the hard-hit regions, there was no role for regional policy in assisting national economic regeneration since the impact of such policy was purely diversionary, without any contribution to agreggate expansion. The 1960s argument for regional policy as the spatial dimension of Keynesian demand management was thus discarded, together with demand management itself, as government economic policy turned to so-called 'monetarist' theory for its inspiration. According to the new thinking, demand management policies could not be used to raise aggregate demand, nor to replace, at least on a permanent basis, jobs diverted from non-assisted areas by regional policy.

In line with such thinking, and with a general ideological preference for less intervention and more reliance upon market mechanisms, the Conservative Government disposed of several elements of the existing spatial policy and planning framework. Industrial Development Certificates were first suspended and then abolished, together with Office Development Permits. The Location of Offices Bureau, operating under difficulties since its somewhat confusing change of role in 1977 (Damesick 1979), was closed. The Regional Economic Planning Councils, set up originally as part of the new regional planning machinery of the mid-1960s, were dissolved, dismissed as 'talking shops' of little value. More than once, government ministers indicated their deep reservations over the value of regional planning. Any attempt at regional *economic* planning was decidedly out of favour. Thus, it was announced in 1979 that there would be no formal government response to the Northern Region Strategy. Published in 1977, this Strategy had already failed to elicit a response from the previous Labour Government. As a wide-ranging economic development plan for the Northern region, including significant public expenditure implications, it went far beyond central government's capacity for, or commitment to, regional planning. In so far as the latter was to be tolerated at all under the new Conservative administration, it was to be confined to strategic land-use issues.

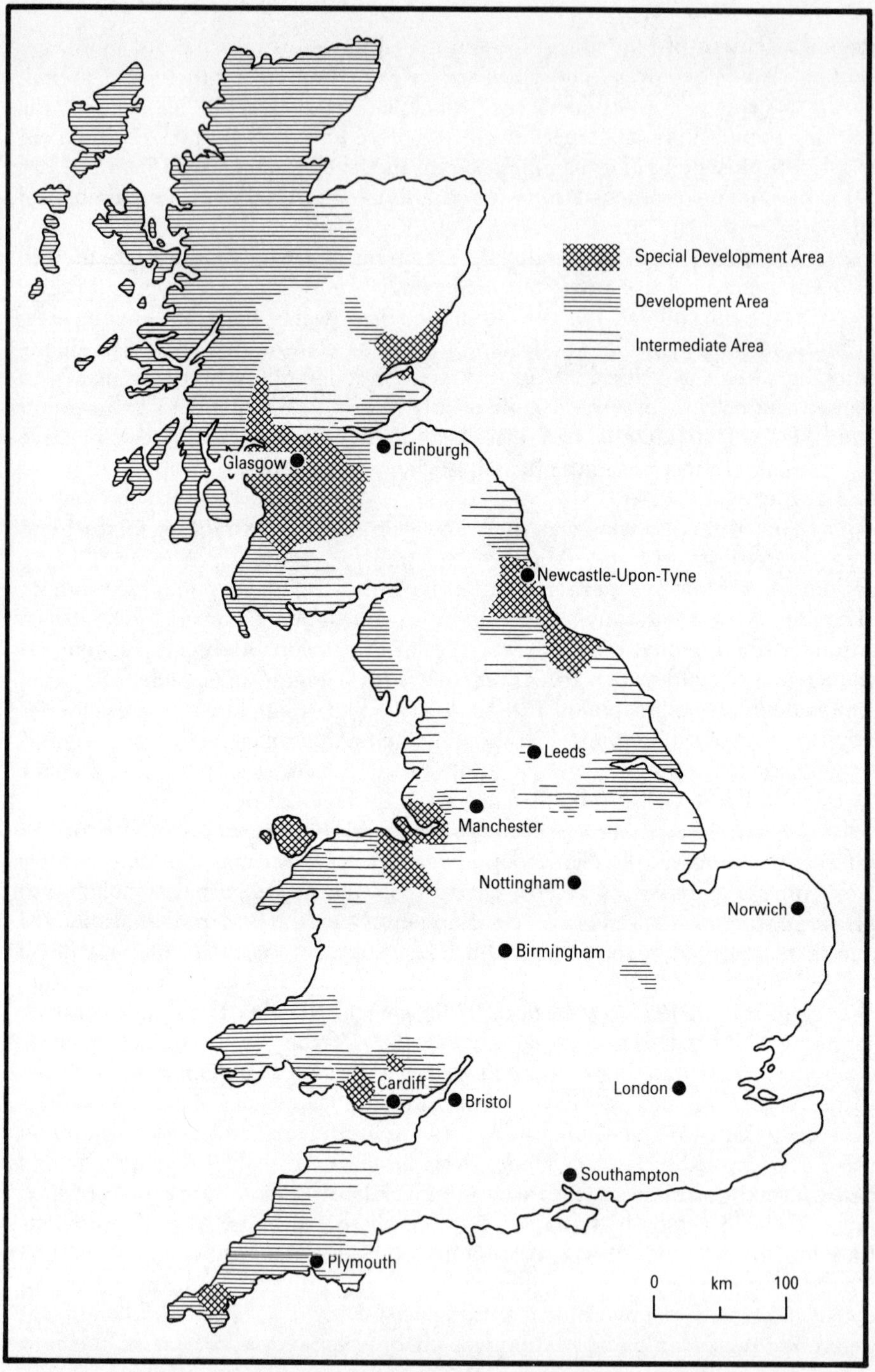

Figure 3.2. Assisted Areas, 1982

The development of the urban programme

The late 1970s and early 1980s were not a period of total disengagement from spatial policy. While the strength and scope of regional policy and planning were diminished, new initiatives and agencies appeared under the growing urban programme. The inner areas of the country's conurbations had, of course, long been recognized as having serious problems. Traditionally these were associated with the overcrowded and unsatisfactory housing conditions of the inner cities, prompting policies of planned population dispersal combined with redevelopment at lower residential densities. In the 1960s there had been increased policy attention to the 'social' problems of the inner areas, including those associated with the concentration of ethnic minority populations. In the 1970s, however, perceptions of the 'inner-city problem' changed quite fundamentally, and in the process posed a major challenge to regional policy. First, the problem was now seen to be 'economic' in character, closely linked to the rapid decline of inner urban manufacturing employment. Second, and equally significant, was the recognition that urban economic decline was a feature not only of the northern conurbations but also of London and Birmingham, previously regarded as sources of mobile employment for the depressed regions.

Urban economic regeneration was thus a leading theme in the 1977 White Paper on the inner cities, and in the 1978 Inner Urban Areas Act. A key element of the new policy was the establishment of central–local government partnerships in selected inner-city areas to implement co-ordinated, comprehensive programmes of action. A similar administrative arrangement had already been initiated in 1976 in the Glasgow Eastern Area Renewal project, under the overall co-ordination of the Scottish Development Agency. Local authorities in the partnership areas (and to a lesser extent in the second tier of 'programme' areas) were empowered to assist economic revival in various ways—for example, by making loans and/or grants available for land acquisition, for environmental improvements, and, in industrial improvement areas which they could designate, for the conversion and rehabilitation of industrial and commercial premises.

Resources for the new urban programme were intended to come partly from additional centrally provided funds, but principally from the eventual adjustment of the mainstream spending programmes of central and local government. The allocation of additional urban aid in the partnerships varied, but, given the new emphasis on economic regeneration, it is noteworthy that, in the initial programmes for 1979–82, none of the partnerships proposed to spend more than 30 per cent of aid specifically on 'economic development'. In four areas, the largest share (over 30 per cent) went to education, cultural, and recreational projects, and Lambeth allocated 24 per cent to health and social services projects (Lawless (1981).

The limited volume of additional resources for inner-city policy meant that redirection of main-line public spending was all important to the programme's chances of success. In practice, however, there were major obstacles to any substantial shifts in expenditure, due to the need to meet existing commitments and to inflexibilities created by long-term planning in resource allocations. Moreover, while the Labour Government in 1977–9 did achieve some redistribution of Rate Support Grant funds in favour of the inner cities, the Conservative administration after 1979 was much less inclined to provide such extra support and reversed the shift. Central government policy on local authority finance in the 1980s has, of course, been aimed at the overall reduction of expenditure. The impact of a growing volume of urban programme aid, from £167 million in 1978–9 (at 1984–5 prices) to £348 million in 1984–5, was thus more than offset by reductions in central grants to local authorities, most clearly reflected in the cuts in public-sector house-building and improvement.

While national economic policies arguably worked against the urban programme's aims after 1979, new urban policy initiatives were taken by the Conservative administration, including the establishment of Urban Development Corporations for the London and Merseyside docklands, and the designation first of eleven and later of another fourteen Enterprise Zones. The creation of a New Town-style development corporation for London's docklands had been advocated some years earlier. The Conservative Government's adoption of this idea was based on the arguments that the redevelopment of this area was of national rather than simply local interest, that the existing local planning machinery was inadequate to the task, and that the dockland boroughs were unsuitable recipients for the substantial government funds needed for the area's regeneration. The proposal for a Development Corporation, with independent government funding, planning powers, and responsibility for land assembly and disposal, met strong opposition from local boroughs and community groups, on the grounds that it would remove local democratic control over the docklands' redevelopment. Such opposition was fuelled when the Corporation reallocated some land previously acquired for public housing to private-sector development. This was in line with the government preference for private, rather than public, investment in urban redevelopment, and the Corporation has had some notable success, backed by fairly substantial public funding, in marketing the docklands to private investors.

In similar vein, Enterprise Zones were originally proposed as an experiment in allowing unfettered market forces to operate in carefully selected inner-city areas where prospects for regeneration by other means seemed poor. The concept was attacked from the left (Anderson 1983; Massey 1982) as an expression of anti-planning ideology; but in practice the extent of deregulation in the Zones has been fairly modest, mainly involving streamlined planning procedures. The chief attractions of Enterprise Zones are substantial financial inducements for industrial and property investment, which in fact bear a remarkable resemblance to the initiatives traditionally available under regional policy. Their role in practice as 'mini-Assisted Areas', rather than as an instrument of inner-city policy, is also evident in the designation of Zones in places like Corby, Scunthorpe, Telford, Invergordon, and the Medway Towns in response to local emergencies.

Initial monitoring of the Zones (Roger Tym and Partners 1984; Bromley and

Morgan 1985) indicates that, while significant investment and renewal has taken place in some, the greatest impact has tended to occur in Zones where public-sector agencies and funding have played a leading role in infrastructure provision, site preparation, etc.; these include the Isle of Dogs Zone in the London docklands, where the Development Corporation has been active, and the Clydebank Zone, with Scottish Development Agency involvement. It also appears that in general the Zones have so far had a greater impact in the diversion of development, often at a local or subregional scale, than in generating genuine net additions to economic activity.

The 1981 riots and after

From 1979 the inner cities were caught in the twin grip of deepening recession and increasing constraints on public spending. In the spring and summer of 1981, serious outbreaks of public disorder took place in several inner urban areas—Brixton in London, Toxteth in Liverpool, and the Moss Side area of Manchester. The immediate causes of the disturbances were linked to strained relations between police and local communities in these areas, but the riots served to focus attention on the wider context of deprivation and high unemployment in the inner cities. Michael Heseltine, then Environmental Secretary, made a two-week fact-finding visit to Merseyside and, reportedly shocked by the scale of urban dereliction he encountered, returned to ask the Cabinet for a major injection of public funds for the area. Instead, as 'Minister for Merseyside', he acquired a brief to head a 'Task Force' for the area, comprising civil servants from several government departments and private-sector managerial secondees.

This initiative stemmed from a government belief that a significant part of the city's problems lay with the inability of its local authorities to respond adequately to urban decline and to use existing resources effectively. The Task Force had no overall strategy as such; it was a project-based, practical problem solving unit, aiming to mobilize private-sector involvement in urban regeneration, and working with existing agencies to show how programmes could be better organized to tackle specific problems (Parkinson and Duffy 1982).

The dynamic of the Task Force relied heavily upon Heseltine's personal commitment and charisma and his status as a Cabinet minister. When he moved from the Department of the Environment, a lower profile for the Task Force was inevitable. Moreover, as Heseltine admitted to the House of Commons Environment Select Committee, the Task Force did not produce any substantial shift in main-line spending in favour of inner Liverpool, nor did it lead to any national or local changes in organizational arrangements for greater co-ordination of policies affecting the inner city (Parkinson and Duffy 1982). Its wider and longer-term significance for inner-city policy probably lay in the influence that experience of this type of intervention had upon subsequent initiatives, including the establishment, in April 1985, of 'inner-city action teams' for Hackney/Islington and the partnership areas in Manchester/Salford, Birmingham, Newcastle/Gateshead, and Liverpool.

Another Heseltine initiative in the aftermath of the 1981 riots was the establishment of the Financial Institutions Group, comprising representatives from banks, building societies, insurance companies, and pension funds, to advise the DoE on the mobilization of private investment for urban renewal. On a visit to the USA to learn from urban policy experience there, the Group were impressed with the Urban Development Action Grant (UDAG) scheme as a means for 'leveraging' private funds for urban renewal (Boyle 1985). A similar initiative, Urban Development Grant, was thus introduced into the UK urban programme in 1982 (Jacobs 1985).

Urban Development Grant (UDG) is paid to projects jointly funded by the public and private sectors which meet 'special needs'—such as job creation and housing—in deprived urban areas. Local authorities in the designated areas are invited to plan projects with private sector partners, and to submit bids to the DoE for 75 per cent of the public funding component. In the first round of operation, approved projects averaged a public/private funding ratio of about 1:4, and by the end of 1983 such projects involved £53 million of UDG and £229 million of private investment. A parallel scheme (Local Enterprise Grants for Urban Projects, LEG-UP) was launched by the SDA in Scotland in 1982 and in the first two years of operations £11 million of LEG-UP funds levered £46 million of private investment (Zeiger 1985).

Interestingly, in 1982–3, 47 per cent of projects approved for UDG were in Greater London and the West Midlands, which together attracted 58 per cent of all UDG funding, with only 28 per cent going to urban areas in the North and North West regions (Goodhall 1985). Since UDG is allocated on a competitive basis, the low share of the latter regions may reflect restricted opportunities to attract private investment there by comparison with London and the West Midlands. Moreover, the average leverage achieved on UDG projects was higher in London and the West Midlands; thus their share of total UDG-aided private investment was even greater at 63 per cent, as against only 20 per cent in the North and North West.

The issue of UDG allocations highlights a more general point concerning the overall thrust and philosophy of Conservative urban policy. An emphasis upon economic regeneration, and upon public funds being used principally to underpin and encourage private investment, was evident in the 1977 Inner Cities White Paper, but has become more pronounced in the 1980s—the interest in leveraging is part of this trend. This is a clear shift from the urban programme approach of the 1960s and earlier 1970s, when there was greater concern with social and community development objectives, and also when many analyses identified private-sector investment strategies as a key causal factor in urban decline. In a sense, what was formerly seen as part of the problem came to be heralded as the solution to inner-city decay (Boyle 1983). Of course, it can be argued that the role of urban aid is precisely to bridge the gap between 'unviability and profit', as Patrick Jenkin did in announcing the new City Action Teams; but this avoids the issue of whether an urban programme geared essentially to commercial criteria will produce a distribution of aid, either spatially or in terms of the types of projects that are assisted, which meets the welfare needs of the inner cities.

The evolving policy framework

Urban programme expenditure in 1984–5, together with spending on Urban Development Corporations and Derelict Land Grant for urban renewal, totalled £502 million (Boyle 1985: 206). This does not include any estimate of the considerable Exchequer costs of Enterprise Zone incentives, but it exceeded total regional policy spending in England and Wales. Expenditure by local government on economic development has also grown substantially since the 1970s (Chandler and Lawless 1985; Wilmers and Bourdillon 1985). A survey by the Association of District Councils in 1984 found almost 90 per cent of councils claiming some form of involvement in local economic development. Space precludes any attempt at a comprehensive review of the many local authority economic initiatives implemented over recent years, which include provision of land and premises, loans and grants to local industry, enterprise workshops, business advisory and information services, and area promotion. The regional chapters which follow cover a range of examples and such initiatives must clearly be acknowledged as an important and growing element in the policy framework for regional and local economic development in the 1980s. The EEC Regional Development and Social Funds also emerged as increasingly significant sources of aid in some areas (see, for example, Chapters 6 and 7).

Thus, as the coverage of Assisted Areas was reduced in the early 1980s and total regional aid cut, spending and effort by both central and local government on a new range of initiatives increased, producing a more localized and complex pattern of aid for economic development which cut across the boundaries of Assisted and non-Assisted areas as defined for regional policy purposes (see Figure 3.3). By 1984–5, the total aid dispensed through these localized policy initiatives must have exceeded total regional preferential assistance in Great Britain (£610 million) by a considerable margin.

The new initiatives appeared in an *ad hoc*, incremental fashion, without a clear view of how the different elements of the total package of spatially focused aid were meant to fit together, or how such aid should relate to various sectoral non-spatial policies of industrial assistance. The urban programme was the responsibility of the DoE working with the local authorities in the areas designated under the Inner Urban Areas Act, while the Department of Trade and Industry retained separate responsibility for regional policy. This administrative division clearly reflected the development of urban and regional policy as competing, rather than necessarily complementary, aspects of government intervention. Enterprise Zones fell within the DoE's remit, but were not formally a part of either urban or regional policy. To complicate the picture further, different and partially separate arrangements for the administration of spatial policy obtained in the three 'national' regions of Scotland, Wales and

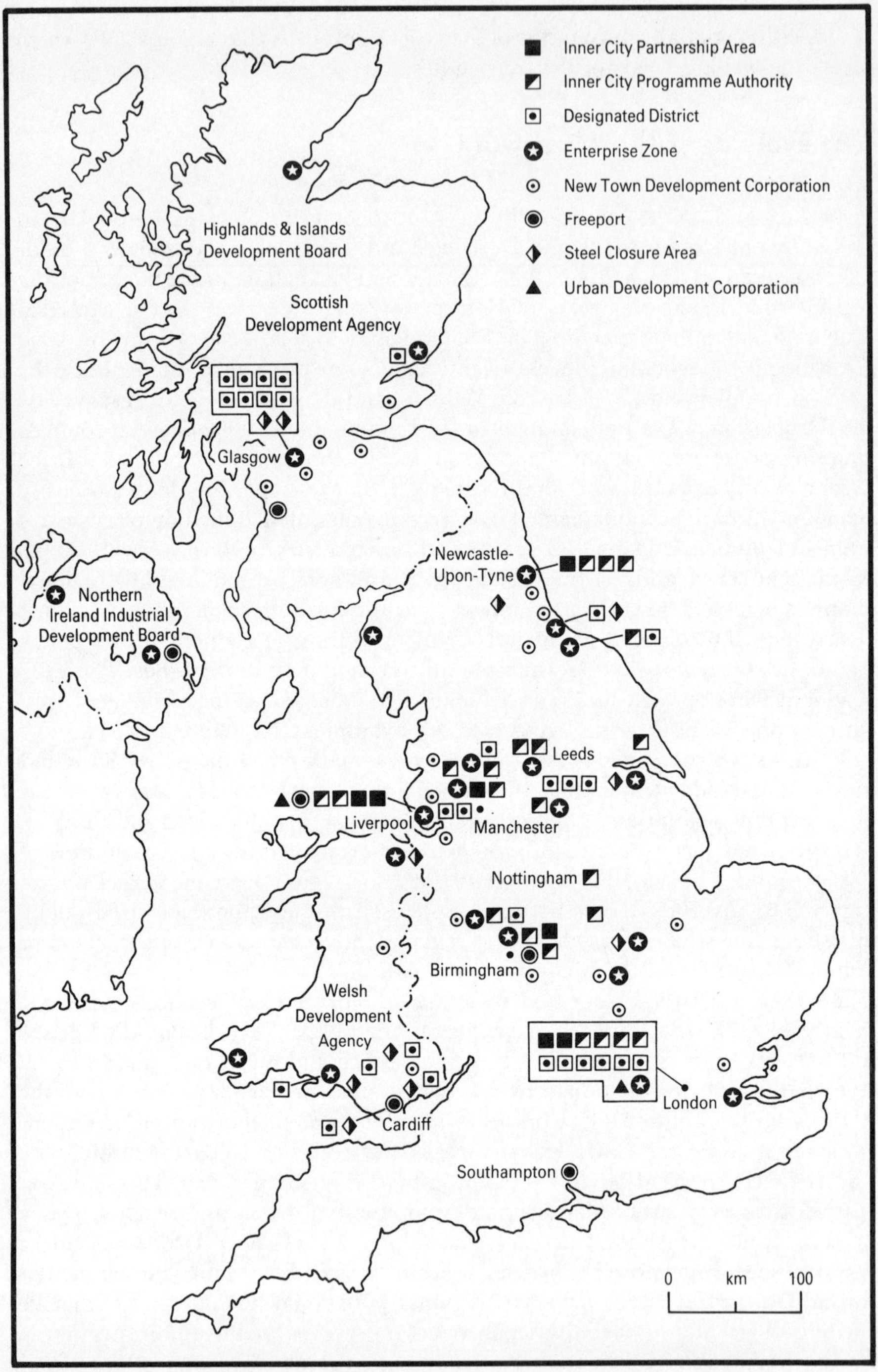

Figure 3.3. Government-sponsored local development initiatives, 1984

Northern Ireland, which have their own territorially based ministers and government departments.

Against this background the Regional Studies Association (1983), in an inquiry into regional problems in the UK, concluded that the evolution of spatial policy had produced by the early 1980s 'a highly diffuse and largely uncoordinated, if not confusing, delivery of policy and aid, involving a multiplicity of agencies operating at different spatial levels'. In so far as central government found cause for concern in this situation, it was inclined to criticize local authorities for their lack of coordination and potentially wasteful duplication of effort in such fields as industrial promotion and provision of business advisory services. Hence the Government's unsuccessful attempt in 1982 to curtail the powers in these fields available to local authorities under Section 137 of the Local Government Act. Defenders of local initiatives, such as Mawson and Miller (1983), on the other hand, place the blame for a lack of coordination in economic development policies squarely upon central government. Cameron (1985) argues that the perceived inadequacies of the Government's own regional and urban policies forced local authorities faced with rising unemployment to undertake what he terms '*sauve qui peut*' measures of various kinds. On the issue of duplication, the last word goes to Mawson and Miller as to the real nature of the problem:

> there is no hard evidence to suggest that industrialists are confused by a plethora of advice centres; . . . the situation may well be the reverse—that the majority of industrialists are unaware of the existence of such services. (Mawson and Miller 1983: 38)

Background to the 1983 Regional Policy White Paper

The revisions to regional policy made in 1979 were directed at the reduction of public expenditure, and did not involve any basic reappraisal of the policy's aims or operation. The structure of regional incentives introduced in the 1972 Industry Act thus remained intact, while geographical coverage was reduced. Interestingly, the 1979 changes may have halted the rise in regional policy spending, but they did not in the short term produce very large savings compared with the last two years of the previous Labour administration. Annual expenditure on regional preferential assistance averaged £933 million in 1979–83, compared with £1031 million in 1977–9 (both figures at 1984–5 prices). The largest fall occured in the English Assisted Areas (see Figure 3.4), while in Scotland regional policy spending actually increased between 1979/80 and 1982/83, principally because of a few very large Regional Development Grant payments to oil-related companies. Thus in 1982–3 Scotland accounted for 42 per cent of all RDG payments (Crampton 1984), and in the same year the Scottish Development Agency also received grant in aid amounting to £105 million (1984–5 prices).

As the transition to the new map of assistance was completed in 1982, the prospect of further policy changes was already evident. The fact that the regional unemployment rate in the non-assisted West Midlands stood above that in Scotland was one factor suggesting that further revision of the Assisted

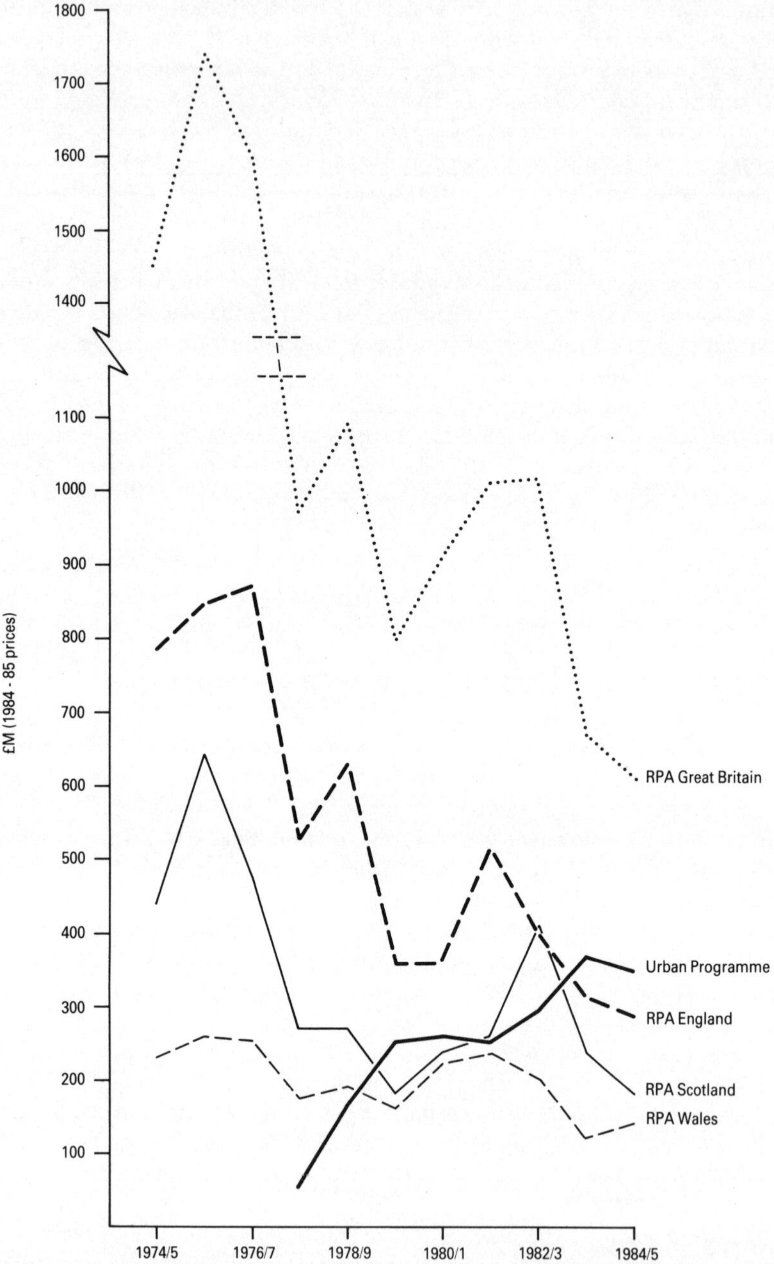
£M (1984 - 85 prices)
1800
1700
1600
1500
1400
1100
1000
900
800
700
600
500
400
300
200
100
1974/5
1976/7
1978/9
1980/1
1982/3
1984/5
RPA Great Britain
Urban Programme
RPA England
RPA Scotland
RPA Wales

Areas map was called for. The Government's short-term response to the declining fortunes of the West Midlands, in advance of the 1983 general election, was to give a junior Industry minister 'special responsibility' for the region (see Chapter 5). Before that, in the context of continuing government concern about the cost of regional policy, its effectiveness, and its relationship with other strands of spatial policy, a major internal interdepartmental policy review had been initiated, leading eventually to a White Paper in December 1983 setting out the Government's intentions for reform of the system of regional incentives, and indicating the likelihood of changes in the geography of assistance.

The difficulties in restraining RDG spending in the early 1980s highlighted a weakness of the RDG scheme that had attracted widespread criticism. RDGs were given automatically for investment in qualifying assets (industrial buildings, plant, and machinery) in the Assisted Areas, and hence the level of aid was not directly linked to job creation, something which Pickvance (1981: 243) found 'a very remarkable feature for a policy whose explicit aim is the reduction of unemployment'. Large amounts of regional aid were thus absorbed by particular capital-intensive industrial sectors and projects for very little or no employment gain. Tyler's (1983) research, for example, showed that the chemical and metal manufacturing industries accounted for massive amounts of regional aid (about one-quarter of the total in 1966–76) for a nil or even negative return in terms of net job creation in the Assisted Areas. It was, however, several North Sea oil terminals that became ministerial *bêtes noires* in this respect, notably Sullom Voe, which was said to have cost £130,000 per job and absorbed one-third of Scotland's regional aid in one year (House of Commons 1985: 310); in addition, these projects had no real choice of location outside the Assisted Areas.

Figure 3.4. Annual expenditure on Regional Preferential Assistance (RPA) in Great Britain, England, Scotland and Wales from 1974–5 to 1984–5, and the Urban Programme in England and Wales from 1977–8 to 1984–5

Sources: Department of Trade and Industry; Boyle 1985.

Notes:

1. Expenditure on a 1984–5 price basis for each year has been calculated by applying the GDP deflator to current price figures.

2. The items included under RPA are Regional Development Grants, Regional Selective Assistance, and expenditure on land and factories in the Assisted Areas by the English Industrial Estates Corporation and the Scottish and Welsh Development Agencies. Regional Employment Premium (discontinued in January 1977) is included in the early years. All RPA figures are gross and include payments to nationalized industries. Figures for 1984–5 are provisional estimates.

3. The figures for RPA are affected by the four-month deferment in payment of Regional Development Grants between June 1979 and November 1982. This reduced the 1979–80 total in Great Britain by about £168 million and raised the 1982–3 figure by up to £165 million (both at 1984–5 prices).

4. Urban Programme expenditure figures cover spending under the Department of the Environment's Urban Programme in Partnership and Programme authorities and other Designated Districts, payments of Urban Development Grant (from 1982–3), and a number of smaller items including inner city research and the Merseyside Task Force.

A second, related charge against traditional regional policy was that it concentrated assistance on manufacturing industry, a sector of overall employment decline after 1966, and that very little support was given to service industries in the Assisted Areas. An Office and Service Industries Scheme (OSIS) had been introduced in 1973 under Section 7 of the Industry Act, although this coincided with a reduction in the volume of office dispersal from London as part of the general slackening of employment mobility in the 1970s. OSIS was a selective and fairly low-key scheme, which did relatively little to offset the regional policy bias towards manufacturing; expenditure on OSIS, at £5–6 million a year in the early 1980s, was dwarfed by RDGs, although it is worth noting that its cost-effectiveness in job creation in the Assisted Areas was superior to the latter.

A further criticism of regional policy was that it had encouraged the growth of externally owned branch plants in the assisted regions, and consequently failed adequately to improve (and, some would argue, actually impaired) the regions' capacity for self-sustaining growth through new enterprise formation and indigenous product innovation. Doubts were also raised about the durability of employment in Assisted Area branch plants, compared with either their parent plants or independent firms. To some extent these criticisms were perhaps underlain by rather too comfortable a view of the merits of 'local control' of manufacturing (see Lloyd and Shutt 1985, for example, for a contrary view). Nonetheless, in so far as the development of branch plant economies in the assisted regions was associated with under-representation of managerial, research, and marketing functions, this did tend to deprive the regions of the skills needed for innovation and diversification, and also reduced local demand for higher-order business services. On the issue of the relative vulnerability to closure of branch plants, the research evidence was somewhat conflicting, producing different results for different periods (Department of Trade and Industry 1983). However, in the case of Northern Ireland, where policy had relied very heavily on attracting inward investment, the evidence points clearly and worryingly to the relative impermanence of many assisted industry projects (see Chapter 11). Elsewhere, some apparent earlier policy successes in steering investment in postwar 'growth industries' to the Assisted Areas subsequently failed to provide a secure foundation for regional growth—motor industry projects in Scotland and Merseyside being notable examples.

In sum, therefore, while some research had identified an appreciable quantitative regional policy effect in diverting manufacturing investment and employment to Assisted Areas in the 1960s and 1970s (Marquand 1980; Department of Trade and Industry 1983), the *qualitative* aspects of the impact gave considerable grounds for concern. The Government's internal review of regional policy thus took place against a background of accumulating criticism of the traditional approach to regional problems and a growing body of opinion that a fundamental overhaul of regional policy, and indeed spatial policies generally, was called for (see, for example, Frost and Spence 1981; Trades Union Congress 1982; Labour Party Parliamentary Spokesman's Working Group 1983; Regional Studies Association 1983; Martin and Hodge, 1983*a*;

1983*b*; Wray 1984). There was, however, no consensus on the direction that change should take; and even if government were finally to be persuaded of the need for reform, it was clear, after the election of 1983, that any new policy would be framed and implemented within a restrictive public expenditure regime.

The 1983 White Paper and subsequent regional policy changes

The White Paper, *Regional Industrial Development*, published in December 1983, reflected the same brand of economic thinking which had shaped UK economic policy since 1979. This was evidenced in the view that 'Imbalances between areas in employment opportunities should in principle be corrected by the natural adjustment of labour markets' (Secretary of State for Trade and Industry 1983: 3). The Government was forced to accept, however, that 'natural' adjustment mechanisms, namely migration and reductions in real wages, could not be relied upon to correct regional imbalances in employment opportunities; and hence a residual social, but not an economic, case for continuing regional policy was acknowledged.

The White Paper also acknowledged some of the existing policy's most widely criticized weaknesses, and proposed that in future regional incentives should be more closely tied to job creation. This was to be achieved by the exclusion of replacement investments and modernization projects which did not create jobs from eligibility for automatic RDGs (again, this change was required by EEC regulations), the introduction of a cost per job ceiling on RDGs, and an extension of aid to service industries. The White Paper also sought a greater emphasis on the encouragement of new and indigenous development in Assisted Areas, but no specific measures were proposed to achieve this. It was indicated that there would be some shift towards selective as opposed to automatic assistance, and also that the Government would seek to maximize the contribution from the EEC to a revised regional aid programme.

On the question of the coverage of a new Assisted Area map and the rates of grant that should apply, and on certain other issues, such as which service industries should be eligible for incentives, the White Paper sought views. The Government's decisions on these matters were announced in November 1984. Before that, legislation was introduced to change the basis of RDG eligibility from qualifying assets to qualifying activities, and to restrict assistance to job-creating projects.

The principal elements of the November 1984 package of changes were:

(*a*) Replacement of the previous three-tier system of Assisted Areas by two tiers (see Figure 3.5). Special Development Areas (SDAs), with their 22 per cent rate of RDG, were abolished; Development Areas (DAs) (15 per cent RDG rate) were retained, but their spatial coverage was reduced compared with that of former SDAs and DAs combined—from 22 per cent of the working population to 15 per cent. Intermediate Areas (receiving selective assistance only) were expanded, mainly to include part of the West Midlands but also to include the north of the large Manchester travel-to-work area, so that the total coverage

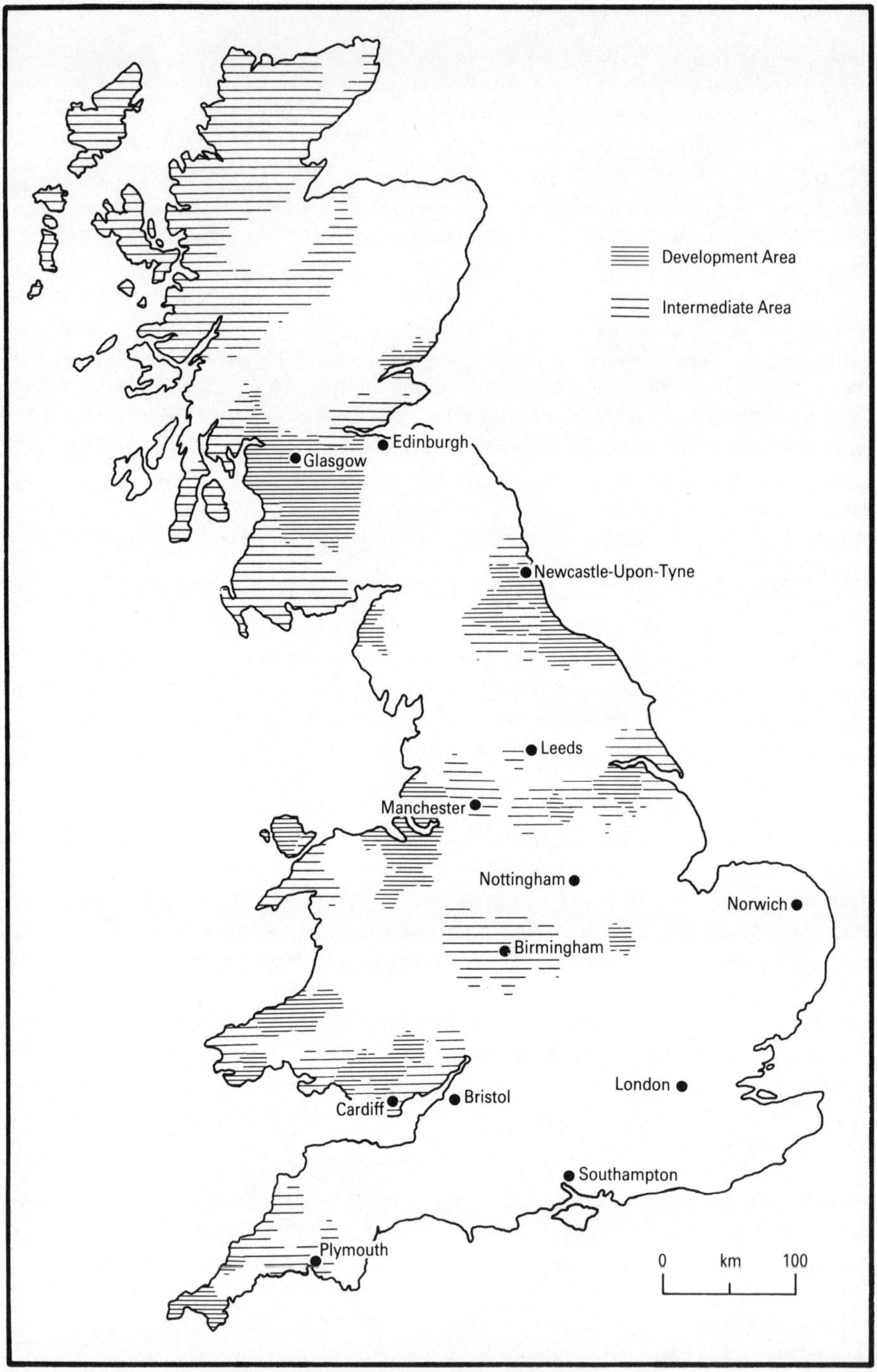

Figure 3.5. Assisted Areas, 1985

of Assisted Areas increased from 27.5 to 35 per cent of the working population.

(*b*) RDGs were to be subject to a cost-per-job limit of £10,000, except in the case of small firms with less than 200 workers. As an alternative, for projects of low capital-intensity, firms could receive a £3,000 grant per job created.

(*c*) A selected number of service activities were included in the qualifying activities for RDGs. These included central office services of multi-locational companies, advertising and market research, computer services, research and development, mail order, and football pools checking.

The Government estimated that the effect of this package and associated changes in RDG eligibility would be to reduce spending on regional policy by £300 million from an otherwise expected level of £700 million by 1987–8. Around £100 million of the expected savings would be made in Scotland, £60 million in Wales, and the remainder in England. An earlier estimate to the Public Accounts Committee had suggested that the exclusion of replacement and modernization investments which did not create jobs from the RDG scheme would, with the existing Assisted Area map, reduce RDG spending by £150–200 million a year, one-third or more of the actual level of expenditure in 1983–4. After the November 1984 changes were announced, Industry Minister Norman Lamont stated that nearly half the total expected £300 million savings 'will come from the requirement to link grants to jobs and the exclusion of replacement investments' (House of Commons 1985: 593). He further noted that the cost-per-job limit on RDGs, at £10,000, would only affect projects in which the investment per new job exceeded about £65,000, which he claimed was twice the average capital-intensity of manufacturing. The larger part of the projected savings would come from the cost-reducing effect of the changes to the map of Assisted Areas: the abolition of SDAs with their higher rate of RDG, and the reduced coverage of areas in which RDGs would be available.

Some increase in RDG spending could be expected to result from the extension of eligibility to selected service industries. It is worth noting, however, that the new £3,000-per-job grant, which might be more commonly taken by less capital-intensive service projects, will partly replace the selective job-creation formerly available under the OSIS scheme, which was terminated in 1984. Regional selective financial assistance was also projected to rise, by 40 per cent by 1987–8, partly in consequence of the extension on Intermediate Areas, and also because some modernization projects excluded from the RDG scheme might get selective assistance instead. These changes help to explain the government expectation that the balance between automatic and selective assistance would approach a 50/50 split under the new system, albeit within a considerably reduced total of regional aid.

Overall, the new map of Assisted Areas reflects the Government's efforts to reduce the costs of regional policy to the UK exchequer while enhancing the opportunities for drawing upon EEC aid for regional development. In the view of Opposition spokesman Geoffrey Robinson:

By extending the map as widely as they can . . . (the government) hope to maximize our take-up of the quota of the European regional development fund . . . It is clear that, if the

ERDF did not exist, we should not have a map or a policy. (House of Commons 1985: 585–7)

Assessing the revised regional policy

The widespread view that traditional regional policy's automatic subsidies to manufacturing investment had become a wasteful and ineffective means of tackling regional disparities in unemployment meant that the reformed system of incentives could expect a fair measure of support in principle. Criticism of the 1983 White Paper and the changes introduced in November 1984, however, tended to centre on their cost-cutting emphasis and the narrowness of their approach to regional development problems—hence Townroe's (1985) characterization of the changes as 'improved tactics but limited vision' (see also Damesick 1984; 1985; Wood 1984; Martin 1985).

While the new policy package may ensure that a reduced regional aid budget is applied more cost effectively, it nonetheless perpetuates the reliance upon a narrow and marginal set of measures to alleviate regional economic problems which has traditionally characterized regional policy in the UK. The role of regional development agencies, perhaps one of the most significant spatial policy innovations of the last decade and one which has attracted considerable interest in some English regions, was ignored in the White Paper. This raises an obvious question: if the government see the Scottish and Welsh Development Agencies as valuable vehicles of economic regeneration, which seems reasonable in the light of their continued operation, why should this approach not be extended to other regions?

The White Paper acknowledged that 'Regional and local economic development is influenced by a wide range of central and local government policy' (Secretary of State for Trade and Industry 1983: 5), but it contained no concrete proposals for better co-ordination of relevant national industrial and manpower policies, the urban programme, and the economic initiatives of local authorities. The White Paper also noted that the Government recognized the need to take account of the regional dimension in such policies as those relating to infrastructure; but, again, such recognition would appear to have little practical significance in the context of the UK's centralized, sectorally based system of public expenditure planning. The call for public investment programmes to be consciously geared to the achievement of regional development objectives is not confined to the obviously disadvantaged regions. It appears in recent statements from the South East local authority standing conference, concerned with imbalances in development within the region (SERPLAN 1985). But, as Short has argued, 'While regional policy, as practised, does not incorporate the wider range of spending that would be incorporated in a regional plan, regional planning, which does recognize the wider elements, is not practised at all' (1982: 108).

Proposals for regional investment budgets and/or for co-ordination of public expenditure planning at the regional level have little chance of political acceptance in present circumstances, given that they will be seen as likely to reduce central government control of public expenditure. In pursuit of the objective of reduced public spending, the upper tier of local government in Greater London and the English metropolitan counties has been abolished, and government 'rate-capping' measures now restrain the revenue-raising ability of individual local authorities which are deemed to be 'overspending' according to centrally determined criteria. The inevitable consequence is the further accretion of power at the centre at the expense of local government.

The policy changes of the mid-1980s seem likely to accentuate several recent trends. A weakened regional policy has given way, on the one hand, to sectoral and other non-spatial schemes of industrial support (the national Support for Innovation scheme, for example, is currently running at £300 million per annum) together with various initiatives aimed at the unemployed (e.g. the MSC Enterprise Allowance scheme), and, on the other hand, to a multiplicity of localized economic development initiatives administered by local authorities and by the DoE. As evidenced in the chapters which follow, the challenge of devising a new and more adequate framework for tackling the UK's spatial development problems remains to be grasped.

References

Anderson, J. (1983), 'Geography as Ideology and the Politics of Crisis: The Enterprise Zone Experiment', in J. Anderson, S. Duncan, and R. Hudson, eds., *Redundant Spaces in Cities and Regions? Studies in Industrial Decline and Social Change*, London, Academic Press.

Boyle, R. (1983), 'Privatising Urban Problems: A Commentary on Anglo-American Urban Policy', Studies in Public Policy 117, University of Strathclyde, Centre for the Study of Public Policy.

——, ed., (1985), ' "Leveraging" Urban Development: A Comparison of Urban Policy Directions and Programme Impact in the United States and Britain" ', *Policy and Politics* 13, 175–210.

Bromley, R. D. F. and Morgan, R. H. (1985), 'The Effects of Enterprise Zone Policy: Evidence from Swansea', *Regional Studies* 19, 403–13.

Cameron, G. (1985), 'Regional Economic Planning—The End of the Line', *Planning Outlook* 28, 8–13.

Chandler, J. A. and Lawless, P. (1985), *Local Authorities and the Creation of Employment*, Farnbarough, Hants., Gower.

Crampton, G. R. (1984), 'Regional and Urban Policy in Britain: An Outline of Recent Expenditure Trends', Discussion Papers in Urban and Regional Economics, Series C, no. 24, University of Reading, Department of Economics.

Damesick, P. (1979), 'Putting LOB in Perspective', *Town and Country Planning* 47, 16–19.

—— (1984), *A Response to the White Paper 'Regional Industrial Development', Cmnd 9111*, London, Regional Studies Association.

—— (1985), 'Recent Debates and Developments in British Regional Policy', *Planning Outlook* 28, 3–7.

Department of Trade and Industry (1983), *Regional Industrial Policy: Some Economic Issues*, London, Department of Trade and Industry.

Frost, M. and Spence, N. (1981), 'Policy Responses to Urban and Regional Economic Change', *Geographical Journal* 147, 321–47.

Goodhall, P. (1985), 'Urban Development Grant—An Early Assessment of Regional Implications', *Planning Outlook* 28, 40–42.

House of Commons Expenditure Committee (1973), Trade and Industry Sub-Committee, *Regional Development Incentives: Report*, Session 1973–4, House of Commons Paper 85, London, HMSO.

House of Commons (1985) *Official Report. Parliamentary Debates (Hansard)*, vol. 71, no. 41 (Thursday, 17 January 1985), cols. 525–604, London, HMSO.

Jacobs, J. (1985), 'UDG: The Urban Development Grant', in Boyle 1985.

Labour Party Parliamentary Spokesman's Working Group (1983), *Alternative Regional Strategy. A Framework for Discussion*, London, Labour Party Parliamentary Spokesman on Regional Affairs and Devolution.

Lawless, P. (1981), *Britain's Inner Cities. Problems and Policies*, London, Harper & Row.

Lloyd, P. and Shutt, J. (1985), 'Recession and restructuring in the North-West region, 1975–82: the implications of recent events', in D. Massey and R. Meegan, eds., *Politics and Method: Contrasting Studies in Industrial Geography*, London, Methuen.

McCallum, J. D. (1979), 'The Development of British Regional Policy', in D. Maclennan and J. B. Parr, eds., *Regional Policy. Past Experience and New Directions*, Oxford, Robertson.

Marquand, J. (1980), *Measuring the Effects and Costs of Regional Incentives*, Government Economic Service Working Paper no. 32, London, Department of Industry.

Martin, R. L. (1985), 'Monetarism Masquerading as Regional Policy? The Government's New System of Regional Aid', *Regional Studies* 19, 379–88.

—— and Hodge, J. S. C. (1983*a*), 'The Reconstruction of British Regional Policy: 1. The crisis of conventional practice', *Government and Policy* 1, 133–52.

—— and —— (1983*b*), 'The Reconstruction of British Regional Policy: 2. Towards a new agenda', *Government and Policy* 1, 317–40.

Massey, D. (1982), 'Enterprise Zones: A Political Issue', *International Journal of Urban and Regional Research* 6, 429–34.

Mawson, J. and Miller, D. (1983), 'Agencies in Regional and Local Development', Occasional Paper 6, Centre for Urban and Regional Studies, University of Birmingham.

Parkinson, M. and Duffy, J. (1982), 'Government's Response to Inner-city Riots: The Minister for Merseyside and the Task Force', *Parliamentary Affairs* 37, 76–96.

Pickvance, C. G. (1981), 'Policies as Chameleons: An Interpretation of Regional and Office Policy in Britain', in M. Dear and A. J. Scott, eds., *Urbanization and Urban Planning in Capitalist Society*, London, Methuen.

Regional Studies Association (1983), *Report of an Inquiry into Regional Problems in the United Kingdom*, Norwich, Geo Books.

Roger Tym and Partners (1984), *Monitoring the Enterprise Zones. Year 3 Report*, London, Roger Tym and Partners.

Secretary of State for the Environment (1977), *Policy for the Inner Cities*, Cmnd. 6854, London HMSO.

Secretary of State for Trade and Industry (1983), *Regional Industrial Development*, Cmnd. 9111, London, HMSO.

SERPLAN (1985), *Developing SE Regional Strategic Guidance: Consultative Regional Statement*, RPC 340, London, The London and South East Regional Planning Conference.

Short, J. (1982), *Public Expenditure and Taxation in the UK Regions*, Farnborough, Hants., Gower.

Sundquist, J. L. (1975), *Dispersing Population: What America Can Learn from Europe*, Washington DC, Brookings Institute.

Townroe, P. (1985), 'Improved Tactics but Limited Vision', *Town and Country Planning* 54, 10–11.

Trades Union Congress (1982), *Regional Development and Planning: A TUC Policy Statement*, London, TUC Publications.

Tyler, P. (1983), 'The Impact of Regional Policy on Different Types of Industry', University of Cambridge, Department of Land Economy (mimeo).

Wilmers, P. and Bourdillon, B., eds, (1985), *Managing the Local Economy*, Norwich, Geo Books.

Wood, P. A. (1984), 'Regional Industrial Development', *Area* 16, 281–9.

Wray, I. (1984), 'Re-structuring the Regions: A Framework for Managing Regional Growth and Decline in the 1980s and 1990s', Occasional Paper no. 11, University of Birmingham, Centre for Urban and Regional Studies.

Zeiger, H. (1985), 'LEG-UP: Local Enterprise Grants for Urban Projects', in Boyle 1985.

CHAPTER 4
The South East

P. A. Wood

A principal theme of this volume is that new approaches are required to regional planning in Britain. This is nowhere more true than in the South East, whose growth characteristics were so crucial to the old framework of ideas (for a full account of planning in the South East until the late 1970s, see Keeble 1980a; Damesick 1982a). Indeed, it is arguable that changes in this region, within the wider context of national economic recession, have been amongst the most influential in undermining traditional regional policy. Today, the notion that the South East Standard Region dominates the pattern of regional growth in Britain is a dangerous over-simplification. It recalls the view of regional planning taken in the 1950s and 1960s, when London was regarded as a dynamo, generating population that needed to be housed and found work in surrounding counties, and employment that could contribute to the revival of other regions.

Any new approach to the problem of regional inequality must face two important changes that have taken place in southern Britain. First, the prosperity and attractiveness of parts of the South East, and their implications for developments in other regions of Britain, are now closely associated with the emergence of what has been termed the 'Greater South East' (Regional Studies Association 1983: 57). The principal zone of economic prosperity in Britain now includes many areas outside the South East Standard Region—in East Anglia, the East Midlands, and the South West—south of the Severn–Wash line, but generally north and west of London. More problematically, however, the prosperity of the South East itself has been tempered by the collapse of significant sectors of the London economy, as well as by intensified economic problems in other areas such as south Essex, north Kent, Portsmouth, some coastal areas and the New Towns.

The dynamo of London therefore no longer generates growth for southern Britain, except possibly in a negative sense. Over recent decades, the releasing of manufacturing and some service activities from the need to locate in or near the city has encouraged the rapid development of other, less urbanized areas. While London still dominates some activities, for example finance, business headquarters, government, and tourism, the economic prospects of many inner Londoners are now no better than those of workers in other conurbations. Indeed, the scale of the city has become a unique liability, intensifying the level of congestion and the rate of manufacturing decline, and creating development challenges whose diversity and huge cost are of national significance. Thus,

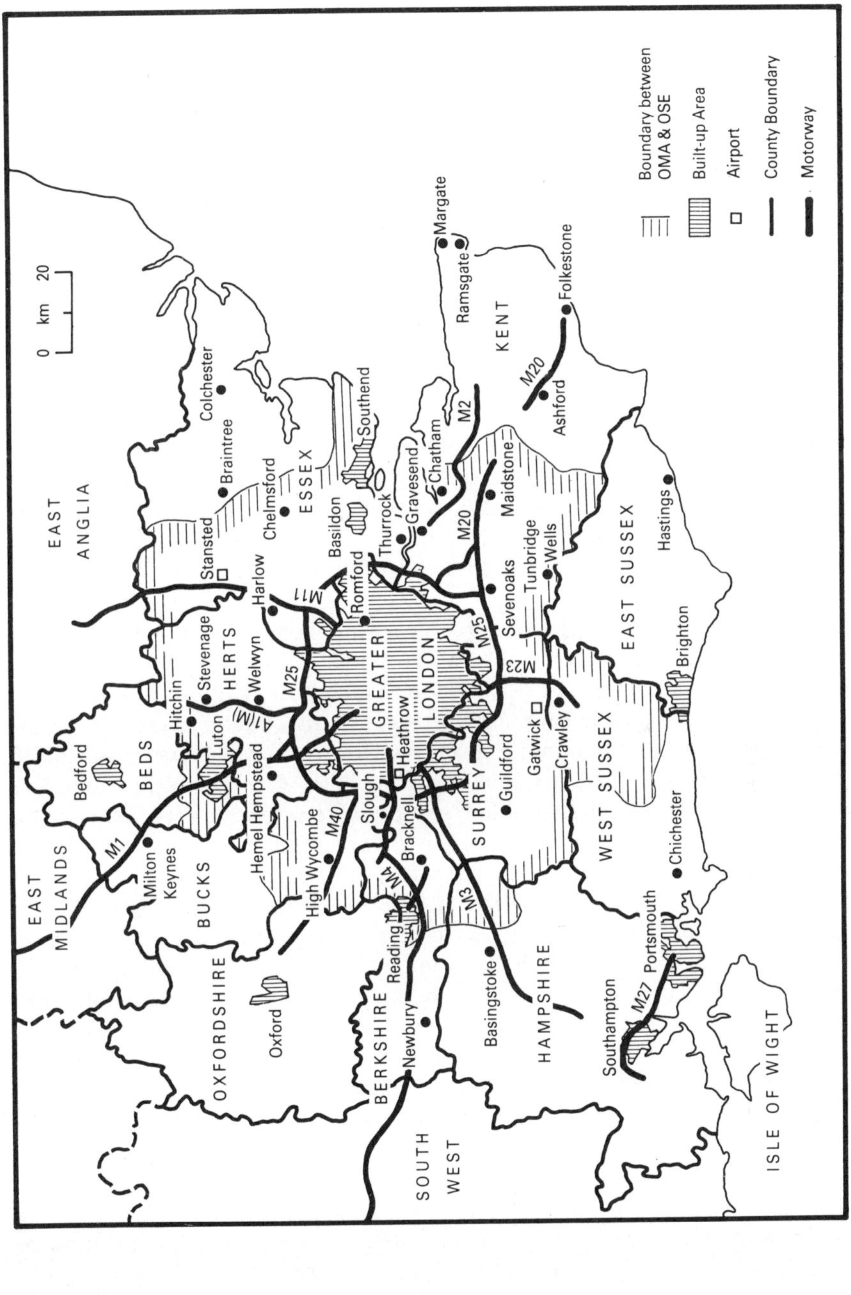

Figure 4.1. The South East

partly because of their scale, proposals for a London motorway system, a third airport, subsidies to public transport or docklands redevelopment have become the focus of particularly intractable conflicts, of a kind not found elsewhere in Britain (Clout and Wood 1986).

In some other parts of the South East, as we shall see, neither location in the region nor proximity to London protected local manufacturing employment from the effects of the recession in the early 1980s. Large private firms in established industries such as motor vehicles, food and drink, oil and chemicals, engineering, or furniture-making, closed or contracted plants, as they did elsewhere in Britain, and public sector cuts in dockyards added to local problems at Chatham and Portsmouth. While demand for certain types of skilled and technically qualified labour is high in some parts of the region, this offers few opportunities for the unemployed elsewhere. The chronic long-term unemployment found in other regions is as yet relatively uncommon in the South East, but the fear persists that some areas may come to acquire it during the 1980s.

In the light of these changes, government's response to the needs of the region since the mid-1970s has been either confused or negative. In terms of so-called 'regional economic policy', the attempt to direct investment away from the South East to other regions has virtually ceased, except for major new projects by overseas firms. Industrial Development Certificate (IDC) limitations on investment in the region were relaxed in the late 1970s and finally lifted in 1980. The South East has been allocated two Enterprise Zones (in London's docklands and north Kent) and a Freeport (at Southampton), and London has received a considerable share of the national budget for Inner Urban Area aid (see Chapter 3; and Hall 1981). At the intraregional scale, traditionally the realm of co-ordinated physical planning policies, the final abandonment of the Regional Planning Council, and effectively of the Strategic Plan for the South East, in 1979 left a strategic planning vacuum. In the first half of the 1980s, this was filled only by occasional letters of guidance from the Secretary of State for the Environment about the desirability of encouraging economic revival in London, protecting the Green Belt, or restraining the impacts of the M25 orbital motorway, to be completed in 1986. The actual responsibility for determining the pattern of change was largely devolved to the indirect efforts of the county and district authorities through their physical planning powers, embodied in structure and local plans. The region lacked an effective framework of monitoring or of guidance that could respond to its growing internal diversity.

This chapter will review the available evidence on recent economic trends in the region. The relationship of these trends to national economic policies will be examined first, followed by the patterns of manufacturing and service employment change within the region. The final section will review the current state of planning in the light of emerging economic contrasts in the region. An effective planning response to the problems of the South East is necessary, not simply for the welfare of its own inhabitants, but also to achieve national economic goals. It will be argued that the region needs a coherent framework of economic monitoring and strategic planning guidance, not to restrict its potential for growth but to facilitate its success and expansion. It will also be demonstrated how arbitrary is the distinction between economic and physical planning in the region, however firmly enshrined that distinction may be in the responsibilities of different ministers of state. While economic contrasts have acute implications for the operation of physical planning controls, physical developments in the region, as in the past, have far-reaching national, as well as local, economic implications. Thus in the current period of rapid change, a means is needed for relating a strategy of physical planning in the South East to the diverse economic requirements of the region's major constituent parts.

Economic policy and the South East

The South East Standard Region has become less self-contained and economically homogeneous in recent decades, as prosperity has dispersed into adjacent regions and decline in some areas has intensified, most notably in London. Nevertheless, this region still apparently dominates patterns of economic change in Britain, because of its great size and its continuing share of national prosperity and growth. Where national forecasts have been employed to explore the regional implications of alternative economic policies in Britain in the 1980s (Cambridge Economic Policy Group 1982), it seems agreed that levels of unemployment in Britain will increase in the 1980s and the gap in job opportunities between the Greater South East and other regions will widen. Nevertheless, it also seems that any expansion in labour demand in the Standard Region is unlikely to compensate for high natural increase in the working population and migration from poorer regions. The persistence of unemployment in the South East at about the levels of the early 1980s therefore seems probable. Manufacturing, construction, the utilities, and transport services will continue to lose jobs, even though some service categories will grow.

The prospects for the South East Standard Region are hardly rosy, therefore, even before account is taken of the polarization between London, with a larger population than any other Standard Region, and the rest of the South East (RoSE). Elias, in a study for the period between 1980 and 1985, demonstrated the significance of different economic policies for this polarization (Elias 1982). He saw a continuing rapid decline in Greater London, through both manufacturing and public service contraction, even under comparatively optimistic assumptions of modest recovery from the recession of the early 1980s. Reflation through increased government expenditure would have favoured employment in the RoSE, and only a policy directly to reduce industrial costs and stimulate demand would favour London. Other aspects of the relationship between Greater London and the rest of the region are also affected by the rate of national economic growth. For example, low growth in the late 1970s seemed to reduce the rate of population decentralization from London, presumably because of low levels of industrial and commercial investment and housebuilding. Faster growth would probably therefore enhance decentralization pressures. Poor national prospects or deflationary policies also reduce the public expenditure available to renew the ageing housing, infrastructure, and services of London and the likely success of redevelopment schemes, such as those in Docklands and other inner-city areas. At the same time, under such conditions the city may nevertheless continue to attract migrants from regions of higher unemployment, adding to its housing, employment, and social problems. While the decline of manufacturing employment in London, as in other industrial centres in the region, seems likely to continue, most forecasts suggest that the principal advantage of the city rests in its national dominance of growing service employment. Nevertheless, the critically important public sector is being severely reduced and, as we shall see, private-sector service employment change in the city was already falling behind national trends in the 1970s.

Two simple but important conclusions about the South East Standard Region emerge from examination of its current national economic role. The first is that no foreseeable economic circumstances are likely to reverse the dominance of its prosperous areas over the rest of the country. Indeed, important elements of government policy, such as support to small firms and innovation, or sustained defence spending, may further enhance the relative prosperity of those areas. Secondly, the problems of the London economy will remain significant in the national pattern of regional economic contrasts. The capital will continue to need special assistance, whether through regional, urban, or local government finance policies. Conversely, restraint on growth in other areas of the region is likely to be necessary, in response to local, if not to national, planning pressures. The principal regional planning policy questions therefore revolve around the types of restraint that will be most effective without being economically damaging, and whether London, other areas in the South East, or areas elsewhere can benefit from the diversion to them of potential investment, which may otherwise fail to materialize.

Patterns of variation within the region

Macroeconomic interpretations of the regional problem in the South East have severe limitations, even when London can be separated from the rest of the region. The pattern of economic contrasts follows no such simple dichotomy. Important contrasts also exist between the west and the east of the region, between urban and rural areas within the RoSE, and between growth areas which cannot attract enough development, such as Milton Keynes or south Essex, and supposed areas of restraint which are too buoyant, such as south Buckinghamshire or parts of Hampshire. Various coastal towns have also fared differently, some suffering tourist decline and a rapidly ageing population, others stimulated by new port developments.

The most disadvantaged areas, in terms of unemployment levels in the early 1980s (more than 10 per cent), were inner London, most of the lower Thamesside areas of Essex and Kent, Milton Keynes, Luton, Stevenage, north Essex (Braintree–Colchester–Clacton), some coastal towns of Kent and Sussex (Margate, Ramsgate, Folkestone, Romney–Hastings, Brighton), Portsmouth and the Isle of Wight (see Figures 4.2, 4.3). In many of these areas, including

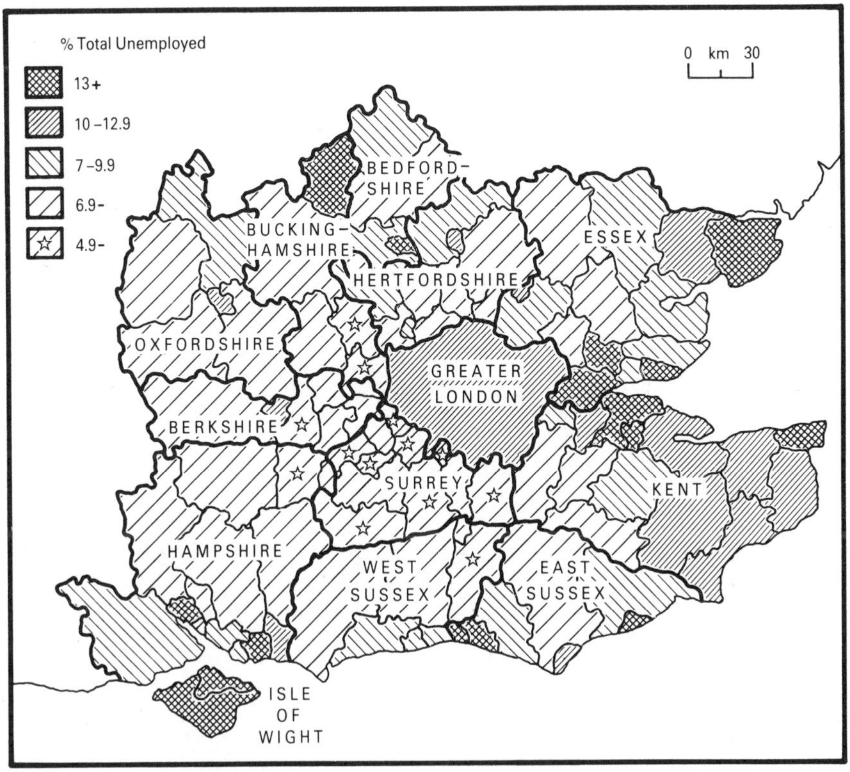

Figure 4.2. Unemployment rates, 1984, the South East

inner North London, Stevenage, Luton, Thurrock, Gravesend, and Portsmouth, employment in manufacturing and related services had been declining in the 1970s, and these were areas of real economic distress. Elsewhere also, especially in Milton Keynes and Essex, growth in the working population had outstripped the capacity of the areas to generate or attract new jobs. In contrast to these areas, employment growth and low unemployment were general in much of the region west of a line from Chichester to Bedford, especially west and south of London. Although manufacturing work had expanded in some areas even during the recession, by far the most general stimulus to prosperity in the western half of the region came from office and other service employment. The residential boom in these areas, related to their attraction for new investment, continued commuting of high earners from London, and the decentralization of some activities from the city, has exerted a beneficial multiplier effect on this western zone. This positive combination seems to be present only on a more localized basis in Essex and Kent, in such centres as Chelmsford, Maidstone, Tunbridge Wells, and Sevenoaks.

Population changes within the region, dominated by migration patterns, broadly reflected these economic contrasts during the 1970s. Between 1971 and

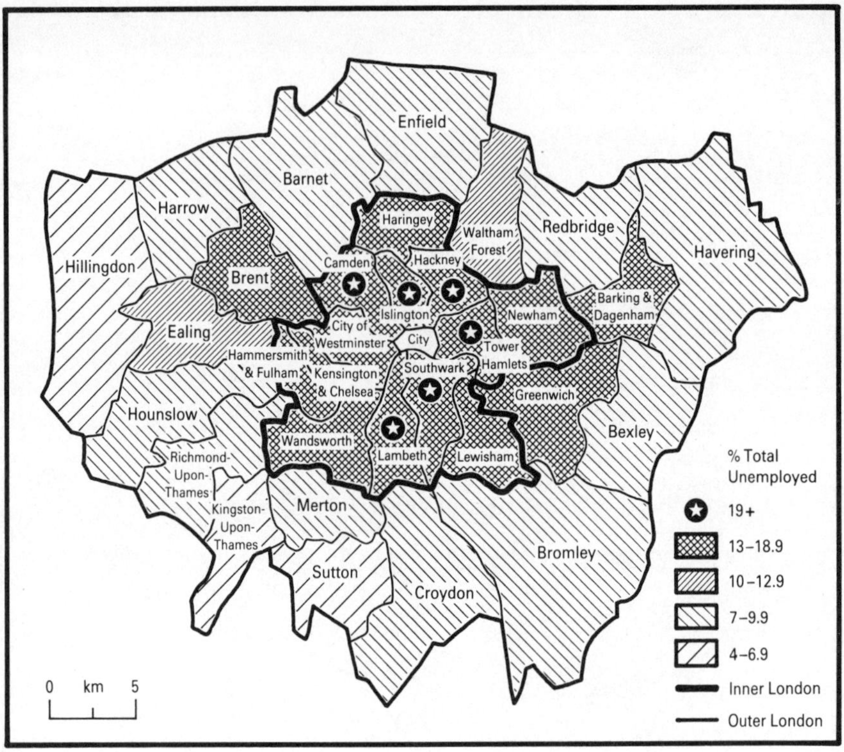

Figure 4.3. Unemployment rates, 1984, Greater London

1981 the population of the South East fell by 0.7 per cent, as gains in the RoSE failed to compensate for a loss of almost three-quarters of a million in London (Table 4.1). After 1982, higher rates of natural increase and reduced net migration out of London resulted in a small increase in the region's population. Population in the RoSE in the intercensal decade grew much more slowly than in the 1960s (6 per cent compared with 18 per cent), because of reduced levels of net in-migration as well as generally lower birth-rates. The numbers in larger towns also fell, even in the prosperous west of the region, including Oxford, Reading, Slough, Watford, and Southampton, as well as Portsmouth, Brighton/Hove, and Southend. Decentralization from such centres favoured the surrounding small towns and rural areas. In the zone of most intense commuting to London dominated by the planning restraints of the Metropolitan Green Belt, population levels were generally stable, with local decline nearer to the city. Population grew fastest in (*a*) Milton Keynes, nearby areas of south Buckinghamshire, and mid- and south Bedfordshire, (*b*) the Basingstoke–Bracknell–Wokingham–Newbury zone, (*c*) the area of Sussex south of Crawley, including Horsham and Arundel, (*d*) much of Hampshire away from the urbanized coastal areas along the Solent, and (*e*) much of Essex beyond the Green Belt. The first three of these areas had been designated as regional

Table 4.1. Population change in the South East, 1971–81, 1981–3 (mid-year estimates)

	1971–81					1981–3
	Natural change	Other	Total change	%	1981 pop.	%
SE region	261	−376	−115	−0.7	17,101	+0.2
Greater London:	91	−814	−724	−9.6	6,806	−0.2
Central boroughs	−2	−122	−123	−19.4	513	−2.7
Inner London	30	−539	−510	−16.7	2,550	−1.6
Outer London	61	−275	−214	−4.8	4,256	−0.2
RoSE	171	438	609	+6.3	10,205	+0.8
Outer Met. Area	178	65	242	+4.7	5,451	+0.5
Outer SE	−7	374	367	+8.4	4,754	+1.2

Sources: Office of Population Censuses and Surveys; SERPLAN 1984; 1985*b*.

growth zones in the 1970 Strategic Plan, and are still referred to as such by the South East Regional Planning Conference.

The reasons for these contrasts in the fortunes of different areas of the South East must be the prime focus of planning concern in the region, and provide the main rationale for concerted action on a regional scale. Other issues related to them include the rejuvenation of Inner London, land pressures within and beyond the Green Belt, the impact of major transport and other infrastructure investments, and environmental conservation problems.

Patterns of manufacturing change

In spite of the dominance of service employment in the South East, changes in manufacturing have generally been given greater emphasis in the explanation of employment and population trends, and in speculation about the future. This emphasis is not wholly justified, as Table 4.2 indicates. Certainly, manufacturing provided the most extreme changes during the 1970s. Between 1975 and 1983, the dominant feature seems to have been the decline of about a quarter of a million jobs in London's manufacturing. These losses had been running at 5 per cent per year in the early 1970s and returned to this level between 1978 and 1981. Even during the intervening economic upturn, between 1975 and 1978, the fall was considerably faster than the national average. After 1978, national output fell and manufacturing employment decline accelerated markedly. The contraction even affected the RoSE, although London's rate of loss was slightly below the very high national rate. Construction and utilities employment followed very similar patterns. After 1981, when Standard Industrial Classification (SIC) changes created a break in the series for London, manufacturing employment losses there continued at rates which were well above the national average, even in the supposed upturn after 1982 (continuing at 5 per cent per

Table 4.2. South East employment, 1981, and changes, 1975–8, 1978–81, 1981–3 (1968 SIC), and 1982–4 (1980 SIC), by sector

	Greater London		Rest of South East		Great Britain	
(a) Employment, 000s (% of total)						
Manufacturing	650	(18.5)	991	(27.3)	5,924	(28.1)
Services	2,650	(75.4)	2,331	(64.1)	13,091	(61.9)
Mining/construction/utilities	211	(6.0)	236	(6.5)	1,762	(8.3)
Total (incl. agriculture)	3,513		3,635	-	21,148	
(b) Changes, 1975–8, 000s (%)						
Manufacturing	−67	(−8.0)	+15	(+1.4)	−217	(−3.0)
Services	−30	(−1.1)	+75	(+3.5)	+332	(+2.7)
Mining/construction/utilities	−17	(−7.0)	0	(0.0)	−60	(−3.1)
Total (incl. agriculture)	−114	(−3.0)	+86	(+2.4)	+40	(+0.2)
(c) Changes, 1978–81, 000s (%)						
Manufacturing	−119	(−15.5)	−101	(−9.2)	−1,193	(−16.8)
Services	−32	(−1.2)	+132	(+6.0)	+214	(+1.7)
Mining/construction/utilities	−15	(−6.6)	−8	(−3.2)	−145	(−7.6)
Total (incl. agriculture)	−167	(−4.5)	+23	(+0.6)	−1,126	(−5.1)
(d) Estimated changes, 1981–3 (September), 000s (%)						
Manufacturing	−60	(−9.2)	−66	(−6.7)	−485	(−8.2)
Services	0	(0.0)	+12	(+0.5)	+111	(+0.8)
(e) Changes, 1982–4 (June), 1980 SIC basis, 000s (%)						
Manufacturing	−66	(−10)	−8	(−1)		(−6)
Services	+31	(+1)	−92	(+4)		(+2)
Mining/construction/utilities	−13	(−6)	−11	(−3)		(−7)
Total	−48	(−1)	+72	(+2)		(−1)

Sources: Censuses of Employment (*a–c*); *Employment Gazette* (*d*); *Employment Gazette, Historical Supplement no. 1*, April 1985 (*e*).

year). Following the earlier losses, manufacturing numbers in the RoSE now stabilized.

In the services, on the other hand, a less spectacular but equally persistent trend throughout the period after 1975 was the emerging contrast of experience in employment change between London and the RoSE. The city lost 62,000 service jobs between 1975 and 1981, while the RoSE gained over 200,000. Although a slight revival seemed to occur in London after 1982, this was still below the national trend, and much less than the continued growth in the RoSE. After 1982, the expansion of banking, insurance and financial employment was supplemented by an apparent revival in the distributive, hotel, catering, and other personal services which benefited both parts of the region, but especially the RoSE. These changes, however, were associated with another significant trend in the service sector: a marked acceleration in the numbers of female, part-time workers, with little impact being made on the availability of male or full-time female jobs. The pattern of service changes will be considered further in the next section.

Detailed evidence for the pattern and nature of manufacturing change in the region is fragmentary. Nevertheless, the causes for the decline of London have been intensively discussed, as part of the wider study of urban manufacturing decline in Britain since the 1960s (Danson *et al.* 1980; Elias and Keogh 1982; Fothergill and Gudgin 1982; Keeble 1980b; Massey and Meegan 1978). The decentralization of investment by large firms and the collapse of the small firms sector across all industries has been widely attributed to the increasing costs, congestion, and inconvenience of operating in cities, spurred by the drive to adopt new technologies and to counter overseas competition. The decline of the cities is therefore associated with the wider restructuring or de-industrialization of the British economy. In London, the loss of over 20,000 jobs in the port has added an extra ingredient, triggering an equivalent amount of other manufacturing and service decline in east London. Further, the unique size of the city seems to have intensified the effects of the general factors that have caused the withdrawal of manufacturing investment from other British cities.

The patterns of manufacturing change outside London are much less clear and, as a result, the reasons for them are the subject of much speculation and not a little myth. Although some areas have benefited from the obverse of the trends that have caused the decline of London, others have suffered a similar experience of large firm rationalization and small firm closure. In 1978, about 30 per cent of the jobs in the RoSE were in manufacturing firms. These were particularly concentrated into the areas to the north west of London, where old-established industrial centres such as Luton–Dunstable, High Wycombe, and Watford were augmented by the post war rash of New Towns, whose development in the 1950s and 1960s was heavily dependent upon manufacturing. These included Stevenage, Hitchin–Letchworth, Welwyn Garden City–Hatfield and Hemel Hempstead in Hertfordshire, and, of course, the more recent growth of Milton Keynes in Buckinghamshire. The continuity of this outer zone of relative manufacturing specialization is enhanced by the importance of manufacturing employment in the suburbs of west and north west London. To the east of London, Essex and north Kent also depend more than the regional average upon manufacturing jobs. In Essex, as in the west, this dependence extends the industrial character of north east London along the river, augumented by other centres such as Romford, Chelmsford, and Colchester, as well as the New Towns of Harlow and Basildon. South Hampshire, of course, is also a significant centre of manufacturing activity, and other more localized concentrations of manufacturing include Crawley–Gatwick in Sussex, Reading, Bracknell, and Slough in Berkshire, Ashford in Kent, and Oxford.

A broad indication of trends in the region's manufacturing capacity, compared with those in commercial office development, between 1974 and 1982 is

Table 4.3. Changes in industrial and commercial office floor-space, the South East, 1974–82

(*a*) Industrial floor-space, 1974–82, 000 m²

	Change	%	1982 stock
South East Region	+90	+0.2	54,802
Greater London	−2,111	−8.7	22,079
Central London	−130	−12.4	919
Rest of London	−1,981	−8.6	21,178
Rest of the South East	+2,200	+7.2	32,700
Outer Metropolitan Area	+700	+3.8	18,900
Outer South East	+1,500	+12.2	13,800
North West RoSE	+831	+11.3	7,236
South West RoSE*	+527	+5.0	11,017
North/North East RoSE†	+440	+5.2	8,838
South East RoSE	+393	+7.5	5,615
*of which:			
Hampshire/West Sussex	+748	+14.3	5,964
Berkshire/Surrey	−236	−4.7	4,750
†of which:			
Hertfordshire	−17	−0.4	4,079

(*b*) Commercial office floorspace, 1974–82, 000 m²

	Change	%	1982 stock	Ratio industrial/ commercial space
South East Region	+5,582	+29.0	24,816	2.2
Greater London	+2,989	+21.2	17,061	1.3
Central London	+1,653	+18.0	10,821	0.1
Rest of London	+1,335	+27.0	6,240	3.4
Rest of the South East	+2,600	+51.0	7,700	4.2
Outer Metropolitan Area	+1,600	+55.0	4,500	4.2
Outer South East	+1,000	+45.0	3,200	4.3
North West RoSE	+386	+45.6	1,234	5.9
South West RoSE*	+1,193	+56.0	3,324	3.3
North/North East RoSE†	+381	+41.4	1,301	6.8
South East RoSE	+492	+51.7	1,443	3.9
*of which:				
Hampshire/West Sussex	+518	+48.4	1,585	3.8
Berkshire/Surrey	+685	+67.5	1,701	2.3
†of which:				
Hertfordshire	+248	+39.8	871	4.7

Source: Inland Revenue (SERPLAN, 1984, Tables 3.17, 3.18).

provided by Table 4.3. The rate of contraction of industrial floor-space in London was much less than that of manufacturing employment (−8.7 per cent from 1974 to 1982, compared with a 31 per cent decline in jobs) indicating the reduced labour-intensity of industrial land use in the city. A similar trend, however, also took place in the RoSE, where for the same period a 15 per cent decline in employment could be compared with a 7.2 per cent increase in floor-space. These comparisons suggest that, over the eight-year period, an expansion of over 20 per cent in floor-space was required simply to maintain levels of manufacturing employment in the region, and probably rather more in London. Between 1974 and 1982, manufacturing floor-space grew faster in the Outer South East, and especially in the western countries of Bedfordshire, Buckinghamshire, Oxfordshire, Hampshire, and West Sussex. Even here, however, the average rate of growth was barely sufficient to sustain employment levels. Elsewhere, contraction in Greater London was augmented by decline in the adjacent areas of Surrey and east Berkshire, to the west and south west, and also in Hertfordshire to the north. In comparison, office floor-space was, of course, much more concentrated into London, even though expansion there was relatively slow. Office growth, however, was most active in the nearby Outer Metropolitan Area (OMA), where manufacturing expansion was slowest, including especially Surrey, Berkshire, and Buckinghamshire.

The best evidence for geographical variations in manufacturing employment change within the region during the late 1970s has come from Dennis, in a Department of Industry paper (Dennis 1981) examining the main components of employment change in Outer Metropolitan and Outer South East (OSE) counties between 1976 and 1980 (Table 4.4). His earlier study of London for the 1966–74 period (Dennis 1978) found that small plants contributed relatively more to closure than larger plants in both Inner and Outer London. After 1976, however, Dennis noted that large plants showed a consistently high loss of employment throughout the South East, but especially in London (Dennis 1981). The highest rates of growth were found, in fact, in small plants (up to 300 workers) in the Outer Metropolitan and Outer South East areas. During the late 1970s, however, the opening of *new* plants made little contribution to the overall pattern of employment change, even in the OSE and the more prosperous parts of the OMA, and job losses through factory closure everywhere swamped the small numbers of jobs created by openings.

The rate of loss from closures was notably high in London (and would probably have appeared higher if smaller firms had been included in Dennis's calculations) and low in some parts of the OSE, including east Kent, Sussex, Hampshire, and Oxfordshire. The poor manufacturing performance of the OMA areas of Surrey/Sussex, Berkshire and Hertfordshire, noted already, was associated with high levels of plant closure and contraction, in spite of significant numbers of jobs in plant expansions. Northern and western Kent showed a similar pattern of losses (not revealed in the floor-space data for the whole county in Table 4.3). Plant closures, although less in London than during the 1966–74 period, affected relatively more jobs in Outer London after 1976, probably reflecting the concentration there of large plants.

Table 4.4. Change in manufacturing employment, the South East, 1976–80 (as percentage of 1976 employment)

	In situ change			Unit turnover			Net change
	Expansion	Contraction	Net *in situ*	Openings	Closures	Net turnover	
	1	2	3	4	5	6	7
Inner London	+7.5	−11.5	−4.0	+0.4*	−7.0*	−6.6*	−10.6
Outer London	+8.5	−10.8	−2.3	+0.4*	−8.3*	−7.9*	−10.2
Outer Metropolitan Area							
Kent	+10.9	−10.0	+0.9	+1.1	−5.3	−4.2	−3.3
Sussex/Surrey	+12.5	−10.1	+2.4	+0.3	−4.3	−4.0	−1.6
Surrey	+11.4	−10.4	+1.0	+0.9	−5.9	−5.0	−4.0
Berkshire	+11.3	−8.9	+2.4	+0.8	−5.9	−5.1	−2.7
Buckinghamshire	+10.7	−6.5	+4.2	+0.9	−4.1	−3.2	+1.0
Hertfordshire	+10.8	−7.9	+2.9	+0.8	−5.8	−5.0	−2.1
Essex	+11.8	−8.1	+3.7	+1.2	−4.7	−3.5	+0.2
Outer South East							
Kent	+13.9	−6.2	+7.7	−1.6	−3.7	−2.1	+5.6
Sussex	+16.3	−7.9	+8.4	+0.7	−3.6	−2.9	+5.5
Hampshire	+13.8	−6.2	+7.6	+0.1	−3.3	−3.2	+4.4
Oxfordshire	+10.0	−7.2	+2.8	+0.5	−2.3	−1.8	+1.0
Bedfordshire/ Buckinghamshire	+15.2	−8.9	+6.3	+1.6	−5.4	−3.8	+2.5
Essex	+14.9	−6.8	+8.1	+0.9	−5.4	−4.5	+3.6

Source: Dennis 1981.

*For units employing 20 or more people only; other areas are for units with 11 or more.

The principal mechanism creating systematic contrasts in the patterns of manufacturing change in the region was the differential expansion of established, small- to medium-sized plants. This was relatively low in London and high in many OSE areas. In addition, the pattern of plant contraction, although less clearly concentric (as we have seen, being high in Surrey, North Sussex, and Western Kent, as well as London), reinforced the generally favourable position for manufacturing in the OSE. The pattern of manufacturing change in the South East in the late 1970s was therefore dominated by the contraction or closure of large plants, especially in Outer London and adjacent areas of the OMA to the south-west, west,and north, combined with the failure of plants of all sizes to develop or expand in London. On-site employment expansion more than compensated for local contractions or closures throughout the OSE (although only just so in Oxfordshire), and in the Buckinghamshire and Essex parts of the OMA. Even in the favoured areas of the region, however, during the recession of 1981–2 and afterwards, the balance of manufacturing employment change undoubtedly moved sharply towards decline.

The local impact of old and new technology

Dennis's data are too crudely defined to allow exploration of the more detailed patterns of local variation in the RoSE. Nevertheless, they hint at the effects of recession on closures and contractions in the old-established industrial areas, especially Surrey and north Sussex, along the lower Thames (south Essex and north Kent), in Luton (Bedfordshire), some of the New Towns (Hertfordshire), and in Reading and Slough (Berkshire), if not so clearly in Oxford and in Portsmouth and the Isle of Wight, where large-scale redundancies also occurred. The distribution and impact of new employment creation in manufacturing, although generally favouring the OSE, are more difficult to characterize. In a period of rapid technological change, the identification of employment 'growth' industries in a conventional sense is virtually impossible. While product innovation may create modest growth in the short term, as we have seen, job losses even in the same areas may far outweigh these gains following the introduction of new, more capital-intensive techniques in the manufacture of established products. If successful innovation in the South East creates new jobs in the longer term to serve a growing demand, these may well require different skills, and be located in different places, possibly even abroad. The close relationship between manufacturing and service employment change and its geographical impacts also raise difficulties in interpreting the full employment effects of new technology.

Evidence assembled by the London and South East Regional Planning Conference, with Department of Industry assistance, in the early 1980s illustrates the difficulties (SERPLAN 1984, Table 3.19, Figs. 3.9–10). The distribution of employment in the broadly defined 'innovative' employment categories of instruments, electrical equipment, and aerospace in 1978 shows a concentration in Outer London (except to the east) and north Surrey, in the New Towns of Stevenage, Harlow, Basildon, Bracknell, and Crawley, in Chelmsford, Portsmouth, the Isle of Wight, and the Medway area. The growing western part of the region notably lacked these activities, and they have evidently not protected the areas which do possess them from decline. In fact, the large plants which dominate these areas have reduced employment needs in recent years, irrespective of their industrial structures. Clearly, these days, a legacy of nominal 'growth' industries provides few clues to an area's strength of employment demand.

The Department of Industry has also examined the distribution of new-technology firms in electronics founded between 1970 and 1980. There were particular concentrations around west London, but comparatively low representations of new innovative firms in Surrey, north Kent, Essex, the Isle of Wight, and most of the New Towns. Relatively high numbers occurred, however, in the Newbury/Reading area, Slough, and south Buckinghamshire. This pattern certainly conforms more closely to the popular image of the 'Thames Corridor' as a focus for innovation, but the numbers of jobs involved in the South East amounted to little more than 5,000 in ten years. On the other hand, over 39,000 jobs were created in 1980–1 alone in new firms in software and computer service activities. These were overwhelmingly (62 per cent) concentrated in London, with significant numbers also in Surrey, Berkshire, Buckinghamshire, and Hertfordshire (SERPLAN, 1984, Table 3.19)—all areas of office rather than new manufacturing development.

Another analysis by SERPLAN of the distribution in the South East of a limited range of the most obvious 'new technology' SIC groups from the 1981 Census also illustrates the difficulties of interpreting local employment impacts (see Table 4.5). For manufacturing, the regional share was little more than the national average, but high proportions occurred in Hertfordshire, Essex, Berkshire, Hampshire, and the Isle of Wight, and especially in the two 'growth zones' designated in the 1970s: Reading–Wokingham–Aldershot–Basingstoke and Crawley–Burgess Hill. Even in these areas the scale of employment hardly compensated for the decline of traditional manufacturing. On the other hand, such new technology manufacturing was poorly represented in Inner London, Oxfordshire, East Sussex, Kent, and, perhaps most surprisingly, Milton Keynes. It is difficult to believe that this distribution adequately reflects the future growth potential of these varied areas.

The identification of 'new technology' services is even more open to question, since innovative methods pervade all types of service activity, and their employment effects are even more ambiguous than in manufacturing. The figures nevertheless suggest that computer services and research and development activities were not particularly concentrated in London, casting some doubt on the significance of the Department of Industry results cited above. Much greater shares were found in Oxfordshire, the Reading–Wokingham–Aldershot–Basingstoke area, Surrey, and Bedfordshire. Particularly low levels occurred in East and West Sussex, the Isle of Wight, Milton Keynes, and Essex. Again, the implications of this evidence for future local employment demand in various parts of the South East are not at all clear.

Thus, the spatial impact of innovation on jobs, both directly in manufactur-

Table 4.5. New-technology employment,* the South East, 1981: percentage of total jobs in areas and location quotients (LQ), compared with Great Britain

	Manufacturing			Services		
	No. ('000)	%	L.Q.	No. ('000)	%	L.Q.
Great Britain	700	3.3		175	0.8	
South East	246	3.4	1.05	96	1.3	1.63
Greater London	76	2.2	0.66	32	0.9	1.11
(Central London)	(4)	(0.4)	(0.13)	(9)	(1.0)	(1.21)
Inner London	16	0.8	0.24	16	0.8	0.99
Outer London	61	3.9	1.18	16	1.0	1.26
Rest of the South East	169	5.8	1.77	64	2.2	2.67
OMA	114	7.5	2.29	32	2.1	2.52
OSE	55	4.0	1.21	32	2.3	2.83
Counties/'Growth Areas'						
Bedfordshire	7	3.5	1.07	3	1.7	2.07
Berkshire	18	5.8	1.77	13	4.0	4.89
Buckinghamshire	7	3.3	1.01	3	1.7	2.09
East Sussex	3	1.6	0.48	—	—	0.21
Essex	25	5.6	1.71	3	0.6	0.74
Hampshire	27	4.9	1.50	9	1.6	1.98
Hertfordshire	39	9.5	2.89	6	1.5	1.83
Isle of Wight	3	7.0	2.13	—	—	0.05
Kent	11	2.3	0.70	4	0.9	1.06
Oxfordshire	2	0.8	0.24	10	5.0	6.13
Surrey	16	4.8	1.45	11	3.2	3.93
West Sussex	12	4.8	1.48	1	0.5	0.66
'South Hampshire'	20	5.8	1.76	5	1.4	1.70
Milton Keynes	1	1.5	0.45	—	—	0.87
'Area 8' (Reading/ Basingstoke, etc.)	19	6.9	2.10	12	4.3	5.20
Crawley/Burgess Hill	7	6.8	2.08	—	—	0.43

Source: SERPLAN 1985*b* Table 3.10.

*Defined as SIC groups 3302 (data-processing equipment), 3441, 3442, 3443 (telephone, telegraph apparatus, electrical instruments, radio and electronic capital goods), 3453 (electronic components), 3640 (aerospace), 3710 (measuring instruments), 3732 (optical instruments), 8394 (computer services), and 9400 (research and development).

ing and through the creation of supporting service activities, is highly differentiated between sectors and functions. The overall scale of new employment creation is small, and sensitive to the decisions of large firms and government agencies. Job losses may far outweigh its effects. The contribution of small firms to growth or innovation, with high risks of failure and only exceptional cases of significant success, is very modest. Attempts to divine the sources of new manufacturing employment growth in various areas of the South East outside London, therefore, remain very generalized. The existence of government research and development establishments, of corporate headquarters, of innovative small firms, of rapid access to airports or to international communications offer some general causes for optimism, but little reliable guidance to the distribution of new manufacturing production and employment itself (Department of Industry 1982; Gould and Keeble 1984; Oakey *et al.* 1980; 1982; Thwaites 1982; Breheny *et al.* 1983).

One of the main assets of some areas of the region is the concentration of professional, scientific, technical, and managerial skills which other regions lack, and the associated nexus of information exchange and ideas extending far outside Britain. Undoubtedly, the growth of some service employment can be related to these assets of expertise and communication, but again their implications for manufacturing are by no means straightforward. In fact, one result of such a concentration, which may well be affecting London and parts of the OMA already, could be to drive out manufacturing investment to other regions with cheaper land and labour, in Britain or abroad. This is an alarming prospect because of the decline of old-established industries and the continuing growth of the working population in many areas. The polarization of employment opportunities that is already occurring in London, between qualified, largely white-collar workers in high-technology activities and office-based services, and the unqualified, low-waged, or unemployed in other services and a rump of locally oriented manufacturing, may well extend to other areas of the South East. These fears demonstrate the increasingly subsidiary nature of what happens to manufacturing employment in 'new' industries in relation to broader shifts in labour demand, especially in the services.

Three principal conclusions arise from this discussion of the fragmentary evidence available in the mid-1980s about manufacturing trends in the South East. First, employment creation in the region would have best been served during the 1970s by giving attention to the conditions which allow successful *established* small and medium-sized firms to develop and expand, rather than by placing hopes too heavily on new plants and new firm formation. Secondly, although market, technological, and corporate considerations lie behind changes at the subregional level, where potential investment is available in the region, local land availability and controls, and other planning policies such as transport investment, have strongly influenced patterns of change. For example, until the mid-1970s, land-use planning in London showed little awareness of the trend of manufacturing decline in its treatment of established industries. Although, according to the Greater London Council, there was a high take-up of planning permissions for industrial development in the early 1980s, especially in the central and western areas of London, we have seen that total available floor-space was rapidly declining (SERPLAN 1984, para. 3.41). The operations of the land market were still squeezing manufacturing out of the city.

Elsewhere, the highest level of land commitment through planning permissions to new industrial and warehouse development was found in the western half of the region, beyond the Green Belt, in Buckinghamshire, Berkshire, and north Hampshire (Basingstoke), and in outer west London, a significant cause, as well as a result, of the pressures for growth. In contrast, the largest areas of vacant land awaiting industrial development were in east London and the lower Thames areas of Essex and Kent, together with Milton Keynes, Stevenage, Ashford, and the Colchester–Clacton area of north east Essex (SERPLAN 1984, Figs. 3.7–8). Thus, contrasts in the land market operate not only between London and the rest of the region, as Fothergill and Gudgin (1982) emphasize, but also between the west and east of the RoSE. This evidence indicates that opportunities exist for regional economic and physical planning priorities to influence patterns of change, if appropriate planning mechanisms were to be in place.

Finally, it is also clear from the evidence reviewed here that the employment-generating effects of manufacturing itself in the South East are uncertain, and probably severely limited. The principal dynamics of employment change are certainly to be found in the service sector, to which we shall now turn.

Service activities in the South East

In spite of its overwhelming regional importance, the pattern of service employment in the South East is even more poorly monitored than manufacturing. The national dominance by the region of many office-based activities is widely regarded as its major source of economic strength (Westaway, 1974). Much service activity is concentrated in London (53 per cent in 1981, compared with its 40 per cent share of regional population), but there have been marked shifts outwards in recent years. With the decentralization of the workforce, such a move is desirable in certain respects, for example to reduce commuting pressures into London. The employment opportunities offered by different types of service vary widely, however, and the significance for London's poorer workers of the decline of some services in the city is a matter of prime concern. Unemployment in London is largely a service industry phenomenon. In 1981, 62 per cent of male and 85 per cent of the female unemployed had last worked in services, particularly in personal services, distribution, and catering. Only the male-dominated construction industry showed higher rates of unemployment than these types of activity.

The role of service jobs in the growing areas of the western half of the region has already been outlined. Much expanding, skilled, information-based, managerial, technical, and professional employment in the service sector, here as well as in London, is oriented to the needs of production. The high proportions of such 'planning and control' activities in the manufacturing plants and headquarters of the South East also contribute similar functions. The further effects of this high income growth on consumer services reinforces the significance of services for economic change around the region. Conversely, of course, decline in transportation and communications services, and in public-sector employment has adversely affected east London, the Medway Towns, and Portsmouth.

Producer and public services have for long been basic components of these economies, and their decline demonstrates that dependence on services can result as easily in local contraction as in local growth.

Local diversity in service employment is therefore highly significant. Here, however, we must illustrate the issues raised by service industrial change in the region by comparing trends in London and the RoSE, because detailed information is available only at this level of generalization. The dominant pattern, like that in manufacturing, is a net dispersal of service activities away from London. This has, however, proceeded to a greater degree in some services than in others and, in the late 1970s, still showed varied trends. By 1981, service jobs in the region were almost equally divided between London and the RoSE. In Table 4.6, variations about this average are shown by distinguishing between those service activities that were already better represented in the RoSE and those in which Greater London still predominated. As might be expected, the former include broadly 'consumer-oriented' functions such as retailing, education, medicine, other professional services, personal services, and construction, with smaller numbers in the utilities and motor repair. In nearly all of these the relative dispersion of employment from London was continuing, whether as a result of growth in the RoSE and decline in London (utilities, retailing), faster growth in the RoSE (medicine, motor repairs) or faster decline in London (education, construction). Only 'other professional' and personal services grew in London at similar rates to the RoSE and this was probably because these categories in the city include more business and tourist-related functions than in other parts of the region. Following transportation developments and manufacturing decentralization, three types of material-handling producer services were also now more important in the RoSE than in London: dealing in industrial materials and machinery, road haulage, and sea and port activities.

Regarding the long-term pattern of employment change, more significance should probably be attached to the business, tourist, and government activities which London still dominates. The most rapid decentralization of these between 1975 and 1981 was in wholesaling (following the other distribution activities) and air transport. On the other hand, the pattern of postal and telecommunications employment shifted outwards only marginally during the period. The modest growth in London's *office-based* business services, including insurance, banking, accountancy, legal services, and other commercial activities, was far exceeded by their rate of expansion in the RoSE. The different nature of growth in the two areas is again possibly disguised by the classification, since some growth in the RoSE must in fact have been in consumer-oriented financial and legal activities rather than in business services. Nevertheless, there is ample other evidence for the movement of business employment away from the city to cheaper, more convenient, and pleasanter sites elsewhere in the South East, especially in the western OMA counties, as Table 4.4 indicated (Goddard and Smith 1978). These activities are particularly affected by innovations in telecommunications and in office management procedures, especially in more routine functions.

Table 4.6. Service employment in Greater London and the RoSE, 1981, and changes, 1975–81

	Greater London		RoSE	
	No. ('000)	% change	No. ('000)	% change
Total service employment (incl. construction/utilities)	2,857	−3	2,562	+9
(i) Services represented more than average in the RoSE				
Construction	162	−13	172	−9
Utilities	45	−17	59	+8
Road haulage	20	−35	30	−3
Sea transport/ports	21	−48	36	−2
Retail distribution	305	−5	360	+6
Dealing in industrial materials	47	−7	57	+21
Education	224	−12	338	−1
Medical	216	+6	246	+16
Other professional/scientific	68	+8	87	+5
Motor repairs	61	+3	103	+29
Personal services	165	+19	148	+19
(ii) Services represented more than average in Greater London				
Rail transport	61	−7	25	−5
Road passenger transport	34	−4	24	−16
Air transport	51	−4	16	+43
Postal/telecommunications	122	−7	67	+3
Misc. transport/storage	64	+24	37	+49
Wholesale distribution	123	−14	91	+18
Insurance/banking	221	+3	103	+27
Other business services	241	+7	115	+53
Accountancy/legal services	63	+12	33	+23
Recreational services	223	+1	187	+19
National government	141	−18	109	0
Local government	174	−4	139	−6

Source: *Department of Employment Gazette*.

The effects of *tourism and entertainment* activities on the growth of personal services in London has already been suggested. Its impact on recreational and 'miscellaneous transport' services (including travel agents) must also have been significant, although in both cases growth was much faster outside London. Up to the early 1980s, the tourist boom in London, although affecting several sectors of employment, seemed to be making a relatively modest impact on employment when placed in the context of the continuing decentralization of the resident population and its spending power in the region.

The reduction in national *government* employment between 1975 and 1981 was clearly more severe in London than in Britain as a whole. This tendency seems unlikely to be reversed in the foreseeable future. Similarly, it is unlikely that the relative stability of employment in London's local government during the period will continue into the late 1980's, especially after the abolition of the GLC. The prospects of public-sector employment growth elsewhere in the region, however, are also slim. The relatively stable levels of employment in road and rail passenger transport activities in London are also unlikely to be sustained by policy trends in the future.

Thus a combination of the continuing decentralization of nearly all activities, whether or not they are still relatively concentrated in London, technological change in telecommunications and administrative procedures, and the contraction of public sector employment suggests that services may no longer offer a sound basis for employment growth, or even its retention in London. Of course, some service employment decline is to be expected, following population decentralization. The economic health of London's basic national and international service functions is vital, however, and should not suffer the same neglect and planning complacency in the 1980s that afflicted its manufacturing and port activities in the 1960s. Planning for its deprived inner and dockland areas also needs to recognize this situation (Damesick 1982*b*).

Elsewhere in the South East, producer and consumer needs will continue to stimulate service demand, reinforcing economic contrasts between different areas. Some service functions, however, particularly in business services, in distribution and storage activities associated with motorway, airport, and seaport investments, in some government administration, and in large-scale recreational activities, are relatively footloose within the region, or at least within some subregions. If services are to play an increasing role in the economic prospects of London and different areas of the RoSE, the potential for influencing the geographical pattern of service employment in the region must also be exploited to serve the region's planning needs

Economic planning needs in the South East

In a region as prosperous, but also as internally diverse, as the South East, the possibility of tapping the economic potential of its growth areas for the benefit of job creation elsewhere might be expected to be a natural topic for debate. Such a strategy, if it were thought to be practical in the circumstances of the 1980s (and there would have been little doubt in the 1960s), would require some form of regional programme to guide the direction of change. In fact, since the mid-1970s, increasing emphasis has been placed not on 'industrial mobility' between areas, but on the encouragement of local activities as the basis for economic revival. It seems to have become widely accepted that, in a period of recession and general employment decline, little investment is available for diversion to areas that need jobs, and that policies to enforce this would threaten the basis of economic recovery itself. Thus, the assumption that no scope exists for planning the transfer of industrial or service employment within the South East is a regional version of the national emphasis on indigenous regional growth.

There are at least two fundamental objections to this view. The first is that it will almost certainly lead to an accelerating contrast in employment opportunities between economically favoured and weak areas. It abandons the belief that the amelioration of inequality of employment demand is worthwhile, even if removal of such inequality cannot be expected. The second objection is less one of principle, and more a matter of practicality. At the subregional scale within the South East, and possibly at the interregional scale also, the distinction between the encouragement of existing or potential local enterprise and the transfer of investment resources between areas is more apparent than real. Each of these tactics is appropriate at different stages in the cycle of a firm's innovation and adoption of technological change. In the 1950s and 1960s, the scope for job-creating investment in high unemployment areas was at its greatest when large numbers of new jobs were becoming available in the mass application of established technology (See Chapter 1). Today, however, with labour-shedding the rule in established manufacturing, much innovative investment has still to create new employment on a large scale. The innovative phase, with its modest and specialized employment needs, may be separate in time and place from the later needs, if any, for a large labour force. These may well be most effectively served in other areas, with very different economic characteristics. Similarly, if small firms are successful, they do not necessarily seek to grow only in their areas of origin.

Thus the simple notion at the basis of traditional regional policies, that surplus jobs created from stable, growing industries could be directed elsewhere, may no longer be valid. Nevertheless, the notion that indigenous growth alone can or should form the basis for local economic revival is equally too simple. Given a reasonable level of general economic growth—and the success of any employment strategy will depend on this—the encouragement of *both* local innovation and the channelling of job-creating investment towards areas of labour surplus will be possible and probably necessary. It is these opportunities that regional policies should be designed to tap, not to restrict growth and enterprise but to facilitate success and expansion.

Similar flexibility is required in relation to service employment. It is at last becoming more widely recognized that much of this is 'producer-oriented', as much a part of the evolving system of production as employment in formally defined manufacturing itself. Indeed, as processes of production have become more complex and the division of labour more elaborate, a growing proportion of 'manufacturing' jobs has been diverted to managerial, technical, and administrative functions. The distinction between these activities and those found in many independent services, for example in financial, legal, and consultancy firms, has become increasingly arbitrary as the producer-service sector has grown (Wood 1984; 1986*b*). In addition, many conventional consumer services are becoming increasingly controlled on a national basis, so that the patterns of their higher levels of employment, in particular, no longer simply follow the distribution of population.

The South East as a whole possesses a powerful comparative advantage in producer services, and in the location of headquarters and divisional functions of large firms. Although this has caused wide concern in other regions, it is also creating growing inequality within the region itself. In 1984, regional industrial policy was at last modified to recognize the potential mobility of some producer services and the contribution they might make to employment growth in assisted areas (Secretary of State for Trade and Industry 1983). The same potential for service-job creation exists in the problem areas of the South East, whether in Inner London, Docklands, or the centres of decline in the RoSE. Office decentralization in the past, of course, favoured some limited areas of suburban London and the RoSE, as did the location of research and development and many public-sector facilities. The potential for influencing the regional distribution of service jobs has therefore been demonstrated within the South East in the past, and their increased employment significance suggests a need to continue such efforts in relation to modern regional planning needs.

The pressures for a public policy framework to guide regional patterns of development are likely to strengthen as a result of the continuing decline of employment in existing industrial areas and growing opposition to 'overheated' development in some growth areas. Public actions, of course, have been influential in the past developments of these contrasts, especially through investments in the motorway system, the New Towns, and Heathrow Airport, and in research and development, defence, and higher education establishments. It is arguable that public investments of these types effectively underpinned the growth and success of the M4 Corridor. Patterns of land release for housing around the region, through structure plan regulation, also imply public guidance of private-sector investment. The simplest case for regional planning is therefore that public expenditure patterns, having always been highly influential in guiding private investment, should more explicitly reflect regional planning priorities. Such a view does not imply any particular level of public spending, but it requires a rational allocation in relation to long-term regional economic and social needs. Within the South East, such an allocation involves modification of land-use regulation and public-sector investment patterns, which have conventionally been the realm of physical planning policy.

Physical planning in the 1980s

Planning in the South East operates at several poorly co-ordinated levels in the mid-1980s.

1. Statutory land-use planning, based on county structure plans, including the Greater London Development Plan (GLDP). All of these were approved between 1976 (GLDP) and 1982 (Essex), and some subsequently formally altered in the early 1980s (East Sussex, Kent, Oxfordshire). A major revision of the GLDP was undertaken in 1983–4, but the results were not accepted by the

Secretary of State for the Environment in view of the intended abolition of the GLC. In Bedfordshire, Buckinghamshire, East Sussex, Hampshire, Hertfordshire, and Oxfordshire, proposed alterations were under consideration by the Secretary of State in 1984, and reviews were on hand in every other county. Thus, structure plans in no sense offer an unchanging framework for development in the region. They represent essentially sub-regional and local responses to the changing prospects for development, within guidelines set down by central government. In a region such as the South East, during a period of rapid economic, social, and geographical transformation, these local responses are inevitably defensive in areas that are under the pressure of growth, while containing a good deal of wishful thinking in areas of stagnation or decline. Without strategic guidance, they cannot rationally allocate land for future housing needs, order the land-planning response to the decline of established industries and the rise of high-technology and service industries, control the impact of major motorway schemes (especially the M25, which in the late 1980s will create entirely new pressures for development), or manage Green Belt control and conservation.

Until 1979, the Regional Economic Planning Council provided a forum through which these wider issues could be discussed between local and central government, even though it had been decreasingly active after the review of the Strategic Plan for the South East in 1976 (South East Joint Planning Team 1976). After 1979, however, a different and more distant form of dialogue replaced this Council.

2. So-called *strategic guidance* from the Department of the Environment to county and district authorities on the implementation of various aspects of planning. In the South East, three communications had been received by late 1984:

(*a*) In August 1980, a letter from the Secretary of State to the Chairman of the (then) Regional Standing Conference sketching the wider aims of the Conservative government within which planning in the South East should be pursued. In fact, of course, ministerial views are implicit in the approved modifications of structure plans, and by 1984 a new letter was urgently being sought by the Conference in the light of subsequent events (SERPLAN 1984, iii, 1985*a*). In 1980, however, priority was given to improving the attractions of London for people and firms; making adequate provision for orderly development elsewhere, particularly in designated 'growth areas' identified in the structure plans; encouraging industrial and commercial developments, especially in small firms and growth industries; improving some transport links (especially completing the M25 motorway); and safeguarding the Green Belt and rural areas. Emphasis was placed on stimulating the private sector in industry, commerce, and house-building, and the restraint of public expenditure. While support for new economic developments was urged, emphasis was also placed on making full use of existing land, labour and infrastructure assets in the larger towns and in parts of London. New and expanded town schemes were being scaled down or terminated, and the Industrial Development Certificate and Office

Development Permit schemes had already been abolished. The setting-up of the London Docklands Development Corporation (see below) and the Enterprise Zones, the release of public-sector land holdings, and support for inner urban Partnership Areas were commended as representing positive help to London. Outside the city, the preferred strategy was one of concentrating a high proportion of the half-million new dwellings proposed by 1990 into selected growth areas, rather than in scattered development.

(*b*) A draft letter of guidance in September 1983 was issued on the impact of the M25 on land-use planning in the South East. This letter reasserted the objectives of the 1980 guidance, but urged a positive response to the development pressures generated by the new motorway. In particular, the steering of development towards the eastern part of the region was recommended through the provision of sufficient land—even though, as we have seen, a land surplus already existed there—while the western counties were also encouraged to be flexible in providing land for development. The economic threat posed by the motorway to London would be dealt with by pressing ahead with proposals for improved links to the M25. Outside London, as in the 1980 letter, local authorities were recommended to concentrate development in existing urban areas and neglected sites, even though additional land provision would probably be needed. Strict control on Green Belt land release would be retained.

(*c*) A draft circular of guidance on Green Belt land policy, issued in 1984, suggested some very limited and selective relaxing of controls in unspecified areas of low-quality Green Belt land to provide for pressing housing needs, and to reinforce the case for sustaining controls elsewhere. This circular was subsequently withdrawn as a result of widespread protest from local authorities and other local interests, and replaced by a version which much more stoutly reaffirmed the traditional protection of the Green Belt (Munton 1983; 1986).

As Damesick (1982*a*: 109) has commented, the Conservative administration's profound disinterest in regional planning, encouraged by the earlier failure of the Labour Government to lay down a clear strategy for the region, has undermined political commitment to regional policy in recent years. In spite of this, local planning authorities of diverse political persuasions in the region still believe strategic guidance to be necessary (see *3* below). Unfortunately, the guidance received between 1980 and 1984 was at best platitudinous and at worst ambivalent in addressing the problems of Inner London, lower Thameside, the disposition of motorway impacts, the allocation of land for housing, or the response to development pressures in the west of the region. Relying heavily on the contribution to change of the private sector, the strategic guidance showed little appreciation of the close relationship of this to patterns of public investment.

Exhortation, or 'planning by good intention' (Damesick 1982*a*: 105), has replaced considered analysis of the economic mainspring of regional change, such as technological innovation, the evolving role of the service sector, urban de-industrialization and decentralization pressures, the dynamics of growth-area development and the huge impacts of 'non-spatial' economic policies on different areas. The political failure to take a strategic view even of the most permanent legacy of past strategic thinking, the Metropolitan Green Belt, was demonstrated by the debacle of the 1984 draft circular. Even though, as Munton (1986) argues, modification of Green Belt policy will become increasingly inevitable in the late 1980s, the Department of the Environment retreated in face of powerful, but almost entirely locally based, political pressures. That political commitment to a form of regional development strategy *can* be mustered is demonstrated in London's docklands, where ample finance has also been made available, even against the opposition of local councils (see 4 below).

3. The London and South East Regional Planning Conference (SERPLAN). The demise of the Regional Planning Council in 1979 brought this consultative body (formerly known as the Standing Conference), representing county and district planning authorities throughout the region, into new prominence. It has published annual monitors of regional trends, progressively charting the impact of the recession on the region and, as far as possibly from secondary data, outlining its internal diversity. Studies have been undertaken of changing patterns of commuting, infrastructure needs, the impacts of the M25, the growth of small households, transport, the Green Belt, and housing supply. The role of the Planning Conference is severely limited, since it represents an uneasy coalition of county and district interests (including, until its abolition in 1986, the GLC) and receives little encouragement in its aims from the Government; but it is the only body which has lobbied for a regional view of some of the critical planning issues in the South East. Most significantly, in spite of disagreements that have threatened its survival, the local authorities still see a need for such a body, with its wider view of economic and social trends in the region than land-use planning alone can provide.

In 1984–5, SERPLAN took concerted action to stimulate a revival of regional strategic planning in the South East, and published a consultative statement as the basis for an agreed approach by its member authorities to the Department of the Environment. The hope was that this would stimulate the Secretary of State to update and extend the guidance offered earlier in the decade. The statement (SERPLAN 1985*a*) looked forward to the needs of the 1990s, especially for 460,000 extra dwellings, compared with the required 600,000 in the 1980s. Its emphasis was upon maintaining and adapting the established housing stock, while locating up to two-thirds of the new dwellings in existing towns and conurbations. The rest, apart from Milton Keynes and South Hampshire, were to be located to serve largely local needs through small-scale developments. This strategy was thus very much in line with the established guidance principles, if less clearly in line with the reality of events in the region.

In fact, as well as the completion of the M25, several new developments in the mid-1980s some arising from government decisions, were exerting new pressures. Stansted Airport was given permission to expand, thus (it was hoped) closing the debate on the third London airport. There was a revived interest in the Channel tunnel. Perhaps most pressing was the proposal from Consortium Developments, a group of major building firms, to construct a series of new 'villages' in the region. Some might possibly be located in the Green Belt and others in the overdeveloped west, although the first to be proposed was in Essex, at Tillingham Hall.

In the light of these and other developments, it is hardly surprising that SERPLAN sought a reiteration of established guidelines. The consultative statement went rather further, however, in re-emphasizing the need to direct development pressures from the west to the east, and towards reviving London and other older settlements. It urged the better co-ordination of land-use policies with both public investment and certain types of revenue expenditure (such as Manpower Services Commission programmes or transport subsidies). Overall, SERPLAN's aim was now to achieve an agreed 'spatial framework to guide public spending' through 'sensitively operated restraint' in the west, co-ordinated infrastructure, land-supply and environmental improvements in the east, and more intense support for Inner London, lower Thameside, the coastal towns, and older industrial towns in the RoSE. Given that agreement on the strategy can be gained among SERPLAN's members, thereafter, the opportunities for effective regional action still remain firmly in the hands of the Secretary of State.

4. While SERPLAN has attempted to fill the strategic planning vacuum in the South East, other *ad hoc* devices have also been used to serve particular needs which are beyond the scope of local land-use controls. These include the London Docklands Development Corporation, which arose in 1981 from central government antipathy to the development strategy and political tactics of the Dockland boroughs and the GLC over the area's renewal. Their planning powers were overruled by this strategic planning body, established to implement (as far as possible) private-sector redevelopment. The designation of the Isle of Dogs Enterprise Zone was also intended to help this process. Rather less commitment has been shown to the inner urban area Partnership schemes, originating in 1978, and representing another form of 'strategic' approach to widespread problems of decline in London and other cities. The programmes were sustained until 1984, but the changing emphasis towards the 'leverage' of private sector economic development, especially through the Urban Development Grant scheme, rate-capping of local authorities' main programme expenditure, and greater Department of the Environment control of the approval of projects, is progressively reducing the public resources available to inner-city areas (Wood 1986*a*).

The *ad hoc* treatment of strategic planning issues was also to be found in the continuing saga of public inquiries into the third London airport and major motorway schemes, within and outside London (for example, on sections of the M25, and the M11 link in North East London). The conflicts which prolonged these inquiries arose partly from disputes about traffic forecasts, but also from an inability to reconcile local and regional strategic needs. As long as the latter are so poorly articulated and half-heartedly pursued, this element of conflict will remain unresolved. As in Docklands and the Partnership Areas, ministerial decisions determine the ultimate outcomes, even if they are that nothing is done. Many more conflicts, however, are resolved on an incremental basis, within the processes of preparing and agreeing structure plans, and the responses to particular proposals by land developers. In the long term, the sum of such *ad hoc* proposals may change the face of the South East as radically as an airport or a motorway, but at present no focused public debate about development trends is possible because of the absence of detailed monitoring and the vacuum in strategic planning ideas. In fact, although hardly a perfect model, the principal body in the region with strategic powers which could resolve local differences over housing, transportation, and economic development provisions, the GLC, was abolished in 1986.

Conclusion: the place for a regional perspective

The mid-1980s is not a particularly auspicious period in which to argue the case for comprehensive, still less for administratively effective, regional planning. Regional considerations today, as they have in the past, challenge powerful central and local government lobbies in Britain, and they 'bureacratize' the process of administering change by raising awkward questions which take time and wider consultation to be answered. It is so much easier in the short term to proceed by *ad hoc* means in the names of responding to market forces, respecting local autonomy, or seeking economies in public spending. It is nevertheless clear that a regional perspective cannot be avoided in the South East either in economic analysis or in the administration of physical planning. The principal question raised in this chapter has been not whether a regional overview is needed, but whether such an overview could be more effectively deployed to serve local and national needs than the current *ad hoc* approach.

In the author's view, like that of the councils represented on SERPLAN, the answer to this question is strongly affirmative. The pressures of change in the region will continue to build as contrasts between areas grow, and as the effects are felt of major public actions such as the completion of the M25 and the release of land for urban development outside London. Local efforts directly to influence economic development, except possibly in Docklands, are unlikely to make a significant difference to regional patterns of change. On the other hand, there is widespread concern that use-class and other locally administered planning constraints in growth areas are impeding new, regionally significant industrial growth (Department of Industry 1982). The net effect of the confused and ill-co-ordinated local efforts to respond to change is unlikely to be the stimulation of enterprise required by national policy. Even basic information about development pressures is lacking (in the absence of Industrial Development Certificates and Office Development Permits), and we have no way of knowing how the administration of planning is affecting investment or job creation.

This chapter has suggested, at various points, that there may be scope for guiding investment from growth areas to declining areas within the South East, in both manufacturing and producer services. It is envisaged that judicious land-use planning, infrastructure investment, and selective economic development policies, undertaken at a subregional scale and co-ordinated at a regional level, could manipulate the spatial impacts of the M25, as both the Secretary of State and the Planning Conference have advocated, and also patterns of development, for example, in lower Thameside, the M4 corridor, along the M11 towards Cambridge, the M1 to the north, and the M3 to the south west.

Even though a revival of the long-distance redirection of investment from the South East may seem unrealistic in current conditions, some shorter-distance redistribution could be actively encouraged as a means of realizing the region's employment growth potential more fully. Such a strategy of spreading sub-regional growth more evenly might well extend beyond the very arbitrary boundaries of the South East, to include the 'Greater South East' and adjacent regions, especially the Midlands or South Wales, through economically and physically linked corridors or growth nodes (for example, Milton Keynes–Northampton–Peterborough).

No such conception of the spatial planning challenge facing the South East economy will emerge from the current chaotic policy framework, even allowing for the efforts of SERPLAN. This suggests that a new framework for economic and physical planning is needed, probably in the form of a regional agency, which could develop the co-ordinating role of the Planning Conference and exert more positive powers to seek agreement on the future of critical sub-regions. The monitoring of key trends is also urgently needed in this rapidly changing region, to inform central and local government agencies and private investors about development opportunities. Without such intelligence, and the planning processes which can build upon it, conflicts of interest within the region will continue to grow, undermining the wider implementation of regional policy in Britain more persistently even than in the recent past.

References

Breheny, M., Cheshire, P., and Langridge, R. (1983), 'The Anatomy of Job Creation? Industrial Change in Britain's M4 Corridor', *Built Environment* 9, 61–71.

Cambridge Economic Policy Group (1982), 'Prospects for the UK in the 1980s' *Cambridge Economic Policy Review* 8(2).

Clout, H. D. and Wood, P. A., eds., (1986), *London: Problems of Change*, London, Longman.

Damesick, P. (1982*a*), 'Strategic Choice and Uncertainty: Regional Planning in South East England', in Hudson, R. and Lewis, J., eds., *Regional Planning in Europe*, London Papers in Regional Science 11, London, Pion.

—— (1982*b*), 'The Potential for and Impact of Office Development in the Inner City in London, *Progress in Planning* 18(3), 189–267.

Danson, M. W., Lever, W. F., and Malcolm, J. F. (1980), 'The Inner City Employment Problem in Great Britain: A Shift-share Approach', *Urban Studies*, 12, 193–20.

Dennis, R. (1978), 'The Decline of Manufacturing Employment in Greater London: 1960–74', *Urban Studies* 15, 63–73.

—— (1981), 'Changes in Manufacturing Employment in the South East Region Between 1976 and 1980', London, Department of Trade and Industry.

Department of Industry (1982), *Location and Mobility of New High Technology Companies in the UK Electronics Industry*, SE Regional Office mimeo.

Elias, P. (1982), 'The Regional Impact of National Economic Policies: A Multi-Regional Simulation Approach for the UK' *Regional Studies* 16, 335–44.

—— and Keogh, G. (1982), 'Industrial Decline and Unemployment in the Inner City Areas of Great Britain: A Review of the Evidence', *Urban Studies* 19, 1–15.

Evans, A. W. (1973), 'The Location of Headquarters of Industrial Companies', *Urban Studies* 10, 387–95.

Fothergill, S. and Gudgin, G. (1982), *Unequal Growth: Urban and Regional Employment Change in the UK*, London, Heinemann.

Goddard, J. B. and Smith, I. J. (1978), 'Changes in Corporate Control in the British Urban System, 1972–77' *Environmental and Planning A*, 10(9), 1073–84.

Gould, A. and Keeble, D. (1984), 'New Firms and Rural Industrialization in East Anglia', *Regional Studies* 18(3), 189–202.

Greater London Council (1985), *The London Industrial Strategy*. London.

Hall, P., ed. (1981), *The Inner City in Context*, London, Heinemann/Social Science Research Council.

Keeble, D. (1980*a*), 'The South East', Chapters 4–6 in Manners, G. *et al.*, *Regional Development in Britain*, 2nd edn., Chichester, Wiley.

—— (1980*b*), 'Industrial Decline, Regional Policy and the Urban–Rural Manufacturing Shift in the United Kingdom', *Environment and Planning A*, 12, 945–62.

Massey, M. and Meegan, R. A. (1978), 'Industrial Restructuring Versus the Cities', *Urban Studies* 15, 273–88.

Munton, R. J. C. (1983), *London's Green Belt: Containment in Practice*, London, Allen & Unwin.

—— (1986), 'The Green Belt', in Clout and Wood.

Oakey, R. P., Thwaites, A. T., and Nash, P. A. (1980), 'The Regional Distribution of Innovative Manufacturing Establishments in Britain', *Regional Studies* 14, 235–53.

—— (1982), 'Technological Change and Regional Development: Some Evidence on Regional Variations in Product and Process Innovation', *Environment and Planning A* 14, 1073–86.

Regional Studies Association (1983), *Report of an Inquiry into Regional Problems in the United Kingdom*, Norwich, Geo Books.

Secretary of State for Trade and Industry (1983), *Regional Industrial Development*, Cmnd. 9111, London, HMSO.

SERPLAN (The London and South East Regional Planning Conference) (1984), *Regional Trends in the South East (The South East Regional Monitor, 1983–4)*, London.

—— (1985*a*), *Developing SE Regional Strategic Guidance: Consultative Regional Statement*, RPC 340, London.

—— (1985*b*), *Regional Trends in the South East*. RPC 369, London.

South East Joint Planning Team (1976), *Strategy for the South East: 1976 Review*, London, HMSO.

Thwaites, A. T. (1982), 'Some Evidence of Regional Variations in the Introduction and Diffusion of Industrial Products and Processes Within British Manufacturing', *Regional Studies* 16, 371–81.

Westaway, E. J. (1974*a*), 'Contact Potential and the Occupational Structure of the British Urban System', *Regional Studies* 8, 57–73.

—— (1974*b*) 'The Spatial Hierarchy of Business Organizations and its Implications for the British Urban System', *Regional Studies* 8, 145–55.

Wood, P. A. (1984), 'Regional Significance of Manufacturing–Service Sector Links: Some Thoughts on the Revival of London's Docklands', in Barr, B. M. and Waters, N. M., eds., *Regional Diversification and Structural Change*, Vancouver, Tantalus Research.

—— (1986*a*) 'Economic Changes' in Clout and Wood.

—— (1986*b*), 'The Anatomy of Job Loss and Job Creation: Some Speculations on the Role of the 'Producer Service Sector', *Regional Studies* 20(1), 37–46.

CHAPTER 5
The West Midlands

M. Marshall and J. Mawson

The West Midlands region (see Figure 5.1) centres on the Metropolitan County, including Birmingham, Coventry and the Black Country, and encompasses the surrounding shire counties of Warwickshire, Staffordshire, Shropshire, and Hereford and Worcester. The regional economy is dominated by one of the largest concentrations of manufacturing industry and employment in the country. As such, it has suffered disproportionately from the decline of UK manufacturing over the past two decades. Industrial decline in the West Midlands was particularly rapid during the post-1979 recession, when the region suffered the fastest growth in unemployment of any UK region. Over one-third of the manufacturing jobs that existed in the Metropolitan County in 1978 had disappeared by 1983, involving a loss of some 225,000 jobs and a trebling of the unemployment rate.

Until recently, successive governments have neither recognized nor responded to the region's economic problems. The prevailing attitude was that the West Midlands would 'bounce back' given a cyclical recovery in the national economy. Central government only began to accept the long-term, structural nature of the area's problems in the early 1980s, when unemployment levels exceeded those in the traditional assisted areas. Several local authorities in the West Midlands became aware of the region's deepening economic problems some five to ten years earlier, but tended during the 1970s to advocate central government aid to create the conditions for regional economic recovery. Since the 1979–81 recession, however, many local authorities have devoted more attention to their own role in fostering local economic development and, in a few cases, have launched radical new initiatives to support industry and employment in their areas.

Industrial change and economic decline

With the onset of recession in 1979, the West Midlands suffered an acute acceleration of its economic decline. A decade earlier, the region had been one of the most prosperous in the country, with very low unemployment levels, high earnings, and above-average standards of living. By early 1980s, the weaknesses of the region's dependence upon a narrow band of manufacturing industries became starkly evident. While the region was badly affected by the international recessions of 1974–5 and 1979–81, it is important to recognize that the economy has experienced a series of progressive structural shifts.

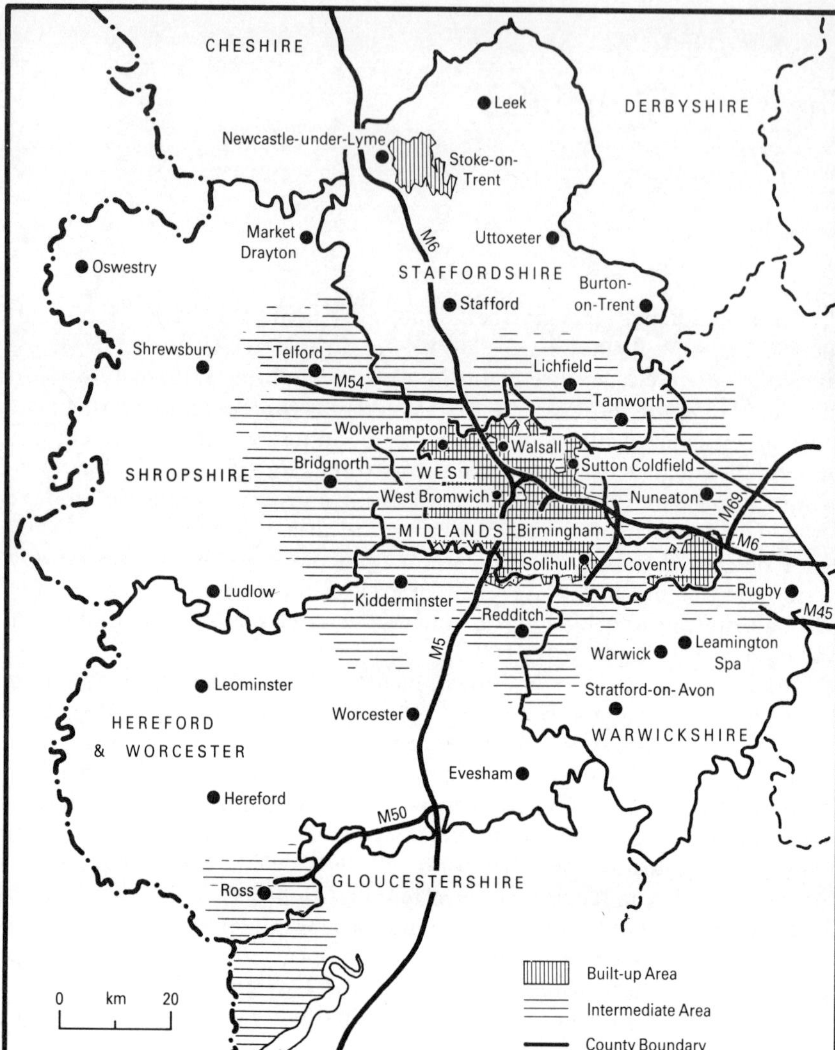

Figure 5.1. The West Midlands

The West Midlands' economic problems need to be viewed in the context of these longer term changes (Batley 1984). The past prosperity of the region relied upon the adaptability of its industrial structure, with both the local business community and the workforce able to adjust to changing national and international economic circumstances. From the late eighteenth century onwards, the regional economy was founded upon its basic industries, notably coal, iron, and steel production, and especially metal-working. When these industries declined in the late nineteenth century, they were replaced by growing engineering industries such as cycles, motor vehicles, machine tools, and aircraft which adapted the old-established metal-working skills.

The experience of the West Midlands in the interwar years contrasted sharply with that of other industrial regions. Unemployment rates were generally lower than in most parts of Britain (although high in some heavy industrial areas), and the region's recovery from depression was more rapid. Rearmament in the late 1930s stimulated further growth of the vehicle and aircraft industries. The dynamism of the West Midlands economy continued into the postwar period, when the region reinforced its position as Britain's leading manufacturing centre.

After the Second World War, the West Midlands vehicle, aircraft, and engineering sectors were boosted by exports to European markets starved by the wartime destruction of their domestic productive capacity. The gradual loss of these markets during the 1950s, as European producers recovered, was, however, more than compensated for by the expansion of British home demand. In the economic cycles of the 1950s and 1960s, the West Midlands' industries suffered less acutely during the downturns and were the first to emerge from each trough, leading the rest of the country. Protected from structural unemployment, West Midlands workers enjoyed high wages and high activity rates, leading to family income levels second only to those in the South East.

During the 1960s the prosperity and resilience of the West Midlands economy began to be undermined as its industries, representative of British industry at large, failed to match the levels of investment and productivity achieved by its chief international competitors. These underlying weaknesses were only fully exposed, however, with the slowdown of world growth after the mid-1960s and the ensuing period of intense international competition. The competitive weakness of British manufacturing was compounded by an overvalued pound. West Midlands manufacturing therefore entered the 1970s in a poor position to withstand the economic shocks that characterized the decade. By its conclusion, successive recessions, intensified competition, and lack of investment had together brought about the imminent collapse of its industrial base. The events of the early 1980s completed this process.

Despite massive job losses, the West Midlands nevertheless remains heavily dependent on manufacturing industries for its employment base, as shown in Table 5.1. In 1981 some 40 per cent of the region's workforce was employed in manufacturing, compared with 28 per cent nationally. Over half of the manufacturing workforce were engaged in the four key sectors of vehicles, metal goods, mechanical engineering, and metal manufacture. This dependence was even greater in the Metropolitan County, where these sectors employed 67 per cent of the manufacturing workforce.

The concentration on metal-related manufacturing stems partly from its very success in the 1950s and early 1960s, and from the failure of the regional economy to develop or attract new industries. The lack of diversification amongst established firms, and the processes of merger and concentration,

Table 5.1. West Midlands employment structure, 1981

	West Midlands Region		West Midlands County		Rest of region		Great Britain	
	No.	%	No.	%	No.	%	No.	%
Primary	55.6	2.7	2.9	0.3	52.7	6.0	1,006.5	5.0
Manufacturing	804.2	39.5	498.9	42.8	305.3	34.9	6,057.5	28.4
Construction	94.0	4.6	50.8	4.4	43.2	4.9	1,089.4	5.1
Services	1,077.5	53.0	610.7	52.4	466.8	53.3	13,100.7	61.5
Total	2,003.7	100.0	1,164.6	100.0	869.1	100.0	21,314.1	100.0

Source: Department of Employment.

Notes:
1. Employees in employment given in thousands.
2. Total includes adjustment for unclassified employees.

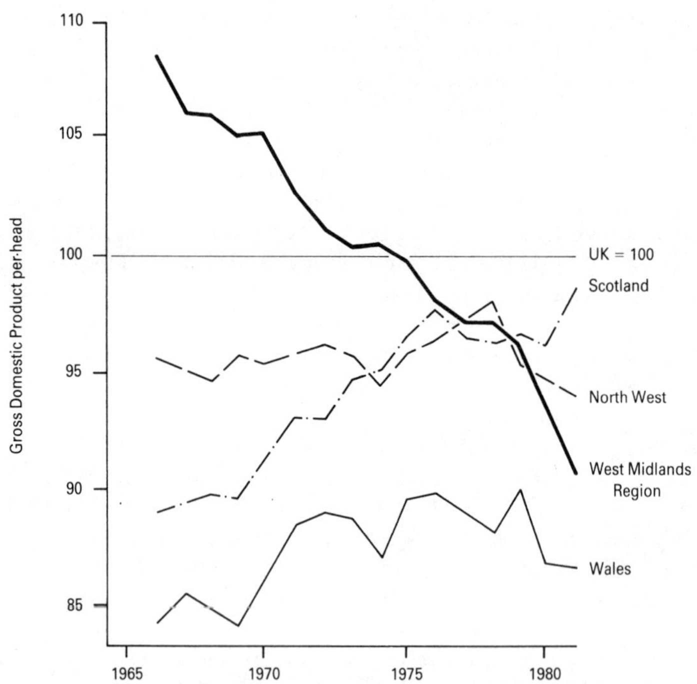

Figure 5.2. Gross domestic product per head, West Midlands and selected regions

created an economy heavily dependent upon a relatively small number of giant companies in a narrow range of industries. From the mid-1960s onwards, many of these companies, faced with a decline in their markets, overcapacity, and falling profits, began to rationalize and restructure their production activities. In many cases this meant diversification away from, and disruption of links with, the region's traditional industries in the search for new markets and products (Flynn and Taylor 1984).

Not surprisingly, since the mid-1960s GDP per head in the region, so heavily dependent on manufacturing performance, has fallen consistently by comparison with other parts of the country. In 1965 the region enjoyed a GDP per head over 8 per cent above the national average, second to the South East. By 1981 this had fallen to almost 10 per cent below the UK average, well below some other regions traditionally regarded as depressed (see Figure 5.2). This trend has been paralleled at both county and region levels by low levels of net output, a poor investment record, and low levels of productivity, (Mawson and Taylor 1983). Mawson and Smith, for example, in a comparative study of net output per employee across all manufacturing industries and regions for the period 1958–76, found that only Northern Ireland had a worse record (Mawson and Smith 1980). A shift-share analysis carried out for the Economic and Social Research Council Birmingham Inner City Study indicated that a large proportion of employment decline in the county over the past fifteen years can be attributed to factors other than purely national trends or structural mix (Taylor 1985). Economic processes influencing changes within key sectors and companies are clearly most significant.

Sector performance and prospects

The vehicle industry occupies a pivotal position in the West Midlands economy. It is not only the largest single employer but also sustains substantial proportions of West Midlands employment in the metal-based and engineering sectors. It has been estimated that around 4,000 firms in the region are dependent upon the British Leyland/Austin Rover Group, equivalent to over 30 per cent of total employment in the region (Bessant *et al.* 1984). The West Midlands motor industry consists of three main sectors: vehicle manufacturers and assemblers, most importantly British Leyland and Talbot; component suppliers, of which the larger and more sophisticated supply car components and sub-assemblies while others supply basic castings, forgings, and fabrications; and suppliers of equipment such as cutting and forming tools, mechanical handling and processing equipment, and robots. After the late-1970s the industry suffered considerable contraction of output, capacity, and employment. Within the Metropolitan County, redundancies announced by major companies between 1979 and 1985 included 28,000 by British Leyland, 3,000 by Talbot, 8,500 by GKN, 10,000 by Lucas, 3,000 by Tube Investments, and 4,000 by Dunlop. Up to 1982 the majority of jobs shed were among the major car assemblers. After 1982, however, most job losses were in the supply-base of component and equipment manufacturers, which cut capacity in line with reduced demand from their assembler customers.

The problems of the component and equipment suppliers are interrelated and mutually reinforcing. Declining demand, leading to excess capacity, intense competition, and lower prices, combined to give poor financial performance, accentuated by over-reliance on loan capital. Hence firms were unable to finance training, purchase of new equipment, and product innovation. In some cases, suppliers were unable to meet the requirements of assemblers in terms of quality and price. This in turn added to the spiral of decline. One result of these problems was a trend towards fragmentation of longstanding national and regional linkages. The traditional policy of assemblers in squeezing domestic suppliers on price was intensified by increasing the volume of imported components. In response, several large component suppliers, such as Lucas and GKN, have reduced their dependence upon West Midlands demand by cutting capacity in the region and expanding their European operations. These processes underlie the successive rounds of plant closures, contractions, and redundancies announced by such companies in recent years. In the long run this process may be self-defeating, since car assemblers will continue to require a viable component- and equipment-supplying base in Britain. Thus, while the process of rationalization and restructuring among car assemblers is now substantially complete, it is still under way among the component and equipment suppliers, and its outcome remains uncertain.

While the motor industry is of vital strategic importance to the West Midlands economy as a whole, outside the conurbation several localities are equally dependent upon other traditional industries. Examples include carpets in the Kidderminster area and, most notably, the Staffordshire pottery industry, which accounted for more than one-quarter of the county's manufacturing employment in 1981. The West Midlands carpet industry was badly affected by weak demand and fierce competition from imports in the late 1970s. Sales fell by 29 per cent between 1977 and 1982, while imports more than tripled. The internal weaknesses of the carpet industry, affecting productivity and sometimes quality, have been compounded by reduced domestic demand and the high value of sterling in the early 1980s, initially against the dollar and later against European currencies, boosting the price advantage of overseas manufacturers. With a few notable exceptions, falling profitability again prevented companies from investing in the new technology required to reverse the spiral of falling market shares. Economic policies to boost demand, both from consumers and from new construction, and to stabilize the pound at a relatively low level in European markets, could enable the industry to recover its markets and competitive strength.

Nearly 20,000 jobs were lost in the Staffordshire pottery industry between 1971 and 1984, with 6,000 redundancies announced after 1981 alone. Exports fell 15 per cent between 1980 and 1982, while the industry's home market share shrank by 25–30 per cent. Problems of increased competition from overseas producers drawing on cheap labour were compounded by design and productivity deficiencies, weak domestic demand, high interest rates, and high exchange rates in the early phase of the recession. The industry has responded with revised marketing strategies backed by improved designs and more emphasis on quality production—factors which distinguish the Staffordshire industry from its overseas rivals.

Under-investment and uneven technical advance

The dependence of the West Midlands economy on nationally declining manufacturing industries does not provide a complete explanation for its economic plight, since the major West Midlands industries have declined at a faster rate than have the same industries nationally (Trades Union Congress West Midlands Regional Council 1982). A number of explanations have been presented to account for this poor relative performance, including weak management and bad industrial relations associated with the very large assembly plants which have come to dominate the West Midlands in the postwar era (Liggins 1978). In relation to the typical small or medium-sized, locally owned firms, which act as subcontractors or component suppliers, a study of their performance in the period 1980–3 highlighted the weakness arising from years of dependence on a single market for their product, leaving them vulnerable and lacking in managerial capacity to diversify (Tym *et al.* 1983). The failure of many family-owned firms to reinvest profits in more successful periods, their resistance to taking in outside equity, and the difficulty of gaining unsecured loans has meant that such companies have been starved of development capital. Forced to borrow short-term at a time of high interest rates, many went to the wall in the recession of the early 1980s.

Capital investment per employee in West Midlands manufacturing industry in 1981 was only four-fifths of the UK average, the lowest of all regions (see Table 5.2). Investment levels have been especially depressed in the region's key industries. Of eleven UK regions, the West Midlands ranked sixth in 1981 for investment per employee in vehicles, ninth for metal goods, and eleventh for mechanical engineering. Significantly, a survey in 1983 of the country's top thirty-one pension funds found that they considered the West Midlands a poor investment prospect, and many were considering withdrawing from the area altogether (Debenham, Tewson and Chinnocks 1983).

A critical element in the pattern of declining investment in the West Midlands relates to the policies of the large multi-plant and multinational companies which command a substantial proportion of the regional economy. In 1978 the ten largest companies in the West Midlands region (excluding British Leyland) were GEC, GKN, Cadbury, Dunlop, Lucas, Tube Investments, IMI, Delta, Glynwed, and BSR, which together employed around one-fifth of the manufacturing workforce. Between 1978 and 1982 the combined UK workforce of these companies fell by 31 per cent and, while a regional breakdown of this employment decline is not available, readily observable evidence of local plant closures and contractions indicates that a substantial proportion of job losses in these companies took place in the West Midlands (Gaffikin and Nickson 1984; Flynn and Taylor 1984). Gaffikin and Nickson

Table 5.2. Capital investment per employee in manufacturing, UK regions, 1981

	Total £'000	Rank			
		All manufacturing	Metal goods	Eng.	Vehicles
North	1,063	4	3	4	11
Yorkshire and Humberside	814	9	10	7	10
East Midlands	804	10	4	5	9
East Anglia	953	6	1	10	8
South East	906	8	8	8	2
South West	915	7	6	6	5
West Midlands	719	11	9	11	6
North West	985	5	11	9	7
Wales	1,575	1	7	2	1
Scotland	1,295	2	5	1	4
N. Ireland	1,157	3	2	3	3
UK average	951	—	—	—	—

Source: Central Statistical Office.

show that there has been a marked increase in the share of the world sales of these companies accounted for by overseas production, and also that this has been to the detriment of British exports.

In the Metropolitan County, the top twenty-five companies, including British Leyland, controlled 48 per cent of manufacturing employment in 1977. Analysis of their corporate strategies shows that, faced with over-capacity and falling profit margins, companies had already embarked on a programme of rationalization and restructuring before 1979. From 1972 to 1982 these companies reduced their workforces by almost 40 per cent (Flyn and Taylor 1984). Home-based companies, such as Birmid Qualcast, emphasized the need to reduce their dependence on the motor industry, diversifying into central heating and lawn-mowers in the early 1970s, with these profitable divisions located outside the region. Many other companies stressed the importance of improving their overseas profile and cutting their dependence on the UK market. The abolition of exchange controls in 1979, together with more buoyant overseas economies, especially in North America and Europe, and the attractions of a cheaper non-unionized workforce, particularly in South East Asia, led to an acceleration of overseas acquisitions during the 1970s. Glynwed, for example, spent £41 million between 1980 and 1983 in acquiring six USA companies. GEC now has 50 per cent of its sales coming from abroad, while BSR has been transformed from a primarily West Midlands-based company into one with its main production activities in South East Asia. The BSR workforce declined by 57 per cent between 1977 and 1981, while overseas employment increased sevenfold.

Disinvestment from the region by multinationals has been accompanied by continuing low levels of industrial movement into the West Midlands. A survey for the period between 1979 and 1983 identified only forty-five companies employing more than twenty manufacturing workers moving into the West Midlands or between its districts (Roberts and Duncan 1984). Of these, about one-third originated from outside the region, including six from abroad, located almost exclusively in the shire counties, particularly in the New Towns of Telford and Redditch. The New Towns have benefited substantially from incoming industry in the past, often at the expense of the region's older urban areas, and they may continue to do so in the future, like other areas in the shire counties. The Metropolitan County has attracted a negligible number of mobile firms in the postwar period, and seems to have little chance of improving this performance in the future. Indeed, a joint survey carried out in the Black Country by the regional CBI and Federation of Civil Engineering Contractors described prospects for attracting new industry to this area as 'hopeless' without major public-sector investment to renovate the area's industrial infrastructure (Osman 1984).

The West Midlands region is distinctive in that more than half of its manufacturing industry is located within the conurbation (Fothergill and Gudgin 1979). Given the problems of declining infrastructure, traffic congestion, ageing plant and equipment, and a shortage of space for modern factory layouts, there can be little doubt that this concentration has presented a constraint on economic growth and new investment. In 1982, for example, there were some 4,800 acres of derelict land in the Metropolitan County, an increase of over 1,000 acres since 1974, much of which reflects the closure of major industrial installations. Estimates suggest that the amount of empty industrial property grew threefold between 1981 and 1985 to around 30 million square feet, 30 per cent of which dated from before 1960 (West Midlands Forum of County Councils 1985).

Low levels of private investment in the West Midlands have been aggravated by central government industrial policies and inadequate levels of public-sector resource allocation as described in more detail below (Bentley and Mawson 1984). The pattern of private and public sector investment in the West Midlands is also reflected in the uneven adoption of new product and process technologies between different industrial sectors (Marshall 1985). Research on the diffusion of robotic technology in West Midlands industry indicates a relatively high level of adoption amounting to 20 per cent of the UK total (Dickson and Fleck 1984). This level of robotic diffusion in the West Midlands is closely related to vehicle manufacturing, where some 66 per cent of the West Midlands County's robot stock is employed, with 21 per cent in the metal-manufacturing, metal goods, and engineering sectors.

The pattern of robot use undoubtedly reflects government support to West Midlands vehicle manufacturers, such as in the roboticized Austin Metro assembly lines at Longbridge. Conversely, low levels of support to other manufacturing sectors, coupled with wider recessionary effects inhibiting private-sector investment, account for the backwardness of the West Midlands in other areas of technological advance. Several studies have drawn attention to the low ranking of the West Midlands relative to other regions, both in the number of *new* product and process innovations and in the diffusion of *existing* advanced technologies (Oakey *et al.* 1980; Howells 1984; Gibbs and Edwards 1983).

As well as suffering poor rates of technological advance in its traditional metal-based sectors, the West Midlands has experienced negligible growth in new, high-technology sectors, unlike some other industrial areas (most notably Central Scotland). A recent study of semi-conductor production in the UK noted:

> the hitherto buoyant Midlands regions . . . economically dependent on mechanical engineering, and not heavily favoured with assisted area status, reveal a marked lack of production facilities. . . . the Midlands is developing a distinctly backward air, as the traditional problem regions experience technical advance in their mass-production industries. (Cooke *et al.* 1984)

Service development

The concentration of manufacturing industry in the West Midlands is mirrored by an underdeveloped service sector. In 1981, services accounted for 52 per cent of employment in the region compared with 61 per cent for Great Britain as a whole. Between 1976 and 1981, service employment in the region grew by 4 per cent, slightly higher than the national average of 3.8 per cent. Between 1981 and 1984, however, service growth in the West Midlands fell to half this rate, in line with national growth of 1.9 per cent, so that there was little evidence of any 'catching up' process.

Within the service sector, employment in business and professional services grew faster than for Great Britain in the decade up to the mid-1980s. This was offset to some extent, however, by losses in government services, distribution, and transport and communications. The most rapid growth of service employment took place in the shire counties, although the West Midlands county showed growth above the national average in business, professional, and miscellaneous services. The decline of distributive employment in the Metropolitan County in recent years has nevertheless been greater than nationally, largely due to job losses in the retail sector, although there was again some growth in the shire counties.

These patterns suggest that future growth of the service sector in the region is unlikely to compensate for the contraction of manufacturing. No doubt there will be continued service growth in the shire counties accompanying the drift of population from the conurbation. Apart from population-led services, however, the West Midlands generally lacks the potential for autonomous service-sector development. With a few exceptions, such as the National Exhibition Centre and some tourist centres, West Midlands services tend to be dependent upon local markets, and lack the national and international links enjoyed by London and the South East. The service sector is not an 'alternative' to manufacturing in the West Midlands, but remains directly or indirectly tied to local industry.

New jobs created in the service sector have been far outweighed by losses in manufacturing and seldom provide realistic alternative employment for the skilled male workforce shed by the region's manufacturing base. The bulk of new service jobs created in recent years have been low-paid, unskilled, and largely taken by part-time female workers, who accounted for nearly 30 per cent of service employment in the region in 1981.

Employment, unemployment, and incomes

From the mid-1960s to the late 1970s, total employment in the West Midlands hovered around 2.4 million. Although by 1979 manufacturing had declined by about 200,000 jobs from its 1966 peak of 1.2 million, service employment rose by about 150,000. After 1979, however, the service sector remained fairly static, while manufacturing shed a further 250,000 jobs by 1983. The rapidity of this loss led to a dramatic rise in unemployment, considerably faster than the national rate, as illustrated in Figure 5.3.

Official unemployment in the West Midlands stood at 341,400 in mid-1985 comprising 238,600 men and 102,800 women. The regional unemployment rate of 15.1 per cent was well above the rate for Great Britain of 13.0 per cent. Within the region, district unemployment rates ranged from 8 per cent in Stratford-upon-Avon to 20 per cent in Birmingham, the Black Country, and the Wrekin, including the New Town of Telford. Only at the smaller, ward level, however, was the full scale of the problem affecting many localities apparent. Within the Metropolitan County, ward unemployment rates ranged from 3 per cent in Knowle, Solihull, to 45 per cent in Sparkbrook in inner Birmingham. Some forty-five wards in the region suffered unemployment rates greater than

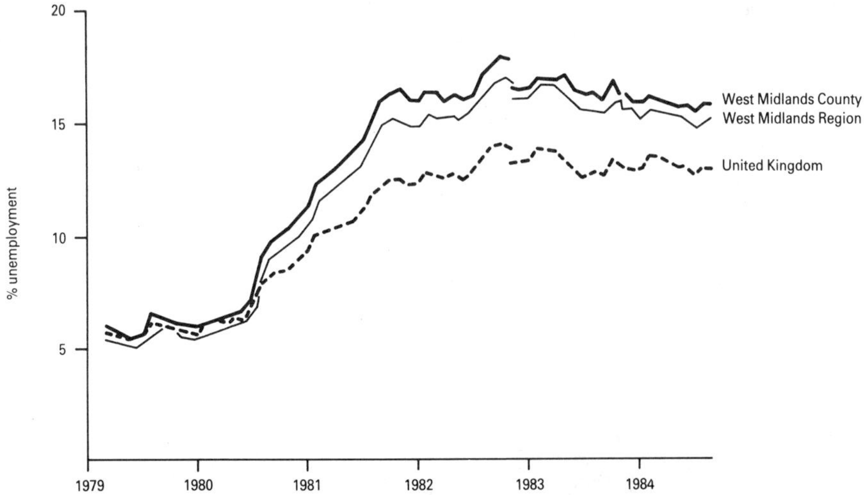

Figure 5.3. Unemployment rates, West Midlands and UK, 1979–84

25 per cent, two-thirds of them in the Metropolitan County. Unemployment among the region's ethnic minorities, disproportionately concentrated in inner urban areas, was double that of the white population. In 1981, some 23 per cent of black workers in the region and 24 per cent of Asians were unemployed, compared with the white unemployment rate of 12 per cent.

While the rate of growth in unemployment slackened in 1984–5, the stagnation of job prospects in the West Midlands was evidenced by the growing scale of long-term unemployment. In 1974 the region had the second lowest proportion of long-term unemployed in the UK. By 1984, however, 46 per cent of the region's unemployed had been out of work for over a year, a higher proportion than any UK region apart from Northern Ireland. Long-term unemployment was no longer confined to certain vulnerable sections of the labour force such as unskilled or older workers. The largest group of unemployed men in the region were aged twenty-five to fifty-four, half of whom had been jobless for over a year.

The rapid decline of industry and employment in the West Midlands has been accompanied by falling earnings and growing numbers of people living on subsistence incomes (Low Pay Unit 1983). In 1972, male manual workers in the West Midlands were top of the ten-region pay league, earning 4.2 per cent more than the national average. By 1982 they had slumped to eighth place, 3.3 per cent below the national average. As a result of these rising unemployment and deteriorating earnings trends, it has been estimated that as many as one in three households in the Metropolitan County live on or below the poverty line, defined as 40 per cent above the subsistence level of supplementary benefit (West Midlands County Council Economic Development Committee 1983).

To conclude this discussion of the West Midlands' economic decline, some appreciation of the scale of the region's problems can be gained by examining them in a wider, European context. In 1984 the European Commission published a 'synthetic index' measuring the relative intensity of regional problems in the EEC, based on GDP per head combined with unemployment rates (Commission of the European Communities 1984). The West Midlands County ranked the 21st worst out of 131 EEC administrative areas.

This index may understate the scale and intensity of economic decline in the conurbation since the 131 areas encompass regions with different types of regional problems. It has been suggested that the index masks the problems faced by declining industrial regions since they are ranked along with underdeveloped rural regions (Wabe 1984). Computation of a separate index for industrialized regions alone revealed that the West Midlands County experienced the greatest relative employment losses of all EEC regions for the previous decade, except for one small region in West Germany.

Central government policy

The critical condition of much of West Midlands industry today makes it difficult to believe that until quite recently the region was regarded as the prosperous industrial heartland of the British economy. During the heyday of redistributive regional policies from the 1950s to the early 1970s, the West

Midlands, along with the South East, was an industrial 'donor', expected to forego some of its expansion in favour of the Assisted Areas.

It has been a long-held view in the West Midlands that the operation of the Industrial Development Certificate policy, whereby firms were required to apply to central government for permission to expand their factory floor-space above a certain threshold and were induced to move to government-assisted areas, had a debilitating effect on the economic growth of the region. The policy operated throughout the post-war period with varying force, and was finally suspended in January 1982. At its height, from the mid-1960s to the early 1970s, up to 25 per cent of applications in employment terms were refused. Thereafter, however, it was very rare for a project to be turned down. Research undertaken by the Department of Industry at that time suggested that few firms were encouraged to move after refusal; rather, the majority would take over dilapidated factories or would squeeze more production from existing premises. This must have had a serious impact on efficiency and productivity. The absence of advanced factory building was clearly another inhibiting factor and, although assistance under Section 8 of the 1972 Industry Act was available within the region, it is likely that IDC policy prevented some large-scale projects from being undertaken. In terms of the loss of employment, this was mainly associated with large-scale moves in the motor vehicle industry which certainly disrupted regional industrial linkages.

While in practice the implementation of the IDC policy virtually ceased after the early 1970s, officially it was still pursued up to 1982. Critics have argued that it stifled potential projects, since businessmen believed that they would not secure permission for expansion. Such arguments remain difficult to prove; and while the IDC policy was damaging to the region, its effects have been overstated (Bentley and Mawson 1985). It has to be remembered that in the 1960s, when the policy was being rigorously pursued, there was a serious shortage of labour in the West Midlands and the policy therefore contributed to relieving 'overheating' pressures. Data on factory movement suggests that regional policy may have been responsible for diverting some 39,000 jobs out of the region between 1960 and 1974. However, Tyler (1980) argues that the impact was much less, and further that most of the jobs diverted out of the region were replaced by new jobs from within the West Midlands. In addition, the loss of employment in the conurbation due to plant movement was always a small proportion of total employment decline.

Turning to the allocation of public expenditure, the regional accounts for 1978 were analysed by the Cambridge Economic Policy Group and showed that the West Midlands suffered the highest deficit on government expenditure and transfers of all UK regions (Cambridge Economic Policy Group 1980). Excluding the £2.6 billion of assistance to British Leyland after 1976, West Midlands firms received a mere £57.1 million of government industrial aid between 1972 and 1983, amounting to just over one per cent of total Industry Act expenditure in that period (Bentley and Mawson 1984). While constraints on industrial development in the region were relaxed in the late 1970s, only in November 1984 did a major part of the West Midlands itself become an Assisted Area.

Responses to decline

Before this change, central government had responded to the region's increasing difficulties with a succession of *ad hoc*, uncoordinated measures. The Black Country District of Dudley was awarded an Enterprise Zone in the first round of designations following the 1980 budget, and a second Zone was subsequently added in Telford. In April 1983, Coventry MP John Butcher was appointed as a junior minister at the Department of Trade and Industry with special responsibility for the West Midlands. After much eleventh-hour lobbying, Birmingham Airport was among those locations selected in February 1984 to take part in the Government's Freeports experiment. The West Midlands has also benefited from a number of industry-specific schemes, such as the short-lived Small Engineering Firms Investment Scheme (SEFIS).

The only consistent programme of central government support for local economic development has been the Urban Programme. This provided 75 per cent of the cost of projects developed under the Birmingham Inner City Partnership (total allocation in 1985–6 of £24.5 million) and the Urban Programme areas of Coventry (£4.3 million), Wolverhampton (£4.8 million), Sandwell (£4.5 million), and Walsall (£55,000). These allocations helped a number of the local economic projects developed by the West Midlands County Council and the metropolitan districts discussed below, although only part of the Urban Programme allocations were available for such projects. For example, only £8.1 million of the Birmingham Inner City Partnership Programme in 1985–6 was allocated to 'economic' projects.

At least part of the explanation for central government's failure adequately to respond to the West Midlands' problems lay in the unsatisfactory organizational arrangements for the co-ordination of policy, both nationally and at regional office level, between the Department of Trade and Industry, the Department of Environment, and the Manpower Services Commission. In theory the co-ordination mechanisms for economic and labour market policies at the regional office level are vested in the Planning Board, but this meets infrequently and does not have sufficient authority. Officials liaise, on an informal basis, on projects and schemes where there is overlap. However, these mechanisms simply do not provide sufficient scope for policy debate and co-ordination in a strategic sense.

Co-ordination is not helped by differing styles of organization of the Departments. In the case of the Department of Trade and Industry, for example, the role of its regional office primarily reflects the Department's national preoccupations. Outside Assisted Areas, the Department does not have an acknowledged territorial economic role, except to encourage the relocation of mobile industry. Its regional office in the West Midlands has therefore primarily functioned to administer national schemes. Even schemes with very strong local relevance, such as SEFIS, were managed from outside the West Midlands (in this case, in Swansea). Although the DTI's actions have major geographical implications, the Department has never succeeded in relating its national industrial policy to these consequences. The activities of the Industrial

Reorganization Corporation in the 1960s, the National Enterprise Board and Sector Working Parties in the later 1970s, and the DTI's present multiplicity of innovation support schemes have not entailed an explicit regional dimension. The establishment in 1983 of a regional 'Team for Innovation' by the West Midlands' new minister was the first small step in this direction.

While the DTI has a small research capacity, this has not been used as an input into policy formulation. Since the early 1970s, for example, the regional office was aware of the long-term structural problems facing the area. Nationally, however, the DTI was not able to incorporate such a view into its policy framework. In the late 1970s, political pressures from the Labour strongholds of Scotland, Wales, and the North of England precluded the Government from contemplating any diversion of resources to the West Midlands, particularly in view of the commitment to Welsh and Scottish devolution. The West Midlands was placed on the Assisted Area map in 1984 by the Conservative Government only in the context of an overall cutback in regional aid, by which time it was suffering higher levels of unemployment than some of the traditional Assisted Areas.

The changing geographical focus of economic problems during the 1970s, especially the accelerated decline of inner-city areas, set against a backcloth of rising unemployment, accentuated the problems of co-ordination between the DTI and the Department of the Environment. The DoE has a greater and more significant regional presence than the DTI, and considerable autonomy of action over the management of its financial programmes. It also has a higher grading of staff, with a greater proportion of senior administrative posts and a more direct relationship with the local agencies concerned with job creation. The DoE has been engaged in a variety of territorial programmes of economic development, including the provision of resources under the Urban Programme, designation of Enterprise Zones, production of industrial land registers, encouragement of Enterprise Trusts, and management of local authority capital programmes (including submitting applications for infrastructure projects to the European Regional Development Fund), as well as overseeing the process of strategic and local planning. All these activities have a regional economic impact, yet there is no systematic mechanism for coordination with DTI programmes of regional and industrial support.

Paradoxically, the appointment in 1983 of a minister with special responsibility for the West Midlands seems to have confused the situation further. In practice, he was only given responsibility for a limited range of DTI activities. Yet he was widely perceived as the minister responsible for *all* matters affecting the region, providing an illusion of co-ordinated departmental activity which served only to obscure the reality. The appointment was widely regarded in the West Midlands as no more than a cosmetic political exercise. The minister was certainly given neither the powers nor the resources to match the scale of the region's problems. His main achievements were: the establishment of a 'Team for Innovation' to promote take-up in the region of the DTI's various Support for Innovation schemes; the securing of partial funding for the West Midlands Industrial Development Association, set up jointly by the regional CBI and local authorities to promote overseas investment; and the co-ordination of public- and private-sector funding to develop small factory and workshop units. His much publicized plans to develop a 100-acre industrial site in the Black Country as a 'flagship' for the region, as well as to establish a prestigious 'Centre of Excellence' demonstrating advanced manufacturing technology systems to promote the development of a Rugby–Telford 'high-technology axis', were shelved because of lack of finance.

In announcing his resignation in November 1984, to coincide with the designation of the West Midlands Assisted Area, Mr Butcher stated: 'The Government has ended regional policy discrimination against the West Midlands and provided access to hitherto unavailable national support for industrial development' (Department of Trade and Industry 1984). While the award of Intermediate Area status to much of the central industrial core of the West Midlands was widely welcomed by employers' organizations, trade unions, and local authorities as an overdue recognition of the region's severe problems, there was also widespread concern, particularly among local authorities, that this action fell far short of the measures required to regenerate the regional economy. Several local authorities, especially Birmingham City Council, expressed disappointment that they had not been awarded top-tier Development Area status and, in the case of Stoke-on-Trent, that they had failed to receive Assisted Area status at all. The choice of travel-to-work areas (TTWAs), enlarged in a review shortly before the regional policy changes, as the basic units for designating Assisted Areas masks the intensity of unemployment in smaller localities in the region, which is at least as acute as in several Development Areas. In addition, the West Midlands will continue to be disadvantaged in relation to other areas of the UK receiving maximum levels of grant aid for investment projects; in an era of slow economic growth and restraint on public expenditure, 'intermediate' regional assistance is likely to be a much less effective stimulant to local economic development than in the past.

EEC finance and macroeconomic policies

Many local observers believed that the most important aspect of the West Midlands' new Assisted Area status would be enhanced access to the European Regional Development Fund (ERDF), for example for local projects in Birmingham, most notably the city's planned International Convention Centre. The West Midlands had fared badly in the past, since support from a number of the EEC's financial instruments (including the European Social Fund, European Investment Bank, and European Coal and Steel Community funds as well as the ERDF) is directly or indirectly tied to Assisted Area status. Between 1973 and 1982 the West Midlands was awarded only 1.5 per cent of the total grants and loans made available to English regions from EEC sources (Mawson and Gibney 1984). Until very recently, the only ERDF support for a West Midlands project was £297,000 in 1978 for the development of an industrial estate at Oswestry (Shropshire), which at that time enjoyed Intermediate Area status. Although the region's position was marginally improved by a temporary dispensation in 1984, which allowed the Metropolitan County's Urban Programme areas to receive ERDF aid pending the outcome of the UK Government's Assisted Area review, these amounts remained small compared with those received by other regions. During 1984, the West Midlands received only 4.9 per cent of the total £372.7 million allocated to the UK from the ERDF.

Even after 1984, the West Midlands will be only a second-tier assisted region, and will not receive the same priority as the Development Areas in project applications to the European Commission. Moreover, the European Commission has itself on several occasions criticized the British Government's failure to respect the principle of additionality with respect to ERDF receipts. The House of Lords Select Committee on the European Communities in 1983 also noted that UK government departments already took into account expected ERDF payments when setting ceilings for local authority capital expenditure on infrastructure (House of Lords Select Committee on the European Community 1984). 'The only tangible benefit local authorities thus gain,' suggested the Committee, 'is a reduction in interest charges and capital repayments over the life of the project.' Moreover, money made available from the Fund for industrial aid is in reality no more than a book-keeping exercise, whereby central government forwards the name of specific companies which have already received assistance in order to recoup its outlay. No additional aid therefore accrues to the region.

The limited steps taken to support industry and employment in the West Midlands were, of course, launched against a backcloth of macroeconomic policies which have had damaging consequences for British manufacturing in general, and for the West Midlands in particular. The abolition of exchange controls in 1979 facilitated the ability of West Midlands-based multinationals to transfer investment abroad. Cutbacks and closures in the nationalized industries and public sector in general have directly contributed to the loss of employment. At the same time, tight monetary constraint, and relatively high exchange and interest rates, have inhibited West Midlands exporters, encouraged import penetration, and discouraged the long-term investment needed to improve manufacturing productivity and competitiveness.

Earlier attempts by the 1964–70 and 1974–9 Labour Governments to intervene in the restructuring of leading companies and sectors, initially via the Industrial Reorganization Corporation (IRC) and later through the National Enterprise Board (NEB) and Sector Working Parties, were seldom wholly successful. The consolidation of British Leyland by the IRC, and subsequent intervention by the NEB, had major consequences, not only directly for the West Midlands motor vehicle assembly industry but also indirectly for the region's motor component, equipment, and material suppliers. While public funds invested in British Leyland over the past decade have helped to create a restructured and efficient assembly sector, the interlinked component, metal manufacturing, and foundry sectors were left to 'sink or swim'. Plant closures and reduced capacity at BL have meant that many small- and medium-sized suppliers have seen their major source of orders cut back or disappear altogether. As the company has been subjected to increasing government pressure to survive without further public funding, it has sought cheaper sources of components, equipment, and materials from abroad or used this threat to force local suppliers into suicidal pricing arrangements. Pressure on local suppliers is likely to intensify in the future as profitable sections of BL are privatized.

Nevertheless, from the viewpoint of West Midlands interests, perhaps the single most important measure undertaken by central government was the long-delayed decision in June 1985 to approve Austin Rover's corporate plan. This included provision for £250 million of public investment to enable the company to develop and manufacture its own new engine rather than buy standard engines from Honda. The consequences for West Midlands industry and employment if Austin Rover had become a mere kit assembler of foreign-produced parts would have been nothing short of disastrous.

Local government responses

While central government has been slow to recognize, let alone respond to, the West Midlands' deepening economic decline, as long ago as 1974 the newly formed West Midlands County Council published the consultation report *A Time For Action*, drawing attention to the deterioration of the region's industrial performance and suggesting that the dynamism that had carried the region through previous national economic downturns was coming to an end (West Midlands County Council 1974; see also Wood 1976, ch. 8). Until the early 1980s, however, local authorities in the region maintained a relatively passive stance towards the local economy, tending to see industry and employment as the preserve of central government macroeconomic and regional policies. The unprecedented collapse of industry and employment in the late 1970s, and an apparent unwillingness on the part of central government to support the regional economy, led many authorities in the West Midlands to reconsider their role in local economic development. For the most part, local responses to economic decline have been confined to traditional forms of infrastructural support. In a few cases, however, local authorities have begun to develop new styles of intervention in the economy. In the case of the West Midlands County Council, a wide range of local economic initiatives were launched which represented a radical break from previous approaches.

Industrial development in the shire counties

Local authority economic initiatives in the shire counties of Warwickshire, Staffordshire, Shropshire, and Hereford and Worcester have been predominantly restricted to development of industrial land and premises, coupled with promotional activities aimed at attracting new industry. Policies and programmes for industrial land development are set out in County Structure Plans within overall planning guidelines for the region as a whole set down in the West Midlands Regional Strategy, a non-statutory framework drawn up by the West Midlands Forum of County Councils in the wake of the abolition of the Regional Economic Planning Council in 1979.

Industrial land development in the shires has always been precariously balanced against the needs of the Metropolitan County. Until the early 1980s, land-use policies were preoccupied with planning for projected levels of industrial movement and population overspill from the metropolitan area. After 1979, however, growing recognition of economic decline in the conurbation led to a shift in policy towards more restrictive development, in accordance with an agreed Regional Strategy to foster economic regeneration in the older urban areas. The precarious nature of this new consensus was periodically revealed in inter-authority disputes over particular development site prosposals, as well as over shire county projections for future land requirements for industrial development. The Metropolitan County Council's view that new development in the shires should wherever possible be confined to sites adjacent to the conurbation, so as to contribute to economic regeneration of the county, has conflicted with the shire counties' need for new development to relieve their own pockets of economic decline, and those of the region's rural west, with its distinctive social and economic problems.

The conflict is particularly strong in relation to North Staffordshire, suffering the most severe economic problems outside the Metropolitan County and, unlike the conurbation, without Assisted Area status. In the early 1980s, the number of local authority initiatives to revitalize the economy of Staffordshire increased substantially. Considerable investment was made in development projects, most notably the National Garden Festival at Stoke in 1986 on the site of the former Shelton steelworks, a partnership scheme with substantial contributions from the County and Stoke councils as well as central government. Some 100 acres of the site will be made available subsequently for industry, warehousing, and commercial uses. Other economic-based schemes funded by the County and district councils included industrial estates of various types and sizes at Newcastle-under-Lyme and Tamworth, and a science park at Keele University.

Complementary to the development of new industrial sites, most authorities in the West Midlands have to varying degrees engaged in marketing and promotional activities aimed at attracting new firms and industries to their areas. The establishment of the West Midlands Industrial Development Association (WMIDA) in 1983, on the initiative of the regional CBI with financial backing from local authorities and the DTI, has helped to a limited extent to co-ordinate overseas promotion activity. Initially this agency enjoyed support from all five county councils in the region, but in 1985 the West Midlands County Council withdrew from WMIDA, on account of the agency's apparent lack of success and in accordance with the Council's own industrial strategy of supporting existing industry rather than attracting firms from elsewhere.

Throughout the 1970s, the New Towns at Telford and Redditch were a source of direct government investment in the region and made a major contribution to its economic development (West Midlands Forum of County

Councils 1984). Both New Towns enjoyed considerable success in new-job creation; by 1981 there were 16,700 jobs on the Development Corporations' industrial estates—less than one-third of them, despite the original intention, in firms originating in the West Midlands County. The New Towns have demonstrated their ability to attract new employment in high-technology industry and from abroad. Nevertheless, after 1980 the coincidence of rapid growth in the workforce with the decline of traditional industries resulted in serious unemployment problems. Although the infrastructure and economic base of the New Towns will continue to support industrial and employment growth, the run-down of the Development Corporations will lead to a loss of direct government investment in their development.

Responses in the Metropolitan Area

With mounting unemployment and accelerating industrial decline, virtually all the metropolitan district councils in the West Midlands County took steps to regenerate economic activity and employment in their areas. Initiatives included industrial promotion and advice, provision of loans and grants, establishment of industrial improvement areas, refurbishment and construction of new factory units, development of new enterprise workshops, support for business advice centres, and tourism development. A survey undertaken for the 1983–4 financial year revealed that, excluding assistance from the Urban Programme, Walsall, Sandwell, Wolverhampton, and Solihull were spending between £250,000 and £1 million a year on economic development projects, Dudley and Coventry around £1.5 million, and Birmingham some £15 million (Mawson and Naylor 1984).

After 1980, Birmingham City Council devoted increasing attention to improving the city's industrial infrastructure, and by 1984 had refurbished almost 300 old factory units and constructed over 100 new units to provide accommodation for small businesses. The city's new enterprise workshops provided a supportive environment for new firms, and over seventy had left the workshops and were still in business in 1985. The City Council also offered financial assistance in the form of loans and grants to small firms through its Business and Employment Scheme. Between 1979 and 1984 some 300 businesses had been assisted, involving the creation or preservation of around 3,000 jobs.

In addition, the City Council took steps to diversify Birmingham's industrial base by encouraging the development of high technology industry and the growth of services and tourism. Aston Science Park, owned and managed by Aston Technology Limited, a company jointly financed by the University, the City Council, and Lloyds Bank, was established in 1981 to provide accommodation for firms using facilities at Aston University. Following the decision in 1972 to build the National Exhibition Centre, the Council also invested heavily in the development of tourism. Subject to substantial financial support from the EEC, an International Convention Centre was planned as a major new business and tourist development in the city centre. Other initiatives included a campaign to establish regular motor racing on Birmingham's streets, and the city's bid to host the 1992 Olympic Games.

The four Black Country district councils of Wolverhampton, Walsall, Dudley, and Sandwell have each prepared land for industrial development, and constructed new small units, use being made of central government Derelict Land and Urban Programme grants. Counselling and advice for small and start-up businesses were provided through local agencies such as the Walsall Small Firms Advice Unit, Sandwell Enterprise, and Wolverhampton Enterprise Limited. The Black Country districts, particularly Dudley, also attempted to exploit the tourist attractions afforded by the area's industrial heritage through improvement of canal facilities and support for industrial museums.

At the other end of the metropolitan area, the city of Coventry, faced with the consequences of the restructuring and closures of large plants in the engineering and motor vehicle sectors, which dominated its local economy, had responded with a 'low-key' strategy concerned mainly with infrastructural measures (Healey and Clarke 1984). As a substantial landowner in the city, the Council became involved in site construction and small unit construction as well as in the refurbishment or redevelopment of several former factory sites. With assistance from the County Council a number of new enterprise workshops were constructed, and through the Coventry Corporation Act loans and grants were made available for the erection or improvement of buildings or development of sites, as well as rent guarantees and loan-free periods. To promote the development of new-technology business in the city, the Council became involved in the establishment of Warwick Science Park.

Solihull, in the rural and suburban belt between Coventry and Birmingham, was the only district within the Metropolitan County which experienced relatively low unemployment levels. Under Conservative control it undertook little explicit economic development activity, except to minimize the rate burden on local firms. Economic decline in the County did not have a serious impact in the district until the early 1980s, when unemployment levels began to exceed 20 per cent in the former Birmingham overspill estates of Kingshurst and Chelmsley Wood. In 1983 the District Council's first review of local economic development led to a limited programme of support to small units and marketing of sites for high-technology industry.

The role of the County Council

It was against the backcloth of the dramatic collapse of the local economy and the perceived inadequacy of existing central government and local authority policies that the County Council launched its economic regeneration strategy in 1981. This was based on the assumption that it was necessary to establish a strategic conurbation-wide approach, based on close knowledge of the local economy, and with financial and staff resources on a sufficient scale to be capable of providing an integrated programme of economic and social initiatives. The proposals represented a significant shift from the County's previous programme in terms both of scale and of nature of policies. Specifically, there was a commitment to make use of the County's 'Section 137' two-penny rate. This section of the Local Government Act is a general enabling power which allows a local authority to undertake any measures which it deems to be in the interests of the area, and which are not covered by powers elsewhere in the Local Government Act. In the West Midlands this amounted to some £8 million per annum, and allowed the county to move away from the earlier approach characterized by limited main programme support for small firms (less than half a million pounds of grants per annum), a rent and rates subsidy scheme, infrastructural measures, and industrial promotion and advocacy.

To give clear political and organizational thrust to the programme, the Council established an Economic Development Committee (EDC) and an Economic Development Unit (EDU), which by the summer of 1985 had grown to be one of the largest and most innovative local authority economic departments in the country, with an establishment of eighty-five staff and a budget of £19 million. It was recognized that the County's initiatives alone would not resolve the severe economic crises facing the area. Nevertheless, it was believed that by taking effective measures of economic regeneration, even within the severe resource constraints, it would be possible to show that there was an alternative to what were seen as economically debilitating and socially divisive national policies. The EDC's approach was guided by a wide-ranging local economic strategy, drawn up before the 1981 elections and elaborated in the light of further research on the local economy and practical experience (Edge 1981; West Midlands County Council Economic Development Committee 1984*a*; Mawson *et al.* 1984).

The EDC's industrial strategy gave priority to support for medium-sized manufacturing companies in West Midlands' traditional industries. The view was taken that new firms and industries moving to the West Midlands, or emerging in the area, would play only a small part in providing future jobs compared with companies already there. Thus the Council sought to increase investment in established local companies, and to encourage local firms to improve business planning and technological development. Although there were a range of different agencies providing investment finance to companies, these were often unwilling to enter into risk-sharing investment. Too often they provided short-term loans and were preoccupied with investment in land and property, rather than in productive industry. Concern that there were few regionally based financial institutions available to provide long-term development capital and other financial services to local firms prompted the Council to set up its own Enterprise Board.

The West Midlands Enterprise Board (WMEB) was established in February 1982 as a company limited by guarantee and controlled by a board of directors, the majority of whom were county councillors, with others selected for their industrial or commercial expertise. Its purpose was to provide a source of equity and long-term loan finance for medium- to large-sized local manufacturing firms, and those engaged in productive services. The initial funding of WMEB came from the EDC, with an annual grant which by the end of the 1984–5 financial year totalled £12.4 million. However, efforts were made to tap other funding sources and, in conjunction with a London merchant bank, the West Midlands Regional Unit Trust was launched to attract public- and private-sector pension funds which initially raised £4.5 million in 1985. Typical situations in which WMEB invested included helping expansion where this was beyond the capacity of existing shareholders, companies' retained earnings, or bank borrowing; financial restructuring, where a company's borrowings were high in relation to its equity; management buy-outs as a result, for example, of changes in the parent group's corporate strategy or of the parent group going into receivership; and mergers and takeovers which led to increased efficiency.

After three years of operation, the WMEB had approved thirty-eight investments totalling £9 million in thirty-one companies. Total finance raised through the investments was £54 million, which meant that the WMEB had been able to lever £4 from the private sector for each £1 it had invested. The Board had experienced losses through the closure of three companies, but this rate was well within the limits of failure accepted by equivalent private-sector development capital organizations. Recorded profits at the end of the 1984–5 financial year were £300,000, a figure forecast to rise to £500,000 per annum. The companies employed 4,500, at a cost to the WMEB of £1,900 per job. In the absence of WMEB involvement, the activities of all these companies would have been constrained and some would have failed, a fact recognized by Sir George Young, Under Secretary at the DoE, in announcing government approval for the 1985–6 WMCC grant to the Board (Young 1985).

In terms of investment and business development, the WMEB was not the only initiative launched by the EDC. An interest relief scheme was introduced in 1982 in conjunction with the Industrial and Commercial Finance Corporation to reduce the burden of high interest rates on companies considering further employment-creating development with the County. By the summer of 1985, thirty-eight loans in thirty-six companies had been made, involving £1.3 million spent to support £14 million of associated investment, preserving 2,497 jobs, and creating 725, at an average cost of £1,900 per job. All Enterprise Board and County Council investments were governed by a principle that private-sector firms should be held accountable for their use of public funds. The EDC replaced the practice of giving grants by one of making loans and equity (share) investments. Assisted companies were required to enter into planning and investment agreements covering, amongst other things, employment practices and future business plans, as well as ensuring that the investment and any associated jobs were retained in the area for a specified period of time.

Another important role played by the County was in the provision of business advice. A Business Development Team was established in December 1984, employing seconded staff from a leading management consultancy to help small/medium-sized firms in metal-based and engineering activities to introduce management techniques and business planning, and to assist in securing development capital and public-sector financial support. In an eighteen-month period the Team provided up to twenty days' free consulting advice to some thirty firms. Other business advice initiatives included a team to provide comprehensive advice and training for the ethnic minority community in inner-city areas of the conurbation.Support was also given through the Urban Programme to over a dozen community-based organizations concerned with employment and training initiatives for disadvantaged groups. A Clothing Resource Centre was established to provide a computer-aided design facility and training centre for the rapidly growing clothing sector, dominated by Asian-owned firms within the County.

Worker co-operatives have also been encouraged: commercially viable businesses owned and controlled by their members. In 1982 three Co-operative Development Agencies (CDAs) were established serving Birmingham, the Black Country, and Coventry; and subsequently co-op centres were established to provide a range of accommodation and shared business services. The EDU established a Co-operative Finance Company with a revolving loan fund. Between 1981 and 1985 the number of co-operatives grew from six to seventy-eight, employing 426 people at a cost of £2,500 per job, or £4,000 when all overhead costs were taken into account. There had been nine failures in this period, of which five occurred before the establishment of the CDAs.

Turning to the question of infrastructure, industrial units and freehold sites were provided, including the clearance and redevelopment of derelict or vacant land and buildings. In 1984, however, a new 'land and premises' scheme was launched to tailor infrastructure measures to the needs of specific companies. This policy was designed to ease medium or large firms' cash-flow so that they could relocate to new, purpose-built premises or expand existing premises, as well as carry out financial restructuring. By the summer of 1985, six companies had been assisted at a total cost of nearly £2 million, involving some 1,350 jobs.

To assist local companies to introduce new technology, the EDU launched two major initiatives (West Midlands County Council Economic Development Committee 1985*a*; Marshall 1985). In 1983 it became a joint founder of Warwick Science Park in collaboration with Coventry City, Warwickshire County Council, and the University, with the objective of facilitating technology transfer and information exchange between university research and the commercial exploitation of high-technology products and processes. The Park achieved the fastest start-up rate of all science parks in Britain, and offered a range of size of units to allow companies to expand on site. By mid-1985 some twenty-nine research-based companies located there, of which three quarters were involved in electronic or computer-based manufacturing systems, or in mechanical and electrical engineering development fields with relevance to the needs of local industry. To foster the introduction of new products, processes, and materials into existing West Midlands firms, the EDU also set up a Technology Transfer Centre, based at Aston University, in 1985. Within the context of the County's sector strategy, technical consultants worked with client firms to assess their technological needs, and to help in gaining access to research, and development capital.

The provision of training programmes was another key element of the County's economic strategy, given the collapse during the recession of skill training through apprenticeships offered by companies (70 per cent reduction between 1979 and 1983 in the engineering industries) and the run-down and closure of skill-training centres and the Industry Training Boards. Over 3,000 training places were provided on an annual basis (the largest training agency in the West Midlands) through various co-operative initiatives with ITBs, local colleges, voluntary groups, the County's Community Programme, and training centres. Over forty schemes covered a wide range of training activities, with a specific emphasis on disadvantaged groups. Every training scheme was designed to provide quality training in areas with significant employment potential. Eighty-eight per cent of trainees subsequently found relevant employment.

The Economic Development Committee's industrial strategy was paralleled by a community strategy which recognized that economic issues were not simply about job creation and investment, but also concerned access to opportunities, the distribution of incomes and, ultimately, living standards (West Midlands County Council Economic Development Committee 1984*b*). Efforts were therefore made to redirect the economic dimensions of the Urban Programme away from its heavy capital expenditure and infrastructure orientation towards more direct people-based initiatives (Burgess and Ham 1985). The Community Strategy involved measures to increase the take-up of welfare benefits, attack illegal low pay, provide counselling and self-help initiatives for the unemployed, and assist community-based employment schemes. Some of the key initiatives included the establishment of a West Midlands Low Pay Unit, and the operation of a welfare benefits team within the EDU, which succeeded in securing an additional £9.5 million per annum of benefits to West Midlands households.

Future directions

The decision taken by central government to abolish the Metropolitan County in March 1986 posed serious problems for the future development of local economic initiatives within the conurbation. One of the most important lessons from the activities of the County Council concerned the advantages to be derived from undertaking economic development on a strategic, conurbation-wide basis. Clearly, the demand for major public investment projects cannot always be generated within the confines of a single local authority, and economic problems and processes in the metropolitan areas spill over local boundaries. The economic problems of the conurbations are so complex, large-scale, and interrelated that there is a need for a concomitant response in terms of resources and specialist skills. At the time of abolition, however, the District Councils, with the exception of Birmingham (see Birmingham City Council 1985), had committed comparatively little staff resources or finance to local economic development. While they were increasingly aware of the need to undertake such initiatives, the Councils were handicapped by committee and departmental structures which were ill-equipped to deal with this important new area of local government activity (Mawson 1986). Given the increasing financial pressures on the District Councils brought about by rate-capping and the consequences of abolition, they were not in a position to expand their activities to any significant extent.

In functional terms the abolition of the County meant the loss of a central source of intelligence on the County's economy, thus making it more difficult to organize a lobby on behalf of the area. It also meant the loss of an agency capable of undertaking innovative initiatives and major investment projects. In respect of the Urban Programme, for example, the County's team of twenty-three officers had been responsible for the development of a number of pioneering economic schemes. These could only be undertaken by the District Councils if they were to recruit substantial additional staff, and even then might well not be effectively replaced because of the expertise built up at the County level, and the economies of scale which it had been possible to exploit. Similar arguments applied in the case of the County's training programmes, co-operative development, voluntary employment schemes, and the welfare and low pay campaigns.

Such a point of view, however, was not shared by the Government, whose position was clearly stated in the White Paper 'Streamlining the Cities' in a single reference to economic development:

> Borough and District Councils already have powers to assist industry in their areas. The Government consider, therefore, that no specific arrangements are required to replace the role of the GLC and the Metropolitan Councils in assisting local industry and in drawing on the Urban Programme or Urban Development Grants. (Department of the Environment 1983)

While the Government was to some extent correct in its statement about the question of powers, there nevertheless remained a serious problem concerning resources and, specifically, the decision not to allow the Metropolitan Districts to secure the product of the County's Section 137 two-penny rate after abolition. Section 137 has proved a most valuable and flexible source of monies for economic development, yet the effect of removing a tier of government in the conurbations was effectively to halve the amount of monies potentially available for economic initiatives. The surrounding prosperous rural areas, with their two-tier system of County and District Councils, will retain the potential to raised 4 pence (West Midlands County Council Economic Development Committee 1985*b*).

Ending on a more optimistic note, however, the District Councils by the summer of 1985 had all become members of the Enterprise Board; and, with the Board's financial position secure, decisions were taken to widen its role from a purely investment agency to take on a number of activities previously undertaken by the County, including economic analyses, helping co-ops, technology transfer, the Clothing Resource Centre, and a major training centre in Birmingham. With this wider range of functions, WMEB became the first strategic conurbation-wide economic development agency in the country under local authority control.

Conclusions

Since 1980 the West Midlands region has suffered an unprecedented collapse of its industry and employment. Between 1980 and 1984, total employment in the region fell by 16 per cent, involving the loss of some 360,000 jobs, while the regional unemployment rate climbed from under 6 per cent to over 15 per cent. Around 11,000 companies were liquidated in the region between 1981 and 1985, while every key West Midlands industry suffered major cutbacks and closures. During 1984 alone, over 1,300 local companies failed and 10,000 redundancies were announced in the Metropolitan County—in a year which the Government insisted was the third of an economic recovery! Not surprisingly, West Midlands industrialists were asking, 'Recovery, what recovery?' (Smith 1984).

The West Midlands' present economic difficulties are not simply an outcome of the national cyclical downturn. Cyclical factors have certainly intensified and accelerated the region's decline; but that decline must ultimately be explained by longer-term underlying weaknesses in the region's industrial structure, and in the performance of key industries and companies. While it seems unlikely that the West Midlands will regain the levels of manufacturing output, capacity, and employment attained in the past, analysis of prospects for the region's future development points to no realistic alternative to retaining and building upon surviving elements of the West Midlands manufacturing base. The development of new industries and growth of services may play a role in the future regeneration of the regional economy, perhaps in some parts of the region more than others, but their impact will be relatively marginal.

Government measures after 1979 to support industry and employment in the region were largely limited to *ad hoc*, uncoordinated, and under-resourced gestures. It is still too early to assess the impact of the region's newly gained Intermediate Area status; but, regardless of the eventual level of regional aid awarded to the West Midlands, such aid will continue to be allocated in a reactive fashion, depending upon applications from individual firms. There will be no attempt to target and co-ordinate public investment in accordance with any overall plan for a regional economy. Government commitment to a market-led process of industrial rationalization, even in its own terms, scarcely ensures the survival of the most productive capacity. Many medium-sized West Midlands manufacturing companies with viable long-term prospects disappeared in the recession because of short-term cash-flow problems. Reorganization of the region's industry through a process based on survival of the lucky, as much as the 'leanest and fittest', is unlikely to produce the most favourable industrial fabric conducive to future recovery.

In the mid-1980s the Government insisted that it had no intention of departing from the national economic policies which many saw as a major factor contributing to the decline of West Midlands manufacturing industry and employment. Indeed, regional forecasts by Cambridge Econometrics suggest that a continuation of present macroeconomic policies under prevailing conditions of moderate international growth will lead to the loss of a further

147,000 manufacturing jobs in the West Midlands between 1986 and 1996, on top of the 350,000 job losses that have already taken place since 1980 (West Midlands Forum of County Councils 1985).

Economic initiatives of the type implemented by the County Council's Economic Development Committee have sought to demonstrate the possibility of an alternative to prevailing central government policy. Even with substantially more resources available, there is obviously a limit to what can be achieved at the local level. Accepting the urgent need to arrest the decline in the West Midlands manufacturing base, this can only occur through planned reflation and improvements in the national economic environment. The 'pump-priming' demand-management policies of the type adopted by successive British governments in the 1950s and 1960s are, however, unlikely in themselves to solve the problems faced by Britain's industrial regions. Rather, what is required, along with the expansion of the national economy, is the channelling of public- and private-sector investment into key sectors, firms, and specific areas. This would necessitate institutional changes at the national level, as well as the establishment of a network of regional and local development agencies, with an enhanced role for local authorities in the sphere of economic regeneration. The role of local economic development policies is potentially of great significance within the context of a national strategy for economic regeneration.

References

Batley, R. (1984), 'An Historical Sketch of Industrial Change and its Social Impact in the West Midlands County', ESRC Inner City in Context Research Programme, West Midlands Study, Working Paper no. 12, University of Birmingham, Joint Centre for Regional, Urban and Local Government Studies.

Bentley, G. and Mawson, J. (1984), 'Industrial Policy 1972–1983: Government Expenditure and Assistance to Industry in the West Midlands', ESRC Inner City in Context Research Programme, West Midlands Study Working Paper no. 6, University of Birmingham, Joint Centre for Regional Urban and Local Government Studies.

—— and —— (1985), 'The Industrial Development Certificate and the Decline of the West Midlands: Much Ado about Nothing', ERSC Inner City in Context Research Programme, West Midlands Study, Working Paper no. 15, University of Birmingham, Joint Centre for Regional, Urban and Local Government Studies.

Bessant, J., Jones, D., Lamming, R., and Pollard, A. (1984), 'The West Midlands Automobile Components Industry: Recent Changes and Future Prospects', West Midlands County Council Economic Development Unit Sector Report no. 4, Birmingham, West Midlands County Council.

Birmingham City Council (1985), *An Economic Strategy for Birmingham 1985—86*. Birmingham City Council.

Burgess, P. and Ham, B. (1985), *Innovative Approaches to Economic Development within the Urban Programme: A Case Study of the West Midlands*, PTRC Conference on Economic Development.

Cambridge Economic Policy Group (1980), 'Urban and Regional Policy with Provisional Regional Accounts 1966–78', *Cambridge Economic Policy Review* 6(2).

Commission of the European Communities (1984), *The Regions of Europe: Second Periodic Report on the Social and Economic Situation and Development of the Regions of the Community*, Brussels, European Commission.

Cooke, P., Morgan, K., and Jackson, D. (1984), 'New Technology and Regional Development in Austerity Britain: The Case of the Semiconductor Industry', *Regional Studies* 18(4), 277–89.

Debenham, Tewson and Chinnocks (1983), *Money into Property 1970–83*, London, Debenham, Tewson and Chinnocks.

Department of the Environment (1983), *Streamlining the Cities*, London, HMSO.

Department of Trade and Industry (1984), Press notice, 28 November.

Dickson, K. and Fleck, J. (1984), 'Robotic Applications and Employment in the West Midlands', West Midlands County Council Economic Development Unit, Sector Report no. 5, Birmingham, West Midlands County Council.

Edge, G. (1981), 'Priorities for Economic Development in the West Midlands', Statement to the West Midlands County Council Economic Development Committee, Birmingham, West Midlands County Council.

Flynn, N. and Taylor, A. (1984), 'De-industrialization and Corporate Change in the West Midlands', ESRC Inner City in Context Research Programme, West Midlands Study, Working Paper no. 8, University of Birmingham, Joint Centre for Regional, Urban and Local Government Studies.

Fothergill, S. and Gudgin, G. (1979), 'Regional Employment Change: a Sub-regional Explanation', *Progress in Planning* 12, (3).

Gaffikin, F. and Nickson, A. (1984), *Jobs Crisis and the Multinationals: The Case of the West Midlands*, Birmingham Trade Union Group for World Development.

Gibbs, D. C. and Edwards, A. (1983), 'Some Preliminary Evidence for the Interregional Diffusion of Selected Process Innovations', in Gillespie, A., ed., *Technological Change and Regional Development*, London, Pion.

Healey, M. and Clarke, D. (1984), 'Industrial Decline and Government Response in the West Midlands: The Case of Coventry', *Regional Studies* 18(4), 303–18.

House of Lords Select Committee on the European Communities (1984), *European Regional Development Fund, Session 1983–84, 23rd Report*, London, HMSO.

Howells, D. (1984), 'The Location of Research and Development: Some Observations and Evidence from Britain', *Regional Studies* 18(1), 13–29.

Liggins, D. (1978), 'Changing Role of the West Midlands Region in the National Economy', in F. Joyce, ed., *Metropolitan Development and Change*, London, Saxon House.

Low Pay Unit (1983), 'Poverty Wages in the West Midlands', *Low Pay Review* 15.

Marshall, M., (1985), 'Technological Change and Local Economic Strategy in the West Midlands', *Regional Studies* 19(6), 570–78.

Mawson, J. (1986), 'Local Economic Development Initiatives', In K. M. Spencer *et al.*, *Crises in the Industrial Heartland: A Study of the West Midlands. ESRC Inner City in Context Research Programme*, Oxford, Oxford University Press.

—— and Gibney, J. (1984), Memorandum of Evidence to the House of Lords Select Committee on the European Communities, 1984.

——, Jepson, D., and Marshall, M. (1984), 'Economic Regeneration in the West Midlands: The Role of the County Council', *Local Government Policy Making* (November), 61–72.

—— and Naylor, D. (1984), 'A Summary of Local Authority Economic Development in the West Midlands', ESRC Inner City in Context Research Programme, West Midlands Study, Working Paper no. 16. University of Birmingham, Joint Centre for Regional, Urban and Local Government Studies.

—— and Smith, B. M. D. (1980), *British Regional and Industrial Policy During the 1970's: A Critical Review with Special Reference to the West Midlands in the 1980*, University of Birmingham, Centre for Urban and Regional Studies.

—— and Taylor, A. (1983), 'The West Midlands in Crisis: An Economic Profile', ESRC Inner City in Context Research Programme West Midlands Study: Working Paper no. 1, University of Birmingham, Joint Centre for Regional, Urban and Local Government Studies.

Oakey, R., Thwaites, A., and Nash, P. (1980), 'The Regional Distribution of Innovative Manufacturing Establishments in Britain', *Regional Studies* 14(3), 235–253.

Osman, A. (1984), 'Westminster Blamed by Employers for Midlands Blight', *The Financial Times*, 18 March

Roberts, B. and Duncan, A. (1984), *Mobile Manufacturing Firms in the West Midlands: An Investigation of the Process of Locational Choice*, Birmingham, West Midlands County Council.

Roger Tym and Partners/Arthur Young McClelland Moores and Co. (1983), *West Midlands Investment Study: Report to the West Midlands Enterprise Board*, London, Roger Tym and Partners/Arthur Young McClelland Moores & Co.

Smith, A. (1984), 'Mood of West Midlands: "Recovery, Recovery, What Recovery?' *Financial Times*, 10 April.

Taylor, A. (1985), 'Employment Change in the West Midlands', ESRC Inner City in Context Research Programme West Midlands Study: Working Paper no. 3, University of Birmingham, Joint Centre for Regional, Urban and Local Government Studies.

Trades Union Congress West Midlands Regional Council (1982), *Our Future: A Planned Programme of Economic and Social Advance*, Birmingham, West Midlands TUC.

Tyler, P. (1980), 'The Impact of Regional Policy on a Prosperous Region: The Experience of the West Midlands', *Oxford Economic Papers* 32, 151–62.

Wabe, J. Stewart (1984), *Regional Impact of De-industrialization in the European Community*, University of Bath, Centre for European Industrial Studies.

West Midlands County Council (1974), *A Time for Action*. Birmingham, West Midlands County Council.

West Midlands County Council Economic Development Committee (1983), *Family Income Trends*, Report to the EDC, December 1983.

—— (1984*a*), *Action in the Local Economy*, Birmingham, West Midlands County Council.

—— (1984*b*), *Economic Review No. 2: Tackling Poverty*, Birmingham, West Midlands County Council.

—— (1985*a*), *Economic Review no. 3, Jobs and Technology*, Birmingham, West Midlands County Council.

—— (1985*b*), *Research Paper no. 6, Resources for Economic Development*, Birmingham, West Midlands County Council.

West Midlands Forum of County Councils (1984), *The Role of the New and Expanded Towns in the West Midlands Region*, Birmingham, West Midlands Forum of County Councils.

—— (1985), *Regenerating the Region: A Strategy for the West Midlands*, Birmingham, West Midlands Forum of County Councils.

West Midlands Region Confederation of British Industry (1983), *Manufacturing in the West Midlands: Problems and Prospects*, Birmingham, West Midlands CBI.

—— (1985), *Innovation and Technology in West Midlands Industry: Survey on Progress*, Birmingham, West Midlands CBI.

Wood, P. A. (1976), *The West Midlands*, Newton Abbot, David & Charles.

Young, Sir George (1985), 'Greater London Enterprise Board', *Parliamentary Debates (Hansard)*, 26 July 1985, 1485–94.

CHAPTER 6
The North West

M. R. Bristow

Introduction

Despite the somewhat more mellow contemporary images projected by the television series 'Coronation Street' and 'Brookside', in many people's perceptions North West England (see Figure 6.1) remains a place of cotton, clogs, and mill towns. While current realities are much more complex, that image from the past reflects former regional economic strength based upon a few dominant industries, which once gave the region a brief leading role in the world economy, and prompted the claim that 'what Manchester does today, the world does tomorrow'.

This early economic supremacy and confidence was already being eroded by the turn of the century. The region's current problems are thus merely one episode in a much longer saga of economic change and decline. Nevertheless, the region's problems in the 1980s seem of a different order than before. In particular, as Spence *et al*. (1982: 289) argue,

> the previous regional hegemony of the provincial conurbations has been undermined by relatively recent changes in the corporate organization of industrial production. In essence, the nation [and particularly the North West with two such conurbations] is left with a number of large cities whose functions within the national urban system no longer correspond with their size.

This dominance of the two problem conurbations of Liverpool and Manchester over the economic fortunes of the North West lies at the heart of the region's current malaise.

Two important national trends are fundamental to an understanding of the 'regional problem' in North West England. Unlike in earlier decades, especially the 1960s, Britain's population is now effectively stable, so that growth in one area must be balanced by decline elsewhere, creating spatial policy options which may not be so palatable, socially or politically, as the differential growth choices of the past. The second national factor is that in the mid-1980s the economy was still recovering from a major economic recession which had effectively lasted for almost a decade, and which had accelerated and accentuated longer-term changes in both national and regional industrial structures.

Since the 1960s, decentralization from the cores of the country's million cities has dominated intraregional migration patterns (Spence *et al*. 1982). In the case of the North West, a substantial part of this movement took the form of planned

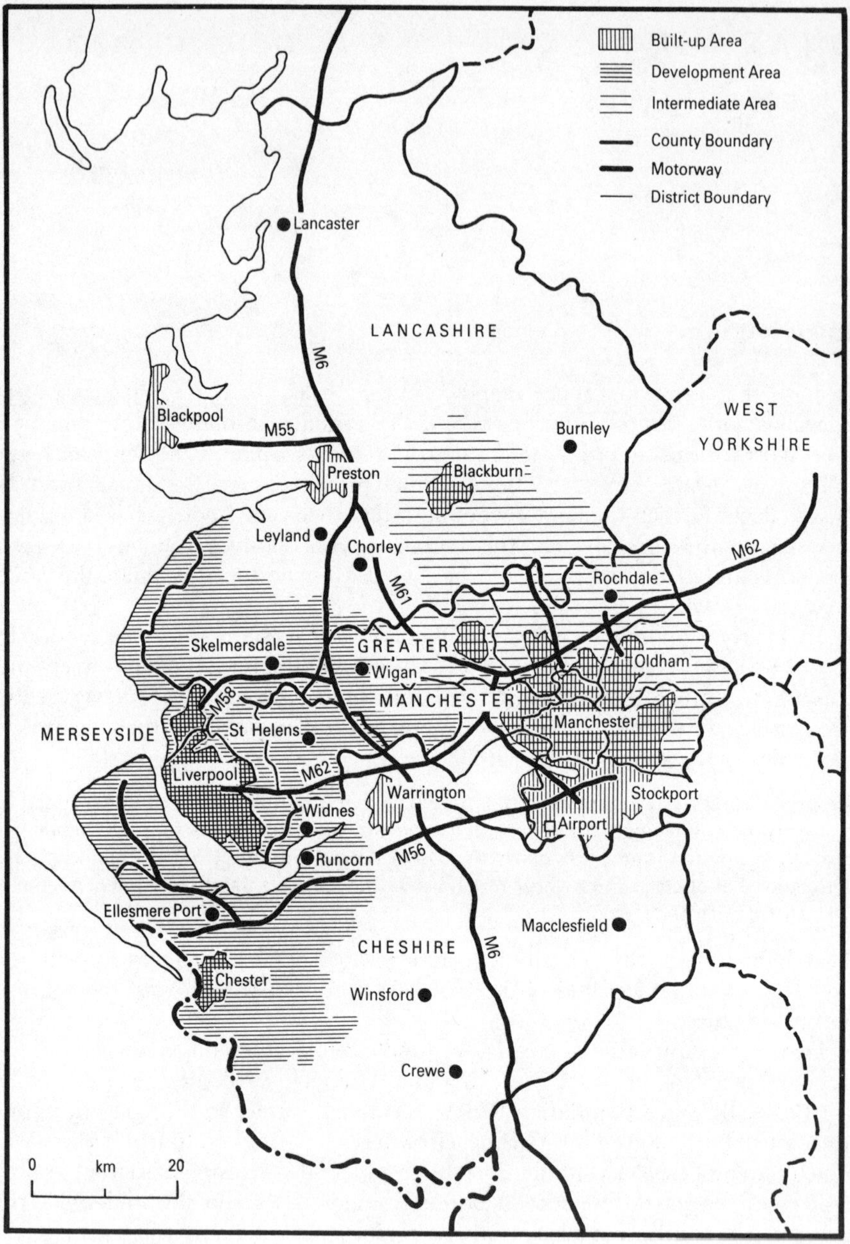

Figure 6.1. The North West

overspill. Also, in the 1970s and 1980s, net employment growth, nationally and regionally, mainly involved females, particularly part-time workers. The loss of manufacturing employment from the larger cities, and the polarization of professional and managerial employment into the South East, have also had particularly severe effects on the North West's conurbations, where service and office job growth failed to offset massive manufacturing employment decline in the economic downturns of the 1970s and 1980s (Lloyd and Shutt 1983).

The changing distribution and composition of population in the region has reflected national trends. Ageing of the population of the region's urban core areas has been one outcome of the expansion of the urban-based daily travel-to-work patterns of the employed, younger, and more mobile and affluent groups, a trend only partly offset by the popularity of the region's coastal resorts as retirement centres. Population shifted from urban cores to suburban rings, and then into the outer metropolitan areas surrounding the two conurbations, as a consequence both of overspill policies and of the preferences of private migrants. As Spence has argued, 'many of the problems of Britain's declining regions now appear to be exacerbated by changes in the intraregional distribution of population' (Spence *et al.* 1982: 282). The implication is that the functional and administrative organization of the nation's urban system may well be out of line with its evolving spatial structure. In the North West in particular, the functioning of present travel-to-work areas and economic linkages has created a mismatch with administrative arrangements and infrastructural provision in the conurbations, with major implications for the effectiveness of social and economic policies of both central and local government.

The North West in the mid-1980s: population and employment trends

The North West is the smallest UK region by area, but has the second largest population. This reflects the high density of population in all four county areas, but especially in the two former metropolitan counties of Greater Manchester and Merseyside. The populations of the latter areas fell markedly in the 1970s (Table 6.1), particularly in their core cities of Manchester and Liverpool. Although the populations of Cheshire and Lancashire increased, the region as a whole experienced a net fall of over 2.5 per cent between 1971 and 1981, the largest of any region in the country (North West County Planning Officers 1985). Population decline is expected to continue, with a further projected fall of over 2.5 per cent by the year 2001.

In terms of industrial structure, in the North West agriculture is less important to this densely populated region than to any other, while manufacturing accounted in 1981 for a third or more of employment in three out of its four counties—Merseyside being the exception, with 28 per cent of its workforce in this sector. Over the region as a whole, the broad sectoral breakdown of industrial employment was close to the national average, although the region derived a relatively high proportion of its GDP from manufacturing. The regional gross value added per employee also lay close to the national average,

Table 6.1. Population change in the North West (mid-year estimates, thousands)

	1971*	1976	1981	1991	2001
North West Region	6,597	6,560	6,460	6,319	6,285
Merseyside	1,657	1,586	1,525	1,424	1,354
Greater Manchester	2,729	2,680	2,624	2,548	2,516
Lancashire	1,345	1,363	1,382	1,394	1,432
Cheshire	867	896	928	453	981
Manchester	546	494	464	445	434
Liverpool	605	551	519	466	426

Sources: *Regional Trends* 1985, Central Statistical Office; Population Projections, Office of Population Censuses and Surveys.
*1971 Census figures.

but this masked large intraregional variations. In Cheshire, for example, the influence of the petroleum and chemical industries produced a gross value added per employee in 1981 which was 21 per cent above the national average, and an even higher capital expenditure per employee, at 67 per cent above the national average.

The region's current problems are, of course, closely related to the recent impact of industrial change and restructuring under the conditions of recession. The level of redundancies in the region by 1984 was well below its 1980 peak (Table 6.2), reflecting the national cyclical pattern, but there was still a continuing upward trend in the region's unemployment figures (Table 6.3). With large-scale collapse of the region's manufacturing, and the consequent permanent loss in its stock of jobs, the North West has recently undergone an irreversible structural economic change, with far-reaching social and political consequences. In examining the incidence of recent change and consequent

Table 6.2. Confirmed redundancies in the North West, 1977–84

	North West	Great Britain
1977	31,736	158,360
1978	37,617	172,563
1979	40,705	186,784
1980	92,595	493,766
1981	91,739	532,030
1982	67,117	400,416
1983	51,019	326,638
1984	37,646	230,212

Source: Manpower Services Commission, Labour Market Quarterly Reports, North West Region.

Table 6.3. Unemployment in the North West, 1980–4 (annual average percentages)

	Male	Female	Total
1980	10.3	5.9	8.5
1981	15.7	8.3	12.7
1982	18.5	9.4	14.7
1983	19.8	10.4	15.8
1984	19.6	11.1	16.0

Source: Manpower Services Commission, Labour Market Quarterly Reports, North West Region.

policy interventions, two possible spatial frameworks of analysis are available—local authority areas (as for the period 1974–86) or travel-to-work areas. Policies based upon both spatial aggregations are currently in force. Here the four county areas of the region are used as a spatial framework to examine recent trends in more detail, as a background to subsequent discussion of central and local government policy approaches.

Merseyside

Merseyside has come to epitomize problems associated with the North West's economic decline, although the specific causes of its own malaise centre on the postwar contraction of the port of Liverpool. With the relative decline of the North Atlantic and other deep-sea-route traffic, and the growth of trade with Europe, there was a general shift from Britain's west coast ports to the east, and especially to the smaller ports outside the registered dock-worker scheme such as Dover and Felixstowe. Liverpool was additionally disadvantaged by its poor productivity, reflected in longer than average times spent by ships in port, compared with ports like Felixstowe which were less hindered by traditional labour practices and old infrastructure. Traffic through the port of Liverpool fell by 51 per cent between 1970 and 1982. Employment in the docks was down to 10,500 by 1975, and shrank to less than 2,000 by 1985.

Within a declining total population—a loss of over 8.5 per cent during 1971–81, and forecast to fall a further 11 per cent by the end of the century—the socioeconomic structure of the former Merseyside county has effectively polarized into the higher-status private residential areas concentrated on the Wirral and in Sefton, where at least 50 per cent of households have access to a car, and the public housing areas in the inner city and the overspill estates. In the three central wards of inner Liverpool in 1984, unemployment rates were 35 per cent or greater, and car-ownership rates below 15 per cent. In the inner city, smaller and older households inhabited a housing stock in which there was an increasing number of voids, even though basic housing amenities and the incidence of overcrowding had been improved.

Between September 1978 and January 1984, employment in the Merseyside county area fell by around 13 per cent, including over 19,000 redundancies. Three-quarters of this drop was in manufacturing industry, and a substantial proportion involved plants brought to the outer areas of the conurbation in the boom years of the 1960s. On the other hand, the inner area of Liverpool and Birkenhead saw major job losses from contraction and closure among the dominant employers in its shipbuilding, electrical engineering, and food and drink industries from the mid-1960s (Lloyd 1979). Even in the aftermath of the recession in 1984, further major job losses were forecast in Merseyside, suggesting a fall in total employment from around 541,000 in that year to 490,000 by 1990 (Merseyside County Council 1984). At the beginning of 1985, the Merseyside county contained, in whole or in part, the four travel-to-work areas with the highest unemployment rates in the North West region—Liverpool (21.1 per cent), Widnes and Runcorn (19.7 per cent), Wigan and St Helens (19.4 per cent), and Wirral and Chester (18.8 per cent) (see Figure 6.2).

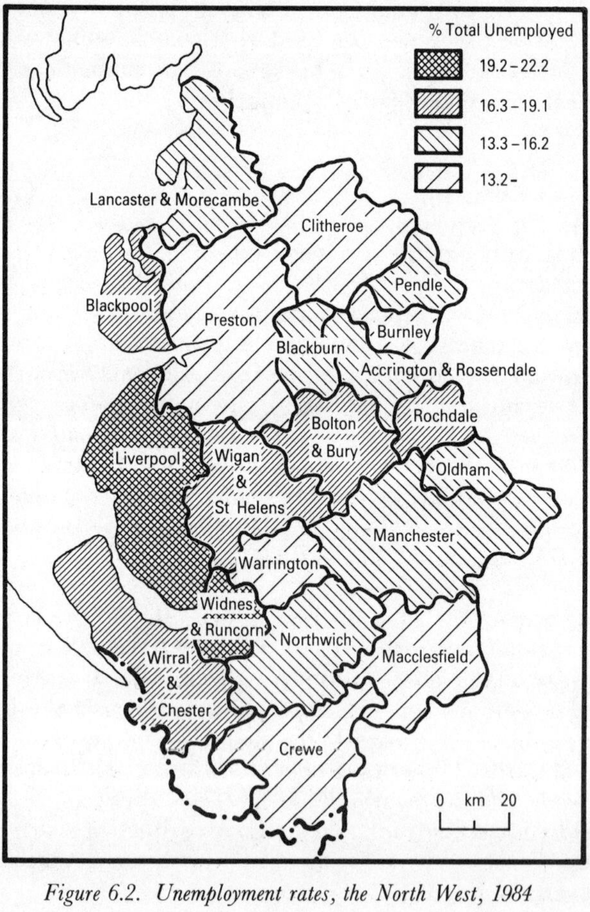

Figure 6.2. Unemployment rates, the North West, 1984

Despite the upward national trend in the proportion of the working-age population in employment between 1971 and 1981, activity rates in the public housing areas of Merseyside actually fell, notably in Knowsley and St Helens, and the proportion of the working-age population with jobs declined from 69 per cent to 59 per cent. In the inner-city areas, the proportion of the population of working age in employment in 1981 was only 48 per cent, compared with 72 per cent in the higher-status residential areas of the conurbation. Statistics such as these are an important part of the social backdrop to the Toxteth riot of 1981. In the higher-status areas of the conurbation, rising activity rates during the 1970s had tended to offset increases in unemployment, but even here, with the onset of deep recession at the end of the decade, unemployment worsened very considerably, with a rise from 11.6 per cent in 1978 to 19.4 per cent in 1984.

Greater Manchester

In Greater Manchester the 1970s also saw overall population decline, although at only just half the rate of decline in Merseyside (−4.3 per cent compared with −8.5 per cent). There were, however, major differences in population changes within the county area. The inner-city core of Manchester and Salford continued an earlier trend of population decline from the 1960s, producing a loss in the 1970s of just over one-quarter of the resident population, while the outer built-up areas lost population for the first time (−1.8 per cent). Only in the outer metropolitan ring, outside the continuous built-up area and including some adjacent areas (particularly in Cheshire) beyond the county's administrative boundary, was there a population gain (3.4 per cent), although at a slower rate than in the previous decade (11.0 per cent) (Law *et al.* 1984). Cumulatively, over the thirty-year period 1951–81, population densities in the inner-city areas of the conurbation were halved, while, overall, those in the remainder of the conurbation stayed roughly the same; a result of both planned redevelopment, a process largely completed by the 1970s, and reductions in average household size. Over this period the inner city saw the replacement of its private housing stock, a great deal of it in 'Coronation Street'-type terraces and much admittedly of poor quality, by a sea of one-class public housing, only interrupted spasmodically in the 1980s by isolated pockets of new, privately built housing (Robson 1980).

Throughout Greater Manchester, the pattern of both private and public housing provision has been determined largely by land availability and allocations. Available land within the south of the county became used up in the earlier growth periods of the 1950s and 1960s, so that in the 1970s more attention was paid, particularly by the private sector, to the northern boroughs within the conurbation, or to areas like Macclesfield outside the county to the south. As in Merseyside, this long-term development process has led to social polarization. In inner-city areas like Hulme in Manchester, over 50 per cent of the available labour force were unemployed in the mid-1980s, contrasting sharply with the large concentrations of population (over 150,000 each) in generally more upwardly mobile and affluent households in the boroughs of

Trafford and Stockport in the south west and south of the conurbation. 'The geography of wealth and poverty in the Greater Manchester area is thus very clear-cut. The poor are concentrated in the inner city, in council estates which were built to take the overspill, and in the older industrial centres to the west, north, and east of Manchester' (Law *et al*. 1984: 32).

In employment terms, changes in national economic circumstances have had particularly severe impacts upon Greater Manchester, especially as large parts of the conurbation received only minimal assistance from traditional regional policy. During the 1970s overall, employment declined in the conurbation at a rate four times that of the population, largely reflecting the contraction of the previously dominant manufacturing sector in the conurbation's economy, which had provided 45 per cent of employment in 1971. Manufacturing shed one-third of its workforce by 1981, but even then this sector still accounted for a somewhat larger share of the conurbation's job stock than it did in the country as a whole, a position which rendered Greater Manchester vulnerable to further job losses in the early 1980s. Moreover, offsetting gains in service employment occurred at only three-quarters of the national rate of increase, and there was a significant loss of service and office jobs from Manchester's central business district during the 1970s. Even in the early 1970s, despite the large amount of office development recently completed or in progress at that time in central Manchester, including that associated with the massive Arndale shopping complex, there were worrying signs that the central business district was not managing to capture and maintain a level of service employment commensurate with its status as the leading business centre for a conurbation of two and a half million people, let alone the wider regional hinterland with six and a quarter million people (Tym and Partners 1981). Already the attraction of London to the highest-order financial, professional, and business services was working to the detriment of central Manchester. On a local scale also, the city centre suffered throughout the 1970s from competition from growing suburban centres, especially in Trafford and Stockport, where office rents in new developments were lower and parking much easier both for office workers and for the increasing number of shoppers using new and expanded retail facilities (Damesick 1979; Tym and Partners 1981; Law 1985).

The impact of job loss and employment decentralization at the district level within the conurbation was notably different, sufficiently so to induce the government to retain some of its northern boroughs in the Assisted Area map when most of Greater Manchester lost Intermediate Area status in the 1979 regional policy revisions. In the new 1984 map, a larger area of the north of the conurbation was given Intermediate Area status, departing from the practice adopted everywhere else of using whole travel-to-work areas as the basis for designating Assisted Areas. This north–south division within the conurbation does nonetheless reflect the fact that the poorest-performing districts have been those like Salford, Wigan, Rochdale, and Oldham which have suffered most from the manufacturing industry shakeout, while the most resilient were the southern districts of Trafford and Stockport, with more affluent populations and associated employment growth in consumer services. In the conurbation as a whole, but especially in the inner city, the vulnerability of small businesses to site dislocation through redevelopment, and to recession, tended to offset gains through new-firm births. Elsewhere, mergers and consolidation amongst the larger manufacturing firms, especially in textiles, and the contraction of the major firms in the Trafford Park industrial estate, resulted in many plant closures and job losses in the central and northern areas of the conurbation. The prospect of technical change now making inroads into office-based employment and general retrenchment in public sector services only add to a generally poor prognosis for a significant improvement in the area's employment stock in the rest of the 1980s.

The Shire Counties: Lancashire and Cheshire

If gloom is cast across the region by the recent economic performance of the two conurbations, the North West's shire counties might be expected to offer more hopeful prospects. Even here, however, the current situation cannot be considered wholly favourable. In Lancashire, after 1972, the population was naturally declining. As elsewhere in the region, there were significant intra-county variations, with growth taking place mainly in the southern and western areas as a consequence of planned and private migration from the conurbations and other urban areas into the New Towns of Skelmersdale and Central Lancashire (Preston–Leyland–Chorley), and into the smaller towns and rural areas generally. Overall, there has been an urban–rural shift of population and a movement from the north and east towards the south and west of the county. In consequence, the associated growth in the working-age population has placed demands for more jobs upon the county's economy which, even though below the level of demand predicted in the 1970s, that economy is ill-prepared to meet in the 1980s.

The key problem for Lancashire is the vulnerability of its employment base. Not only is service employment currently under-represented, despite a large leisure-oriented sector, but the 34 per cent of the workforce employed in manufacturing are heavily concentrated (1 in 5) in the vehicle and aircraft industries—the dominant industry group in the county since 1978. These two sectors are made up largely of the commercial vehicle division of British Leyland and defence-related plants of British Aerospace; hence their vulnerability to external shocks is considerable. Job growth in the county in the 1970s came almost entirely from the service sector, but recession at the end of the decade brought severe job losses overall. In the three years 1979–82, no less than 40 per cent of textile industry employment and 21 per cent of the jobs in the vehicles sector were lost, and over 6,000 jobs from the service sector. Projections made in 1984 of the county's employment levels over the next five years forecast at least a continuing shortfall, additional to the existing pool of unemployed, and at worst a widening gap between availability and the resident labour force.

Cheshire is commonly regarded as the most prosperous county in the North West. Even here, however, by the mid-1980s change was not proceeding as previously expected, with major discrepancies between planners' projections and actual trends in population change and migration, and increasing levels of unemployment. Local authority land-use planning in Cheshire in the late 1970s had proceeded on the basis that, in general, land for new housing should be made available only to meet demand from new household formation within the existing population. Provision for migration into the county was to be limited to the two New Towns of Runcorn—almost completed—and Warrington, and the district of Ellesmere Port adjacent to the Wirral (Cheshire County Council 1978). This marked a major policy shift from the acceptance in the 1960s of major migration flows from the two conurbations. A review of the workings of the new policy in the early 1980s (Cheshire County Planning Department 1982) showed that it was effective in all parts of the county, with the notable exception of those areas nearest to Greater Manchester (primarily in the Macclesfield district), where continued outward population pressures from the conurbation had by 1980 almost exhausted the land allocations for private house-building. Despite this situation, planning policies in the 1982 County Structure Plan revisions sought to maintain existing settlement policies for the remainder of the decade. Thus, continuing outward pressure from Greater Manchester was met by increasing resistance from the recipient areas to the south, a conflict not unlike those in some growth areas around London, and reminiscent of Cheshire's earlier successful opposition in the 1950s and 1960s to new-town proposals to house Manchester's overspill.

In employment terms, on the other hand, the same Structure Plan revisions of 1982 reflected a strong reaction to the somewhat unexpected effects of recession upon the county. A relatively favourable county-wide unemployment rate of 5.5 per cent in 1979 had deteriorated to 14.0 per cent by early 1983, a level maintained for the following two years. Moreover, major closures in towns like Winsford and the spillover effects of the Shotton steelworks closure in Clwyd had sent the unemployment rate to over 20 per cent in some local areas within the county. Job creation and employment support thus became a cornerstone of local authority planning policies in Cheshire, as in other areas of the North West. Perceived job needs are now a key determinant of industrial land allocation policies, sweeping away previous restrictions on land release imposed for fear of too rapid local expansion.

Restructuring and the North West's economy

As already noted, economic decline is by no means a new phenomenon for the North West. The well-documented saga of the decline of the region's textile industry since the 1920s is but one example; the loss of Liverpool's port functions and the decline of coalmining in the Wigan area are others. The significant difference in recent events is that, whereas earlier problems could be traced to the contraction of particular localized sectors of economic activity, which it was once thought could be overcome by government-aided infusions of new industry (underlying, for example, the references to a Merseyside 'economic miracle' in the 1960s (Rodgers 1972)), over the last decade the North

Table 6.4. Employment changes in the North West, 1978–82

	No.	%
Manufacturing:		
Food, drinks, tobacco	−13,400	−12.7
Chemicals	−15,300	−14.3
Metals and engineering	−89,800	−21.4
Textiles and clothing	−72,400	−40.8
Other manufactures	−44,300	−23.9
Services:		
Construction	−28,700	−21.1
Transport and communications	−25,100	−14.6
Distributive trades	−10,800	−3.4
Public services	−7,200	−4.3
Private services	+29,300	+3.7

Sources: Lloyd and Shutt 1983; *Employment Gazette*.

West has been overtaken by generalized economic decline affecting virtually all industrial sectors in almost every part of the region.

In the North West as a whole, the four years 1978–82 saw a net loss of 235,000 manufacturing jobs, amounting to 24 per cent of the 1978 total (Table 6.4). While the traditional textiles and clothing industries continued their long-term decline, they were joined by the engineering, electrical, and vehicles industries, which collectively lost a fifth of their job stock in the region over the four-year period. Even former growth sectors like petrochemicals proved not to be immune from decline, with threats to Shell's Carrington plant near Manchester, and the announcement of the loss of 1,000 jobs at the Stanlow complex in early 1985.

In seeking to understand the severity of this latest phase of economic decline in the region, it is important to recognize that the North West's manufacturing sector had, by the 1970s, become dominated by large corporate enterprises, often multinational in character. Just fifty-four firms, each employing more than 2,500 workers, accounted for 46 per cent of the region's manual workforce in manufacturing in 1975, with the thirteen largest among them employing no less than 25 per cent of this workforce (Lloyd and Shutt 1983). In the following five-year period, these firms shed almost a quarter of their manual employment as the result of amalgamation, fragmentation, and closure arising from corporate strategies designed to meet changing world market conditions. An important point to note with respect to the potential for effective local responses to this process is that the changes produced by corporate restructuring were not locally determined. The individual locality found itself the passive recipient of employment changes decided elsewhere, in response to external influences beyond local control.

Table 6.5. North West region: employment change by establishment size 1973–81

	Manufacturing				Services			
	Census units	%	Employees	%	Census units	%	Employees	%
1–49	+1,740	+15.7	+7,197	+5.2	−9,375	−11.1	−230,503	−27.9
50–99	−265	−18.9	−18,974	−19.2	+161	+8.9	+10,322	+8.1
100–499	−485	−28.8	−155,323	−42.7	+142	+9.7	+18,020	+6.1
500+	−151	−37.1	−186.838	−36.3	+58	+17.5	−171,905	−38.0
Total	+839	+5.8	−353,938	−30.6	−9,130	−10.4	−275,606	−16.2

Source: Shutt and Whittington 1984, based on Annual Census of Employment data.

As Table 6.5 shows, employment in establishments with more than 500 workers fell substantially in both the manufacturing and service sectors between 1973 and 1981. Net job growth was confined to small manufacturing establishments and medium-sized operations in services. This growth was spatially uneven, with the smaller shire county towns gaining disproportionately over the two conurbations, Merseyside in particular. The underlying economic health of the region also does not look good from the point of view of new firm formation. North West England ranked only sixth out of the ten British regions in the number of new VAT registrations per thousand of the working population in 1981–3, and the ratio of new firm births to firm deaths was the lowest in the country (with the Northern region) (Table 6.6). In general, it appears that the depressed state of regional demand created a 'crowded platform' of market niches for new firms in the North West, leaving little room for real growth.

When compared with the scale of decline in manufacturing (Table 6.4), the loss of 42,000 construction and service industry jobs (−8 per cent) over the four years 1978–82 looks less serious at first sight. Nonetheless, the decline in services is worrying for the long-term economic health of the region, and the overall rate of decline masks wide variations. The largest contraction outside the manufacturing sector occurred in construction, with a loss of over 20 per cent of the workforce as a result of the general economic downturn and cuts in public sector capital programmes, especially in roads and housing. The transport sector also shed labour heavily as restructuring of the North West's ports—continued contraction in Liverpool, the closure of Preston, and virtual shutdown in Manchester—took place, together with increasing economies in public transport operations in the region. Decreases in employment in the distributive trades and government services, although not so large, were equally

Table 6.6. New VAT registrations per thousand of working population

Region	1981–83	Rank	Ratio of new firm formation to firm cessations 1982
South West	18.9	1	1.24
South East	17.6	2	1.28
Wales	15.9	3	1.32
East Midlands	14.8	4	1.27
West Midlands	14.7	5	1.33
North West	13.4	6	1.21
Yorkshire–Humberside	13.1	7	1.24
East Anglia	12.4	8	1.27
North	11.4	9	1.21
Scotland	10.8	10	1.29
Northern Ireland	n.a.	n.a.	—

Source: Shutt and Whittington 1984.

important, in that their impact was concentrated on the inner areas of the conurbations. Only in some private business and consumer services was there a modest growth in jobs over the four year period. In locational terms, that growth tended to go to areas that were already relatively prosperous—the metropolitan fringes and the more buoyant rural centres—rather than to the central business districts of the two conurbations.

To sum up, North West England recently experienced a major restructuring of its capital and hence its employment stock, which had differential impacts upon its spatial and settlement structure. Analysis of the impact of recession upon the industrial heartland of the region, still the two conurbations, has shown that dependence upon large branch plants of major industrial companies—some, like the motor industry, established in previous rounds of regional policy aid—proved particularly detrimental to the economic health of Merseyside, while in Manchester, inner urban locations with obsolescent sites and premises reduced the competitiveness and viability of the city's manufacturing industry. In the shire counties, rather different problems emerged. In some smaller towns, dependence upon large employers based on single-product sectors in manufacturing, often dominating local labour markets, brought economic vulnerability and major job loss as firms contracted or restructured to maintain viability.

In terms of specific job types and skills, it seems most unlikely that recent employment losses will ever be replaced. Restructuring of this kind—with the scrapping or replacement of industrial plant and buildings, and the concomitant scrapping of human skills and the need for retraining—means fundamental changes to the life-styles of many of the region's households, and presents a major challenge to policy-makers.

Policy responses

These recent changes in the North West occurred in spite of continuing attempts to support the economy of the region through both traditional regional policy and, latterly, urban programme assistance. Earlier it had been hoped that technological innovation and investment multipliers would flow from the implantation of large units of capital in the 1960s on Merseyside and in the region's New Towns, contributing to self-generating growth. As well as regional industrial restructuring by these means, policy-makers had also sought significant spatial restructuring. As early as 1959, consultants appointed to investigate the problems of north east Lancashire were arguing that 'the problem should be viewed, not as one of moving work to the workers, or *vice versa*, but as one of moving the work, and the workers if necessary, to the places where it will be most efficiently performed' (Economist Intelligence Unit 1959: 150). The efficacy of industrial 'growth poles' has been increasingly questioned, and recent events reveal the failure to secure self-sustaining growth by such means in the North West. Nevertheless, the issue of necessary spatial restructuring still remains. It is still unclear in the North West whether a concentration of resources in the new urban areas linked to the M6 corridor would be the most efficient way of renewing the economic strength of the region, or whether attempting to adapt the older towns and cities to new economic and social uses is a better way of using national and regional resources.

The last decade has seen a proliferation of support policies, from both central and local government, to meet perceived economic and social problems in the North West. Two additional elements of policy emerged alongside traditional regional policy efforts to ameliorate local unemployment. The mid- to late 1970s saw increasing realization of the problems of the older urban areas, especially in terms of inner-city deprivation. Research on the North West's urban areas contributed its share to government's understanding and recognition of these problems—the studies of Oldham and inner Liverpool (Department of the Environment 1973; 1977) are well known—while Manchester was the chosen venue for the announcement of the Labour government's inner-city initiative in 1977. A dichotomy emerged, however, between regional and sectorally based industrial support policies, and the newly developed set of policies designed to improve conditions in the most deprived urban areas. This was emphasized by the administrative split between the two organizing ministries—Industry and Environment. A second change after the late 1970s was the proliferation of local economic initiatives by both the private and local public sectors. The result of the development of these three forms of policy was a bewildering array of interventions, all designed to influence or ameliorate various aspects of economic and social change in the region, but often seeming to be uncoordinated, if not actually at variance with each other.

Merseyside, for example, has a history of Assisted Area status stretching back to 1949; by the early 1980s, not only was it a Special Development Area, it also contained an Inner City Partnership Area, an Enterprise Zone, and an Urban Development Corporation, and some of its constituent boroughs were designated as Programme Authorities under the Inner Urban Areas Act. Alongside these central government measures were local authority initiatives and self-help business support schemes originating in the private sector—the first of these in the North West, the St Helens Trust, being in Merseyside. It is not surprising that one organizational response to this plethora of assistance was the development of business information and advisory offices providing 'signposting' services. These included the private-sector business enterprise trusts, local authority industrial assistance departments or companies, now common throughout the region, and central government agencies like the DTI's Small Firms Information Service. In Merseyside, too, following the Secretary of State for the Environment's visit to the area after the 1981 riot in Toxteth, an attempt was made to secure better co-ordination of central government initiatives through the Task Force experiment—a group of locally based civil servants and private-sector secondees headed by the Secretary of State. This concept has since been extended to urban partnership areas elsewhere in the country, in the form of City Action Teams.

In the Manchester conurbation, the policy picture over recent years has been, if anything, even more confused. Before the 1970s, the conurbation received relatively little economic support, apart from the coalfield area of Wigan (intermittently from as early as 1946) and specific aid schemes related to the rundown of the cotton industry, which affected most of the northern ring of textile towns. It was not until after the report of the Hunt Committee (Secretary of State for Economic Affairs, 1969), and the later large-scale extension of Intermediate Area status in the 1972 revisions to regional policy, that Manchester was brought more fully into the regional aid programme. This assistance was subsequently removed after the 1979 cutbacks in regional aid, only to be partially reinstated in the November 1984 package of changes, when the northern half of the Manchester travel-to-work area was again designated an Intermediate Area. Industry in the conurbation has thus not benefited from a consistent regime of regional policy support, creating obvious difficulties in long-term business planning.

As on Merseyside, the Manchester conurbation also has a Partnership Area and three Urban Programme authorities, in Bolton, Rochdale, and Oldham, as well as the Trafford Park/Salford Docks Enterprise Zone. However, past uncertainties over central government support led, if anything, to greater local authority involvement in economic development. At county level, the Greater Manchester Council not only set up its own industrial aid company—the Greater Manchester Economic Development Corporation—but also established its own office in Brussels to facilitate a direct campaign for EEC assistance. An important direct result of this campaign was the implementation of a textile areas aid scheme late in 1984 which brought £25 million of EEC support for environmental improvement and textile worker retraining in the northern towns of the conurbation and adjacent areas of Lancashire and West Yorkshire. The County Council was also very active in seeking Urban Development Grant aid, perhaps most notably in the case of the Manchester Central Station Exhibition Hall project, which opened in 1985 on a site which had lain derelict for almost twenty years. This project was particularly significant in that it was based on a carefully negotiated package involving central government, a major local authority, and private-sector finance, and was aimed directly at an aspect of what has long been perceived as one of the North West's major drawbacks—a general obsolescence in the urban infrastructure and environment (North West County Planning Officers 1985). The loss of the county authority in 1986 would seem to be a serious setback to Manchester, given the Council's recent success in generating local economic support measures.

The major policy lessons from the conurbations seem twofold: the need for better co-ordination of approaches, and for long-term consistency of support measures. Rather different lessons can be illustrated from the experience of the shire counties in the region. In Lancashire, for example, the impact of central government industrial and other policies has been a major factor in local economic development. The effective nationalization of British Leyland and subsequent government funding for the company was a major influence on the employment fortunes of the Leyland area, following the initial boost in the 1960s from the formation of the British Motor Corporation under the former Industrial Reorganization Corporation. Yet this government support seemed unable to create an industry sufficiently competitive to withstand the recessionary pressures of the early 1980s, when there was a severe contraction of commercial vehicle manufacture and associated employment in both Lancashire and Cheshire. In Lancashire's other major industrial sector, aircraft manufacture, local employment is vulnerable to changes in defence policy. Elsewhere in the region, the presence of British Aerospace as a large local employer in Woodford near Manchester (the Nimrod programme) and Chester (European Airbus project) makes these local economies heavily dependent upon major contract decisions in the public sector. These cases illustrate the important influence of national policies upon the economic fortunes of particular localities, even when such policies have no explicit spatial basis. This of course opens up the much wider policy issue of the regional and local impacts of central government's expenditure programmes in general, and the question of whether these should or could be used as part of overall support policies for the regions.

External control versus local initiative

Since the late 1970s, with the Labour Government's moratorium on local authority capital schemes, central government has attempted to control more directly than before public expenditure in the local government sector. Restraints on public spending generally, the problems of the local rating system, and the Conservative Government's 'rate-capping' scheme all affect the ability of local decision-makers in the region to respond to local needs and problems. Alterations to funding levels on the capital side have major impacts upon infrastructure investment in a region, an issue of particular importance in the North West given its special problems of environmental obsolescence. Central government's preferences on the direction of capital spending have also had important local implications. For example, the recent emphasis on private house-building rather than public spending on housing creates a different pattern of housing investment from that required, for example, to improve many interwar/early postwar dwellings, or to replace stock from the deck-access, high-rise era of the 1960s, which many see as the dominant housing issues in the region. Similarly, transport investment priorities favouring roads over rapid transit systems will have a major impact on the future growth and form of the Manchester conurbation, which unlike Merseyside and Tyneside, failed to get a new intra-urban rail system in the 1970s.

The erosion of local choice begun in the increasingly centralized housing and transport investment programme procedures of the 1970s and accentuated by the rate-capping scheme of the 1980s underlies recent central–local government conflicts in the region. The Manchester and (especially) the Liverpool councils featured prominently among those causing particular difficulties for central government in the mid-1980s. By 1985, the need for a major rethink on local government finance was clearly evident, and the issue of reform of the rating system was once more on the Government's agenda.

The problems of effective intervention at the local level, however, go beyond the issue of central control of local public finance. As already argued, the vulnerability of Merseyside's branch plant economy, and of the single-industry-dominated towns in the shire counties, and even Manchester, with its declining manufacturing base and its financial and business services draining away to the South East, all represent in various forms an increasing dependence in the North West upon decision-makers based outside the region.

A more subtle, but related, problem facing the region is that of attitudes. Adversity can breed both resentment and apathy. The realization that decisions affecting the basic viability of the regional economy are no longer solely or even marginally within the control of those in the region can breed resentment at the loss of real choice and independence, and apathy about attempting to change circumstances for the better. Comments about a growing North/South divide in Britain (Robson 1985) and perceptions of an unconcerned government are more easily generated when those in the region feel helpless in the face of economic adversity. That is why, to take but one example, the decision to fragment the local government structure in the English conurbations seems so unwise in the circumstances of the mid-1980s. Although it may be argued that economic initiatives by the local state can have only a limited impact, even at Metropolitan County level, the removal of the upper-tier authorities in the conurbations of the North West will only serve to reduce the institutional capacity both for the articulation of their needs and for meaningful intervention in the local economy.

There has been a recent shift in emphasis in regional development theory towards a greater role for locally based economic decision-making (for example, Friedmann and Weaver 1979; Weaver 1984). Notwithstanding the dominance of macroeconomic forces, it is argued that better utilization of local resources, especially human-based ones, will occur through allowing more local decision-making responsibility. This is analogous to arguments for more local managerial autonomy within large business organizations. These ideas imply a strengthening of the power and institutional capacity of the local state. In the North West, as in other regions, recent moves by local authorities into the economic arena represent steps in this direction. However, recent policies on the reform of local government structure and finance reveal a central government reluctance to recognize such arguments, or to devolve real power within the already highly centralized state in Britain.

Weaknesses of the present policy framework in the North West

The North West has successively endured a spatially and temporally varied pattern of regional policy assistance, the application of sectorally based industrial subsidies, a complex programme of urban aid measures, and finally an increasing avalanche of locally based economic initiatives, all operating over separate, contiguous, or sometimes the same sub-areas of the region, and initiated, planned, and controlled by a variety of central and local, public and private organizations. As some have observed, it has become '*ad hocery*' run riot, with initiatives, money, and effort all chasing decreasing amounts of investment and employment in what at times has appeared to be a zero-sum game.

Against this background, the main current need is to improve radically the co-ordination and delivery of policy, particularly at the local level. The local government reforms of 1985–6 hinder rather than assist that objective. Nevertheless, the proliferation of aid programmes demands unification of aims and implementation at the regional and subregional level. With regard to central government involvement, the administration of urban policy requires better integration with regional support. There is also the spatial dimension to consider. If one agrees with Parr (1979) and Spence *et al.* (1982) that existing spatial structures are to some extent obsolescent, then administrative systems tied to such structures will not operate efficiently in the new economic and social circumstances of future decades.

The riots in Toxteth in Liverpool in 1981 forcibly underlined the bankruptcy of attempting to meet urban decay and deprivation by uncoordinated policies initiated by different central government departments and inadequate local authority resources. Yet the government response of setting up the Merseyside Task Force did little to solve this fundamental problem. Industrial support remained the prime prerogative of the Department of Industry, for example, despite loan support from the Department of the Environment's Urban Programme. The political confrontation in 1984–5 between an ever-more strident local authority in Liverpool and centrally imposed spending constraints only aggravated central–local government relationships, rather than fostering an aura of partnership. As yet, it seems, the state has not found an administrative consensus capable of responding effectively to the North West's worst area of economic decline and social deprivation.

Attempts to encourage private-sector involvement in economic regeneration have also been unfruitful, except with or through public support measures. The much-vaunted privatization of some problem council housing estates in Knowsley, for example, was only possible with substantial local authority support, while inner-city private housing investment has required publicly subsidized land provision. Also, while the Liverpool Garden Festival of 1984 represented a major success for public funding and the Urban Development Corporation, the announcement in early 1985 of a £7 million art gallery for Liverpool's dockland did not seem greatly relevant to the problems of Merseyside's unemployed.

On the other hand, the successful efforts of the Greater Manchester Council to tap EEC resources, and the development of local economic strategies and professional support teams in many districts in the early 1980s, suggest that there is a political will among authorities in the North West to help themselves. Such local initiatives gain little support from central government policies to rein back local spending, and to control local political independence and power bases.

Between these central–local tensions, there remains an important regional dimension. In the North West, for example, a choice in investment terms lies between concentrating resources around the central regional spine of the M6 motorway and the New Towns or, alternatively, continuing to pump resources into the (some might argue 'bottomless pit' of the) two conurbations; between facilitating current economic and demographic changes within the region, or frustrating and redirecting them to attempt the resuscitation of the urban structures of the past. The nearest attempt to confronting these issues was the Merseybelt strategy of the 1974 *Strategic Plan for the North West (Department of the Environment 1984)*, prepared jointly by central and local government. However, implementation was largely left to the County Structure Plans, which favoured development of the existing urban cores; and these longer-term strategic objectives could well be frustrated by administrative fragmentation in the conurbations after 1986.

The case for regional planning

The clear administrative implication of this analysis is a need for a thorough revision of the machinery of policy co-ordination and implementation at the regional and sub-regional level, clearly illustrated in the North West by the case for considering the Mersey valley as a whole. The effective integration of physical and economic planning which is required should ideally be based upon an extension of local authority planning powers rather than upon the introduction of a separate, regionally based, economic development organization. In summary, the inefficiences of the present diversity of approaches and responsibilities argue for much greater integration of efforts, the setting of meaningful priorities, and providing the practical means of implementation which only a locally based governmental organization with real power, finance, and responsibility could achieve.

The task of any regional planning body in the North West, however, would never be easy. For business, effective self-determination has been removed from the dominant players in the region's private sector to decision-makers based outside. In the public sector, the region's voice has never been particularly strong in modern times; it has not been seen as politically marginal and therefore important in national policy terms. Locally, also, there has been no impetus fully to develop regional political, planning, or economic organizations. Even NORWIDA (the North West Industrial Development Association) lacked sufficient regional backing to keep it alive in the 1980s, although a revamped regional promotional agency, INWARD, was revived from the ashes. The only real regional institution was the North West Economic Planning Council, a purely advisory body with scarcely a policy outcome to its name.

It is worth noting, however, that in the absence of the Economic Planning Council after 1979, the North West's county planning authorities did co-operate in the preparation of a profile report on the region, published in early 1985, intended for use in supporting cases made to central government and the EEC for a range of assistance to tackle the region's problems, and in highlighting opportunities for renewed economic growth. A County Planning Officers Housing Subgroup also produced a series of technical reports, including one in 1985 on the region-wide position regarding land availability for housing in mid-1983 (Housing North West 1985). Even this level of regional co-operation on planning matters, and in presenting a strong, unified voice on the region's needs, has been made that much more difficult with the abolition of the North West's metropolitan counties in 1986.

For the North West, the 1984 changes in regional policy represented an opportunity missed rather than one grasped. The revised regional policy does allow greater scope for the use of selective assistance, thus creating the potential for more sensitivity to regional needs; but regional aid will continue to be implemented by central government officials with central perspectives in mind. As long as centralism continues to be a dominant political trend in Britain, then all that can be hoped for in the North West is a rather more sensitive and efficient means of transmitting regional requirements to the centre by modest institutional and procedural changes, and occasional modifications of national policies to ameliorate their impacts upon the region's cities, towns, and rural areas. Such incremental and marginal adjustments, however, do not seem likely to provide a very secure foundation for the region's future growth and prosperity, which demands a more fundamental and thorough review of the region's administrative structures than so far seems possible.

References

Cheshire County Council (1978), *County Structure Plan*, Chester, County Planning Department.

Cheshire County Planning Department (1982), *County Structure Plan–First Alteration. Consultation Report*, Chester, County Planning Department.

Damesick, P. (1979), 'Office Location and Planning in the Manchester Conurbation', *Town Planning Review* 55, 346–66.

Department of the Environment (1973), *Making Towns Better: The Oldham Study. Environmental Planning and Management*, London, HMSO.

Department of the Environment (1974), *A Strategic Plan for the North West*, London, HMSO.

—— (1977), *Change or Decay: Final Report of the Liverpool Inner Area Study*, London, HMSO.

Economist Intelligence Unit (1959), *A Study of the Prospects for the Economic Development of North East Lancashire*, London, Economist Intelligence Unit.

Friedmann, J. and Weaver, C. (1979), *Territory and Function: The Evolution of Regional Planning*, London, Edward Arnold.

Housing Sub-Group (1985), *Housing Northwest Technical Report no. 5, Land availability for housing: Situation at mid-1983*, Manchester, North West County Planning Officers Group.

Law, C. M. (1985), 'The Spatial Distribution of Offices in Metropolitan Areas: A Comparison of Birmingham, Glasgow and Manchester', *Manchester Geographer*, New Series, 6, 33–41.

——, Grundy, T., and Senior, M. L. (1984), *The Greater Manchester Area*, Comparative Study of Conurbations Project, Working Paper no. 1, University of Salford, Department of Geography.

Lloyd, P. E. (1979). 'The Components of Industrial Change for Merseyside Inner Area: 1966–75', *Urban Studies* 16, 45–60.

—— and Shutt, J. (1983), *Recession and Restructuring in the North West Region: The Policy Implications of Recent Events*, North West Industry Research Unit, Working Paper Series no. 13, University of Manchester, Department of Geography.

Merseyside County Council (1984), *Merseyside County Employment Prospects to 1990/91*, Liverpool, Merseyside County Council, Department of Development and Planning.

North West County Planning Officers (1985), *The North West. Profile of an English Region*, Manchester, North West County Planning Officers Report, Greater Manchester Council Planning Department.

Parr, J. B. (1979), 'Spatial Structure as a Factor in Economic Adjustment and Regional Policy', in D. Maclennan and J. B. Parr, eds., *Regional Policy. Past Experience and Future Directions*, Oxford, Robertson.

Robson, B. T. (1980), 'The County Housing Market', in H. P. White, ed., *The Continuing Conurbation. Change and Development in Greater Manchester*, Farnborough, Gower.

—— (1985), *Where is the North? An Essay on the North/South Divide*, Manchester, City of Manchester Public Relations Office (published on behalf of the North of England Regional Consortium).

Robson, B. T. and Bradford, M. G. (1984), *Urban Change in Greater Manchester–Demographic and Household Change 1971—81*, University of Manchester, Department of Geography.

Rodgers, H. B. (1972), 'The North West and North Wales', in G. Manners, D. Keeble, B. Rodgers, and K. Warren, *Regional Development in Britain*, London, Wiley.

Roger Tym and Partners (1981), *Capital of the North: The Business Service Sector in Inner Manchester/Salford*, Report to the Inner Manchester/Salford Partnership, London, Roger Tym and Partners.

Secretary of State for Economic Affairs (1969), *The Intermediate Areas. Report of a Committee of Inquiry under the Chairmanship of Sir Joseph Hunt*, Cmnd. 3998, London, HMSO.

Shutt, J. and Whittington, R. (1984), *Large Firm Strategies and the Rise of Small Units: The Illusion of Small Firm Job Generation*, North West Industry Research Unit, Working Paper Series no. 15, University of Manchester, Department of Geography.

Spence, N., Gillespie, A., Goddard, J., Kennett, S., Pinch, S., and Williams, A. (1982), *British Cities: An Analysis of Urban Change*, Oxford, Pergamon.

Weaver, C. (1984), *Regional Development and the Local Community: Planning, Politics and Social Context*, Chichester, Wiley.

CHAPTER 7
Yorkshire and Humberside

P. Foley and D. H. Green

The Yorkshire and Humberside region, covering 6.3 per cent of the United Kingdom (15,422 km^2) and with a population of 4,854,000 (8.7 per cent of the UK total), consists of the Metropolitan Counties of South Yorkshire and West Yorkshire, Humberside, and the more rural county of North Yorkshire (see Figure 7.1). The region possesses a long and illustrious industrial tradition. Wool textiles are synonymous with West Yorkshire, coal and steel with South Yorkshire, and fishing with the Humberside ports. The success of these industries led many commentators to regard Yorkshire and Humberside as a prime example of a basic industrial region. In 1983 it produced 32 per cent of the nation's steel, 29 per cent of its coal, and over 70 per cent of its textiles. These industries also dominate particular areas of the region; for example, 80 per cent of the male workforce in some mining villages are employed at the local pit. Other industries which might have diversified the employment base in these areas in the past did not establish themselves. High wage rates offered by some successful basic industries have to be seen as one cause of this. The subsequent decline in the fortunes of these basic industries has thus had a profound effect in some parts of the region.

Economic growth and decline have followed a very uneven pattern throughout Yorkshire and Humberside. At the same time, little has been done at a regional level, to reduce the localized effects of decline by attempting to divert growth from healthier parts of the region. This is primarily because regional planning has never been vigorously undertaken within Yorkshire and Humberside which, unlike some other English regions, has not been distinguished by its regional strategic thinking. Because there has been no strategic framework for change, planned development within the region has largely been dependent upon the policies and attitudes of the Yorkshire and Humberside local authorities. These authorities have all followed very localized concerns, promoting their own best interests rather than the collective interests of the region. This chapter outlines the recent economic fortunes of the region against this background of uncertain strategic thinking.

Recent economic change

Yorkshire and Humberside has traditionally been an average region when compared with the rest of the United Kingdom. The recent recession nevertheless affected Yorkshire and Humberside more than many other regions, primar-

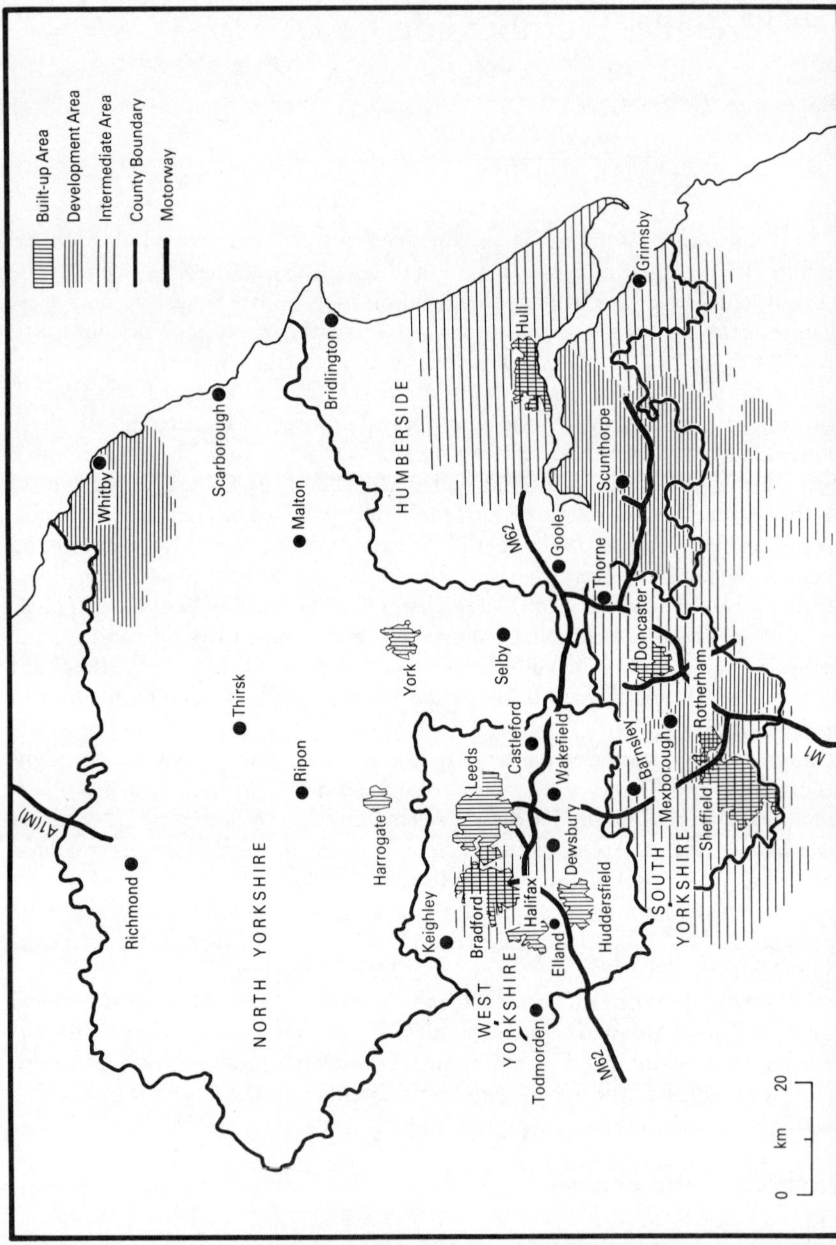

Figure 7.1. Yorkshire and Humberside

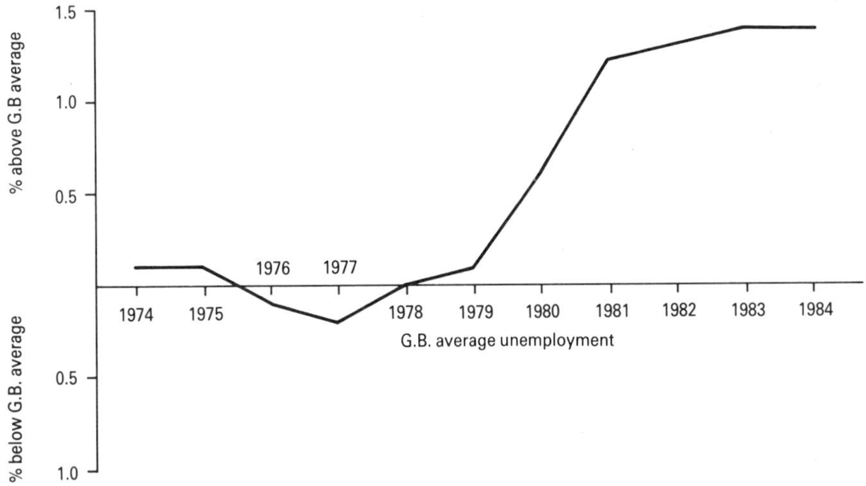

Figure 7.2. Yorkshire and Humberside: unemployment in relation to Great Britain, 1974–84
Source: *Employment Gazette*.

ily because of its over-reliance on basic industries. Until 1979 the region's unemployment rate closely followed the national figure. After that date, unemployment in the region rose above the national rate. This difference increased until 1984, when a very slight fall occurred (see Figure 7.2). Regional per capita GDP figures also reveal the region's recent relative decline. Until 1978 the regional per capita GDP was about 95 per cent of the UK average. This figure slowly declined to 92 per cent in 1982. By then, only Northern Ireland, Wales, and the West Midlands had a lower per capita GDP than Yorkshire and Humberside.

The region is now amongst the poorest 25 per cent of European Community regions. The European Commission's index of regional problems, compiled from GDP and unemployment figures, ranked the combined Yorkshire and Humberside areas twelfth out of the thirty-four UK groupings, with an index of 82.5 (EEC average 100). But even from this analysis disparities within the region were evident. Humberside had an index of 74.0, South Yorkshire 78.9, and West Yorkshire 80.3, while North Yorkshire was the most prosperous with an index of 97, placing it seventh in the UK (West Yorkshire Metropolitan County Council 1984).

It can be seen from Figure 7.3 that the diversity of unemployment within the region is considerable. North Yorkshire, traditionally a prosperous agricultural region, has enjoyed considerable indigenous industrial growth, and has proved attractive for industries relocating factories from nearby urban centres. Growth in the tourist industry has further increased the area's prosperity. Harrogate is one of the country's fastest-growing conference venues and, with its surrounding areas, is a rapidly growing commuter settlement for people working in the

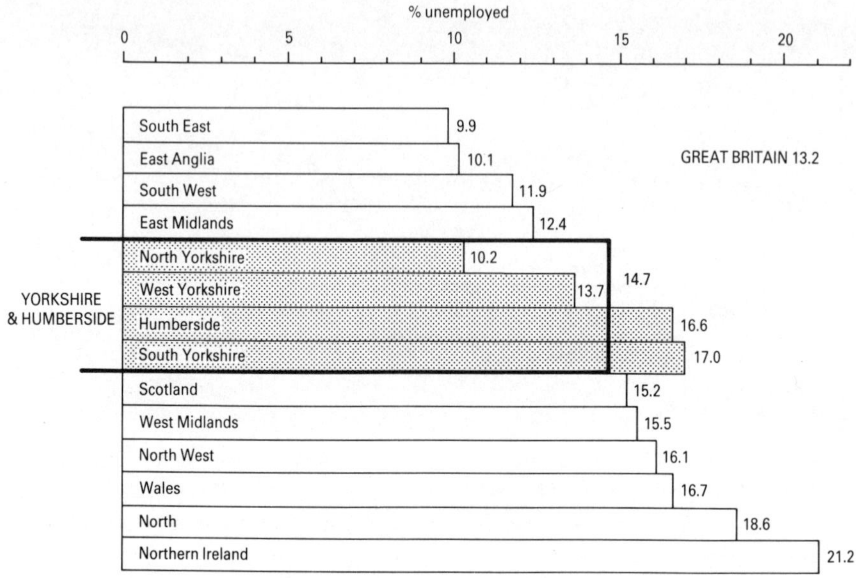

Figure 7.3. Yorkshire and Humberside: subregional unemployment, 1984
Source: *Employment Gazette*.

West Yorkshire conurbation. Consequently, North Yorkshire has become one of the UK's more prosperous areas. With unemployment at only 10.2 per cent in November 1984, it compares favourably with the UK's two leading regions of the South East and East Anglia (9.9 and 10.1 per cent unemployed respectively). However, even within North Yorkshire there is considerable diversity. The county has four areas with unemployment of less than 8 per cent (Malton, Pickering and Helmsley, Ripon, and Settle). It also contains Yorkshire and Humberside's area of highest unemployment, Whitby, on the Yorkshire coast, with 21.7 per cent unemployment, which was one of only three areas of the UK to be upgraded to Development Area status in the revised regional industrial policy of November 1984. These figures illustrate the need to look at local as well as regional or county patterns of unemployment and industrial decline when determining priorities within the region.

The remaining three county areas of Yorkshire and Humberside shown in Figure 7.3 have unemployment rates above the national average. In West Yorkshire this has generally been only just above the national average, but South Yorkshire and Humberside have unemployment 3 or 4 per cent above the national figure. Fothergill and Gudgin (1982), in their shift-share analysis of regional employment change in the UK between 1952 and 1979, found that in Yorkshire and Humberside 'poor industrial structure has been an important cause of decline'. The region's over-reliance on declining industries (poor industrial mix) accounted for a 13.2 per cent decline in employment relative to

Table 7.1. A comparison of UK and Yorkshire and Humberside industrial structure, 1971 and 1981

Industrial sector	Yorkshire and Humberside (% employment)		United Kingdom (% employment)	
	1971	1981	1971	1981
Primary	6.5	6.0	3.4	3.3
Manufacturing	40.5	31.1	38.2	28.6
Construction	5.5	5.4	5.7	5.3
Services	47.5	57.5	52.7	62.8
	100.0	100.0	100.0	100.0

Source: MSC unpublished data and *Economic Trends* (HMSO).

the UK as a whole. Only Northern Ireland had a greater employment loss due to an adverse industrial structure.

Overall decline in Yorkshire and Humberside has been accompanied by changes in the relative importance of different industries within the region's labour market. The region has above UK average employment in primary and manufacturing industries and below average employment in service industries (see Table 7.1). Between 1971 and 1981, changes in the Yorkshire and Humberside and UK figures were very similar. Both underwent a transition from the manufacturing to service sector, with the former sector declining by about 9.5 per cent and the latter gaining by approximately 10 per cent. The region's greater-than-average reliance on the manufacturing sector is one reason why it has suffered more than many others during the recent recession.

Between 1971 and 1981 manufacturing employment in Yorkshire and Humberside decreased by 208,000. This represented a loss of over a quarter of all manufacturing jobs in the region (see Table 7.2). Job loss also occurred in the primary industries (16,400 jobs, a loss of 13 per cent) and construction (6,200 jobs, a loss of 6 per cent). These losses were only partially offset by a 15 per cent rise in service-sector employment (138,400 jobs). The result of these changes was an overall decline of 92,200 (5 per cent) in the size of the employed workforce in Yorkshire and Humberside between 1971 and 1981.

Change has also taken place in the relative proportion of men and women employed in the region. All areas, with the exception of North Yorkshire, have undergone a decline in male employment and an increase in female employment (see Table 7.2). Between 1971 and 1981 women increased their relative share of the Yorkshire and Humberside workforce from 37 to 42 per cent. In all cases, except North Yorkshire, the rise in female employment has not been sufficient to offset male employment decline. North Yorkshire is an exception in both cases because both male and total employment have risen. Labour market

Table 7.2. Employment change in Yorkshire and Humberside industrial sectors, 1971–81 (all figures in thousands)

Administrative county	Primary		Manufacturing		Construction		Services		Total 1971	Total 1981	Change 1971–81
	1971	1981	1971	1981	1971	1981	1971	1981			
Humberside											
male	15.0	8.7	85.5	64.6	20.9	16.0	86.6	82.7	208.0	172.0	−36.0 (−17%)
female	2.7	2.5	29.6	24.8	1.0	1.6	73.7	90.0	107.0	118.9	+11.9 (+11%)
total	17.7	11.1	115.1	89.4	21.8	17.6	160.3	172.9	314.9	291.0	−23.9 (−8%)
North Yorkshire											
male	11.1	11.9	35.5	38.0	13.7	14.6	63.5	65.7	123.8	130.2	+6.4 (+9%)
female	2.5	2.9	15.1	12.3	0.8	1.5	60.8	81.2	79.2	97.9	+18.7 (+21%)
total	13.6	14.9	50.6	50.3	14.5	16.1	124.3	146.9	203.0	228.2	+25.2 (+12%)
South Yorkshire											
male	59.0	52.5	163.7	115.6	27.3	23.0	103.8	112.5	353.8	303.6	−50.2 (−14%)
female	3.0	3.2	60.1	43.0	1.5	2.3	119.8	151.9	184.4	200.4	+16.0 (+9%)
total	62.0	55.6	223.7	158.6	28.8	25.3	223.6	264.4	538.1	503.9	−34.2 (−6%)
West Yorkshire											
male	30.0	25.2	255.0	184.5	36.3	34.9	205.1	216.9	526.4	461.5	−64.9 (−12%)
female	1.8	1.9	130.9	84.5	2.9	4.2	197.0	247.7	332.6	338.3	+5.7 (+2%)
total	31.8	271.0	385.9	269.0	39.2	39.1	402.2	464.6	859.1	799.8	−59.3 (−7%)
Yorkshire and Humberside totals											
male	115.1	98.3	539.7	402.7	98.2	88.5	459.0	477.8	1,212.0	1,067.3	−144.7 (−12%)
female	10.0	10.5	235.7	164.6	6.2	9.6	451.3	570.8	703.2	755.5	+52.3 (+7%)
total	125.1	108.7	775.3	567.3	104.3	98.1	910.4	1,048.8	1,915.1	1,822.9	−92.2 (−5%)
Change in Yorkshire and Humberside 1971–81	−16.4 (−13%)		−208.0 (−27%)		−6.2 (−6%)		+138.4 (+15%)		−92.2 (−5%)		

Source: MSC unpublished data.

Note: Owing to rounding, totals may not agree.

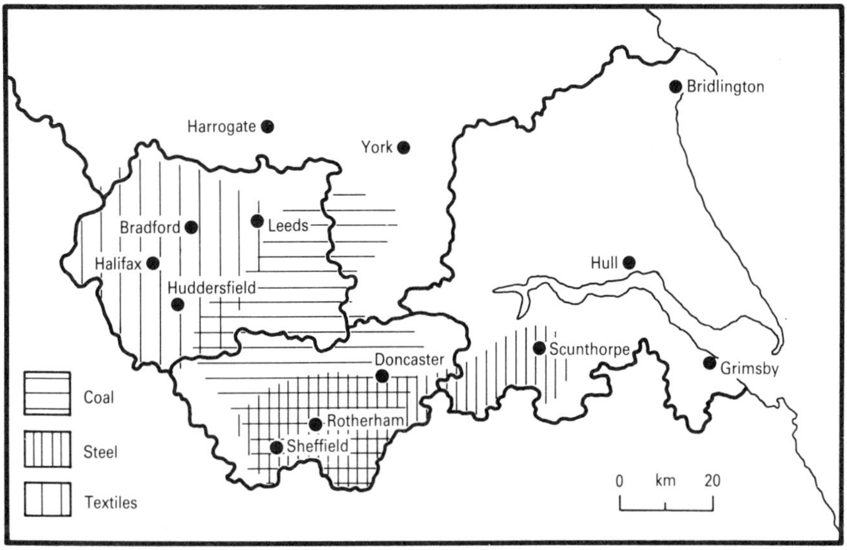

Figure 7.4. Yorkshire and Humberside: location of basic industries

changes have been characterized by a decline in the male-dominated manufacturing industries and growth, predominately female-oriented, in service industries. These changes have stimulated major alterations in the domestic roles of family members, creating new conflicts and stresses as traditional roles have been reversed.

An examination of three of the regions' traditional industries will help to quantify and explain some of the causes of job losses. The three industries chosen are textiles and clothing, metal manufacture, and the coal industry (see Figure 7.4). Fishing in the Humberside ports, the fourth traditional industry associated with the region, has also lost a large proportion of its workforce (63 per cent between 1971 and 1981), but its relatively small size (the industry in Humberside only employed 5,700 people in 1971) and its geographical concentration around the Hull area have not caused the effects of its decline to be felt as widely as the loss of over 120,000 jobs, between 1971 and 1981, from the other three traditional industries. This is not, of course, to diminish the particularly acute local problems caused by the decline of the fishing industry, but reflects the relatively greater importance in Humberside and elsewhere in the region of job loss from the other three industries.

Textiles and clothing

Despite all the problems the textile and clothing industries have suffered, the West Yorkshire conurbation still remains extraordinarily dependent upon this sector for employment. The region's wool textile industry is located mainly in Bradford, Calderdale, and Kirklees, in the west of the county (see Figure 7.4).

The clothing industry is mainly located in Leeds, to the east of the county, although there are also some clothing firms in a number of other towns and cities such as Barnsley, Hull, and Thirsk.

In 1965 over 20 per cent of West Yorkshire workers were employed in these industries. In some areas the figure was even higher, e.g. 54 per cent in Elland and 35 per cent in Keighley (Warren 1980). During the 1960s and 1970s, Yorkshire's wool textile industry was seriously affected by foreign competition. The industry was incapable of competing with cheaper imports, primarily from the developing world. Many of the difficulties stemmed from the use of obsolete machinery. For instance, in 1969 over 60 per cent of the looms used for worsted weaving had been installed before 1939. The major route for regaining competitive efficiency and economic survival was by lowering costs, through the replacement of obsolete machinery and increased mechanization. The 'Scheme for Textiles' introduced under the 1972 Industry Act assisted the modernization of the industry. It is estimated that, between 1973 and 1978, 60 per cent of the industry's assets were modernized at a cost of about £86 million (19 per cent government-funded). This had the desired effect of changing the industry from a low-productivity, craft-based, labour-intensive sector into a more capital-intensive industry making use of new technology (Department of Industry 1978). Despite losing 42,700 workers, 30 per cent of the workforce, between 1975 and 1981, the industry still provides jobs for 75,400, nearly 10 per cent of West Yorkshire employees. The industry is still under pressure, with increased imports from the United States and Europe now causing greater damage to the industry than those from less developed countries. Job losses from the industry continue.

Metal manufacture

The metal-manufacturing industry in Yorkshire and Humberside is centred on the steel-producing plants of Sheffield and Rotherham in South Yorkshire and Scunthorpe in Humberside (see Figure 7.4). The region's steel industry is impressively diverse. As well as common carbon grades of steel, a whole range of more specialized products, including the finest alloy steels, are also manufactured in the region. In Sheffield and Rotherham a high proportion of plants produce specialized steels, such as stainless steel, high speed and tool steel, and alloy steels. Within the industry there has been no lack of investment in new techniques of production. But much of the investment has been at the melting and forging (the primary or initial) stage of production. This investment stragegy has been criticized, particularly in Sheffield and Rotherham, because the expertise of these areas lies mainly in the steel-finishing end of the production process (City of Sheffield Department of Employment 1984). The crisis in the steel industry and decline in demand has meant that much of the investment in primary processes has never been used, or has been used only for short periods.

In July 1980 Ian McGregor was appointed Chairman of the British Steel Corporation (BSC) to try to reverse the £1,619 million in losses which had been accumulated by BSC since nationalization in 1967. His appointment coincided with the deepening of the recession and a consequent decline in demand for steel, with a 6 per cent fall in world consumption, and a 28 per cent fall in consumption in the UK. A number of other factors also contributed to BSC's problems. The Government's withdrawal of state financial contributions, in line with the EEC's ruling on subsidies, and increased competition from cheap foreign steel both had a detrimental effect on the industry. Between 1980 and 1983 BSC reduced steel-making capacity in the UK and made over 100,000 workers redundant. Combined with earlier job losses caused by the substitution of new technology for labour, this had a devastating affect on the metal-manufacturing industry. In 1975 there were about 94,000 employed in metal manufacturing in the region, but by 1981 this figure had fallen to 59,600, a decline of 37 per cent in seven years.

Detailed information on the proportion of employees working for BSC and the private sector are not available for the whole region, but a recent study (City of Sheffield Department of Employment 1984) gives an indication of the probable distribution. In 1979 BSC controlled 54 per cent of steel industry employment in Rotherham and Sheffield. Since that date redundancies from BSC and the private sector have occurred on a broadly similar scale. Recent estimates suggest that employment declined by 12,400 between 1979 and 1985, with only 26,000 people now employed in the industry in Sheffield and Rotherham.

The coal industry

The importance of the coal industry for Yorkshire and Humberside, and the future of the industry in the UK, was brought dramatically to the attention of the country by the miners' strike which lasted for a year between March 1984 and March 1985. The region's coalfield, in South Yorkshire, West Yorkshire, and the Selby area of North Yorkshire (see Figure 7.4), produces over a quarter of national coal output (National Coal Board 1984). A large market for coal exists locally; the steel industry has coke-fired ovens and Central Electricity Generating Board power stations consumed over 18 million tonnes of locally mined NCB coal in 1983–4 (Central Electricity Generating Board). The region's power stations meet 20 per cent (43 billion units) of the demand for electricity in England and Wales.

The Yorkshire and Humberside coal industry currently employs 78,000 people (Yorkshire and Humberside County Councils Association 1983), but its future, despite the efforts of the miners' strike, is still unclear. Cheaper foreign sources of coal, new technology , and new finds in other areas of the country, particularly in the Vale of Belvoir, all contribute to make the future of the Yorkshire and Humberside coal industry a very complex and uncertain issue (Manners 1981).

According to the National Union of Mineworkers, the closure of Yorkshire and Humberside's NCB pits which were not making a profit would mean the loss of 32,700 jobs, two-thirds in the Barnsley and Doncaster areas (National

Union of Mineworkers 1984). However, the industry's future has been in doubt before. National Coal Board estimates made in 1967 envisaged a steady reduction in employees to only 18,500 by 1980 (Warren 1980). This forecast, based on an increasingly competitive energy market in the UK in the late 1970s, was considerably revised in the NCB's 1974 *Plan for Coal* report (National Coal Board 1974). Yorkshire and Humberside benefited considerably from the investment scheme outlined in the 1974 report. Of five major new mining investment projects, four were in Yorkshire, at Selby, Thorne, Royston, and Kinsley. The Selby coalfield is the largest current investment project in Britain, and when fully operational it should produce 10 per cent of the nation's deep-mined coal. Despite this and other investments in the region's coal industry, job losses still occurred, although far smaller than the losses in metals and textiles. Between 1975 and 1982, 8,000 jobs were lost, a decline of 9 per cent in the workforce. The future of the industry is unclear; but, as Fothergill, Gudgin and Mason (1984) point out, the Government's long-term programme for the construction of ten major nuclear power stations could greatly reduce the importance of coal in electricity generation. Fothergill and Gudgin estimated that a nuclear power station created 600 jobs whilst a coal-powered station created over 10,000 jobs, the majority of them in mining and associated works. When the results of the Sizewell 'B' inquiry are announced there will be a clearer understanding of how Britain's future electricity requirements will be met. If the nuclear power option is accepted, the future of many Yorkshire pits could be in doubt.

Secondary problems associated with job losses

Yorkshire and Humberside's textile, metal-manufacturing, and coal industries lost 91,200 jobs in the six-year period between 1975 and 1981, equivalent to 60 per cent of the increase in unemployment which took place in this period (151,700). The decline of these three basic industries had very significant effects on the regional economy, often going far beyond the direct loss of jobs. An examination of the secondary effects of decline in the region's basic industries will illustrate some of the additional problems associated with plant closure and redundancies.

Decline in the textile industry has not only created redundancies amongst employees, but has also led to many old industrial buildings becoming redundant. As well as representing a particular architectural tradition and local heritage, because of their location, they (or their sites) often represent the only area available locally for employment growth (Green and Foley 1982*a*). When a textile plant closes in West Yorkshire, local authorities are often faced with the twin problems of trying to find employment for a redundant workforce and new uses for redundant buildings (Green and Foley 1983).

In 1983 West Yorkshire County Council, in association with Greater Manchester Council, commissioned a study of redundant mill premises. The resulting report (Tym and Partners 1984) revealed a total of nearly 10 million square feet of floor-space available in West Yorkshire in complexes larger than 15,000 square feet. This represents about 4 per cent of industrial floor-space in the county. Of this total, 61 per cent was multi-storey accommodation, predominantly in textile mills built before 1950. The Roger Tym report advocated the demolition of between 2 and 4 million square feet of this type of industrial floor-space in West Yorkshire. This recommendation has been criticized by some commentators (*Planning* 1984) for failing to see the value of rehabilitation for many mills. Green and Foley (1982*b*; 1983) found that conversion of mills could often be completed far more cheaply than the cost of building new units (£2.17 per sq ft against £20 or more for new units). Consequently, it was often possible for developers to charge relatively low rents in converted premises and still gain higher rates of return than they would have achieved by the construction of new premises. Such low rents were often responsible for enticing new small companies to start up in business. More than half the companies interviewed in the Green and Foley (1982*b*) study were new business start-ups. Conversion can thus return a redundant building to productive use, and can help to create jobs in the local economy. Although such action is not possible with all older premises, it is an option which is increasingly being promoted by many West Yorkshire authorities.

The problems of finding new uses for redundant industrial buildings are not confined to textile closure areas. Decline in the South Yorkshire and Humberside steel industry has also left a legacy of old buildings, but these are much more difficult to re-use. Steel and other metal production premises are tall (40 to 60 feet high), single-storey buildings designed to disperse the heat generated during the melting and forging process. Their size and poor heat retention make them largely unusable for other purposes. Vast areas of previously productive steelworks have therefore been demolished in the old steel-producing heartland between Sheffield and Rotherham.

Sheffield City Council (City of Sheffield Department of Employment 1984), in a study of redundancies in South Yorkshire, attempted to quantify the effect of job loss in the steel industry on other sectors of the economy. The report estimated the impact of the difference between an average worker's take-home pay and unemployment benefit on local spending power in the county. The average difference in income per job lost was £50 per week or £2,600 per annum. Thus, for every 1,000 redundancies from the steel industry, £2.6 million less would be available to be spent locally. Some of the 37,000 workers made redundant from the industry between 1975 and 1982 will have been able to find new employment. The loss of income for those who could not find a job, or who might otherwise have entered the industry but have remained unemployed, will nevertheless have a considerable effect on the local economy. This loss of purchasing power, combined with a fall in orders to industrial suppliers resulting from closures or contraction, helps to explain an EEC estimate that for every steel job lost, two additional jobs are lost in non-steel firms (City of Sheffield Department of Employment 1984).

One reason why the miners' strike lasted so long is that mining communities are traditionally single-industry towns. In some mining towns and villages, up to 80 per cent of the male workforce is employed at the local colliery; closure can thus have a devastating effect. The effects of pit closure in mining villages has long been realized. The Hunt Committee, in 1969, reviewing the possibility of regional assistance to the Yorkshire coalfield area, 'found no other problem which was comparable in scale, given the size and speed of the rundown and the key position of the industry in the area'. At that time out-migration, or commuting to jobs in larger nearby urban centres, was possible. Nowadays such opportunities elsewhere are limited.

The possibilities of attracting new industries to pit villages are not enhanced by the drabness of many mining settlements, and the unsightliness of a landscape often dominated by huge pits and waste-heaps. Considerable additions to the area of waste-land can accrue as a result of mine closures. Derelict pit-gear, railway sidings, and general waste can be a major problem and produce an unattractive environment for incoming investors (Green 1977). In a migration study in 1969, the main reason given for moving from the coalfield area was the poor environment (Yorkshire and Humberside Economic Planning Council 1970). Since that date efforts have been made to improve the situation, but as fast as some areas are reclaimed more colliery waste is produced. In 1979 colliery waste production was running at about 20 million tonnes per annum. Since about 90 per cent of colliery waste is deposited close to the pithead, it is the local environments of the pit villages that suffer most. Consequently, when pits close, workers are left not only jobless but also, often, with a much poorer environment.

In 1974 Yorkshire and Humberside had 4,069 hectares of land despoiled by the coal industry (Commission on Energy and the Environment 1981). This was 46 per cent of all colliery waste land in the UK. In the same report the Flowers Commission singled out the Yorkshire coalfield as an area where Government should provide additional funds for the clearance of coal dereliction. Although the NCB is now creating better landforms, by progressive restoration and landscaping as tipping takes place, the recent reduction of the Derelict Land Grant to the region will do little to improve existing derelict land. The grant was reduced from £9 million in 1980–1 to £4 million in 1982–3, at a time when grants to all other regions (except the Northern region) were generally being increased (Yorkshire and Humbershire County Councils Association 1983).

Plant closures and redundancies will not always have these severe long term effects, if employees can find new jobs and buildings are returned to new uses. In Yorkshire and Humberside, however, in areas where the basic industries of metal manufacture, coal, and textiles predominate, there are few alternative job opportunities, and new users for redundant buildings are scarce.

The framework for change

The declining fortunes of Yorkshire and Humberside might have been expected to produce a more co-ordinated response to the increasing problems of unemployment and economic decline within the region. At present, specific problems are being tackled by individual district councils with, in a few cases, coordination and financial assistance from their respective county councils. There are several groupings of authorities within the region dealing with specific issues, such as the Yorkshire Textile Areas Group (YORTAG), concentrating on problems of the textile industry, the Yorkshire and Humberside Development Agency, whose remit is principally promotional, and the Conference of Chief Planning Officers. But a more developed approach to regional planning is needed to deal with the problems of spatial and sectoral differentiation within the region. The abolition of the Metropolitan Counties, the replacement of structure plans with Unitary Development Plans, and the failure of previous attempts to co-ordinate strategic planning in the region do little to raise hopes that an appropriate strategic framework will be forthcoming.

In Yorkshire and Humberside, as in other regions in the country, a Regional Economic Planning Council and Board were established in the mid-1960s. The Council produced several reports in its formative years. *The Review of Yorkshire and Humberside* (Yorkshire and Humberside Economic Planning Council 1966) was not a plan but an information and problem-analysis document. Area reports of a similar informative but non-planning nature followed: Halifax and Calder Valley (YHEPC 1968), Doncaster (1969*a*) and Huddersfield and Colne Valley (1969*b*). These studies culminated in the Yorkshire and Humberside Regional Strategy produced in 1970. The document presented a very superficial approach to regional planning and policy development. Broad policy objectives were introduced without any consideration being given to their implementation. Subsequent reports by the Economic Planning Council and Board continued in the same vein. Even the *Strategic Review 1975* (YHEPC 1976) failed to provide a much-needed framework to co-ordinate economic regeneration within the region. It failed to take advantage of the major changes, both economic and political, which had given new vitality and optimism to those involved with planning in the region, between the original strategy and the review. These changes were of great significance to the region and included the designation of Intermediate Area status in the Yorkshire coalfield and North Humberside in 1969, which was subsequently extended to the whole region in 1972; the introduction of regional development grants for new industrial building, and selective financial assistance under the 1972 Industry Act; the wool textile scheme started in 1973; and the transfer of part of the Northern Development Area to the region in 1974. The reorganization of local government which took place in 1974 resulted in the formation of the Metropolitan Counties of West and South Yorkshire, and the shire counties of Humberside and North Yorkshire. Other political changes included the creation of a regional Water Authority, Regional Health Authorities, and the county-based Passenger Transport Executives.

The 1975 *Strategy Review* expressed policy at a level of generality and flexibility which could not influence the development of structure plan policies. It did not present a coherent case for more investment and aid from central government. An explanation of this failing lies in part in the essentially 'average' nature of the region. At a subregional level, problems clearly existed (see for example Kingston upon Hull City Council 1970), but their significance was less evident from the regional perspective. The problems of presenting a coherent case for regional strategy were accentuated by the political and administrative structure of the region and the associated power bases. Before 1974, political and administrative power was based on the three Ridings, East, North, and West, and the county boroughs. Of these, the West Riding and the county Boroughs saw themselves as dominating thinking and planning in the region. In 1966, the West Riding County Planning Department in fact produced a document, *A Growth Policy for the North*, which could easily be mistaken for a regional strategy. The traditional political power base was very strong; authorities were proud and independent. After 1974 this position was repeated in the contrasts between the two Metropolitan Counties (West and South Yorkshire) and the shire counties (North Yorkshire and Humberside). The development of regional strategic thinking remained very difficult. The strategic framework was dominated by the two Metropolitan Counties, whose abolition in 1986 has thrown this framework into disarray yet again.

The precise impact of abolition of the Metropolitan Counties on the region is uncertain. While the Counties have campaigned enthusiastically to demonstrate their value to the region, there has been no detailed study of their effectiveness. The impact of specific policy initiatives in economic development, for example, is easily demonstrated, but at the wider strategic level, assessment is less tangible and clear-cut. There are, however, several areas in which the loss of the Counties will be significant.

Firstly, the Metropolitan Counties had taken on a role which is strategic in a wider sense than that implicit in their statutory role of preparing Structure Plans. With the weak position of regional planning in the region, both West Yorkshire and South Yorkshire County Councils had taken the regional initiative. With their demise this initiative will wither, unless a new, regionally based authority appears. The regional office of the Department of the Environment is not equipped, either politically or in terms of manpower, to deal with this problem. Secondly, in their approach to structure planning both authorities had been remarkably successful in presenting a county identity, and in linking together disparate views and approaches at the conurbation level. Ten years is a very short time in which to forge together the antagonisms and rivalries of the individual towns and cities within these conurbations. Nevertheless, there are indications that their strategies have been successful. This is reflected in activities as diverse as waste disposal, highways, direct industrial investment, and passenger transport. Most particularly, the counties had begun to succeed in the strategic approach to the co-ordination of policies to deal with industrial change. It is arguable that it is at this less tangible level that the major loss of the Metropolitan Councils will be felt, with a return to the more parochial power base of pre-1974 days. Thirdly, as Dumsday (1983: 331) has argued, 'It is fair to say that in West Yorkshire the County Planners have been the bulwark of the declining communities of the West.' Districts, such as Calderdale, with a poor rate base must view the removal of West Yorkshire County's resource-equalization capability with some trepidation. The more prosperous areas such as Leeds are unlikely to take a very philanthropic view of the plight of their less well-resourced neighbours.

The Unitary Development Plans which will replace the Structure Plan in the Metropolitan Counties will do little to overcome these problems. Whilst the Secretary of State for the Environment will issue regional strategic guidance to provide a wide view of planning against which each metropolitan interest can draw up its plan, the recognition and solution of problems will be transposed to a smaller rather than a larger scale. The larger-scale assessment will be technical, rather than (as at present) based on the attempt to gain political agreement.

The current framework for industrial change

The dramatic change in fortunes of the region, and the lack of a regional approach to employment and economic issues, has led most authorities in the region to develop their own strategies for economic regeneration. The approaches vary significantly between authorities, from the opportunistic in Wakefield, through the minimal interference of Calderdale, to the powerfully ideological of Sheffield. All are inevitably based on local self-interest; few consider the wider regional implications of their actions. In terms of size, the approaches of Sheffield and Leeds are most significant. Both authorities have been reorganized to form an Employment Department, which in Leeds has been combined with the Estates Department. Both departments were established with a strong commitment to the local authority's role in the local economy, and place particular emphasis on the training needs of minority groups. The Sheffield department has a workforce of over sixty, whilst the Leeds department is organized on an area team basis and employs over one hundred.

Most of the authorities in the region offer financial assistance in the form of loans and grants for a variety of purposes, including employment subsidy, refurbishment, and small-firm start-ups. Only West Yorkshire saw fit to establish an Enterprise Board. The Board was set up to fill a gap in the funding market in the region. Its objective is primarily economic, carrying out an investment policy to preserve, protect, and promote jobs. Although funded by the local authority, the Board is an independent company, and is consequently protected from the abolition of the County Council. The Board sees its role as maximizing the availability of external finance for projects it believes are viable and beneficial. It acts as a broker rather than as a bank. After initial scepticism from within the region, the Enterprise Board has gained the confidence of industry and local authorities. In November 1984, the Board negotiated £10 million funding from the Bank of Nova Scotia, which will protect it from the 'withering away' which central government sees as the future of all Boards once the Metropolitan Counties are abolished.

As in many regions in the UK, the growth in local employment initiatives in the public, private, and voluntary sectors has been dramatic. With this, there has followed the inevitable inter- and intraregional competition for jobs, both externally and indigenously generated. An analysis of this type of competition in Humberside (Ritchie *et al.* 1984) showed that there were no less than 180 agencies offering advice and assistance to small businesses. A similar pattern is repeated in the case of employment-creating incentives offered by local authorities. This is an area in which the regional perspective has failed to produce an overall strategy, and has again allowed a free-for-all in employment creation, leading to a massive duplication of services and personnel as well as competition between areas. Even the Metropolitan Counties have been unable to resolve this problem in pursuance of their Structure Plan employment policies.

The problem of strategic co-ordination is reflected in the way authorities within the region have responded very differently to the designation of Enterprise Zones. Four Zones have been designated within the region, at Wakefield, Rotherham, Scunthorpe, and Glanford (on the site of the former Nypro (UK) factory at Flixborough). The zones vary in size, ownership, and locational environment. Sheffield and Bradford, amongst others, decided not to apply for Enterprise Zones, fearing the effect on the local economy of short-distance moves and the lowering of land values in the surrounding area observed by Syms (1984) in the case of Trafford Park in Manchester. With policy initiatives such as Enterprise Zones, a local perspective dominates the more strategic view of the county or region. Both the Rotherham and Wakefield Enterprise Zones were opportunistically developed against the wider needs of the conurbation, and inevitable conflicts have followed their attraction of companies and jobs from surrounding, equally depressed areas.

Increasing assistance to the Yorkshire and Humberside region

The decline of the Yorkshire and Humberside region has meant that it has become eligible for increasing amounts and sources of funds to assist in the economic regeneration of the region, from a previously very low level of assistance. These funds have undoubtedly helped the region, but they have also highlighted the lack of a co-ordinating framework to administer effectively their distribution within the region. In many cases individual districts or counties are competing for funds; anomalies are apparent, as in the ability of Wakefield, a relatively prosperous part of the region, to apply for Urban Development Grant money across the whole of its area, because of the designation of an Enterprise Zone in a very small part of the district. The eligibility of Leeds to apply for the European coal and steel closure funds is even more of an anomaly.

Some of the major funding schemes available within the region include:

(*a*) *Regional policy*. Whilst there was a considerable level of indignant comment over the redrawn Assisted Area map of late November 1984, the new two-tier system gave Development Area status to the Rotherham, Mexborough, Scunthorpe, and Whitby travel-to-work areas. Intermediate Area status was given to six travel-to-work areas: Barnsley, Bradford, Doncaster, Grimsby, Hull, and Sheffield. Two areas, Grimsby and Hull, were downgraded from Development Area status, whilst the four former Intermediate Areas of Bridlington, Goole, Richmond, and Scarborough were excluded.

In general, the redrawn map highlighted the problem areas within the region, particularly those of the steel-producing Don valley and Scunthorpe. Only Bradford was singled out in West Yorkshire. This clearly reflects the emphasis on unemployment levels in UK regional policy, which does not adequately recognize the importance of other indicators of economic decline. The paradox of non-quota EEC funding for the textile areas of West Yorkshire while the area is not designated for Assisted Area status clearly highlights this fact.

(b) Assistance from Europe. Yorkshire and Humberside has taken advantage of several financial instruments available from the European Community. The specific problems of parts of the region have given access to a wide variety of funds. All of South Yorkshire and the Scunthorpe, Leeds, Wakefield, and Castleford travel-to-work areas are eligible for aid under the European Coal and Steel Community treaty. The majority of West Yorkshire's travel-to-work areas and Sheffield, Scunthorpe, Grimsby, and Hull are eligible for 'non-quota' funds from the European Regional Development Fund's textile scheme. 'Non-quota' aid is used to finance, with national authorities, specific regional development programmes which help to overcome problems caused by the Community's structure, or by decisions taken in other areas of policy (Commission of the European Communities 1982). All areas can apply for finance from the European Agricultural Guidance and Guarantee Fund.

The parts of the region designated as Assisted Areas under British regional policy received European Regional Development grant aid of £75.2 million between 1975 and 1983. These grants were used in thirty-nine projects in the industrial and service sectors and 407 infrastructure projects. Of the large investments (over 10 million ECU), ten were related to the water industry and sewerage, and four grants were made to the Rotherham and South Yorkshire Navigation canal project. The majority of the small investments went to industrial projects.

The continuing level of support will be affected by the change in British regional policy Assisted Area boundaries. The region is, however, well-placed to benefit from the changes in the European Regional Development Fund's non-quota funds. In November 1982 the Commission published proposals for non-quota money to be available in Textile Areas. West Yorkshire County Council has been heavily involved in the lobbying for this particular fund, and produced its case in the STAR report (West Yorkshire Metropolitan County Council 1979), which argued for support for the country's textile industry in general and that of West Yorkshire in particular. The non-quota scheme approved in 1984 will provide funds to cover a variety of job-creating projects in the textile areas of the region. Of particular significance is the funding which will be available for the conversion and refurbishment of older textile buildings for use by small businesses. Of the £67.5 million recently made available in the UK under this scheme over a four-year period, the travel-to-work areas of Bradford, Dewsbury, Halifax, Huddersfield, Keighley, and Todmorden will receive approximately 30 per cent.

The European Coal and Steel Community Treaty has funded many projects in the region, related to investment in the industry, research and development, and particularly retraining, with £32.5 million granted for retraining steel workers in the period between 1973 and 1983. In 1982, parts of West and South Yorkshire were designated Coal Closure Areas, which gave access to low-interest loans for small businesses. Recent non-quota fund allocations have greatly benefited the region. Assisted Areas in Humberside and South Yorkshire will receive £5.6 million, approximately 25 per cent of the £22 million given to the UK.

(c) Aid for inner urban areas. Many of the region's inner urban areas, particularly the inner cities of Bradford, Hull, Leeds, and Sheffield, face serious problems of urban decay. Estimates of local unemployment rates as high as 30 and 40 per cent are not uncommon within some areas of the inner cities. The 1978 Inner Urban Areas Act gave designated authorities powers to undertake additional expenditure so that 'they may participate more effectively in the economic development of their areas' (DoE circular no. 68/78). Under the Act, Bradford, Hull, Leeds, and Sheffield are eligible for funds as Inner City Programme Districts, and Barnsley, Doncaster, and Rotherham have Designated District status. The powers under this Act have been used by many local authorities to develop Industrial Improvement Areas. In Sheffield the success of the Wellington Street Industrial Area, the first designated, has encouraged the local authority to designate four more. In the Wellington Street Area, jobs were created or saved at a cost of £1,450 per job, and every £1 the local authority spent 'levered out' £2.50 from the private sector (City of Sheffield MDC 1983).

Conclusion

The Yorkshire and Humberside region has suffered considerable economic problems in recent years. The region's industrial tradition was built on coal, steel, and textile industries. These industries, with the possible exception of coal, whose future is still in the balance, have suffered severely during the recent economic decline. They lost 91,000 jobs between 1975 and 1981, accounting for 60 per cent of the increase in unemployment which took place in the same period. As well as the basic problems of job loss, there have been other associated problems. The decline in local purchasing power has had detrimental multiplier effects within the local economy. Where job losses are related to company closure, new uses often have to be found for redundant buildings. The multi-storey nature of textile mills and the poor heat-retentive qualities of steel industry buildings makes their re-use considerably more difficult than in many other areas of the country, where lower-storey buildings predominate. Due to the geographically concentrated nature of the region's traditional industries and their dramatic decline, problems have had a very localized impact.

The region's declining fortunes have made it eligible for increasing amounts and sources of financial assistance to help alleviate the problems of decline. The localized nature of many of these problems raises questions about how effectively funds will be distributed. There is no strategic framework for planning change within the region, and there is a lack of co-ordination in allocating resources. The Metropolitan Counties had taken a leading role in trying to distribute resources in some of the worst affected parts of the region. There are indications that these county strategies were achieving their objectives. Abolition will be detrimental to many of the declining Metropolitan Districts which have a poor rate base from which to finance their own policies for regeneration. The Metropolitan Counties have helped these districts to a disproportionate degree (relative to the normal allocation of funds). The ability of these smaller districts to compete with larger neighbours such as Bradford, Leeds, and Sheffield for the various sources of aid now available must be in doubt. Their own resources will probably be stretched to the limit to produce and process applications and finance initiatives to overcome particular local problems. The region is facing an uncertain future, especially in those areas which were reliant upon the region's traditional industries of coal, steel, and textiles. This future could be even more uncertain with the abolition of the Metropolitan Counties. The lack of any alternative framework to co-ordinate economic change and area regeneration will cause increased problems in the less prosperous districts within the region.

References

British Steel Corporation (1985), *Steel Industry Statistics*, 11 January.

Central Electricity Generating Board (1985), *Yorkshire and Humberside Provides Power for the Nation* (unpublished paper).

City of Sheffield Metropolitan District Council, Department of Employment, (1984), 'Steel in Crisis', Sheffield.

City of Sheffield Metropolitan District Council, Department of Planning and Design (1983), *Wellington Street Industrial Improvement Area*, Sheffield.

Commission of the European Communities (1982), *Finance from Europe*, London, CEC.

Commission on Energy and the Environment (1981), *Coal and the Environment*, London, HMSO.

Department of the Environment (1969), *The Intermediate Areas*, Report of a Committee under the Chairmanship of Sir Joseph Hunt, Cmnd. 3998, London, HMSO.

—— (1978*a*), *Inner Urban Area Act*, London, HMSO.

—— (1978*b*) *Inner Urban Areas Act 1978*, London, HMSO Circular 68/78.

Department of Industry (1978), *Wool textile industry scheme*, London, HMSO.

Dumsday, J. (1983), 'Streamlining the Cities', *Town and Country Planning* 15(12), 330–1.

Employment Gazette (1984), November, s24–s30.

Fothergill, S. and Gudgin, G. (1982), *Unequal Growth; Urban and Regional Employment Change in the UK*, London, Heinemann.

——, ——, and Mason, N. (1984), *The Economic Consequences of Sizewell 'B' Nuclear Power Station*, Working Paper no. 5, University of Cambridge, Department of Land Economy.

Green, D. H. (1977), 'Industrialists' Information Levels of Regional Incentives', *Regional Studies* 11(1), 7–18.

—— and Foley, P. (1982*a*), 'Small Industrial Units: Is Conversion a Viable Alternative?', *Estates Gazette* 263, 574–5.

—— and —— (1982*b*), *The Conversion of Industrial Premises to Multiple Units*, Leeds, D. Howard Green Associates.

—— and —— (1983), 'Making Homes for Small Firms', *Town and Country Planning* 52 (1), 17–20.

Kingston upon Hull City Council (1970), 'Yorkshire and Humberside Regional Strategy: Comments,' Kingston upon Hull.

Manners, G. (1981), *Coal in Britain*, London, Allen and Unwin.

National Coal Board (1974), *Plan for Coal*, London.

—— (1984), *Annual Report and Accounts 1983–4*, London.

National Union of Mineworkers (1984), *The Economic Case Against Pit Closure*, Sheffield.

Planning (1984), 'Trouble at Mill', 580, 3 August, 8–9.

Regional Studies Association (1983), *Report of an Inquiry into Regional Problems in the UK*, Norwich, Geobooks.

Ritchie, D., Asch, D., and Weir, A. (1984), *The Provision of Assistance to Small and Medium Enterprises on Humberside*, Paper presented at the National Small Firms Policy and Research Conference, Trent Polytechnic, 5–7 September.

Roger Tym and Partners (1984), *Mills in the 80s*, London, Roger Tym and Partners.

Syms, P. (1984), 'Enterprise Zones—Special Report', *Chartered Surveyor Weekly*, 12 April.

Warren, K. (1980), 'Yorkshire and Humberside', in G. Manners *et al.*, *Regional Development in Britain*, London, Wiley.

West Riding County Planning Department (1966), *A Growth Policy for the North*, Wakefield.

West Yorkshire Metropolitan County Council (1979), *STAR: A Scheme for Textile Area Regeneration*, Submission for the Commission of the European Economic Community, Wakefield.

—— (1984), *Quarterly Review of Economic Development*, November, 16–34, Wakefield.

Yorkshire and Humberside County Councils Association (1983), *A New Deal for Yorkshire and Humberside*, Barnsley.

Yorkshire and Humberside Economic Planning Council (1966), *A Review of Yorkshire and Humberside*, London, HMSO.

—— (1968), *Halifax and Calder Valley; an area study*, London, HMSO.

—— (1969*a*), *Doncaster: an area study*, London, HMSO.

—— (1969*b*), *Huddersfield and Colne Valley: an area study*, London, HMSO.

—— (1970), *Yorkshire and Humberside Regional Strategy*, London, HMSO.

—— (1976), *Yorkshire and Humberside Regional Strategy Review, 1975. The Next 10 years*, London, HMSO.

CHAPTER 8
The Northern Region

R. J. Buswell, A. G. Champion, and A. R. Townsend

The Northern region enters the second half of the 1980s with its economy in extremely bad shape. Its offical level of unemployment is the highest of all the standard statistical regions in the UK except for Northern Ireland, with a further substantial 'discouraged labour force' not registering as unemployed. The number of jobs in the region has been affected considerably more seriously by the post-1979 recession than has employment in the country as a whole. Moreover, all the signs point to a very gloomy outlook for the North, because the region suffers from a number of fundamental structural problems which will prevent it from participating fully in, and from contributing to, any future upturn in the national economy. Despite fifty years of regional policies designed to bring in employment and at times to improve the region's infrastructure, diversify its industrial base, and provide the ingredients for self-sustained economic growth, the North's economy is now weaker and more dependent on external support than at any time in the past four decades. In terms of its people's economic opportunities and life chances, the absolute level of disparities between the North and the South East is wider than ever.

The assessment of the Northern region's situation which we present in this chapter cannot fail to make depressing reading. It is based on our interpretation of the region's experience over the last ten years, which has revealed that the North's problems have not been limited to those of sectoral imbalance and physical obsolescence, but are in fact rooted in more fundamental deficiencies in its industrial inheritance, business environment, and human resources. Our gloomy prognostications are based, too, on our identification of the yawning chasm that separates the current and foreseeable types and levels of policy response from what we believe to be the minimum necessary. That minimum would restrict the gap between regional and national standards to its 1970s dimensions, but it would not produce the shifts in regional balance anticipated in the Barlow Report over forty years ago or in the strategies developed in the 1960s. We deal, in turn, with the problems of industrial structure, the related weaknesses of the North's economy, and the deficiencies in policy response, before going into more detail on our verdict on the region's longer-term prospects. First of all, however, we provide an outline of the North's main features and current difficulties.

The regional context

The Northern region, comprising the five counties of Cleveland, Cumbria, Durham, Northumberland, and Tyne and Wear, has a population of 3.1 million people, making it the smallest Standard Region in Britain after East Anglia and Wales. As outlined by Smailes (1960), it is an essentially rural region in areal terms, dominated by the relatively infertile uplands of the Lake District, the North Pennines, and the Northumbria National Park (see Figure 8.1). In terms of its economic base and settlement pattern, however, it owes its distinctive characteristics very largely to the major developments which occurred during the latter half of the nineteenth century: in mining in the Northumberland/Durham and West Cumberland coalfields and the Cleveland iron-ore field, and in the iron and steel, shipbuilding, heavy engineering, and chemical industries concentrated mainly on the Tyne, Wear, and Tees estuaries, and in a small number of other locations such as Consett, Shildon, Whitehaven, and Barrow (House 1969; Warren 1973; McCord 1979). Even today, despite the more rapid growth of some of the smaller towns and rural areas in recent years, over half of the North's population (56 per cent) is concentrated in Cleveland and Tyne and Wear, which together account for only 7 per cent of the region's land area, while the western half of the region—consisting of the single county of Cumbria since the reorganization of local government in 1974—contributes less than one-sixth of the region's population and employment (North of England County Councils Association (NECCA) 1984).

The North's economic problems are more massive and intractable than those of any other region in Britain. It is now realized that the seeds of this decline were sown by the nature and sheer pace of its past development, and by disinvestment in certain sectors dating from around 1880 (Community Development Project 1977; Hudson 1983*a*). The scale of its problems is reflected in the fact that, ever since the designation of North East England and West Cumberland as Special Areas in 1934, a substantial proportion of the region's population has lived in areas eligible for industrial assistance under UK government regional policy. Even after the 1984 revision, which restricted the coverage of Development Areas to 15 per cent of Britain's working population, the proportion of the region's population within such Development Areas remains as high as 70 per cent, while (including Intermediate Areas as well) 97 per cent of the North East's population continues to live in Assisted Areas compared to the national figure of 35 per cent (see Figure 8.1).

This is not to say that the last fifty years of positive discrimination in favour of these areas have not benefited the North at all. In fact a considerable transformation has taken place in both its industrial structure and its physical appearance. The North gained greatly from the diversion of new manufacturing investment from the more prosperous South, Midlands, and Yorkshire during the late 1940s, and particularly in the decade following the publication of the Hailsham plan, *The North East; A Programme for Regional Development and Growth* (Board of Trade 1963). Despite massive job losses in key male-employing sectors between 1958 and 1973 (117,000 from mining, 25,000 from shipbuilding,

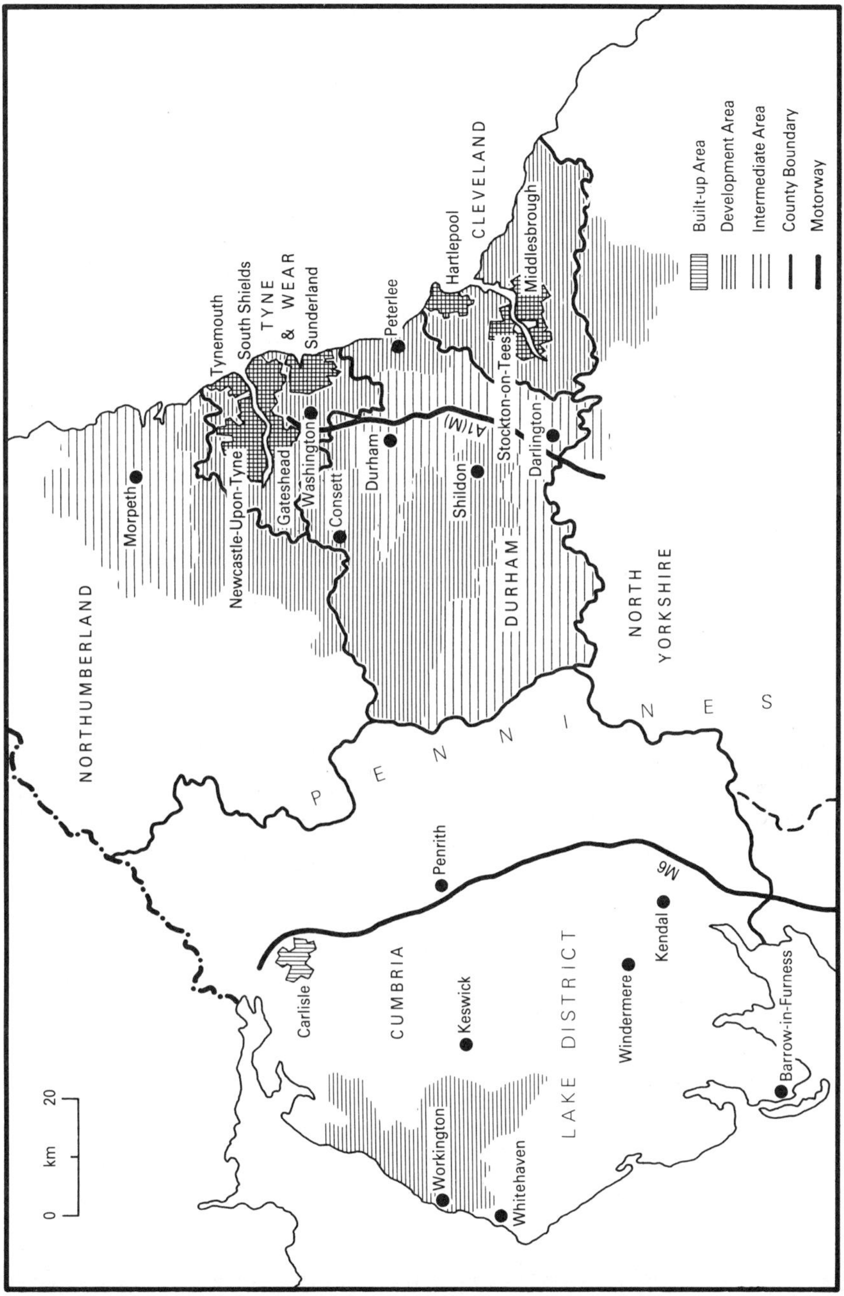

Figure 8.1. The Northern Region

13,000 from metal working), overall employment in the North, including that of females, fell by only 4,000, for these losses were compensated for by the combination of major new investments in chemicals on Teesside, the opening of a variety of activities in the more mobile sections of manufacturing industry, the relocation of parts of central government offices, and the steady growth of the local service sector stimulated by these developments and by the general increase in real incomes (NECCA 1983*b*). Although the calculation of the contribution of regional policy to employment change is fraught with difficulties, not least that of estimating the independent effect of corporate restructuring, it is believed that regional aid may have created over 54,000 jobs in the Northern region between 1960 and 1976 (Marquand 1980). Moreover, a large-scale road-building programme, the expansion of the New Towns programme, slum clearance and housing redevelopment, and the imaginative plans for the upgrading of Newcastle city centre all helped to produce a major change in the physical fabric and external image of the region, intended to pave the way for long-term self-sustained growth.

The region is now a living statement that such investment in infrastructure does not guarantee permanent job creation. Many of these improvements subsequently proved to have been short-lived and superficial in their effects on employment, unemployment, and the region's quality of life in general. The North's new prosperity was profoundly shaken by the world economic recession which began in the mid-1970s and deepened in the UK after 1979, following the increase in the value of sterling and the rise in interest rates (Townsend 1982; 1983). Between 1976 and 1984 the North experienced a higher rate of job decline than any other region in the UK; indeed, in the four years 1978–82 the region's employed workforce dropped by 11.5 per cent, compared with a national fall of 7.3 per cent. Manufacturing was particularly hard hit, with a net loss of 90,000 jobs in the period 1979–82 alone, a 22 per cent drop in only three years. The sectors which suffered most acutely were the steel industry, shipbuilding, mechanical engineering, and electrical engineering, with the worst effects being felt in the conurbations and large towns, and in some smaller communities which experienced the closure of their major industry. Among the latter, Consett lost 4,500 jobs with the closure of its steelworks in 1981, and Shildon 2,600 from British Rail Engineering's April 1982 decision to close its wagon works (Hudson and Sadler 1983; Shildon Action Group 1984).

The unemployment figures, presented on the basis of the 1984 revisions of the travel-to-work areas (TTWAs) in Figure 8.2, portray the inevitable results of the past few years of job shedding, though they do not portray the full outcome. In February 1985, one in four of the registered workforce was without a job in the South Tyneside and Hartlepool TTWAs (25.0 and 24.9 per cent respectively), while Middlesbrough, Bishop Auckland, Sunderland, and Stockton TTWAs all had unemployment rates of 20 per cent or more. In addition, Consett was recording an unemployment rate of over 24 per cent in early 1984 before it lost its separate TTWA status through amalgamation with Newcastle upon Tyne, which recorded a level of 18.3 per cent in February 1985. In fact, only two TTWAs in the North East—Hexham and Berwick—had rates below the

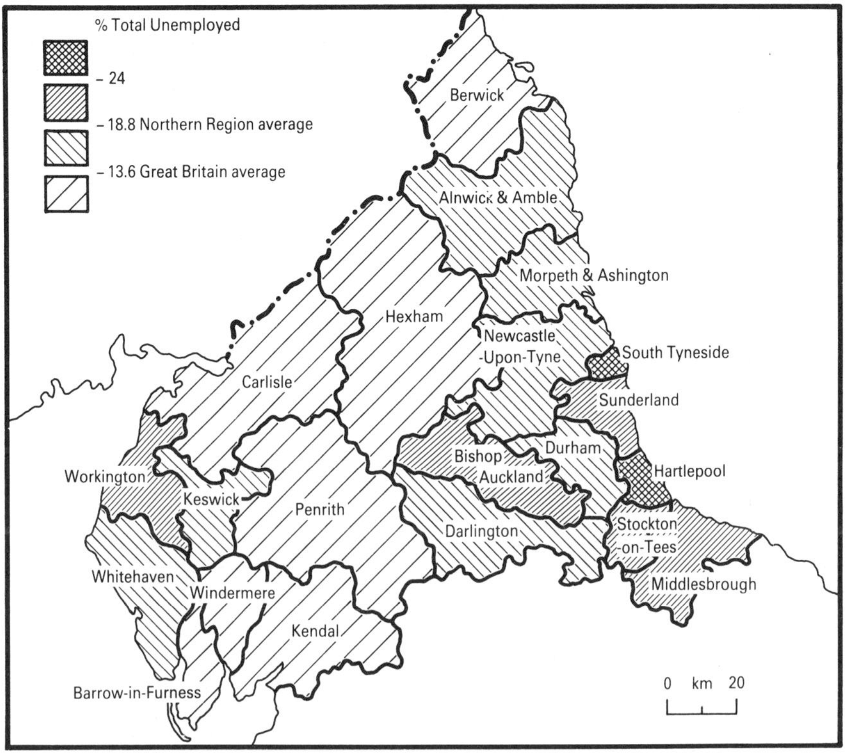

Figure 8.2. The Northern region: unemployment, 1984

national average of 13.6 per cent. Across the Pennines, the problems in Cumbria appear somewhat less severe, with Workington (19.7 per cent) being worst affected, and with two other TTWAs also above the national average. The overall Northern region average had by this time reached 18.8 per cent, an increase by over 10 percentage points since 1976—in contrast to a rise of only 6 percentage points for the South East region. The real margin between these regions in terms of changing levels of job opportunities was, however, even larger than this, because over this period both net emigration of labour and growth of unregistered unemployment were taking place at a faster rate in the North than in the South East (Gudgin *et al*, 1982; NECCA 1983).

The plight of the North in relation to many socioeconomic considerations can be summed up dramatically by calculating the fortunes of a hypothetical group of 1,000 children born into the region and facing the risks and opportunities prevailing in the early 1980s, compared with their counterparts living in the South East (Table 8.1). It can be seen that the probability of a stillbirth or death within one month of birth is significantly higher in the North. When school-leaving age is reached, far more children will stay on at school in the South East, get at least one A-level and go on to full-time higher or further

Table 8.1. The fortunes of 1,000 children: Northern Region and South East Region

	North	South East
Still births per 1,000 live births	8	7
Live births	1,000	1,000
Deaths within one month	8	7
Staying on at school at age 16	270	413
School-leavers, one or more A-levels	124	180
School-leavers, no graded results	743	693
School-leavers going to university	68	82
School-leavers going to other full-time education	84	148
Unemployed, age 20	144	79
Unemployed, age 35	74	41
Economically active, age 35	801	752
Unemployed, age 50	65	37
Economically active, age 50	700	700
Survivors, age 70	618	689

Source: NECCA 1982.

education. After leaving school, there is nearly twice as much chance of being unemployed in the North, a disadvantage which is paralleled throughout working life. Finally, the higher mortality rates in the North mean that 10 per cent fewer will attain the age of 'three-score and ten' (NECCA 1982). Clearly, in spite of the apparent progress made during the 1960s and early 1970s, regional balance seems as remote a possibility as ever. It is this experience of false hopes and dashed expectations that prompts a reappraisal of the nature of the North's problems and the relevance of current forms of regional policy.

The legacy of heavy industry and large plants

The Northern region's role in the national spatial division of labour, and as a traditional 'problem region', gives it more in common with Wales and Scotland than with other English regions. In marked contrast to Lancashire and Yorkshire, the Northern region's manufacturing specialisms date back only to the 1850s, and were concentrated in a small number of towns and plants, which *reduced* in number over time. Thus, iron and steel production had by the 1930s mainly been concentrated in two principal firms in Cleveland, and in those of Consett and Workington. Shipbuilding became concentrated in fewer yards on the Tyne, Wear, and Tees, and at Hartlepool and Barrow. In engineering, most activity was from the start in heavy industry requiring large plants—in marine engineering and armaments near the shipyards, and in locomotive and wagon building. Even in electrical engineering, in which Tyneside was a pioneering area, the specialisms adopted lay at the 'heavy end' of the industry, in the design and manufacture of power-station equipment.

The extent of twentieth-century industrial diversification in the region is often underestimated, yet it is a curious feature that this, too, was often in large plants. In the chemical industry, ICI built up major economies of scale in its development of chemical works at Billingham, founded in the First World War on the basis of local supplies of brine, and at Wilton, also in Cleveland but founded after the Second World War. Heavy postwar investment in large modern plant in Cleveland's chemicals and steel industries is attributable to the modernization of the Tees waterway itself for the international supply of oil and ores.

Even the arrival of modern light industry over the last fifty years has continued the tendency towards large plants, at least in terms of the length of the payroll at each plant. Over the period 1945–65 the size of plants introduced to the North averaged just over 400 employees, the same as for the North West but higher than any of the other regions (Board of Trade 1968). The Department of Trade and Industry's 'Record of Openings' data for subsequent years show that, during the most effective regional policy period of the late 1960s, the size of plants attracted to the Northern region was the highest in the country, with plants opened in 1966–71 averaging 138 employees in 1975, compared with a national average of 79 workers per newly opened plant. The average size of plant openings in the North stayed well above the national average during the first half of the 1970s, after which economic conditions severely reduced the number of large plants being set up anywhere (Pounce 1981; Killick 1983).

The combined effects of the nineteenth-century legacy and of the types of plants attracted to the North since the Second World War can be seen from the 1981 employment–size characteristics of plants employing twenty or more workers (Table 8.2). The most striking features are the 77 per cent of workers that were employed at plants with 200 or more on their payroll, compared with the national average of 66 per cent, and the fact that almost two in every five workers (37.2 per cent) were in plants employing 1,000 or more compared with the overall UK figure of 28.7 per cent. The above-average concentration in large plants was shared by all the constituent counties of the region, except Northumberland with its comparatively small manufacturing base of only 16,900 jobs. Not suprisingly, the heaviest concentration was in Cleveland, with its ICI and British Steel plants (Table 8.2).

The region's distinctiveness within the UK can be further established from Table 8.3. The North stands out in the most extreme position in terms of the proportion of manufacturing workers in units employing 1,000 or more. Several other of the country's smaller regions—East Anglia, the East Midlands, and Northern Ireland—lie at the opposite extreme; but the Northern region is also completely out of line with the UK's larger industrial regions, with their average levels of only 29–31 per cent. Comparison with the 1976 situation reveals that, despite the dramatic fall in the North's number of very large factories as a result of closures and labour shedding, and the consequent fall in the proportion of manufacturing workers in these factories, the changes over this five-year period have done little to reduce the North's distinctiveness within the nation (Table 8.3).

Table 8.2. Manufacturing units by employment size, Northern Region, 1981

Employment size group	North: Units	North: Employment	North: %	% total manufacturing employment in size groups 20 and over: Tyne and Wear	Durham	Cleveland	Northumberland	Cumbria	UK
20–49	635	19,606	6.4	6.8	7.6	4.8	7.9	6.1	10.2
50–99	299	20,853	6.8	7.6	8.8	3.5	9.4	6.7	10.4
100–199	210	29,116	9.6	10.5	7.8	6.9	15.3	10.9	13.5
200–499	208	65,325	21.4	21.6	24.5	18.2	34.1	18.0	21.4
500–999	80	56,580	18.6	20.5 }	51.3 (500–999 and 1,000+ combined)	17.9 }	33.3 (500–999 and 1,000+ combined)	18.2	15.8
1,000+	54	113,293	37.2	33.1 }		48.7 }		40.2	28.7
Total	1,486	304,773	100.0	100.0	100.0	100.0	100.0	100.0	100.0

Source: Business Statistics Office 1983. The table reflects register details held in 1983, at which time most of the employment data included related to 1981. The data relate to manufacturing units with twenty or more employees only.

Table 8.3. Manufacturing units employing 1,000 and over, 1981 and 1976, by UK region

	1981		1976		
	Units of 1,000+	Employment as % of size groups 20 and over	Units of 1,000+	Employment as % of: Size groups 20 and over	Employment as % of: All size groups
North	54	37.2	85	43.9	42.2
Scotland	67	31.1	94	33.0	30.7
West Midlands	83	30.3	130	35.1	32.9
North West	95	29.8	153	32.9	30.8
Wales	32	29.7	50	39.1	37.1
South East	155	29.2	213	28.8	25.6
South West	35	29.1	44	30.0	27.6
Yorkshire and Humberside	61	24.9	90	27.3	25.4
Northern Ireland	9	23.1	17	27.8	26.7
East Midlands	49	22.2	69	24.9	23.3
East Anglia	18	20.3	19	19.0	17.6
Total UK	658	28.7	964	31.4	29.0

Source: Business Statistics Office 1976; 1983. Publication of data ceased after 1979 for size groups under twenty.

More detailed data confirm that industrial structure is an important determinant of the region's large average plant size. The principal factor lies in Division 2 of the 1980 Standard Industrial Classification, composed mainly of 'primary processing industries' which had an average plant size of 285 workers in 1981, compared with the regional average of 205. Within this division, the average size was as high as 435 for the 26,100 workers in metal manufacture, and 399 in respect of the 34,700 workers in chemicals. In Division 3 (the metal-using industries), the largest average plant size was represented by electrical and electronic equipment, with 36,400 workers in plants averaging 314 workers each, many of them semi-skilled female assembly workers in postwar factories.

Further investigation, however, suggests that plant-size structure has an effect on the performance of the region over and above that of industrial sectoral structure by itself. During the period 1978–81, when the North's industrial structure was no more disadvantageous than that of the country as a whole, the North's number of manufacturing workers fell by 80,000 to 339,000, a decline of 19.1 per cent. This compares with a national contraction of only 16.8 per cent, leaving a balance of 2.3 per cent decline to be 'explained' by other factors. The work of Fothergill and Gudgin (1982) attempts to partition the roles of these other factors, and attributes considerable significance to the effect of plant-size structure inherited at the start of the period in 1960, while in Cleveland analysis, disadvantageous plant-size structure contributed the equivalent of a 4.3 per cent decline in the North's manufacturing employment between 1960 and 1975, compared with a 3.1 per cent decline caused by the poor industrial structure inherited at the start of the period in 1960; while in Cleveland plant-size structure and industrial structure were calculated respectively to have caused 6.6 and 1.1 per cent falls in manufacturing employment between 1965 and 1974 (Fothergill and Gudgin 1982: 154, 162).

It appears likely that the disproportionate national decline of large plants from 1976 to 1981 is of continuing importance in the interpretation of Northern region trends. From this analysis it is thus clear that the problem of adverse industrial structure is more complicated than was generally believed from the research of twenty years ago. At that time, various forms of shift-share analysis had suggested that the Northern region would have out-performed the national economy during the 1950s and early 1960s if only it had had the national-average composition of industrial sectors (McCrone 1969). Unfortunately, the correction of these broad sectoral imbalances over the last two decades has ultimately done little, if anything, to bring the overall performance of the region's economy closer to that achieved by southern England. These newly recognized problems of industrial and economic structure are not fully reflected in the standard sectoral tables, and are particularly associated with the fact that both the traditional industries and the new manufacturing plants tend to specialize in the more basic processing and mass production stages of their industrial sectors (Massey 1984)—a characteristic which is reflected in the region's emphasis on large plant size, and which has done little to reduce the vulnerability of the North's economy to trade cycles and overseas competition.

Related weaknesses of the regional economy

The legacy of heavy industry and large plant size which seems to provide such a powerful explanation for the North's depressing economic performance in recent years is now known to operate through a number of factors which we shall describe in this section. These include a high degree of external control over the region's productive plant and economic affairs in general (Smith 1979; Marshall 1979*a*), a limited range of local business services (Marshall 1979*b*), a poor record of local entrepreneurship and management (Storey 1982*a*), and a low representation of research and development activities (Thwaites 1982). These features make for a poor local business environment which, through a circular process of cause and effect, results in low rates of new-firm formation and survival (Johnson and Cathcart 1979; Storey 1981), and in a poor record of innovation development and adoption (Oakey *et al.* 1980; Gibbs *et al.* 1982). They tend to exacerbate the problems of vulnerability to circumstances outside the region, and are also associated with the development of a labour force with an occupational structure biased towards lower skill groups, thereby, it is argued, further undermining the scope for local initiative and the attractiveness of the North for inward investment. This is the kind of vicious circle which researchers and policy-makers in the Northern region reckon that regional policy must now break out of, if it is to stand any chance of achieving long-term improvements (Northern Region Strategy Team (NRST) 1977; Goddard 1979; NECCA 1983). Taken together, these factors have important implications for the future prosperity of the region, and tend to undermine the continuing efforts being made to generate self-sustained growth in its economy.

The problem of external control is probably the single most important stumbling-block, as it is related to most of the other features to a greater or lesser extent. The Northern region constitutes a classic case of the branch-plant economy. Even before the reinvigoration of regional policy in the early 1960s, less than half of the region's manufacturing employment was accounted for by plants owned by firms based in the region, but subsequently the proportion fell dramatically from 48 per cent in 1963 to 22 per cent in 1973. The establishment of new branch plants has contributed to this process, with the branch-plant sector increasing its share of the region's manufacturing employment from 35 to 46 per cent. The greater part of the increase in external ownership has, however, come about as a result of mergers and takeovers. The proportion of the region's manufacturing employment accounted for by factories which had once been owned by local firms but which subsequently moved into the hands of those with head offices outside the region increased from 17 to 31 per cent over this ten-year period (Smith 1979).

The high degree of direct dependence on high-level decisions taken outside the region is also reflected in the extensive role of the public sector in the North's employment (Hudson 1983*b*). In 1981 no less than 395,000 people worked in the public-sector and nationalized industries, 35 per cent of all the jobs in the region. Of these, 56,500 were still in the manufacturing sectors of shipbuilding and steel, and 39,200 in coalmining, these together comprising 6.5

per cent of the region's employment, and clearly operating in the capacity of branches in the sense of having their decisions closely controlled by central government even if some of the headquarters were outside London, as with British Shipbuilders in Newcastle. Similarly, some of the national government offices such as the branches of the DHSS and National Savings, decentralized to Newcastle upon Tyne and Durham respectively, are affected by the 'branch-plant syndrome'. In addition, other branches of the public sector such as education (with 7.4 per cent of the North's workers), health (5.6 per cent), transport (3.4 per cent), and gas, electricity, water, and nuclear fuel (2.3 per cent) are not immune from central government decisions on funding and employment policy, while local government itself (with 4.5 per cent of the region's workers) is nowadays greatly affected by central government attitudes on the scale of rate support, and by its actions on controlling rate levels. Clearly the freedom for local initiative has declined substantially since the early 1960s.

The region's poor achievements in new-firm formation are highlighted in a survey carried out by the Department of Industry in 1980. This showed that, at that time, the North had the third lowest birth-rate of new businesses of any region in the UK, and the second highest death-rate relative to births. This record can be related to the low quality of the region's business environment. In terms of a number of key indicators of barriers to entrepreneurs (Table 8.4), Storey (1982*a*) has shown that the North emerges in aggregate as the UK's worst region. These deficiencies can also be traced back to the legacy of heavy industry and large plants, as identified some years ago with reference to Scotland (Scottish Council 1962). Indeed, Checkland (1976), working on the comparable area of Clydeside, has likened the impact of shipbuilding and heavy engineering on new-firm formation to the sterilizing effect of the Upas Tree, which has such a dense canopy that virtually no vegetation can survive underneath it. Fothergill and Gudgin (1982) also convincingly link together large plant size and low rates of new-firm formation. The reasons include the domination of financial resources and labour markets by those major industries (Lever 1979), the very limited opportunities for the majority of workers to gain enough management experience to encourage them to set up their own businesses (Storey 1982*a*), and the rundown of local business services as the branch plants tend to be serviced by the other parts of their parent companies, or by other firms based outside the Region (Marshall 1979*a*).

It is a similar story for the rate of development and adoption of technological innovations. Early work by Buswell and Lewis (1970) revealed a distinct dearth of establishments for research and development in the Northern region compared particularly with South East England, whether on-site or in reasonable proximity to the production plants—a situation which has largely been confirmed by a more recent survey (Buswell *et al.* 1985). Goddard and Thwaites (1983) identify this as a key reason for the differences between these two regions in the rate of introduction of new products and processes. A large-scale inquiry carried out by the Centre for Urban and Regional Development Studies at Newcastle University showed that 56 per cent of small- and medium-sized firms in three high-technology sectors in the North had failed to introduce a new or

Table 8.4. Indicators of barriers to entrepreneurship, Northern region and South East (regional rankings)

	Northern region	South East
1 % of total manufacturing employment in small plants	9	1
2 % of total manufacturing employment in large plants	11	4
3 % of school-leavers taking degree course	9	3
4 % school-leavers without qualifications	4	2
5 % economically active in managerial and professional classes	7	1
6 % economically active in manual occupations	9	1
7 Savings per capita	3	4
8 % householders who are in owner-occupied property	11	7
9 Average dwelling price	6	1
10 % employment in metals, shipbuilding, and chemicals (high 'barrier-to-entry' industries)	11	2
11 Disposable income per capita	6	1
Total rank	11	1

Source: Storey 1982*a*.

improved product over the previous five years, compared with only 15 per cent of similar firms in the South East. It was also found that, relative to the UK average of 100, the rate of incorporation of microprocessors into products by mechanical engineering firms in the North was 61 compared with a South East figure of 113 (see also Thwaites 1982).

These various observations on external control, new-firm formation, and technological development, taken in conjunction with the adverse aspects of industrial structure mentioned previously, add up to an extremely depressing picture, helping to explain the North's poor employment performance in the early 1980s, and offering little hope for a sustained revival in the foreseeable future. In contrast to the rather simplistic industrial-structure interpretation of the North's problems of twenty years ago, the key elements in regional development are now seen to be technological change, management expertise, industrial relations, training, finance, and the quality of local business services (Goddard and Thwaites 1983). On these criteria, many of the major sections of the North's manufacturing industry come out badly. What remains of its indigenous industry tends to be vertically integrated, with mainly local contact patterns. Meanwhile, the branch plants by definition constitute the outer limbs of their parent organizations, little involved in developing new products and processes but instead engaged primarily in the mass production of well-established lines which are in the older part of their 'product cycle'. They are therefore highly vulnerable to any rationalization required by the changing role of the main company, and are likely to lose jobs from the introduction of new processes.

Perhaps the most serious aspect of the North's problems is the fact that they tend to be cumulative in their effects. The increasing level of external control tends to reduce the possibilities for local initiative in setting up new firms, as the people with sufficient experience become fewer and the stock of local business services diminishes. The likelihood of 'management buy-outs', suggested as one means of saving branch plants from closure and of reducing the degree of external ownership (Storey 1983*a*), is low if their management teams have an essentially 'branch-plant mentality' or a dependence on large employers, and can obtain only very limited support from local advisory agencies and financial institutions. Similarly, with more manufacturing being geared up to routine mass production, the shop-floor labour force becomes progressively deskilled, and therefore declines in its ability to develop or adopt innovations and also loses much of its attraction to inward investment, particularly as it meets greater competition from low-wage labour in the Newly Industrialized Countries.

Policy responses

Central government has been slow to acknowledge the implications of these complex and deep-seated problems. Particularly disappointing was the failure of the 1974–9 Labour Government to come to a decision on the Strategic Plan for the Northern region (NRST 1977); in the event, the decision made in 1979 by the incoming Conservative Government not to implement its recommendations came as no surprise. Equally depressing, but no more surprising, given the Thatcher Government's 'monetarist' ideology and pattern of electoral support, was the selection of regional industrial assistance as a field suitable for spending cuts, also announced in 1979. It was not until 1984 that the results of Whitehall's more thorough review of regional policy were announced and even then the Government itself, not just Northern political groups, saw these changes more as a further cost-cutting exercise than as a fundamental restructuring. While the imposition of a cost-per-job ceiling on regional development grants, and the extension of eligible industries to include some elements of the service sector, reflected some of the thinking embodied in the Strategic Plan, two much more significant challenges were left unsolved—the task of stimulating indigenous growth as opposed to a continued emphasis on attracting inward investment, and the recommendation of greater co-ordination of all forms of place-specific aid and indeed of the development of an explicit regional dimension in all regionally relevant areas of public expenditure.

The reluctance of successive governments to tackle these two major issues has produced some interesting consequences, particularly the involvement of local authorities in economic development activities and the call for some form of development agency covering all or parts of the Northern region. The first steps in the latter direction were prompted by the establishment in 1975 of Development Agencies for Scotland and Wales, which, as shown in Chapters 9 and 10, were given substantial financial resources, powers, and discretion concerning direct and indirect investment for industrial development. The Northern region pioneered the involvement of local authorities in economic regeneration, with the Tyne and Wear Act being approved by Parliament in 1976, and the City of Newcastle starting its annual Economic Policy and Programme in the same year (Cameron and Gillard 1983). The Tyne and Wear Act gave the Metropolitan County Council and five District Councils powers to declare 'Industrial Improvement Areas' (Williams 1982), and to provide forms of loans and grants to firms over and above those available from the Department of Industry—powers which foreshadowed those introduced more widely by central government in the Inner Urban Areas Act 1978. Cleveland County and its four Boroughs have also been very active in formulating economic development policies, particularly since the advent of a Labour-controlled administration at county level in 1981 (Gallant 1982; Smith 1983).

The range and scale of local economic initiatives in the North has increased since these early steps were taken (see Figure 8.3). In Cleveland, most local aid comes through section 137 of the 1972 Local Government Act and is intended primarily for assisting firms and the unemployed, with some £1.7 million being allocated in 1983–4 to more than twenty schemes involving economic regeneration or job creation and retention. Both Cleveland County and its Boroughs are also active in the more traditional area of providing land suitable for industrial or commercial development, and in the provision of premises (Gallant 1982; Smith 1983). Tyne and Wear County Council's budget for economic development in 1983–4 totalled £6.8 million, most of it deriving from Parts 3 and 4 of the 1976 Act; and whereas it had initially concentrated its efforts on land and site preparation and advanced-factory construction, by the early 1980s it was giving more attention to assisting the entrepreneur, improving innovative performance, and giving direct financial assistance as well as advice (Clough 1982; Cameron and Gillard 1983). Newcastle City's Employment Policy and Programme built up to an annual budget of over £5 million by the early 1980s, of which some 45 per cent was received from Inner City Partnership funding under the 1978 Act.

A related aspect of local initiative which also took off impressively in the North in the late 1970s is reflected in the emergence of agencies which offer various forms of assistance to businesses, particularly to small firms. A survey carried out in 1981 by the Durham University Business School (Price 1982) identified over forty such agencies operating in the North East, excluding the services provided directly by local authorities and commercial banks, and not counting educational institutions offering business courses. These agencies were involved in all or some of the following activities—information and advice; counselling services, training in business methods, provision of premises, provision of manpower, provision of finance, and 'signposting' services, that is, informing clients about other agencies which might be of assistance. Constituting a veritable growth industry in themselves these organizations—many

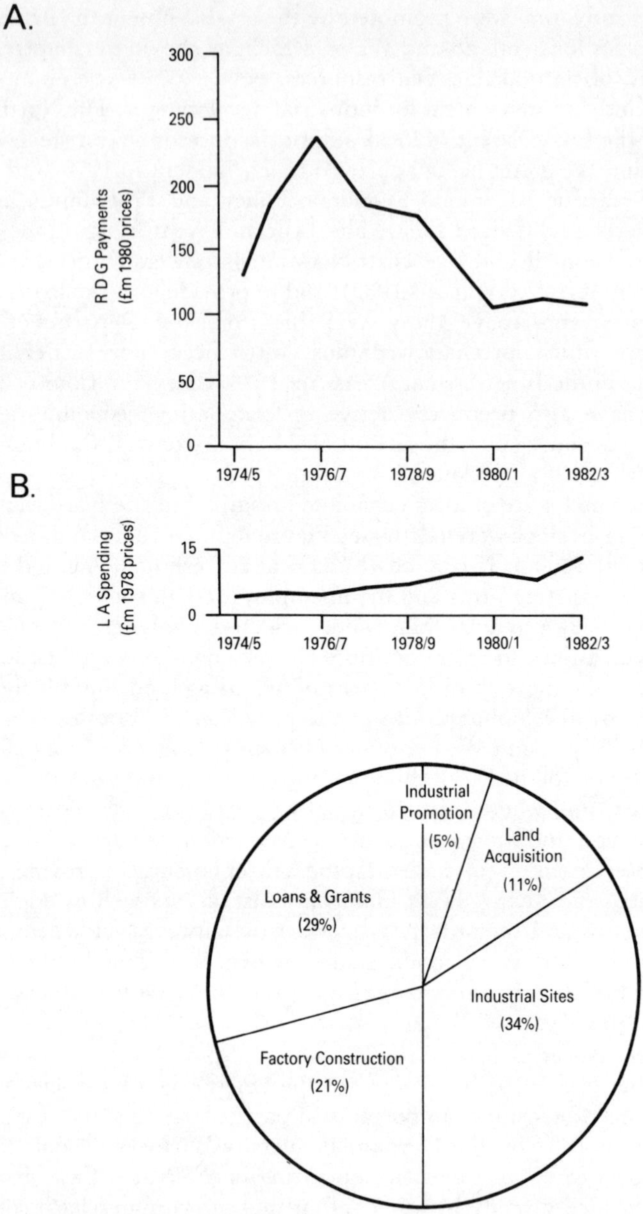

Figure 8.3. (A) Regional Development Grant expenditure, the Northern region; (B) Local authority expenditure on economic development in the Northern Region; annual totals, 1974–83, and allocation, 1982–3

provided on a voluntary basis or with minimal funding—have been helping to offset the region's general shortage of business services, but the overall impression is one of considerable duplication and of potential confusion to the aspiring entrepreneur. This is reflected in the very need for the special 'signposting' bodies, in contrast to the 'one-stop' function which the Scottish Development Agency advertises as one of its main strengths.

The need for the type of co-ordination which a regional development agency could provide in the North East, however, relates only partly to the proliferation of advisory bodies and local-authority economic initiatives, although the duplication of services and inter-authority rivalry for inward investment is not an insignificant problem. The case rests just as much on the multiplicity of separate area-based policies emanating from Whitehall and Brussels. As summed up by Buswell (1983: 26), national spatial policies comprise 'a confusing array of government assistance administered by a number of government departments and agencies and aimed at a wide variety of potential recipients'. The situation of Newcastle upon Tyne in 1985 illustrates this point well. In addition to being in a Development Area (defined on the basis of travel-to-work patterns), the city receives non-quota assistance from Brussels as a shipbuilding area in decline. It is also a Partnership authority under the Urban Programme; but, while this is jointly with Gateshead across the Tyne, the Partnership Area includes only the poorer wards in Newcastle (see Figure 8.4). Finally, as well as

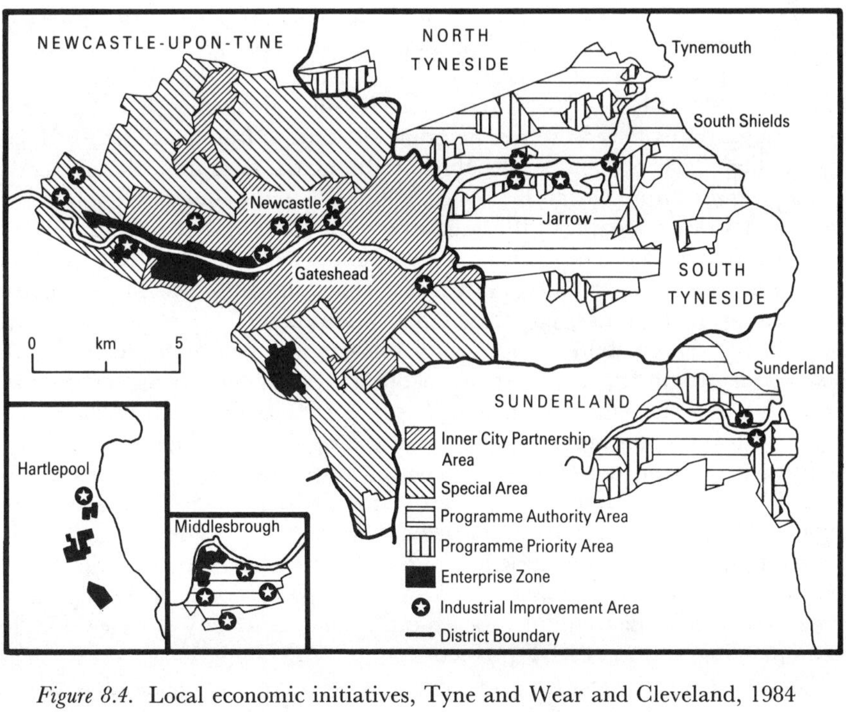

Figure 8.4. Local economic initiatives, Tyne and Wear and Cleveland, 1984

the various local economic initiatives operating in Newcastle under the control of the city or the county, central government initiative has also provided Newcastle with an Enterprise Zone which is split between the city and Gateshead.

The situation in the County of Cleveland is, if anything, even more complicated. With the highest overall levels of unemployment in Britain, the whole County has the benefit of Development Area status, and is thus eligible for the full range of regional policy measures available from Whitehall and from the European Regional Development Fund (ERDF) quota section. Under the Urban Programme, Middlesbrough is a Programme Authority, and was given an Enterprise Zone in 1983. A second Borough in the County, Hartlepool, is a specially designated area under the Urban Programme, and has a three-site Enterprise Zone. The whole county was included in the non-quota section of ERDF in 1982 for both shipbuilding and steelmaking assistance—but note again how this type of aid goes to local-authority areas, whereas ERDF monies go via the Department of Industry to travel-to-work areas. In the rural southeast of the county, on the flanks of the North Yorkshire Moors, is to be found a Rural Development Area in which the Development Commission has funded CoSIRA to build factory units in Lingdale and Liverton. This, then, illustrates the range of sources of non-local aid, involving in all at least four British government departments and five European Community directorates. Add to this the relatively frequent changes in the policy areas and measures (including those of both the Department of Trade and Industry and the Development Commission in 1984 alone) and the case for co-ordination and advice at regional and local levels becomes overwhelming (Buswell 1983).

The Regional Studies Association Northern Branch, in reviewing policy options in 1983 (Buswell 1983), recommended that an agency should be set up with responsibility for administering grant aid derived from local, national, and supranational sources, and for deciding on the spatial allocation of most sectors of public expenditure within the region. One of its main functions should be to produce a strategy dealing with both long-term structural changes and short-term activity, set within a strategic regional framework for the UK as a whole. It should provide information both to aid central government in formulating and monitoring its policies and to help the various bodies to put the policies into effect. A key responsibility of such an agency should be the lubrication of the business environment; for instance, encouraging new technology, stimulating product innovation, supporting local entrepreneurs, building up links between higher education and industry, and striving for greater backing from financial institutions. Among the other more specific responsibilities recommended by the RSA Northern Branch were the direct provision to firms of specialized advice and assistance (including a delivery system for new-technology advice run on lines similar to the Agricultural Development and Advisory Service for farmers), and the preparation of integrated proposals for particular problem areas, such as those required for co-ordinating inner-city policies and for accompanying bids for ERDF projects.

Various alternative options involving lower degrees of devolution than a regional development agency were also considered (Buswell 1983; 78–9). These included granting greater powers and resources to existing local authorities at county and district levels, strengthening the regional offices of central government, and upgrading the role of a regional body like NECCA or the Northern Economic Development Council. It was recognized that each of these would represent some improvement over the present pattern of policy formulation and delivery; but it was felt that, even in combination, these lesser options would not provide a sufficiently effective framework for addressing the major problems which the region faces, particularly in view of the fact that, of all the regions in England, the North is the most remote from the nation's centre of economic and political power.

Outlook for the North

Any assessment of future prospects must be coloured by current circumstances and recent experience; the Northern region in the mid-1980s offers little by way of encouragement. Probably about 11,800 jobs were generated by newly founded manufacturing firms in Tyne and Wear, Durham, and Northumberland between 1965 and 1978, but these were more than offset in the four years 1978–82 by the loss of 42,000 jobs from closures alone (Storey 1983*b*). From 1980 to 1984, notified redundancies from all sectors were running annually at 30–40,000, thus affecting around 3 per cent of the employed workforce each year. Visitors to Tyneside at this time could be forgiven for concluding, on the basis of its regular daily front-page news coverage, that Newcastle's *Evening Chronicle* was published specially to record the demise of the region's 'sunset industries'.

Nor does the national context offer any more hopeful signs. The most important single influence on the absolute level of well-being in the North is the size and performance of the national economy. With central government's emphasis on the reduction of inflation seemingly unshakeable, the chances of a short-term increase in labour demand appear remote. Moreover, allied with the 1984 announcement on the further reduction of regional industrial assistance, and its relegation to a social rather than an economic justification, it is certain that the Northern region will not benefit from any longer-term national recovery as much as will the more prosperous parts of the country. The implications of such a 'minimum spatial policy' are spelt out by the Regional Studies Association (1983: 104–6), and are reflected in regional forecasts that show the shortage of jobs remaining close to its present level until the end of the decade at least (NECCA 1983).

Yet, even if central government were to switch to policies more sympathetic to the plight of the Northern region, it is not clear how much could be achieved in the short term. According to Gudgin *et al.* (1982), adoption of the Alternative Economic Strategy, involving reflation and import controls, could perhaps have increased jobs in the region by as much as 6.8 per cent between 1981 and 1990, but that would not have been sufficient to bring employment back to the 1978 level, let alone restore the situation prevailing in the early 1970s. Moreover, while many of the more radical recommendations put forward by the Regional Studies Association have been supported by the Labour, Liberal, and SDP parties, there is no strong confidence in the region that a change of government at Westminster would lead quickly to the establishment of a powerful regional development agency, or to the introduction of a strong regional dimension to all relevant public expenditure programmes.

In these circumstances it is not surprising that an air of gloom and despondency has now descended on many of the people who remain in the North. The rewards for labour increasing its geographical mobility are slim. In 1983, two-fifths of the region's unemployed had been without work for over a year (half of these for over two years), and 44 per cent of the region's under 20s were out of work (one in five for more than twelve months). Moreover, with three-quarters of the region's 238,000 registered unemployed located in six TTWAs and being spatially concentrated within these, whole communities have been forced to come to terms with mass unemployment, particularly in the older urban areas and on the outlying council estates. Until the miners' strike of 1984–5, apathy seemed to be the main outcome of this course of events; but now it looks much more certain that, without substantial improvements in the near future, there will emerge deeper problems of alienation and withdrawal from national life, and a fuller resurgence of local and regional consciousness based on some alternative to the formal work ethic.

Particularly unnerving is the growth of the feeling, shared by sections of the business community as well as the wider population, that the Northern region is now being abandoned by the rest of the nation. While people have, by necessity, become accustomed to the progressive withdrawal of private investment, there is a suspicion that now they are also being overlooked by Westminster, upon which dependence is very considerable. This feeling is given credence by the halving of the real value of the regional development grant coming to the region since the mid-1970s, and by the reluctance to set up a regional development agency. It is also symbolically induced by decisions not merely to close redundant works but to demolish them completely so that they would never be used again, as seen particularly dramatically in the clearance of the site of the Consett steelworks. In this context the term 'redundant spaces' (Anderson *et al.* 1983) is particularly apposite, and may be beginning to apply to wider areas than individual factory sites. The North is being made increasingly aware of its remoteness within England, its small size (less than half the population of Greater London and, indeed, not much larger than Greater Manchester), and its vulnerability as an area which, having prospered as a result of opportunities grasped in the mid-nineteenth century, has so far failed to find a major new role for itself.

Conclusion

Regional policy in so far as it affects the Northern region is now largely discredited, being based on a potential for the interregional mobility of capital that no longer exists—except marginally for inward investment from overseas, as witnessed by the establishment of Nissan, the Japanese car company, at Washington. Whilst urban policy continues to focus more directly on local problems, especially in the more powerful Partnership authorities such as Newcastle–Gateshead, it was not designed to deal with large-scale unemployment. Local government initiatives, although wholly laudable, will simply never be able to work at a high enough rate to offset the scale of closures and redundancies experienced by the North since the late 1970s. The legacies of heavy industry and large plants, with all the 'Upas Tree' effects which these have brought in their train, cannot be tackled adequately except through a coherent package of policies designed to produce a revival of local entrepreneurial activity and a long-term regeneration of the region's economic base. In this context, it is doubly unfortunate that the *ad hoc* responses of both levels of government to the deepening crisis have only resulted in the proliferation of a set of confused policies, programmes, and geographical areas, and that they have come at a time of rapidly diminishing resources for such policies.

The justification for most intervention remains economic, yet with the present very high levels of unemployment, the problem, at least in the short term, is clearly a social one. Whilst central government has recognized this in its 1983 White Paper on regional industrial policy (Department of Trade and Industry, 1983*a*), it has done little to alleviate the considerable social distress being caused other than through conventional social policy. Local authorities, on the other hand, are made acutely aware of this aspect of the North's problems and have begun to respond with schemes for the unemployed, as has the voluntary sector. Community business ventures such as co-operatives and workshop projects are seen as being one way forward. Such experiments can contribute to the maintenance of communities by providing

> useful and rewarding occupation for otherwise unemployed people in the community, providing goods appropriate to local needs and services that are qualitatively better than those of the private and public [representing] a means of recycling wealth created in the formal economy in a way that satisfies the creative needs of workers in the third sector and the needs of deprived sectors of the local community . . . wealth created and consumed, as far as possible at the local level. (Murgatroyd and Smith 1984: 8)

Yet the number of jobs created and sustained in such enterprises is always going to be small. Moreover, this approach surely smacks of the romantic, and envisages communities largely sustained by local production; surely Byker and Benwell, Consett and Shildon, Port Clarence and Middlesbrough will want to partake of nationally produced and advertised goods and services just as much as more prosperous areas do.

In relation to the formal economy, many key questions must be addressed afresh, in particular concerning the scale of active intervention which should be used to achieve economic regeneration, and the form which this should take. The Strategic Plan for the Northern Region (NRST 1977) put forward a carefully articulated strategy, but this has not been implemented by central government. Many of the current ideas, as summarized in Buswell (1983), also seem to stand a similarly limited chance of being adopted, given the present political climate. It may be the case that government is not directly responsible for the present plight of the North; but any further shift in the policy emphasis away from local/regional issues towards perceived national goals can only accelerate the decline of what Peter Hall has called 'yesterday's regions' (Hall 1981). If 'the geography of Britain is being rewritten every bit as radically as it was in the nineteenth century' (Johnston 1982; 419), then government must be made aware of the consequences. The North may appear small, remote, and increasingly marginal to central government in economic and political terms, but it cannot be neglected without considerable social cost. Many of the solutions currently being proffered for the North's recovery could surely only see results in the longer term, and it appears increasingly likely that they will be overtaken by secular changes already under way. Therefore, policy might be better concentrated on ameliorating the social effects of a considerable shift in the geography of Britain, and thereby helping the North to adjust to changing spatial circumstances.

References

Anderson, J., Duncan, S., and Hudson, R., eds., (1983), *Redundant Spaces in Cities and Regions?* London, Academic Press.

Board of Trade (1963), *The North East: A Programme for Regional Development and Growth*, Cmnd. 2206, London, HMSO.

—— (1968), *Movement of Manufacturing Industry in the United Kingdom, 1945–65*, London, HMSO.

Business Statistics Office, Business Monitor Series, PA 1003, *Analyses of United Kingdom Manufacturing (Local) Units by Employment Size*, 1971–9, 1982, 1983, London, HMSO.

Buswell, R. J., ed., (1983), *The North in the Eighties: Regional Policies for a Decade of Development*. Newcastle upon Tyne, Regional Studies Association Northern Branch.

——, Easterbrook, R. P., and Morphet, C. S. (1985), 'Geography, Regions and Research and Development Activity: The Case of the United Kingdom', in A. Thwaites and R. Oakey, eds., *The Regional Economic Impact of Technology and Change*, London, Frances Pinter.

——, and Lewis, E. W. (1970), 'The Geographical Distribution of Industrial Research Activity in the UK', *Regional Studies* 4, 297–306.

Cameron, S., and Gillard, A. (1983), 'Local Authority Economic Development in Tyne and Wear', in Buswell 1983.

Checkland, S. G. (1976), *The Upas Tree: Glasgow, 1875–1975: a Study in Growth and Contraction*, Glasgow, Glasgow University Press.

City of Newcastle (1984), *Economic Development Policy and Programme 1984–1986*, City of Newcastle upon Tyne, Economic Development Committee.

Clough, R. (1982), 'Tyne and Wear Enterprise Trust—A New Approach to an Old Problem', *Northern Economic Review* 5, 2–10.

Community Development Project (1977), *The Costs of Industrial Change*. London, CDP.

Department of Trade and Industry (1983*a*) *Regional Industrial Development*, Cmnd. 9111, London, HMSO.

—— (1983*b*), *Regional Industrial Policy: Some Economic Issues*, Lodon, DTI.

Fothergill, S., and Gudgin, G. (1982), *Unequal Growth: Urban and Regional Employment Change in the UK*, London, Heinemann.

Gallant, V. (1982), 'Economic and Employment Initiatives in Cleveland', *Northern Economic Review* 4, 11–17.

Gibbs, D., Edwards, T., and Thwaites, A. (1982), 'The Diffusion of New Technology and the Northern Region', *Northern Economic Review* 5, 22–7.

Goddard, J. B. (1979), *The Mobilisation of Indigenous Potential in the UK: A Report to the Regional Policy Directorate of the European Community*, Newcastle upon Tyne, Centre for Urban and Regional Development Studies, University of Newcastle.

—— and Thwaites, A. T. (1983), 'Unemployment in the North, Jobs in the South—The Regional Dimension to the Introduction of New Technology', Discussion Paper 54, Newcastle upon Tyne, Centre for Urban and Regional Development Studies, University of Newcastle upon Tyne.

Gudgin, G., Moore, B., and Rhodes, J. (1982), 'Employment Problems in the Cities and Regions of the UK: Prospects for the 1980s', *Cambridge Economic Policy Review* 8, (2).

Hall, P. (1981), 'The Geography of the Fifth Kondratieff Cycle', *New Society* 958, 535–7.

House, J. W. (1969), *The North East*, Newton Abbot, David & Charles.

Hudson, R. (1983*a*), 'Capital Accumulation and Regional Problems: A Study of North-East England 1945–80', in F. E. I. Hamilton and G. Linge, eds., *Regional Industrial Systems*, Chichester, Wiley.

—— (1983*b*), 'The Paradoxes of State Intervention: The Impact of Nationalised Industry Policies and Regional Policy on Employment in the Northern Region in the Post-war Period', in R. Chapman, ed., *Public policy studies: North-East England*, Edinburgh, Edinburgh University Press.

——, and Sadler, D. (1983), 'Anatomy of a Disaster: The Closure of Consett Steelworks', *Northern Economic Review* 6, 2–17.

Johnson, P. S., and Cathcart, D. G. (1979), 'New Firm Formation and Regional Development: Evidence from the Northern Region', *Regional Studies* 13, 268–80.

Johnston, R. J. (1982), 'And the future?' in R. J. Johnston and J. C. Doornkamp, eds., *The Changing Geography of the UK*, London, Methuen.

Killick, T. (1983), 'Manufacturing Plant Openings, 1976–80', *British Business* 11(11), 466–8.

Lever, W. P. (1979), 'Industry and Labour Markets in Great Britain', in F. E. I. Hamilton and G. J. R. Linge, eds., *Spatial Analysis, Industry and the Industrial Environment*, Vol. 1, *Industrial System*, Chichester, Wiley.

McCord, N. (1979), *North-East England: The Region's Development 1760—1960*, London, Batsford.

McCrone, G. (1969), *Regional Policy*, London, Allen & Unwin.

Marquand, J. (1980), 'Measuring the Effects and Costs of Regional Incentives', Working paper 32, London, Government Economic Service, Department of Industry.

Marshall, J. N. (1979*a*), 'Ownership, Organization and Industrial Linkage: A Case Study of the Northern Region of England', *Regional Studies* 13, 531–57.

—— (1979*b*), 'Corporate Organization and Regional Office Employment', *Environment and Planning A* 11, 553–67.

Massey, D. B. (1984), *Spatial Divisions of Labour*, London, Methuen.

Murgatroyd, N., and Smith, P. (1984), *The Third Sector Economy: An Appraisal of Community Business Ventures in the North East*, Newcastle upon Tyne, Northern Regional Group, Councils for Voluntary Service and Rural Community Councils.

North of England County Councils Association (1982), *The State of the Region 1982*, Carlisle, NECCA.

—— (1983), *The State of the Region 1983*, Carlisle, NECCA.

—— (1984), *A Profile of the Northern Region 1983*, Morpeth, NECCA.

Northern Region Strategy Team (1977), *Strategic Plan for the Northern Region*, Newcastle upon Tyne, NRST.

Oakey, R. P., Thwaites, A. T., and Nash, P. A. (1980), 'The Regional Distribution of Innovative Manufacturing Establishments in Britain', *Regional Studies* 14, 235–54.

Pounce, R. (1981), *Industrial Movement in the United Kingdom, 1966—75*, London, HMSO.

Price, K. (1982), 'Help for Small Business in the North East', *Northern Economic Review* 2, 25–31.

Regional Studies Association (1983), *Report of an Inquiry into Regional Problems in the United Kingdom*, Norwich, Geobooks.

Scottish Council (1962), *Report on the Scottish Economy*, Edinburgh, Scottish Council (Development and Industry).

Shildon Action Group (1984), *Shildon Interim Action Plan*, Sedgefield, Sedgefield District Council.

Smailes, A. E. (1960), *North England*. London, Nelson.

Smith, E. (1983), 'Economic Development Policies of the County and Borough Authorities in Cleveland', in Buswell 1983.

Smith, I. J. (1979), 'The Effect of External Takeovers on Manufacturing Employment Change in the Northern Region between 1963 and 1973', *Regional Studies* 13, 421–38.

Storey, D. J. (1981), 'New Firm Formation, Employment Change and the Small Firm: The Case of Cleveland County', *Urban Studies* 18, 335–45.

—— (1982*a*), *Entrepreneurship and the New Firm*, London, Croom Helm.

—— (1982*b*), 'Small Firms and Economic Recovery', *Northern Economic Review* 2, 14–19.

—— (1983*a*), 'Indigenizing a Regional Economy: The Importance of Management Buyouts', *Regional Studies* 17, 471–5.

—— (1983*b*), 'How Beautiful is "Small"?' *SSRC Newsletter* 49, 18–20.

Thwaites, A. T. (1982), 'Some Evidence of Regional Variations in the Introduction and Diffusion of Industrial Products and Processes within British Manufacturing Industry', *Regional Studies* 16, 371–81.

Townsend, A. R. (1982), 'The Distribution of Redundancies in the North of England', *Northern Economic Review* 4, 3–10.

—— (1983), *The Impact of Recession on Industry, Employment and the Regions*, London, Croom Helm.

Warren, K. (1973), *North East England*, Oxford, Oxford University Press.

—— (1980), 'North East England', in G. Manners, D. Keeble, B. Rodgers, and K. Warren, *Regional Development in Britain*, second edition, Chichester, Wiley.

Williams,. R. H. (1982), 'Tyne and Wear's Industrial Improvement Areas', *Northern Economic Review* 4, 18–27.

CHAPTER 9
Wales

P. N. Cooke

During 1984–5 the National Union of Mineworkers entered into a struggle which was unlike any other in the history of the coalmining industry. The crucial difference between that struggle and comparable events in 1926, 1972, and 1974 was that the terrain of the strike was formed not by the need to protect or enhance wage levels but by the imperative of preserving sources of employment in single-industry localities. The roles of the state in alleviating regional disparities and as a corporate owner of productive capacity are conventionally separated in regional analysis. The argument here is that the nature of state intervention in regional development cannot satisfactorily be compartmentalized in this way. It is only by understanding the nature of structural economic change as mediated by the state that an understanding of why large numbers of coalminers were prepared to suffer the privations of a year's wagelessness can be achieved. Experience led them to mistrust the argument that traditional industry can be painlessly run down, with jobs lost being replaced by new jobs brought in with the judicious application of regional aid instruments.

This chapter might have been titled 'Post-industrial Wales: A Suitable Case for Treatment', because that label, contentious as it is amongst theorists of mature capitalism, forces itself upon the consciousness of anyone who consults the sectoral employment trends of the past decade or so, as revealed by the Censuses of Employment. It also summarizes the fears of Welsh miners, the experience of former steelworkers, and the uncertain future for many still in manufacturing industry. Wherever you look in Wales—urban, rural, north, or south—a similar tale of industrial employment decline for men and women, and growth, first of public, then of private service-sector employment, mainly for women, has unfolded during the 1970s and early 1980s.

Wales came to occupy a particular position in the spatial division of labour of imperial Britain. It was an archetypal basic-industry region, whether providing roofing slate for the burgeoning slums and suburbs of Victorian Britain, steam coal for the imperial merchant and naval fleets, or rails, sections, and brackets for the railroad systems of North and South America. The debate about how to characterize Wales in that imperial division of labour ranges from Hechter's (1975) rather flawed view of Wales as an 'internal colony', culturally and economically oppressed by English industrial and financial power, to G. A. Williams's (1982) interesting conception of the dynamic heart of its industrial strength residing in 'imperial South Wales', almost a country within a country. Thomas (1962) has shown how the Welsh economy of the nineteenth and early twentieth centuries moved to different rhythms from those of the rest of the UK. When the latter was in a cyclical downturn, Wales was usually in an economic upturn, often linked more closely to increases in world demand, especially as the resources of North America were opened up. Thomas argues that during that period Wales was integrated into the Atlantic economy almost as much as it was into the rest of the UK. Smith (1980) has called the South Wales of this period 'American Wales' because of the interchange of ideas, economic activities, and population that occurred between the two countries. Astonishingly, he has shown that South Wales was outstripped only by America in its rate of immigration during the years leading up to the First World War.

All that, of course, came to an end generations ago; yet it still echoes in the stubborness, pride, and solidarity of contemporary miners, and their extreme reluctance to see that history completely wiped away. Now there are perhaps only 18,000 employed in an industry which at its peak in Wales employed more than twelve times as many, and there are more employed in both motor vehicle assembly and electrical engineering in Wales than in either the coal or the steel industries which were so formative in that dynamic economy. To record the changes in the intervening years would take a book. All that is attempted here is to record the recent changes in the structure of the Welsh economy, and to interpret the different forms taken by state interventions as efforts have been made to grapple with the permanent problem of economic adjustment, not to say hangover, from the imperial past. The chaper is in two parts. The first is an account of economic and employment change during the 1970s and early 1980s. The second is an interpretation of the changing forms of state intervention which have been brought to bear on the longer-term restructuring of the Welsh space economy.

Industrial South Wales: corridor growth and coalfield decline

Industrial South Wales (see Figures 9.1 and 9.2) can be conveniently divided into three subregions, each of which makes a good degree of social, economic, and political sense. First, there is the coastal 'corridor' whose axis is the main M4 motorway link eastwards to London. This is a politically conservative area, dominated by service-sector employment and, increasingly, high-technology manufacturing industry; it is socially mixed in the sense of having both a comparatively broad range of social classes and a not insignificant proportion of ethnic minority populations. Next there is the coalfield, socially relatively homogeneous, with a high proportion of its population Welsh-identifiers though not Welsh-speakers. Unemployment is universally high, reaching over 30 per cent in some localities; manufacturing employment is not as substantial as in the corridor area even though the population, at around one million, is significantly higher. Finally, there is the mixed western end of South Wales, where the corridor and coalfield intermingle. The area is socialist, as is the coalfield, but tends to look towards the city of Swansea as its main focus in employment and consumption terms. Socially, it is more heterogeneous than

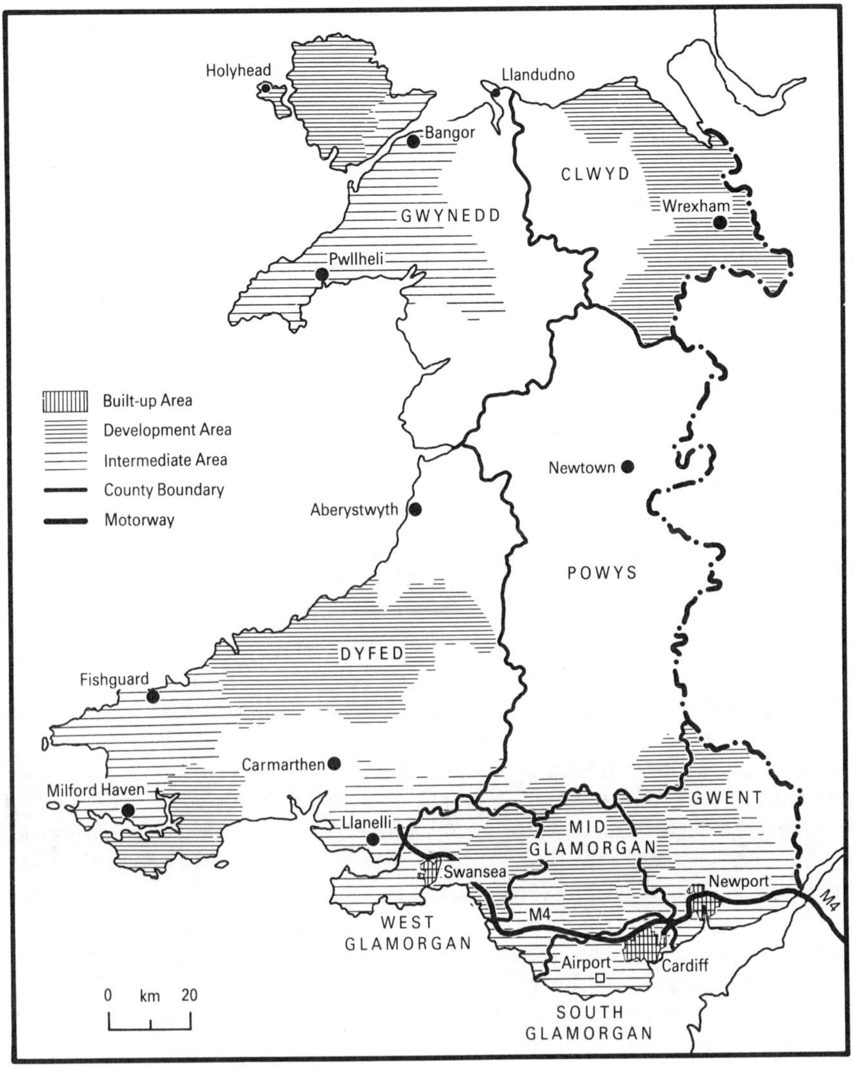

Figure 9.1. Wales

the coalfield, but also more Welsh, in the sense of having a higher proportion of Welsh-speakers.

The coastal corridor

It can be seen from Figure 9.3 that there was employment decline in most manufacturing and extractive industries throughout the 1970s and into the 1980s. Interestingly, the only primary or secondary industrial category not to fit

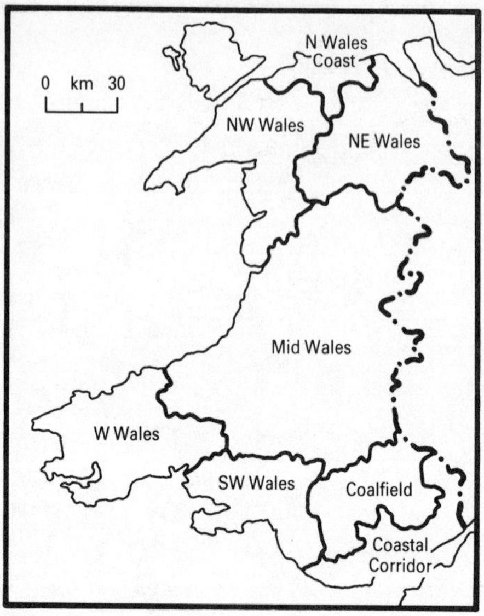

Figure 9.2. Regional subdivisions of Wales

this pattern was the engineering industry. This showed employment growth during the 1976–81 period, a reflection of large-scale inward investment by foreign capital, most notably in the motor vehicles industry, where there was a 78 per cent employment increase (90 per cent for males, 21 per cent for females). The other manufacturing growth sector was electronics and electrical engineering, where 1,130 net new jobs were created, again mostly for men (70 per cent) although the sector has traditionally had a more even gender division of labour than most. The reasons for growth in modern engineering industries is tied to the decentralization plans of large corporations (Ford, for example) and the desire by Japanese producers to gain an EEC foothold. But a key condition for this inward investment has been the availability of finance and factories supplied by government agencies (the Welsh Office and the Welsh Development Agency), good infrastructure (such as motorway links to the UK network) and the suitability of the labour force, for example its familiarity with shift-working, and the preparedness of trades unions to agree to single-union plants and no-strike deals.

Offsetting this employment growth was the massive job loss in metal manufacturing in the 1976–81 period (K. Morgan 1983). This was almost wholly accounted for by the closure and slimming down of steel mills which occurred at the Government's behest after 1978 in particular. From 1971 onwards, 15,000 jobs were lost, of which 11,800 disappeared after 1976. These were overwhelmingly male jobs, though 1,000 women's jobs were also lost in metals after 1976. The other substantial job-shedding sectors were in primary industry (mainly coalmining) and construction, both overwhelmingly male-dominated industries.

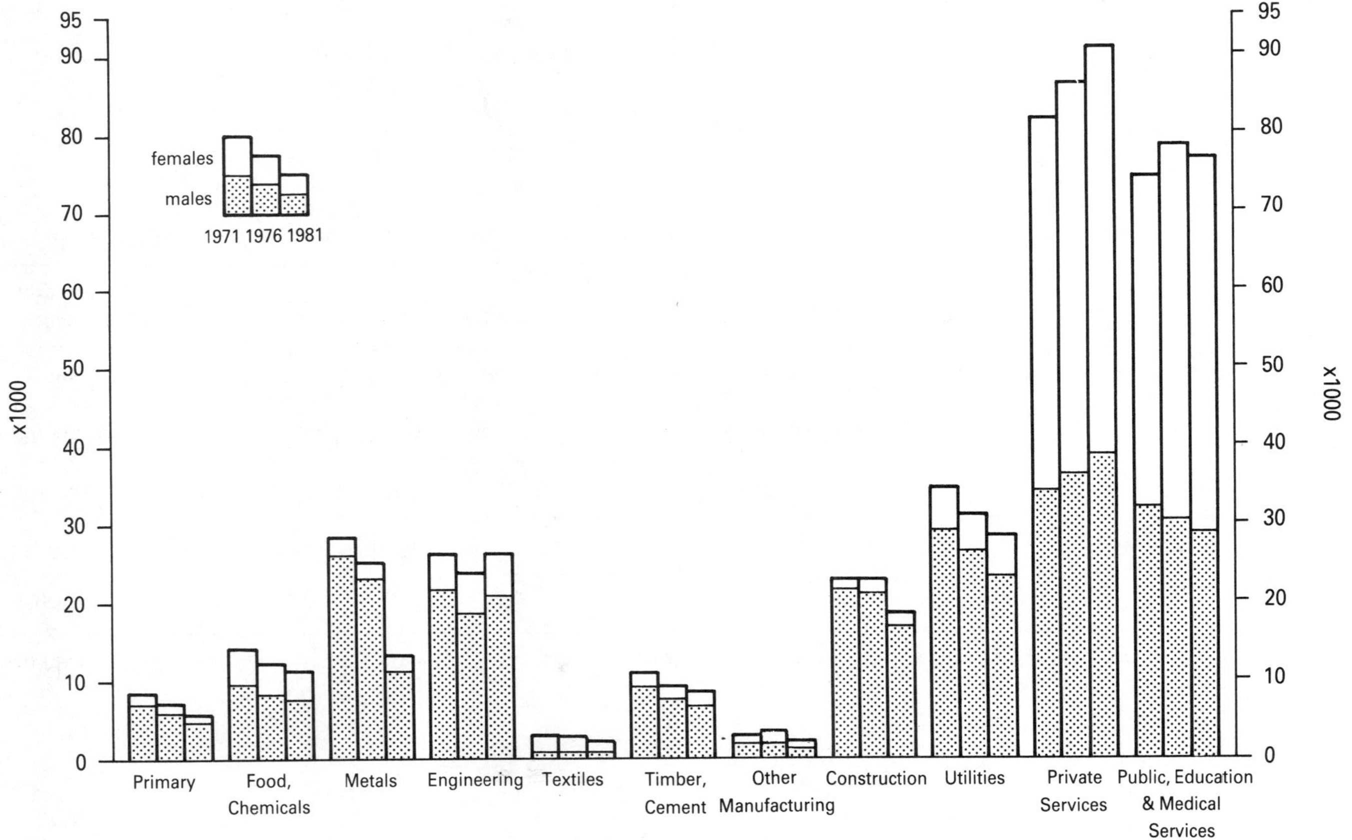

Figure 9.3. Employment change in the South Wales coastal corridor, 1971–81
Source: Manpower Services Commission, Annual Census of Employment Data

Table 9.1. Employment change by subsector (minimum list headings) in the South Wales coastal corridor, 1971–81

5 fastest-growing subsectors				5 fastest-declining subsectors			
1971–6		1976–81		1971–6		1976–81	
1. Education	+4,631	1. Small, private services	+2,132	1. Local Government	−4,613	1. Iron and steel	−11,230
2. Small, private services	+3,444	2. Motor vehicles	+1,860	2. Small machinery	−2,252	2. Construction	−4,056
3. National Govt.	+2,310	3. Business services	+1,534	3. Insulated cables	−1,805	3. Local government	−3,376
4. Public houses	+2,176	4. Radio, radar	+1,417	4. Iron and steel	−1,803	4. Railways	−1,493
5. Telephone apparatus	+1,693	5. Medical services	+1,147	5. Paper and board	−1,510	5. Telephone apparatus	−1,227

Source: Manpower Services Commision, Annual Census of Employment Data.

Moving to the tertiary sector, it is clear that this is where the new jobs appeared in reasonably large numbers, although it is important to draw a distinction between public- and private-sector services. The former grew in number for both males and females up to 1976, but from 1976 to 1981 there was a loss of 2,100 male public service jobs, while those for women during that period grew in number only very marginally. This reflects government policy towards local government, where there was a loss of 3,400 jobs during 1976–81.

The initial surge in public-sector services was associated with office decentralization by national government and the growth of regional government services. Part of the explanation for office decentralization by government was the female labour supply problem in London, and the availability of potential female clerical workers in South Wales (Winckler 1983). This large public-sector labour force injected income into the local economy, and in turn generated demand for private-sector services, where 9,000 new jobs were created in the 1970s, at an evenly increasing pace throughout the decade. Much of this new work was taken by women, and tends to be part-time, low-paid and non-unionized; these jobs are no real compensation for the loss of highly paid, full-time, and well-organized male jobs, particularly in steel. Table 9.1 is a summary of the five fastest-growing and declining subsectors in the coastal corridor.

The coastal corridor has thus moved rapidly away from its historical emphasis on heavy industry, and towards a new specialization in consumer and, to a lesser extent, producer services. There is also an emerging trend towards higher value-added engineering production, centred upon electronic engineering (for example, semiconductor production, consumer electronics) and motor vehicles (for example, motor vehicle engines).

The coalfield

Despite its proximity to the coastal corridor, the coalfield subregion displayed substantially different employment patterns over the 1971–81 period (see Figure 9.4). First, its dependence on primary production remained much greater than that of the coast. However, 9,000 jobs were lost in the decade, mainly in coalmining. This loss of male-dominated employment was compounded by the loss of over 8,000 metal-manufacturing jobs, mainly in iron and steel. However, deindustrialization did not stop there, for in the engineering industry, growing in the early 1970s, nearly 9,000 jobs were lost after 1976, and in textiles another 8,000 jobs, over half of them occupied by females, were lost over the decade. The only manufacturing bright spot was in food, petroleum, and chemicals processing, where 2,300 new jobs were created, mainly in chemicals, over the decade.

Service employment now dominates in the coalfield, though to a lesser extent than on the coast. In 1971 coalfield engineering employment was greater than that in private or public services. By 1981 both service sectors employed more than engineering. As is the case nearer the coast, women predominate in services, but unlike on the coast, private services are growing only marginally

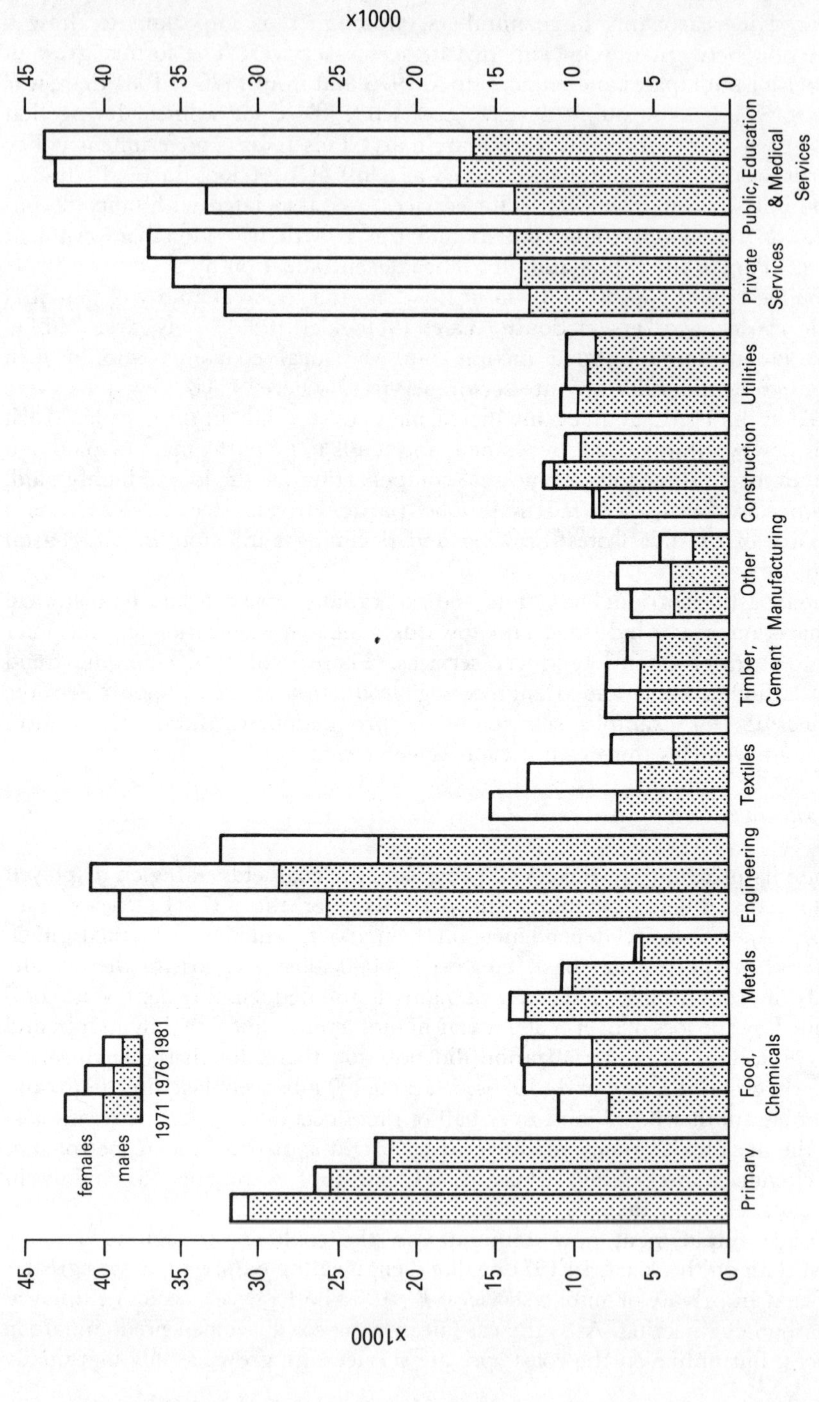

Figure 9.4. Employment change in the South Wales coalfield, 1971–81
Source: Manpower Services Commission, Annual Census of Employment Data

and public services are not in decline. These two features reflect the lack of private regional headquarters, business services, hotels, and so on in the coalfield, and the greater dependence upon the public sector for white-collar employment generally. With the steep decline in male manufacturing employment, this subregion is also becoming proportionately more gender divided in terms of labour market participation.

The employment change in the coalfield represents a dual de-industrialization—the decline not only of the heavy industries which gave definition to the subregion but also of the government-assisted investments of the 1940s and 1960s aimed at providing alternatives to job-shedding basic industry. There are faint signs of a third round of investment in the industries associated with new, electronic technologies (Table 9.2), but it is clear that the coalfield has become services-dependent, with a substantial proportion of female employees. While women became an increasingly important part of the labour force of some manufacturing industries in the 1960s and early 1970s, their proportional share of job loss has become greater than for men in the 1970s and 1980s.

West South Wales

This subregion is centred upon the city of Swansea (with a population of about 100,000) which was a major centre of metal manufacturing (steel, tinplate, nickel) with coalmining in its hinterland. However, Swansea itself has been developing as a service centre for much of the south western area of Wales. It represents a subregion combining the characteristics of both the coastal corridor and the coalfield subregions. Figure 9.5 indicates the subregion's rapidly changing employment profile during 1971–81. Job loss in metal manufacturing, primarily in steel, was of a greater magnitude than elsewhere in south Wales with 16,000 jobs lost, of which nearly 14,000 disappeared after 1976. Engineering declined by over 10,000 jobs. Women's jobs were lost at an accelerating rate, with the male/female ratio slipping from 3:1 to 5:1 in the process. There was no growth in employment outside the services industries at the SIC order level. However, there were large gains in both private- and public-sector services at different points during the decade. A huge expansion of public services by over 14,000 jobs took place in the early 1970s. This was echoed to a lesser extent by a 6,400 rise in private services in the late 1970s, over half as great again as the 4,000 rise in private services earlier in the decade. It is difficult to avoid the conclusion that large injections of public services employment in this and other subregions in south Wales had some subsequent effect on the growth of private services, to some extent offsetting the drop in demand for services caused by de-industrialization. Once again, services are revealed to be a strongly feminized area of economic activity, and increasingly so over time.

West South Wales is clearly a subregion where the extremes of de-industrialization and movement towards a 'post-industrial' economy are most pronounced. Manufacturing industry based on older technologies is everywhere in retreat, and the overwhelming proportion of employment growth is to be

Table 9.2. Employment change by subsector (minimum list headings) in the South Wales coalfield, 1971–81

5 fastest-growing subsectors				5 fastest-declining subsectors			
1971–6		1976–81		1971–6		1976–81	
1. Education	+5,424	1. Medical services	+3,186	1. Coalmining	−5,363	1. Coalmining	−3,625
2. Construction	+3,137	2. Postal services	+731	2. Iron and steel	−2,807	2. Iron and steel	−3,345
3. Local govt.	+2,303	3. Electronic computers	+609	3. Man-made fibres	−1,991	3. Metal industries	−2,416
4. Medical services	+1,399	4. Social clubs	+599	4. Iron castings	−895	4. Paper and board	−1,823
5. Pharmaceuticals	+1,272	5. Electrical goods	+587	5. Construction equipment	−763	5. Local government	−1,823

Source: Manpower Services Commission, Annual Census of Employment Data.

Table 9.3. Employment change by subsector (minimum list headings) in west South Wales, 1971–81

5 fastest-growing subsectors				5 fastest-declining subsectors			
1971–76		1976–81		1971–6		1976–81	
1. National govt.	+7,399	1. Education	+4,177	1. Construction	−4,497	1. Iron and steel	−12,650
2. Education	+4,643	2. Small, private services	+3,404	2. Steel plant	−1,875	2. Construction	−4,061
3. Medical	+2,845	3. Property services	+762	3. Small engineering	−1,656	3. Coalmining	−1,683
4. Plastic products	+1,628	4. Electronics	+664	4. Small manufacturing	−1,239	4. Motor vehicles	−1,577
5. Small, private services	+1,120	5. Social clubs	+528	5. Metal industries	−1,044	5. Local government	−1,238

Source: Manpower Services Commission, Annual Census of Employment Data.

found in government-funded services or, more recently, in those small, private services which seem to reply on consumers employed in the public sector to some extent. There are small signs of growth in high-technology industry (Table 9.3), but west South Wales is a sub-economy where the shift towards a feminized, services base has occurred fairly rapidly.

Mid- and west Wales

These two subregions are predominantly rural. Primary production is basically agricultural, varying from dairy farming in lowland areas to sheep-farming in the uplands. As Figure 9.6 makes clear, male agricultural employment held up reasonably well until 1981, aided considerably by the relatively favourable pricing policy for milk and sheepmeat operated by the EEC Common Agricultural Policy. Since 1984 the 9 per cent cut in EEC milk quotas has disrupted employment among small dairy farmers quite markedly. Female agricultural employment, however, declined during the period, with an almost exactly compensating growth of textiles employment for women in mid-Wales and slower manufacturing but rapid service employment growth for women in west Wales. These two rural subregions have thus been moving away from their traditional primary base and towards a heavy services bias on the one hand and an emergent, though small, manufacturing base on the other. Much of the growth of secondary employment is due to a combination of low-wage labour availability and the efforts of government development agencies to stem out-migration.

Employment grew fastest in medical and educational services, hotels, and retailing in both subregions up to 1976. After 1976 growth was strongest in local government, education, dress manufacture, and research services in mid-Wales, and in west Wales in construction, petroleum refining, and small private services. Both subregions lost agricultural and related employment in the early 1970s, and there has been retrenchment in small private and public services and construction from 1976.

In both areas over half of all employment is now in services, and half of service employees are women. This is a greater services emphasis than in industrial Wales, though not as great as in the coastal corridor of South Wales. These trends can be understood largely in terms of increased UK government expenditure on health and education in the 1970s, and a lagged growth in private services consequent on that investment. Such areas are clearly vulnerable to state cutbacks.

North Wales

This Welsh region contains a traditionally heavy industry area centred on steel and coal in the east, a rural, semi-industrialized, and tourist area to the west, and in the centre, an area of services and manufacturing growth on the coast. The greatest employment change in the region over the last decade was the massive loss of steel employment in north east Wales (see Figure 9.7). There

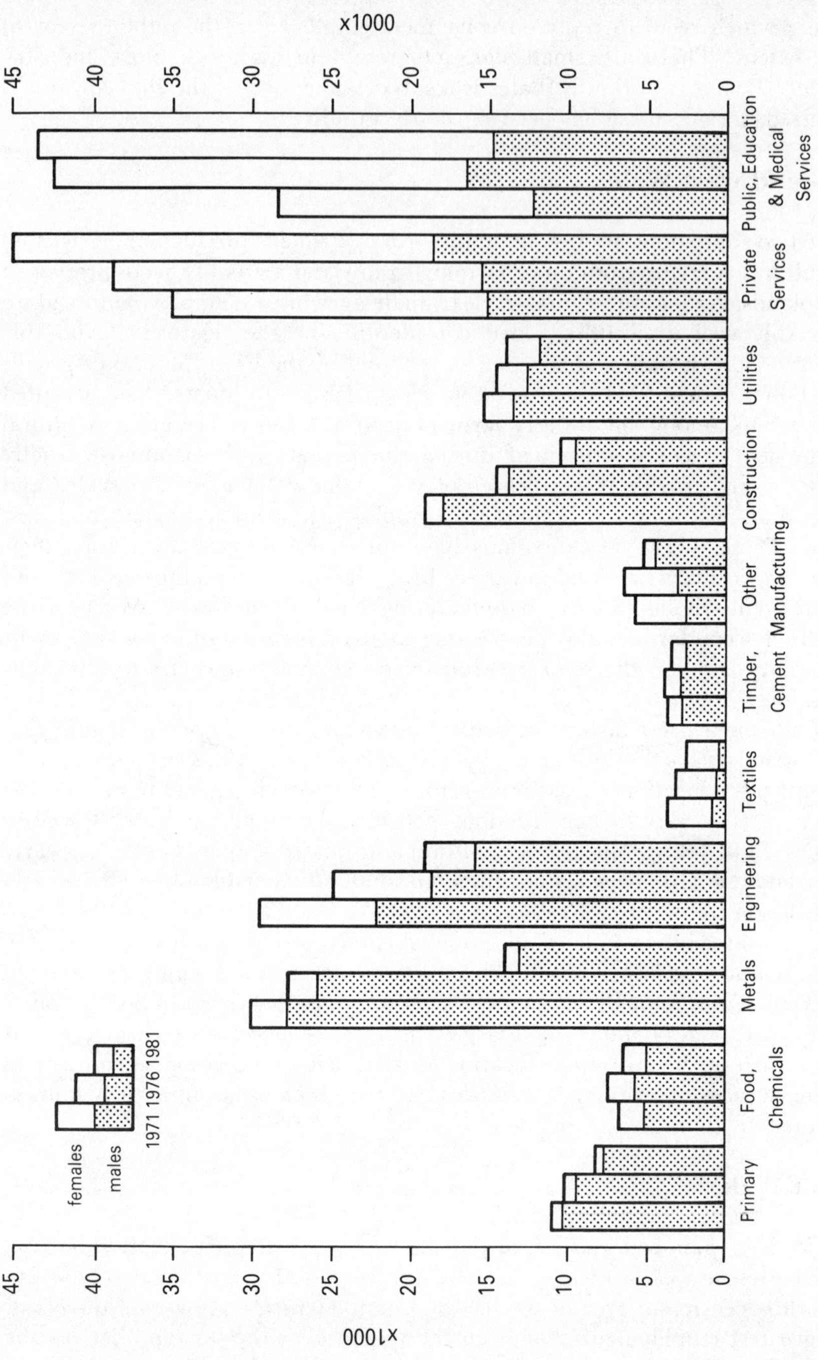

Figure 9.5. Employment change in west South Wales, 1971–81
Source: Manpower Services Commission, Annual Census of Employment Data

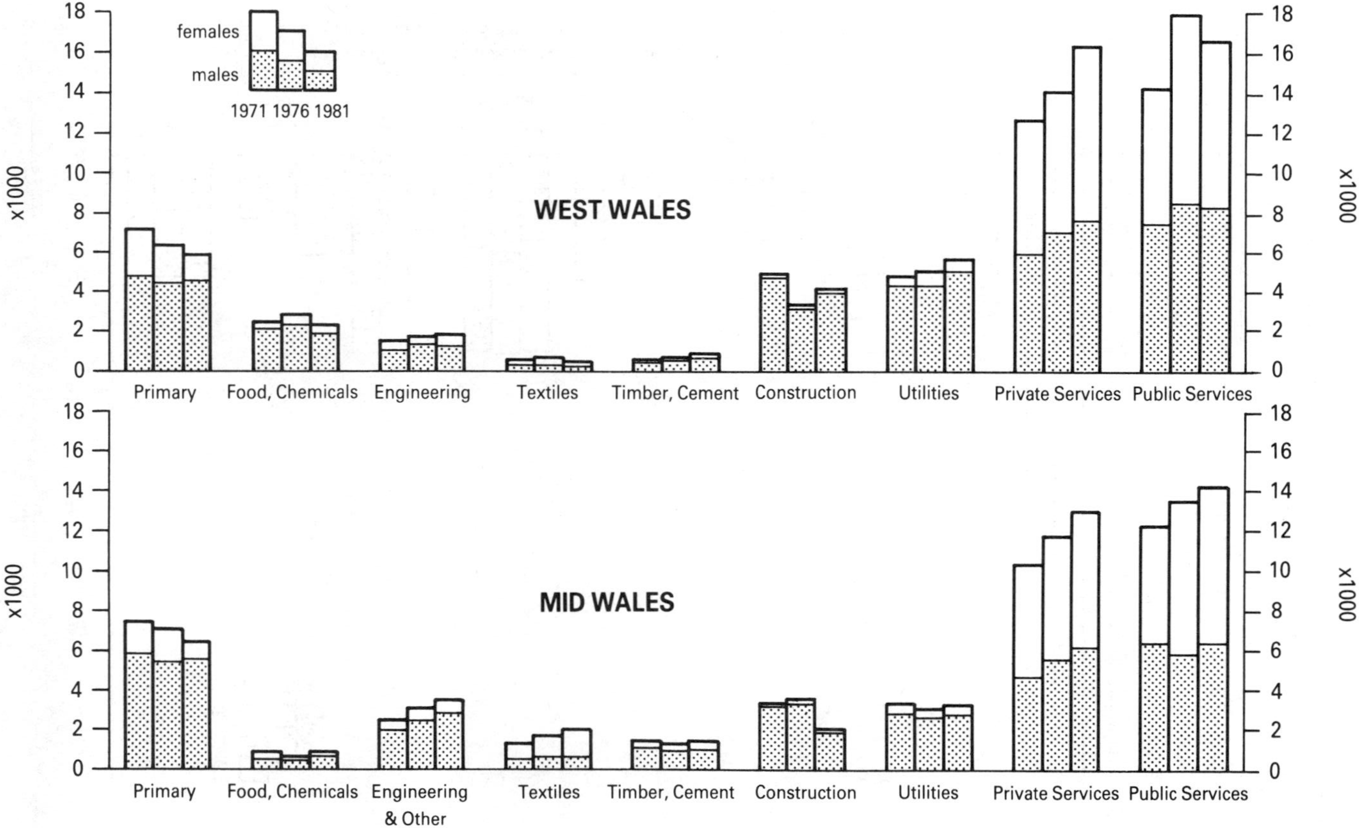

Figure 9.6. Employment change in mid- and west Wales, 1971–81
Source: Manpower Services Commission, Annual Census of Employment Data

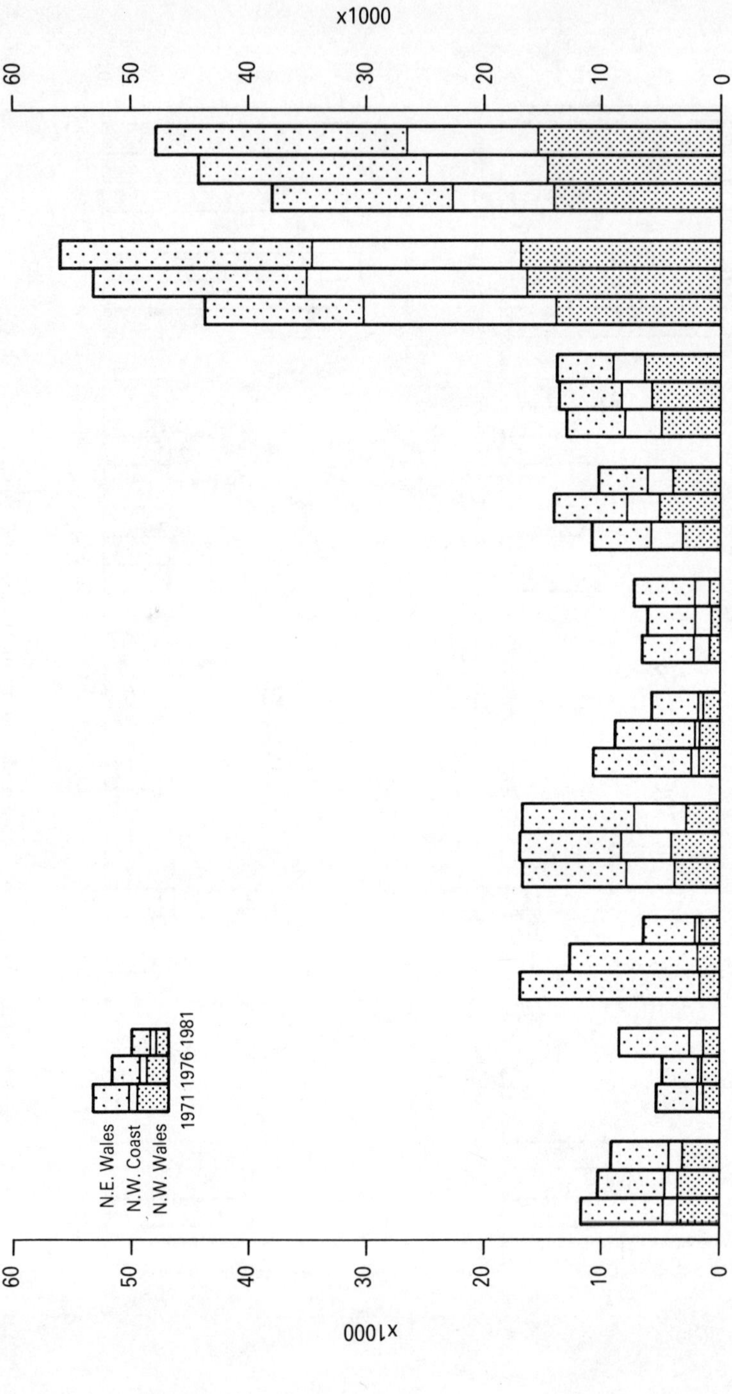

Figure 9.7. Employment change in north Wales, 1971–81
Source: Manpower Services Commission, Annual Census of Employment Data

were also very large increases in service employment, with women predominant in this labour market in the 1970s. Some growth has been registered in engineering, notably aerospace, but there were job losses in coalmining, construction, and man-made fibre industries over the 1971–81 period. In north west Wales, job loss occurred in most sectors excluding services. Notably, small electronics branch plants cut back or closed down. On the North Wales coast, public and private services, especially in medicine, grew consistently, while manufacturing and some private services began to feel the effects of the recession after 1979.

The three subregions, though contiguous, have had the general effects of recession, and in particular the injection of public expenditure and its removal in the nationalized steel industry, impressed upon them differentially. The coast is a centre of tourism services, the north east is becoming very services-dominated, with light engineering emergent, while the north west is dependent on tourism and public services employment. This is the Welsh area where political Conservatism has grown most dramatically. The influx of tourists, some of whom settle, the growth of small private services and public services which inevitably attract in-migrant managers, and the decline in working-class employment in primary and heavy industry are probably changing North Wales more rapidly than anywhere else at present.

State interventions in the restructuring of the Welsh space economy

Wales has experienced massive state involvement in its economic life during the postwar years (Cooke and Rees 1981) and the epithet 'nationalized region' was being employed at the turn of the 1960s in an attempt to fix this growing state-dependence conceptually (Humphrys 1972). By the late 1970s the proportion of the working population employed by the state directly, at slightly under 40 per cent, was demonstrably higher than elsewhere in Great Britain (Parry 1980*a*; 1980*b*). If, in addition, the employed population working in private firms which have decentralized with the aid of regional assistance, and in hill-farming, which only survives through government and EEC subsidy, and the 17 per cent of the workforce unemployed according to official statistics in 1984 are taken into account, then the picture emerges of an economy in which a majority, perhaps as high as 75 per cent, of the population of working age is directly or, in varying degrees, indirectly dependent on resource transfers from the state.

Of course, some of this state-dependence is accounted for by industrial structure. For much of the postwar period the main employers were the coal and steel industries, with rail transport, power generation, and other public utilities also well represented. The ensuing structure fitted in well with the postwar spatial division of labour in Britain. Consumer industries centred on the London–Birmingham axis received cheap inputs from producer regions such as South Wales because public policy recognized that British exports could gain a competitive edge if inputs were priced artificially low. Thus both coal and steel were reorganized early with substantial injections of capital, especially via Marshall Aid, to upgrade technology, and private sector engineering in southern England reaped the benefit. Later, though, the coal industry found itself being starved of internally generated investment, partly because of the huge compensation payments that were legally required consequent upon nationalization, and partly because prices were artificially depressed by government policy. In steel, innovations produced in Wales, such as continuous casting technology, were adopted by competitor countries such as Japan, who then proceeded to invest in super-steel mills with associated economies of scale. Meanwhile, in Britain the only large-scale mill planned was in 1962 actually split in half, with one bit being located in Scotland, at Ravenscraig, and the other in Wales, at Llanwern. This was Harold Macmillan's 'judgement of Solomon' to buy off Scottish protest at rising unemployment levels in 1959, a decision which was subsequently to cost the British steel industry dear (Morgan 1979).

Awareness of structural imbalance in the Welsh economy dates from the interwar years, when some of the earliest state interventions were made in the region to provide employment in consumer goods industries for unemployed coalminers. The Treforest industrial estate, constructed between Cardiff and the coalfield, was one of the first to be opened. In the early postwar years there was a great deal of advance factory building in South Wales, approaching 50 million square feet by the mid-1960s. However, only about 15 per cent of this floor-space was located in the areas where job loss was greatest, in the coalfield; the greater part of the new investment occurred in the coastal corridor between Newport and Llanelli. Simultaneously, steel employment was also shifting to the coast; and it is clear that already in the 1950s the spatial strategy for South Wales assumed the continued run-down of the coalfield communities and a slow but irreversible shift of employment opportunities, and hence population, towards the coastal cities and smaller new or expanded towns.

In the 1960s this process continued apace. In the active stage of regional policy from 1945 to 1951, Wales as a whole received 36 per cent of new plant openings in Development Areas; in the passive phase from 1952 to 1959 the share dropped back to 23 per cent; then in the active, 1960–71 phase it rose slightly to 24 per cent (Moore and Rhodes 1975). Wales was being given less favourable treatment in relation to other Development Areas than it had received in the 1940s when, of course, there were fewer competing areas. Lack of spatial sensitivity meant that most of this new investment was located, as noted before, in advance factories constructed away from the main coalfield unemployment blackspots. Despite the coalfield's Special Development Area status, only one of the large industrial estates constructed on the sites of the huge wartime munitions production complexes was located there, and even then it was on its most northerly edge. Unsurprisingly, it remained relatively unsuccessful. In north east Wales the equivalent facility was also located with market accessibility given priority over the pattern of unemployment blackspots. Employment directly generated by regional policy in Wales in 1960–72 was estimated at between 62,000 and 72,000 jobs (Moore and Rhodes 1975). Nevertheless, unemployment was on average 50 per cent higher in Wales than for Great Britain throughout the period.

The Development Board for Rural Wales

The problems of rural Wales have tended to be overshadowed by the severe employment difficulties experienced in the industrial belts of south and north east Wales. Yet it was often the problems of rural mid-Wales, notably depopulation and the preservation of the language, which were in the minds of politicians and policy-makers when reference was made to the importance of extra assistance being given to meet 'the special needs of Wales' (Rowlands 1972; Cooke and Rees 1984).

Between 1951 and 1961, mid-Wales lost 2.8 per cent of its population and over 5.0 per cent of those aged 0 to 44. Between 1961 and 1971 net migration fell a little to 2.4 per cent, with out-migration in the 0–44 range falling to a just over 4 per cent. However, between 1971 and 1981 the historic pattern of out-migration was completely reversed, as mid-Wales registered a 9.5 per cent net increase in population, which was wholly accounted for by a net surplus of in-migrants. A substantial proportion of this net in-migration is explained by the creation of job opportunities in the Severn valley, especially in Newtown, Britain's smallest New Town, and other market towns which were designated as growth centres by the Development Board for Rural Wales (DBRW, now called Mid-Wales Development), established by Act of Parliament in 1976 R. Morgan 1983).

There were government-financed factories in mid-Wales before the establishment of the Development Board. They had been provided by the Mid-Wales Development Corporation, the Mid-Wales Industrial Development Board, the Development Commission, and the Council for Small Industries in Rural Areas. However, by 1969 there were only 58 enterprises in such factories, 27 branch plants, 16 relocated firms, and 15 new firms (Garbett-Edwards 1972). By 1978 DBRW owned 104 factories, but thereafter a sharp acceleration in factory building brought the total to 219 by 1981, and to 328 by 1984 (DBRW statistics). The profile of economic activity in such factories has changed relatively little since 1969, as Table 9.4 shows. Although it has been suggested (Martin 1982) that the ownership pattern is unlikely to have changed greatly from the branch plant domination of the 1960s, the DBRW strategy has shifted towards the provision of small units for new firms, and that sector has risen

Table 9.4. Development Board for Rural Wales: factory activities, 1969 and 1981

Firm types	1969 (%)	1981 (%)
Clothing	18	10
Engineering	35	41
Timber, paper	5	19
Plastics	5	8
Others	37	23

Source: Martin 1982.

proportionately as a consequence. According to DBRW, its 257 factories in 1982 provided '6,000 job opportunities' (DBRW 1982). Clearly, the use of the vague term 'job opportunities' implies that net job creation was rather less. Manufacturing employment in the region increased by only 1,000 between 1976 and 1981. This undoubtedly underestimates the impact of DBRW; there was an increase of 2,600 private-service-sector jobs in the region, some of which can be realistically assigned to the activities of the Board. Thus it is probable that the real impact of DBRW on mid-Wales employment (1976–81) is somewhere close to the middle of the range from the figure of 1,000 net manufacturing jobs created to the 6,000 'job opportunities' claimed by DBRW.

One final point that should be noted about the impact of the DBRW is that its activities are highly uneven in spatial terms. As noted earlier, much of the investment in new-factory building has been concentrated in the Severn valley. For example, Newtown had 95 of the Board's 257 factories in 1982. Concentration of this kind has been subject to criticism for two reasons. First, the more peripheral, coastal areas have not benefited to the same extent from new investment as those areas close to good communications links with the West Midlands of England. One effect of this is that 25 per cent of in-migrants to Newtown are not from Wales but originate from the West Midlands (R. Morgan 1983). Second, the 'mini-growth pole' policy has been perceived as an urban solution to a rural problem: that is, rural depopulation is still continuing, but Newtown and other, small growth centres are acting as a brake on out-migration to regions outside mid-Wales. Criticism of this urbanization strategy, combined with the decline in capital mobility during the 1970s and 1980s, has led DBRW to pursue a more diffuse strategy, based on encouraging indigenous potential by providing more small factories and workshops, often in relatively small village settings (Williams 1980).

The Welsh Development Agency

The Welsh Development Agency (WDA) was set up in 1976 to further economic development in Wales, to promote international competitiveness, to maintain or safeguard employment, and to help improve the Welsh environment. The means for achieving these aims were through the provision of loan and equity capital, building advance factories, and undertaking derelict land reclamation. The principal innovation, therefore was that the agency could use its own finances to make loans to, or purchase stock in, private companies, and it could set up new companies which were subsequently expected to be sold to the private sector or have shares floated on the stock market. It was not charged with performing an economic planning function for Wales, a position reiterated publicly in 1977 (WDA 1977). Moreover, the WDA was keen to counter the image that it represented 'creeping nationalization', a fear which was present amongst industrialists in Wales given the rhetoric surrounding its sister agency, the National Enterprise Board (Cooke 1980). Rather, it sought to present itself as 'a fairly adventurous merchant bank', 'an industrial property developer', and a 'major land reclaimer' (Gray 1976). The relative success of this presentation is shown by the fact that the WDA became a corporate member of the Confederation of British Industry within three years of its establishment.

The emphasis on its 'adventurous' financial activities as a distinctive feature, by comparison with previous forms of regional policy, might have led observers to expect equity investment to account for the lion's share of the WDA's budget. However, a lower share of its funds was earmarked for industrial investment than was the case with either the Scottish Development Agency or the National Enterprise Board. Even the modest target of 31 per cent of the budget for such investment between 1976 and 1982 was approached only once, in 1977–8, when 26 per cent of expenditure was in equities. The average for the remaining years was 7 per cent. By far the largest proportion of expenditure from 1976 to 1982 was in the building of advance factories; on average 75 per cent of expenditure was in this category. The remainder was allocated to derelict land clearance and environment upgrading.

From the outset the WDA was required by the Secretary of State for Wales to achieve a 15–20 per cent rate of return on capital invested. The complete unreality of such a target is reflected in the statements of accounts for 1981–2 and 1982–3 which show (unlike previous WDA annual reports) the target agreed with the Welsh Office for the financial returns (5.6 per cent in 1981–2; 6.0 per cent in 1982–3) and the actual return earned, expressed as a percentage of the capital base (2.2 per cent in 1981–2; 9.1 in 1982–3). The 'pragmatic' targets agreed with the Welsh Office were exactly half the 'ideal' target determined by the Secretary of State, who has placed the duty on the WDA:

> to be guided in its decisions to invest and to dispose of investments by the aim to achieve over a rolling five-year period a cash return at least equal to the cost of Government borrowing over the same period. (WDA 1983)

In 1981–2 and 1982–3 this cost to the Government was 11.4 and 12.0 per cent respectively. It should also be noted that the substantial increase in return on investment in 1982–83 was largely accounted for by sales of stock and property. Clearly, such inflated rates of return cannot be sustained in the long term, as the WDA's Corporate Plan (WDA 1984) has recognized. Given that, up to 1981–2 there were probably no net returns on investment, only losses—especially in 1980 when more than £2.25 million of investment was written off—then the claim that the WDA was going to act like a fairly adventurous merchant bank has to be treated with some scepticism.

Moving to the WDA's responsibility for safeguarding and creating employment, it is a sobering fact that from 1976, when the WDA began its operations, to 1981 the Welsh economy experienced a loss of 110,000 jobs in the primary and secondary sectors. Clearly, therefore, the WDA has been confronted with a massive and accelerating jobs crisis during its brief history. The major response until very recently has been focused upon the provision of advance factory space. Indeed, during the period 1980–2, when job loss in the South Wales steel industry was of a scale 'never encountered before in a relatively small geographical area' (Select Committee on Welsh Affairs 1980), £48 million of additional government aid was made available to the WDA for new factory

Table 9.5. Welsh Development Agency expenditure on advance-factory building, 1976–7 to 1982–3

Fiscal year	Actual £ million	Constant (1980) prices
1976–7	10.1	12.9
1977–8	14.9	18.0
1978–9	28.5	31.9
1979–80	38.6	38.6
1980–1	60.0	54.0
1981–2	66.3	54.4
1982–3	46.2	35.1

Source: WDA Annual Reports.

Note: Constant prices calculated from the Producer Price Index in Central Statistical Office, (1985).

building. The expenditure profiles on advance-factory construction are shown in Table 9.5.

The key question regarding this substantial construction programme is, of course: how many new jobs were created in Wales as a direct result of advance factory provision? In a review of progress published in 1981 (WDA 1981), the claim was made that 11,000 jobs had been helped into being, with 'prospects and opportunities' for a further 9,000 as a result of the factory-building programme. However, it has recently been demonstrated that such figures must be questioned. By March 1982 the WDA had completed 812 factory units which, when added to those it had inherited, gave a total of 1,225. At that time 40 per cent of the WDA-built units were vacant and available for letting—a very high figure by comparison with the 14 per cent more common amongst private-sector industrial property development companies. In those factories which the WDA owned, 12,954 persons were employed. However, in the advance factories which the WDA had built since 1976, 5,125 persons were employed, less than half the figure claimed. The WDA claim is that, between 1976 and 1981, 300 new tenants had taken leases on their property; but clearly the proportion of these moves which were voluntary rather than WDA-induced, and which resulted from moves between WDA factory units, needs to be taken into account in assessments of this kind (Eirug 1983).

In the 1980s the WDA has moved somewhat from being a 'state enterprise' form of agency, drawing its funds from the public sector, towards a more strongly 'entrepreneurial' style of activity. In 1982 a £1 million (subsequently increased to £2 million) risk capital fund was set up expressly to supply investment capital to new-technology ventures and and small businesses. This move marked the recognition by the Chief Executive of the WDA, endorsed by the Secretary of State for Wales, that enough advance factory space was now available to more than meet likely demand. Consequently the WDA changed direction somewhat, proposing to increase its investment activities by comparison with its property development programme which had made the agency possibly the largest general property developer in Western Europe (Eirug 1983). In early 1985 it was announced that the WDA was to collaborate with the Commercial Bank of Wales to establish a pension fund which would act as a source of industrial investment capital. This was a response to the Welsh Secretary of State's criticism of the City of London for stifling the prospects of industry in Wales through its unwillingness to stimulate investment in areas perceived to be 'remote' from its normal sphere of influence. The WDA also entered agreements with a small number of private pension funds and insurance companies to finance both property development and investment schemes.

A move away from building standardized advance factories towards the provision of a smaller number of 'bespoke' premises for known high-technology companies was accompanied by the establishment of two new bodies—WINvest (in April 1982) and WINtech (in May 1984). The former arises from the need, expressed by the House of Commons Select Committee on expenditure in 1978, to overcome what was seen as confusion and waste caused by the proliferation of agencies engaged in attracting industry to Wales. WINvest co-ordinates the inward investment roles of the WDA and the Welsh Office Industry Department, rather as Locate in Scotland does *vis à vis* the Scottish Development Agency, although, unlike the latter, it has no overseas offices. WINtech, by contrast, is the core of a technology-broking network. It links industry with sources of scientific and technological expertise in universities and other centres of scientific research (Deloitte, Haskins and Sells 1983).

It is clearly too early to judge the effectiveness of these new forms of intervention. The WDA has now chosen to put more of its eggs in the highly competitive, highly internationalized, high-technology basket. In effect, therefore, the WDA has itself written off the traditional industrial structure of Wales and is engaged in the risky business of what might be called substitution restructuring. This approach involves targeting specific new industrial sectors, rather than aiding a plethora of both *in situ* and footloose outside industry, as occurred with traditional regional policy. This contrasts with what might be called 'graduation restructuring', which builds innovative activity on an existing production base by moving up-market from basic to quality products. The substitution strategy has been in existence in France since the 1950s, particularly in Brittany, where electronics was used as the spearhead of modernization. It has resulted in only 13,000 new jobs in electronics over a thirty-year period (Cooke 1985). Nevertheless, a not insignificant presence of high-technology companies, especially in electronics-related activity, has developed in South East Wales since the WDA was established. Moreover, the claim of the Secretary of State for Wales, echoed by the press, is that in the two years 1982–3 and 1983–4, Wales was highly successful in winning around 25 per cent of all mobile investment projects in the United Kingdom (Smith 1985).

New investment on this scale during a severe recession, and after the reductions in regional aid brought about by the redrawing of the Assisted Area map in 1979–82, suggests that the WDA and its subsidiaries, WINvest and WINtech, may well be effective means of augmenting inward investment. It also suggests that, with the further erosion of Assisted Area status in 1984, the co-ordination and forward planning embodied in the WDA's Corporate Plan 1984–90, allied with a predictable level of government funding (set at £50 million per annum 1984–5 to 1986–7), are realistic instruments for future state intervention. Wales may be better prepared to face the reduction of other forms of regional assistance than are regional economies which lack a development agency presence.

Regional policy in the 1980s

It is clear from government pronouncements since the early 1980s that Wales, along with other Assisted Areas, can no longer rely on national measures to help overcome the job loss associated with industrial decline. Successive Industry Ministers (Cooke *et al.* 1984) and the Secretary of State for Wales adopted the position that problem regions must become more self-sustaining, more competitive, and less reliant upon central government than had hitherto been the case.

The first round of cuts in 1979 resulted in the abolition of the symbolic but senescent Welsh Council, along with Regional Economic Planning Councils elsewhere in Britain, the redefinition of the Assisted Areas map, and associated financial reductions. Before 1979 the whole of Wales had been designated for Assisted Area status of one kind or another with around 50 per cent of its population in Special Development Areas, 40 per cent in Development Areas, and 10 per cent in Intermediate Areas. The new Assisted Area map from 1980 progressively reduced the population in the first category to 15 per cent, in the second to 35 per cent, and increased the third to 25 per cent, leaving the remainder unassisted. The reduction of Regional Development Grant (RDG) expenditure was temporarily quite marked, as payment of RDGs was deferred for four months after June 1979; expenditure then climbed sharply before levelling off after 1981–2, as shown in Table 9.6. Moreover, a sudden increase in Regional Selective Assistance (Section 7) acted as some compensation.

In the 1984 round of cuts in regional expenditure, the Bridgend, Cardiff, Newport, Swansea, Cwmbran, and Pontypool Development Areas were downgraded—only the minuscule Tenby Intermediate Area was upgraded. The key element in the downgrading was the loss of entitlement to automatic grant aid, the rationale being that the Welsh M4 corridor (which passes through or near each downgraded area) has been attracting the lion's share of inward investment into Wales as a whole, and is in a better competitive position than the coalfield which received Development Area status. Other downgradings in Wales were in north Pembrokeshire, a small part of Anglesey, and the north western peninsula of North Wales.

There was, understandably, a wide-ranging outcry at the financial effects of the changes. The estimate was that there would be a net reduction of £60 million in aid to Wales, half of the 1982–3 level of RDG expenditure. Within this reduced total, there are likely to be increases in Selective Assistance to

Table 9.6. Regional policy expenditure in Wales (£ millions), 1978–9 to 1982–3

Regional Development Grants		Regional Selective Assistance	
Year		Section 7	Section 8
1978–9	71.4	—	0.9
1979–80	50.7	—	2.4
1980–1	103.5	24.0	0.7
1981–2	122.2	22.0	1.5
1982–3	121.5	26.0	2.6

Source: Welsh Office 1984.

prime projects. An illustration of the prospects for the latter was provided by the proposal of the Laura Ashley dresswear and fabrics company to locate a new plant in an assisted region of the Netherlands, rather than in unassisted mid Wales where the company has its headquarters. A package of £4 million of Selective Assistance was put together by the Welsh Office to top the £2 million Dutch inducement, and the plant is to be located in mid-Wales. Nonetheless, with severe cuts in government aids to industry, combined with a philosophy of self-help through improved regional competitiveness, the effect of the cuts should be viewed in a less sanguine way than recent history might suggest.

Finally, perhaps the more worrying features of the new system for regional aid in Wales relate to the shift of emphasis towards assisting new service employment and applying cost-per-job criteria more generally. It is well established that service-sector employment is less mobile than that in manufacturing because at the bottom end of the hierarchy it is constrained to serving a localized market (and excluded from regional aid anyway), while at the top end, services cluster disproportionately in or near a primate city (Cambridge Economic Policy Group 1980). To the extent that service employment has decentralized to Wales, it has taken the form of public-sector producer services (the Business Statistics Office, Companies House) or state consumer services (the Driver and Vehicle Licensing Office), rather than private-sector services of significant scale and status (Chemical Bank's move to Cardiff being a notable exception). Public-sector decentralization of offices has now ceased; and although the new system makes it theoretically possible for management consultancies, other business services, and R&D activities to become more mobile, the 'social milieu' of Wales, as the *Financial Times* (29 November 1984) puts it, has not shown itself conducive to such activities in the past. Wales actually lost a quarter of its miniscule regional share of R&D services between 1971 and 1976, settling it more firmly at the foot of that particular league table (Howells 1984).

Moving on to the cost-per-job yardstick, it is unlikely that such a measure will shift aid significantly towards job creation because of the capital-deepening force known as 'jobless growth' (Freeman *et al*. 1982). Those sectors, often coincidental with the newer technologies in which output growth is still occurring, are increasing their capital-to-labour ratios quite dramatically in order to survive. New openings are now much less likely to be large-scale employers of labour than hitherto. In areas of high unemployment in Wales, therefore, it is unlikely that the central problem of large-scale job creation will be materially addressed by the new system. Furthermore, for small enterprises, where the cost-per-job yardstick does not apply, the new system may not reap the expected reward precisely because of the kind of industrial and firm-size structure which past regional policy and other state interventions have helped create—namely, one which, through encouraging branch plants and medium- to large-sized factories, is associated with low rates of new-firm formation.

Clearly, regional policy on its own cannot resolve the basic problem of unemployment in Wales. It was public expenditure on services that made the most dramatic impact upon employment levels in Wales during the 1970s. In most, if not all Welsh subregions the employment structure has taken on a distinctly 'post-industrial' appearance. During a period of recession and monetarist government strategy hostile to what is perceived as a 'bloated' state sector, it is difficult to see how rapid increases in employment levels can be achieved without a thoroughgoing redirection of policy towards a more expansionist stance in general economic management.

Conclusions

This chapter has described the main changes in the Welsh economy in recent years and has shown how the pattern of employment growth and decline has been mediated by state intervention in a thoroughgoing way. While the importance of conventional regional policy interventions, and that of new forms of activity such as the Development Agencies and related initiatives, has been recognized, it is equally important to note that interventions by other parts of the state, especially through nationalized industry policy, have contributed massively to the growing problems faced by those responsible for implementing regional development aid. Moreover, the greatest source of new jobs in all areas of Wales has been state expenditure on the expansion of services, particularly education and medicine in the early 1970s. Furthermore, these injections of capital have had a significant multiplier effect upon private-sector consumer services. It is not unreasonable to conclude from this that the most effective way of creating large numbers of new employment opportunities in a relatively short time would be through increased government expenditure on services. Such expenditure would help to counteract worsening conditions in Wales in housing, health, and education. During a period when inflation is reasonably well under control and demand is depressed, a managed reflation of the economy, led by injections of public expenditure in areas of severe need, could make inroads into the problem of unemployment in the worst hit parts of Britain.

Much of the new employment created by state investment in services has benefited women, often new to the labour market but often also finding work which is not particularly well-paid or skilled. Unemployment has been high among males, notably those made redundant by steel and coal industry closures. Moreover, in certain of the newer manufacturing sectors, attracted to Wales by a combination of corporate restructuring and the availability of regional assistance, women were often the dominant workforce, especially in electrical engineering. There are recent signs that changes may be afoot in many manufacturing sectors where, to some extent, men are holding their own or even increasing their representation, particularly in motor vehicle manufacturing. Women's employment is in decline in manufacturing, though it is by no means clear that such job losses result in men replacing them in specific factories. Over 80 per cent of women in engineering in Wales are employed in the lowest 'operative' grades, which are being automated out of existence most rapidly (Engineering Industries Training Board 1981); it is clearly not the case that 'getting women back into the home' would offer any solution to male unemployment.

Lastly, it is undeniable that regional policy and associated Development Agency activities have helped industrial diversification and the creation of job opportunities in Wales. However, the location of jobs created has tended to be removed from the centres of highest unemployment. Special Development Area status has not in the past been of great advantage to depressed communities in the coalfields of Wales. Conversely, Development Area status for some rural, semi-rural, and small urban areas has been an undoubted advantage, but one which they have now lost as a result of the 1984 regional policy adjustments. There has been a contradiction in postwar state intervention in the Welsh economy. On the one hand, regional policy has aimed to diversify employment opportunities, but not in any clearly targeted way. There are now strong signs that interventions by the WDA are moving away from such a tradition. On the other hand, earlier state interventions in basic industries had reinforced subregional specialization in declining sectors. Areas of need and those which benefitted from new-firm openings were often not identical.

It should not be surprising that the coalfield communities of South Wales resisted what was perceived as the destruction of their local economies through the NCB's pit-closure programme. As the result of experience since the 1960s, such communities could see little prospect of adequate alternative employment arising from regional or other aid. Although the 1983 White Paper on Regional Industrial Development reiterated the social justification for regional policy, even where its economic rationale might be questioned, the NCB's narrowly interpreted balance sheet approach now dominates these communities. The dubious ability of existing regional measures to alleviate the distress and decline that will result from the NCB strategy, in line with general economic policy, once again highlights the contradictions in the state's role in the Welsh economy.

Acknowledgements

I would like to thank Mr Terry Watson of the Manpower Intelligence Unit of the Manpower Services Commission in Wales for help in acquiring Annual Census of Employment statistics. For the pleasure of their company and their willingness to talk about issues addressed here, I would like to thank Emeritus Professor Gwyn A. Williams, University College, Cardiff; Dr Kim Howells, Research Officer, South Wales Area of the National Union of Mineworkers; Dr Kevin Morgan, University of Sussex; and Mr Gareth Rees of University College and UWIST in Cardiff.

References

Cambridge Economic Policy Group (1980), 'Urban and Regional Policy with Provisional Regional Accounts 1966–1978', *Cambridge Economic Policy Review* 6(2), Aldershot, Gower.

Central Statistical Office (1985), *Economic Trends: Supplement Edition*, London, HMSO.

Cooke, P. (1980), 'Discretionary Intervention and the Welsh Development Agency', *Area* 12, 269–77.

—— (1985), 'Regional Innovation Policy: Problems and Strategies in Britain and France', *Environment and Planning C, Government and Policy* 3, 253–67.

——, Morgan, M., and Jackson, D. (1984), 'New Technology and Regional Development in Austerity Britain: The Case of the Semiconductor Industry', *Regional Studies* 18, 277–89.

—— and Rees, G. (1981), 'The Industrial Restructuring of South Wales: The Case of a State-managed Region', *Policy Studies Journal* 10, 284–96. Reprinted in S. Redburn and T. Buss, eds, *Public Policies for Distressed Communities*, Lexington, Lexington Books.

—— and —— (1984), 'The Social Democratic State in a Radical Region', in I. Szelenyi, ed., *Cities in Recession: Critical Responses to the Urban Policies of the New Right*, London and Beverly Hills, Sage.

Deloitte, Haskins and Sells plc (1983), *WINTECH: an Initiative for Welsh Industry*, Cardiff, Welsh Development Agency.

Development Board for Rural Wales (1982), *Making an Impact in Mid Wales 1977–1982*, Newtown, DBRW.

Eirug, A. (1983), 'The Welsh Development Agency', *Geoforum* 14, 375–88.

Engineering Industries Training Board (1981), *The Engineering Industry in Wales*, London, EITB.

Freeman, C., Clark, J., and Soete, L. (1982), *Unemployment and Technical Innovation*, London, Frances Pinter.

Garbett-Edwards, P. (1972), 'The Establishment of New Industries,' in J. Ashton and W. Long, eds., *The Remoter Rural Areas of Britain*, Edinburgh, Oliver and Boyd.

Gray, I. (1976), 'Chief Executive WDA', *The Times*, 8 November.

Hechter, M. (1975), *Internal Colonialism: The Celtic Fringe in British National Development 1536–1966*, London, Routledge & Kegan Paul.

Howells, J. (1984), 'The Location of Research and Development: Some Observations and Evidence from Britain', *Regional Studies* 18, 13–29.

Humphrys, G. (1972), *Industrial South Wales*, Newton Abbot, David & Charles.

Martin, M. (1982), *Agricultural Change in Mid-Wales*, unpublished MSc dissertation, Cardiff, UWIST, Department of Town Planning.

Moore, J. and Rhodes, B. (1975), *Regional Policy and the Economy of Wales*, Cardiff, Welsh Office.

Morgan, K. (1979), *State Regional Interventions and Industrial Reconstruction in Post-War Britain: The Case of Wales*, Urban and Regional Studies Working Paper 16, Falmer, University of Sussex.

—— (1983), 'Restructuring Steel: The Crisis of Labour and Locality in Britain', *International Journal of Urban and Regional Research* 7, 175–201.

—— and Sayer, A. (1984), 'Sunrise Industry, Union Sunset?', *Radical Wales* 5, 6–9.

Morgan, R. (1983), 'Population Trends in Mid-Wales: Some Policy Implications', in G. Williams, ed., *Crisis of Economy and Ideology: Essays on Welsh Society, 1840–1980*, Bangor, British Sociological Association (Wales) Group.

Parry, R. (1980*a*), *United Kingdom Public Employment: Patterns of Change, 1951–1976*, Studies in Public Policy no. 62, Glasgow, Centre for the Study of Public Policy, University of Strathclyde.

—— (1980*b*) *The Territorial Dimension in United Kingdom Public Employment*, Studies in Public Policy no. 65, Glasgow, Centre for the Study of Public Policy, University of Strathclyde.

Powell, B. (1979), *New Agencies in Wales*, London, Regional Studies Association.

Rowlands, T. (1972), 'The Politics of Regional Administration: The Establishmentf the Welsh Office', *Public Administration* 50, 333–52.

Select Committee on Welsh Affairs (1980), *The Role of the Welsh Office and Associated Bodies in Developing Employment Opportunities in Wales*, London, HMSO.

Smith, D., ed., (1980), *A People and a Proletariat: Essays in Welsh History 1880–1980*, London, Pluto Press.

Smith, M. (1985), 'Grants Cut: A Traumatic Road Ahead?', *Western Mail Economic Review*, 8 January.

Thomas, B. (1962), 'Wales and the Atlantic Economy', in *The Welsh Economy: Studies in Expansion*, Cardiff, University of Wales Press.

Welsh Development Agency (1977), *WDA Policies and Programmes*, Treforest, WDA.

—— (1981), *The First Five Years*, Treforest, WDA.

—— (1983), *Report and Accounts 1982–3*, Treforest, WDA.

—— (1984), *Corporate Plan of the Welsh Development Agency 1984–1990*, Treforest, WDA.

Welsh Office (1984), *Welsh Economic Trends*, Cardiff, Welsh Office.

Williams, G. (1980), 'Industrialisation, Inequality and Deprivation in Rural Wales', in G. Rees and T. Rees, eds., *Poverty and Social Inequality in Wales*, London, Croom Helm.

Williams, G. A. (1982), 'Imperial South Wales', Chapter 7 of his collection of essays entitled *The Welsh in their History*, London, Croom Helm.

—— (1985), *When was Wales?* London, Black Raven Press and Harmondsworth, Penguin.

Winckler (1983), 'Women, Work and the Recession in Wales', *Cambria* 10, 61–9.

CHAPTER 10
Scotland

J. N. Randall

In geographical terms Scotland is by far the largest of the Standard Regions, accounting for 32 per cent of the area of the UK (see Figure 10.1). It is also an exceptionally varied country, encompassing the densely populated urban concentrations of the Clydeside conurbation and, to a lesser extent, the rest of the central belt; a range of larger and smaller settlements in the eastern part of the country from Aberdeen to the Borders surrounded by attractive and (in the main) good-quality farm-land; and the vast, remote, often mountainous, and scenically outstanding tracts of sparsely populated land in the Highlands and Islands and South West Scotland. Of a population in 1982 of 5.2 million (9.2 per cent of the UK total), some 4 million, or three-quarters, lived in the belt of country bounded by Ayr and Edinburgh in the south and Greenock and Dundee in the north.

At a broad level, Scotland's present distribution of population and many of her economic and social problems can still be seen as a legacy of the rapid industrialization and urbanization which took place in the late eighteenth century and throughout the nineteenth century, in response to natural resource advantages such as local coal and iron-ore deposits, entrepreneurial flair, and access to the world-wide markets of the British Empire. Following the economic collapse of the 1920s and 1930s, the postwar period has seen major planned and unplanned shifts of population mainly within the central belt, with a dramatic decline in Glasgow's population, and the growth of New Towns and some other smaller settlements. There has also been a determined effort by policy-makers to encourage the industrial restructuring of the Scottish economy, and to close the gap between measures of economic welfare in Scotland and those in the UK as a whole. In some ways the changes of the 1970s and early 1980s—which it is the purpose of this chapter to discuss in more detail—can be viewed as a continuation of these trends; but in addition some new factors (notably those triggered by the development of North Sea oil resources) led to new departures. In retrospect the 1970s can be seen as a watershed in Scotland's postwar history and, to some extent, in popular perceptions of her problems and opportunities.

Economic performance 1971–81

Indicators which compare Scotland's economic performance with that of the UK are subject to the obvious limitation that the UK bench-mark may not represent a satisfactory absolute standard of performance, particularly during a

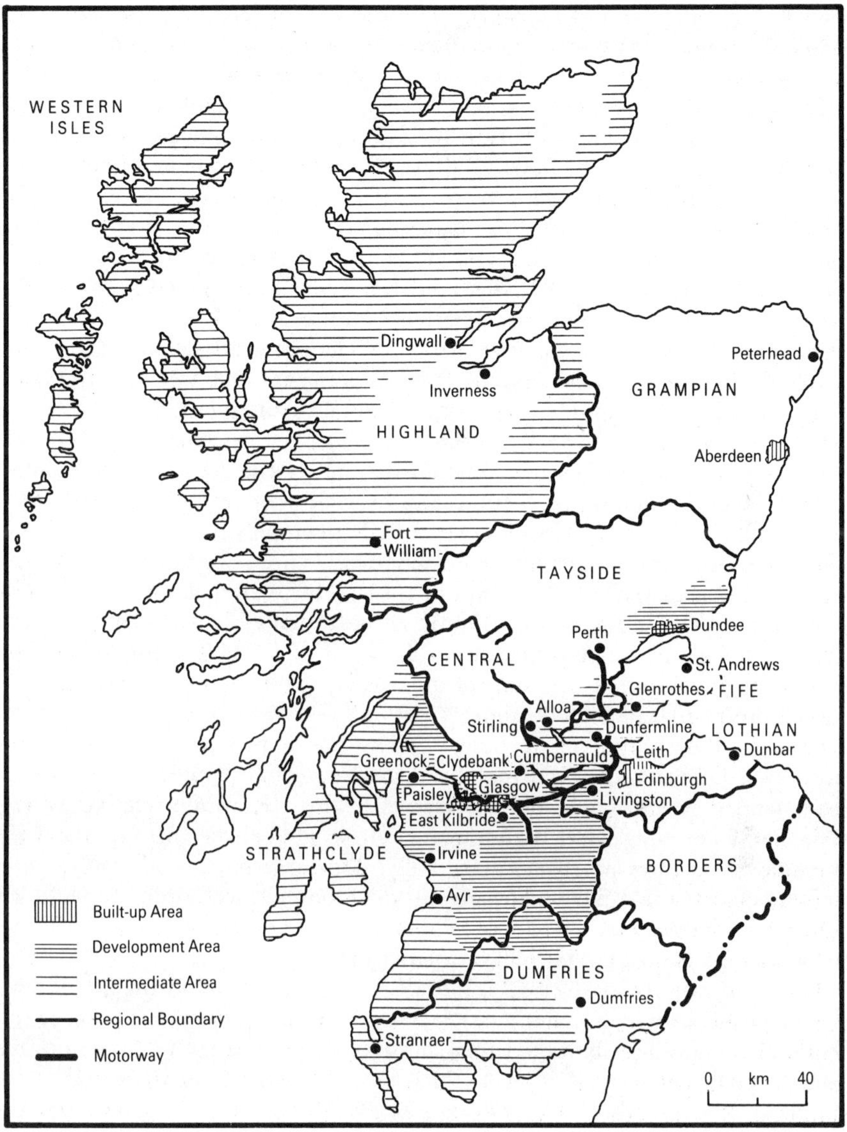

Figure 10.1 Scotland

period of exceptional national economic difficulty such as the 1970s, when unemployment in the UK increased from around 3 per cent in 1971 to over 10 per cent in 1981. Nonetheless, for an economy such as Scotland's, which is very closely integrated with that of the rest of the UK (it is estimated that in 1979 only some 12 per cent of Scotland's gross output, excluding oil and gas extraction, was exported outside the UK), marked and persistent divergence from UK trends is not to be expected. Indicators of relative performance can therefore provide useful pointers to the degree of success which policy and other factors have had within the range of outcomes amenable to their influence.

The main indicators are consistent in suggesting that Scotland made considerable progress during the 1970s in narrowing the gap between Scotland and the UK. Scotland's share of UK GDP (excluding the Continental Shelf region) increased marginally from 8.7 per cent in 1971 to 9.0 per cent in 1981, the first decade since the war when this has occurred, and relative GDP per head continued its upward trend, from 93 per cent of the UK level in 1971 to 98 per cent in 1981. Indeed, by 1981 Scotland was ranked second (after South East England) amongst UK Standard Regions in terms of GDP per head compared with eighth in 1971. Personal disposable income per head also increased more rapidly in Scotland over the decade (from 93 per cent of the UK level in 1971 to 97 per cent in 1981), and average male manual earnings rose from 3 per cent below the UK level at the start of the period to 2 per cent above in 1981. The unemployment rate in Scotland remained some 1–2 percentage points above the UK level throughout the period, and by 1981 was near the top end of this range, although, with the large increase in UK unemployment, the Scottish rate when expressed as a percentage fell dramatically (from around 170 per cent in the early 1970s to about 120 per cent in 1981). The relative improvement in the Scottish economy is also reflected in much lower net emigration: in the period 1961–71 there was a net outflow from Scotland of 327,000 people (over 6 per cent of the population at the start of the period), while between 1971 and 1981 the net outflow was 144,000 (under 3 per cent).

Between 1981 and 1983 the story told by the main economic indicators is more mixed. Scotland's GDP per head, and personal disposable income per head, tended to slip back slightly relative to the UK, while relative average male manual earnings were maintained, and the gap between Scotland and UK unemployment rates narrowed marginally. This may partly reflect short-term factors operating at a particular stage in the economic recession, although it is noticeable that the greater part of Scotland's relative improvement during the 1970s took place in the first half of the decade.

The aggregate trends conceal a more complex pattern of change, and mask serious problems which remain, particularly in some geographical areas within Scotland. It may first be noted that, despite a very marked relative improvement in GDP per head to a level which by 1981 was higher than that of any Standard Region other than South East England, unemployment remains significantly above the UK level (Scotland had the fifth highest unemployment rate among GB Standard Regions in 1981), and net emigration continues on a substantial scale. While comparative rates of increase in the supply of labour are also relevant, this suggests that the increase in Scotland's relative prosperity is not fully reflected in the availability of job opportunities, and that the growth in incomes has been unequally spread.

Geographical inequality also became increasingly evident during the 1970s. The growth of North Sea oil-related employment concentrated in Aberdeen and particular localities mainly in the north and east of Scotland, and the tendency, which has been noted throughout the UK, for smaller settlements to grow more rapidly than larger urban areas has accentuated the contrast which already existed between Clydeside and other parts of Scotland. Over the period 1971–81, employment in Strathclyde region fell by 12 per cent, while in all other regions of Scotland except Tayside employment increased—by around 30 per cent in Grampian and the Highlands and by considerably more in percentage terms in the less populated Shetland and Western Isles (Table 10.1). A similar pattern is revealed by population trends over the decade, with Strathclyde the only region in mainland Scotland to record a fall in population between 1971 and 1980. Average unemployment in Strathclyde in 1983 was 17.3 per cent, compared with 15.0 per cent in Scotland and under 10 per cent in Grampian, Borders, and Shetland.

Factors underlying the trends

During the 1950s and 1960s, an unfavourable industrial structure exerted a depressing effect on the performance of the Scottish economy relative to that of the UK, and was the major factor explaining lower rates of growth of GDP and employment in Scotland during most of this period (McCrone 1969). But throughout the postwar period the structure of Scottish industry has been changing, both through the decline in the traditional industries and through the growth of new industries. Table 10.2 illustrates this in relation to the manufacturing sector. Over the period 1953–78, employment in textiles fell by 52,000 or about a half, in shipbuilding by 30,000 or 40 per cent, in metal manufacture (mainly iron and steel) by 23,000 or 40 per cent, and in mechanical engineering by 17,000 or 17 per cent. These four industries accounted for nearly one-half of all manufacturing employment in Scotland in 1953, but for only around one-third by 1978. In contrast, there was a net job increase in electrical engineering of 31,000 or 157 per cent, in instrument engineering of 10,000 or 150 per cent, and in food and drink of 8,000 or 9 per cent, while much larger growth occurred in both private and public services. The result of this transformation of industrial structure—which reflected partly normal market pressures responding to changed patterns of demand, and partly the encouragement given through regional policy—was that by the 1970s and early 1980s industrial structure was no longer a significant adverse factor (Randall 1985).

This is not to say that structural problems do not remain in some sectors; for example in a continued over-representation in shipbuilding, which accounted for 7 per cent of manufacturing employment in Scotland in 1981 compared with 2 per cent in Great Britain, and an under-representation in some of the faster-growing service industries such as computer software. It is also the case that some parts of Scotland, notably Strathclyde, still experience an unfavourable industrial structure reflecting over-representation of the manufacturing sector, particularly steel, shipbuilding, textiles, and heavy engineering. But for Scotland as a whole in the 1970s, an unfavourable industrial structure was no longer the major handicap it had been in earlier decades, and the more favourable relative performance of the 1970s can partly be attributed to this.

Table 10.1. Employment change, population change, and unemployment, by Scottish region

Region/Island area	Change in employees in employment 1971–81 (%)	Change in population 1971–80 (%)	Change in population 1981–3 (%)	Average unemployment rate 1983 (%)
Borders	10.0	1.8	−0.1	9.5
Central	6.6	3.3	−0.3	15.6
Dumfries and Galloway	16.2	0.1	0.5	13.5
Fife	0.5	3.2	0.4	13.2
Grampian	30.3	7.1	2.0	8.8
Highland	27.3	12.3	0.6	13.8
Lothian	2.3	0.3	−0.6	12.3
Strathclyde	−12.1	−5.8	−1.3	17.3
Tayside	−1.7	0.7	−0.5	14.5
Orkney	27.0	5.2	0.3	11.8
Shetland	118.6	27.2	−11.0	6.8
Western Isles	67.9	−2.1	−0.1	21.7
Scotland	−0.4	−1.2	−0.6	15.0

Source: Census of Employment (column 1), General Register Office, Scotland (columns 2 and 3), Department of Employment (column 4).

Table 10.2. Manufacturing employment change in Scotland, 1953–78

Industry (1968 SIC)	1953		1978		Change	
	Nos.	% manufacturing employment	Nos.	% manufacturing employment	Nos.	(%)
3. Food, drink, tobacco	82,254	12.3	89,971	15.6	+7,717	+9.4
4. Coal and petroleum produces	4,448	0.7	2,716	0.5	−1,732	−38.9
5. Chemicals	29,339	4.4	29,740	5.1	+401	+1.4
6. Metal manufacture	57,678	8.7	34,771	6.0	−22,907	−39.7
7. Mechanical engineering	96,273	14.4	79,706	13.8	−16,567	−17.2
8. Instrument engineering	6,844	1.0	17,132	3.0	+10,288	+150.3
9. Electrical engineering	19,799	3.0	50,889	8.8	+31,090	+157.0
10. Shipbuilding	66,695	10.0	36,501	6.3	−30,194	−45.3
11. Vehicles	37,147	5.6	33,745	5.8	−3,402	−9.2
12. Metal goods	23,714	3.6	25,101	4.3	+1,387	+5.9
13. Textiles	106,407	16.0	54,071	9.4	−52,336	−49.2
14. Leather	3,645	0.6	2,116	0.4	−1,529	−42.0
15. Clothing	27,740	4.2	31,641	5.5	+3,901	+14.1
16. Bricks, pottery, etc.	19,614	2.9	15,008	2.6	−4,606	−23.5
17. Timber	23,131	3.5	16,722	2.9	−6,409	−27.7
18. Paper, printing, publishing	46,390	7.0	42,400	7.3	−3,990	−8.6
19. Other manufacturing	16,049	2.4	15,941	2.8	−108	−0.7
All manufacturing	667,167	(100)	578,171	(100)	−88,996	−13.3

Source: Scottish Manufacturing Establishments Record.

The role of regional policy in speeding up the industrial restructuring of the Scottish economy has already been mentioned. It has been estimated that regional policy may have generated some 100,000 jobs in Scotland over the period 1960–76 (or around 5 per cent of all employment), of which perhaps 70,000 were in manufacturing (around 12 per cent of manufacturing employment; estimates based on the approach used by Moore and Rhodes, 1974). Most analyses attribute the effects of regional policy to the financial incentives available at preferential rates to industry in the Assisted Areas, although it is possible that part of the impact reflects the programme of motorway building and other public investment in infrastructure in Central Scotland following the 1963 White Paper. While the impact of regional policy has probably been less during the 1970s (particularly in the second half of the decade) than in the 1960s, as a result of lower economic growth and higher unemployment throughout the UK and reduced expenditure in the latter part of the period, this was still a factor relatively favourable to the Scottish economy. Despite the much-publicized closure of some of the plants attracted by regional policy (for example the car plant at Linwood in 1981), the evidence is that employment induced by regional policy has declined less rapidly than has employment as a whole. The lessons to be drawn from the experience of regional policy are discussed in more detail in the next section.

It is more difficult to evaluate the impact of regional policy on particular areas within Scotland, partly because of data limitations and partly because it becomes increasingly difficult to disentangle the effects of financial inducements from infrastructure provision at this more local scale. The whole of Scotland was an Assisted Area from 1971 until 1982, when Aberdeen, Edinburgh, and large, predominantly rural areas in Grampian, Tayside, Fife, Lothian, Borders, and Dumfries were downgraded. These changes reinforced the tendency which already existed throughout the 1970s for regional policy to give highest priority to West Central Scotland, the Dundee area, and parts of Fife, including the five New Towns (East Kilbride, Glenrothes, Cumbernauld, Livingston, and Irvine). While information is not available on regional policy expenditure or its impact on individual areas within Scotland, it seems likely that the areas which benefited most, particularly in the attraction of incoming industry, were those settlements within Special Development Areas which had available a good supply of attractive industrial sites and modern premises, notably the New Towns. Between 1960 and 1970 it has been estimated that 60 per cent of the advance factory space in West Central Scotland and 54 per cent in the east of Scotland was built in the New Towns (Henderson 1980). While this proportion is likely to have fallen in the 1970s with a greater concentration of effort on the older urban areas, there seems little doubt that the favourable infrastructure (and accompanying image) of the New Towns enabled them to attract a disproportionate share of new employment. In fact, the New Towns accounted for over a third of the gross job increases provided by manufacturing units moving to Scotland from outside during the period 1973–8 (Randall 1985). Since the mid-1970s, following publication of the West Central Scotland Plan (1974), the establishment of Strathclyde Regional Council (1975), and a number of area initiatives undertaken by the Scottish Development Agency, increasing attention has been given to factory building and environmental improvement in older urban centres within the former Special Development Areas such as Glasgow, Dundee, Clydebank, and Motherwell, although the full effects of this shift in emphasis are still to be seen.

A further factor helping to explain the broadly favourable relative performance of the Scottish economy and the changing distribution of economic activity within Scotland during the 1970s was the growth in North Sea oil-related developments. Employment in companies wholly involved in North Sea oil-related activities grew rapidly from a negligible level in 1971 to 50,000 in 1981 and 67,000 at the end of 1983. The total impact of North Sea oil, including construction activity and the effect on local service employment, had risen to around 100,000 by 1983, an order of magnitude similar to the estimated impact of regional policy over a longer period. But whereas most of the regional policy impact is on manufacturing, the bulk of oil-related employment is associated with services and with the manning of the offshore production platforms, and the geographical impact of oil-related employment is much more concentrated. An increasing proportion (over 70 per cent by 1983) is located in Grampian region, predominantly in and around Aberdeen, which has established itself as the administrative centre of the industry with the best longer-run prospects, while other major but localized centres of oil-related employment include the Cromarty Firth and Shetland. By contrast, Strathclyde accounted for only some 5 per cent of employment in wholly involved companies, under 4,000 jobs, in 1983. North Sea oil therefore helped to accentuate spatial inequalities within Scotland during the 1970s. This effect is evident not only in the contrast between West Central Scotland and North East Scotland but in some areas at a much more local scale, for example Aberdeen and Peterhead compared with most of the rest of rural Grampian, or the platform yard at Loch Kishorn in Wester Ross compared with the rest of the North West Highlands. The areas of influence in terms of daily labour-market areas around isolated oil-related establishments in the north of Scotland can be very limited (although with migrant workers the effects may be extended more widely), while in other areas, such as Shetland and Aberdeen, existing industries such as fish processing, textiles, and paper-making have been affected adversely through pressure on wage levels or labour shortages, at least for a period (McDowall and Begg 1981). Very rapid oil-related growth in some areas has led to population in-migration on a large scale and acute pressure on public infrastructure and local resources—the population of Shetland increased by almost a half between 1971 and 1981. On the whole, North Sea oil has clearly been a favourable development for Scotland and for incomes and job opportunities in the affected areas, but in some cases the balance of economic and social costs and benefits is not self-evident, particularly where growth has already been replaced by decline in oil-related activity.

A final factor which merits discussion is the more general pattern of public expenditure by Standard Region during the 1970s—of which specific regional policy expenditure forms only a small part. Estimates of identifiable public expenditure—which excludes expenditure on defence, overseas aid, and other overseas services which is incurred on behalf of the UK as a whole—suggest that public spending per head has been significantly higher in Scotland than the average for the UK over a long period. This reflects a combination of factors, including the relative need of different parts of the UK (for example, lower incomes and higher unemployment in Scotland) and particular historical circumstances (for example, the high proportion of public-sector housing in Scotland). The estimates suggest that, in the late 1960s and early 1970s, identifiable public expenditure per head in Scotland was around a third above the UK average, while since 1973–4 the differential has reduced to an average of around a fifth higher (House of Commons 1977; 1983). Higher public expenditure in Scotland is likely to have had favourable effects on relative economic and employment performance in a number of ways, for example through increasing general income levels and boosting construction-related employment. As already mentioned, a major programme of infrastructure investment was carried out following the 1963 White Paper, including massive housing redevelopment in older urban areas, the building of motorway links between the cities of the central belt, and the development of five New Towns. Public-sector employment also grew more rapidly than in the UK during the first half of the 1970s, although over the rest of the decade the relative trends were more closely in line. Estimates suggest that, in 1983, public-sector service employment accounted for 47 per cent of all service employment in Scotland compared with 42 per cent in the UK, although the dependence on public-sector employment in services in Scotland is considerably less than in Wales (around 52 per cent) and Northern Ireland (62 per cent) (House of Commons 1984). Within Scotland, public-sector employment is particularly important in Edinburgh, the centre of national administration, and in the administrative headquarters of the Regional Councils, including Glasgow.

Other issues affecting regional development

While the aggregate pattern of change discussed in the previous sections reveals a broadly favourable, if increasingly unequal, relative performance in Scotland during the 1970s, a number of considerations suggest caution in looking into the future. This is partly a matter of how far it is reasonable to expect the factors which helped the Scottish economy in the 1970s to continue with similar effect in the 1980s and beyond, and partly a reflection of a number of other issues which will affect regional development prospects in Scotland. In the former category, it seems unlikely that Scotland's industrial structure will prove a major handicap to relative economic performance, although further structural adjustments seem probable, particularly in industries such as shipbuilding. Regional policy will continue to be a favourable factor, but in a period of higher unemployment and greater international competition it seems unlikely that regional policy can have the same impact as in the more favourable conditions of the 1960s and early 1970s. Following the changes to regional policy announced in November 1984, Scotland's share of the British working population in Assisted Areas has fallen from 25 to 18 per cent, although Scotland's share of areas eligible for Regional Development Grant is slightly higher than before. The growth rate of North Sea oil-related employment is bound to level off after the exceptionally rapid build-up during the 1970s. Public expenditure trends may also show less regional divergence than during the 1960s and early 1970s. Turning to other issues, there seem to be both potential strengths and weaknesses in the Scottish position.

Ownership of industry, entrepreneurship, and self-sustaining growth. In recent years increasing attention has been given to the extent to which plants in the Assisted Areas are owned and controlled from outside the region, and the possible disadvantages of this for the quality of jobs available in the Assisted Areas, in terms of management functions and Research and Development work and the capacity for indigenous entrepreneurship and self-sustaining growth from within the region. It has further been suggested that regional policy has served to exacerbate these problems through the encouragement given to the setting up of branch plants in the Assisted Areas. These are all themes which are familiar in a Scottish context. It has been estimated that over 60 per cent of manufacturing employment in Scotland is ultimately controlled from outside Scotland, the proportion tending to be highest in advanced technology and growth industries such as electronics (Firn 1975). Overseas-owned manufacturing units alone account for around 17 per cent of Scottish manufacturing employment, the proportion rising to 52 per cent in instrument engineering and 43 per cent in electrical engineering (estimates based on Industry Department for Scotland data). There is also evidence that, in 1981, Scotland had a lower proportion of professional and managerial socioeconomic groups and a higher proportion of low-skilled groups than the average for Great Britain (Department of Trade and Industry 1983), while Scotland's share of UK Research and Development employment in private industry in 1981 was only a little over 3 per cent. (Scrimgeour 1984). On the other hand, Scotland retains an important locally based financial sector, centred on Edinburgh.

Entrepreneurial performance is difficult to measure, and the data available provide conflicting evidence. While the number of new-business starts in Scotland in 1982 appeared rather lower than the average for the UK (Department of Trade and Industry 1984), the number and employment in enterprises new to manufacturing in Scotland during the 1970s seems at least as favourable as in the UK as a whole (Randall 1982). A regional index of entrepreneurial potential based on plant structure, education, occupational mix, savings, home ownership, and disposable income, however, ranks Scotland only seventh out of the ten Standard Regions of Great Britain (Storey 1983).

The concept of self-sustaining growth is also difficult to define. It relates partly to the ability of a regional economy to generate new-business starts, and partly to the subsequent growth of smaller firms. While comparative regional figures are not available, it seems disappointing that, of all manufacturing units in Scotland employing over 200 in 1974, only forty had grown from units employing under 100 in 1954 or in the second year after opening (Scottish Office 1980). The extent to which new industries in Scotland have led to the growth of linkages with other parts of the economy, helping to build up an industrial complex which is mutually reinforcing, must also be regarded as disappointing. Various commentators have drawn attention to the relatively low level of purchase of inputs from within Scotland by overseas-owned firms in Scotland, and more generally in the vehicles industry, some parts of electronics, and offshore oil activity (Forsyth 1972; Johnston *et al*. 1971; McDermott 1976). This may reflect partly the fact that the scale of activity in Scotland necessary to support local suppliers has been too low, partly the established practices of firms owned outside the region, and partly deficiencies in the local supply response. There are some encouraging indications that the position is improving in certain sectors, such as electronics, and this industry also provides some good examples of the spin-off of new Scottish-based companies established by the ex-employees of larger branch plants.

Regional policy has been criticized on the grounds that it has accentuated the pattern of external ownership of industry in Scotland, and has been unsuccessful in promoting self-sustaining growth, as shown not only by low levels of industrial linkage within Scotland but also by the closure in the 1980s of major units such as the vehicle plants at Linwood and Bathgate, the Fort William pulp mill, and the Invergordon aluminium smelter. A number of points should be made. First, the evidence from Scotland is that, notwithstanding the closures mentioned above, the overall employment performance of branch plants has been more favourable than that of locally owned manufacturing industry. Secondly, research on the trends in functions carried out by US-owned manufacturing companies in Scotland suggests that in many cases Research and Development functions are being increased, and there is no indication that Scottish plants inevitably become less important within the company over time (Hood and Young 1980). Thirdly, outside ownership (including takeovers of existing plants) can have beneficial effects in some circumstances, through access to the financial resources of the parent company and the introduction of new management and technology. Finally, it is a great over-simplification to attribute the closure of some of the major plants controlled from outside Scotland to inherent defects in regional policy. In the case of Linwood, for example, disadvantages emanating from the size and performance of the companies owning the plant and in the car models built there help to explain the eventual closure—although whether such weaknesses were more likely in the context of a car plant attracted to a relatively peripheral location such as Scotland is a moot point.

The difficulty of promoting entrepreneurship and self-sustaining growth is not a reason for abandoning regional policy. On the contrary, whatever the disappointments, regional policy, and the attraction of new investment from outside Scotland which it has brought, have helped to encourage the longer-term changes that are necessary in the Scottish economy. There is certainly a need to give increasing attention to ways of improving the quality of jobs and upgrading the functions carried out in Scottish plants, and to encourage a more active entrepreneurial climate in terms both of new start-ups and of the expansion of indigenous industry.

The present status of the electronics industry in Scotland illustrates these points. Electronics output in Scotland has increased rapidly in recent years, a growth of 60 per cent occurring between 1979 and 1983 alone, but high labour productivity increases have meant that employment growth has been much more modest—a net increase from around 37,000 in 1971 to just over 40,000 in 1983. Some 40 per cent of employment is in overseas-owned companies (estimates by Industry Department for Scotland). The main strengths of the industry in Scotland are the production of semi-conductors (Scotland accounts for 80 per cent of UK production of integrated circuits), and also personal computers, defence electronics, and industrial instrumentation. This covers a range of different types of activity, from semi-skilled assembly of components, many of which are purchased from outside Scotland, to high-technology research in areas such as artificial intelligence and optoelectronics. In certain respects the Scottish industry compares unfavourably with the functions carried out by electronics plants in the M4 belt of southern England, and there are a number of related activities (such as computer software) where Scotland is under-represented. Nonetheless, there are encouraging signs that progress is being made towards higher-quality jobs and a wider spin-off from the industry. Small high-technology companies in Scotland (some of which have been established by entrepreneurs previously employed in the larger branch plants) appear more likely to have a full time Research and Development capability than their counterparts in South East England or California (Oakey 1984). A wider range of local subcontractors has developed, and it is estimated that IBM alone spends about £40 million a year in Scotland on local goods and services. There is an increasing demand for skilled manpower and, while specific shortages have occurred in some fields, the high output of electrical and electronics engineering graduates from the eight Scottish universities and several colleges of technology, together with their research capability in electronics, is a source of strength to Scotland. While much of the recent expansion of the industry has been located in the New Towns, particularly Livingston, and so has been of less immediate relevance to the problems of Glasgow and older urban areas, it should be remembered that there are also important and growing centres of electronics in older areas such as Greenock, while the shift of population to the New Towns has probably been in the longer-term interests of the Scottish economy. A balanced assessment of the electronics industry in Scotland has, therefore, to acknowledge several weaknesses in the present position. But the overall conclusion must be that Scotland has benefited greatly from a development in which regional policy, particularly through the attraction of inward investment, has played an important part.

Peripherality. An issue which has been of longstanding interest in analysis of the performance and prospects of the Scottish economy is the extent to which Scotland's peripheral location in relation to the major markets of the UK and Europe is a disadvantage to economic development. Since the work of the

Toothill Committee (1961), there has been a tendency to assume that any disadvantage is easily exaggerated, since transport costs in manufacturing industry typically account for only some 2 per cent of gross output (although some 7 per cent of value added). Moreover, the incidence of measured transport costs on Scottish manufacturing industry in recent years appears to be only marginally if at all higher than the average for the UK (Scottish Office 1981), and significantly lower than in Northern Ireland. It has been argued that peripherality may act like a tariff barrier to protect local industry from outside competition, while the development of modern communications has reduced the constraints on accessibility to markets. At the same time, peripherality has historically tended to be associated with offsetting advantages such as lower labour and land costs.

There are signs of a reassessment of this conventional view. This reflects, first, the general erosion of regional labour-cost differentials over the last twenty years, together with rapid increases in land costs in some peripheral areas, particularly those affected by North Sea oil. In these new circumstances, the competitive position of some of Scotland's traditional industries may become more difficult (McDowall and Begg 1981), and any underlying problems associated with location (including the limited development of agglomeration economies in smaller population centres) may emerge more strongly. Secondly, there is increasing recognition of the importance of marketing and ready access to up-to-date information on changing market opportunities to the growth and performance of industry. In this respect, companies in Scotland—particularly smaller companies unable to support marketing offices located in the south of England or Western Europe—may be at some disadvantage compared with more centrally located competitors, despite communications improvement. There is evidence that Scottish industry is more likely than competitors in the south of England to regard location as a disadvantage, and to spend more management effort in minimizing its cost (PEIDA 1985). Thirdly, distance from larger population centres may lengthen the time taken for innovations first tested in these centres to be diffused. Thus the volume of interregional industrial movement to Scotland from the south of England may be reduced, relative to less 'peripheral' regions such as South Wales, North West England, or Yorkshire. The latter factor may be especially important in relation to the attraction of offices and other service industries from the London area, which have shown a tendency to move over relatively short distances.

For these reasons some caution seems advisable in assessing the future relative prospects of the Scottish economy, particularly in the more remote areas, where labour and other costs may not adjust to a decline in oil-related activity as rapidly as they did to its increase in the 1970s. Much of the Highlands is unlikely to attract a wide range of industry, and its scope for satisfactory adjustment to economic change is likely to be small. The traditional industries which have prospered in the more rural areas of Scotland—such as whisky in Grampian and the Highlands and Islands, and high-quality wool textiles in the Borders—are industries with high value to weight, and with markets based on a quality image rather than on low costs (Randall 1985). For the larger centres in the central belt, the problem of peripherality generally seems less; certainly these areas can prove attractive and efficient locations for many types of economic activity—as the successes in electronics demonstrate. But even in central Scotland it seems probable that geographical factors will have an influence on the type of activity most likely to succeed. In general, industries producing low-value, bulky goods or large-scale, standardized products where marginal cost differences are crucial to competitive position are most likely to face difficulties, while those with a high value-added component based on inputs of highly skilled manpower seem best placed.

Infrastructure and environment. The postwar period has been one of major improvement to the physical infrastructure of Scotland. Perhaps the outstanding example of a sustained effort to use public resources to create improved facilities has been in housing. Over 780,000 new dwellings in the public sector were completed in the period 1945–81, and by 1980 54 per cent of the total Scottish housing stock comprised dwellings built since the war, compared with 49 per cent in Great Britain as a whole (Scottish Office 1984). There has been a marked reduction in the incidence of overcrowding and housing without basic amenities, although in 1980 some 5 per cent of the housing stock was below the statutory tolerable standard, and there were additional problems of poor environment and urban deprivation in some housing estates. Substantial investment has also been made in modernizing the transport network, notably the programme of motorway building in central Scotland during the 1960s, and the electrification of the Glasgow–London railway line in 1974. Some £550 million in terms of long-term loans was spent on developing the five New Towns over the period 1947–81 (Carter 1986). Looking at infrastructure in its wider sense, Scotland's educational institutions, particularly in higher education, are regarded highly and make an important contribution to the supply of skilled manpower and research facilities. By 1980 there were eight universities in Scotland (out of forty-six in the UK) with an annual intake of full-time students of around 12,000, as well as several colleges of technology and other central institutions (Scottish Office 1984). A number of the higher-education institutes have built up specialist capabilities in electronics and other high-technology sectors, and links with industry generally compare favourably with the position elsewhere in the UK. Scotland also has a distinctive administrative structure, which is discussed in the next section. The result of this investment and other developments is that infrastructure is probably not a major constraint on the relative performance of the Scottish economy. Particular problems remain, either in certain geographical areas (for example, many parts of the Highlands lack a modern road network, although several of the main links, including that to Inverness from the south, have been upgraded) or in relation to certain types of infrastructure. For example, the range of direct air links from Scotland to the main cities in Europe is limited, while some of the public-sector housing estates on the outskirts of Glasgow and other large cities have a poor physical environment, and other social problems.

The most serious general problem from an economic viewpoint is probably the continued concentration in certain urban areas, predominantly but not exclusively in West Central Scotland, of environmental dereliction on a substantial scale. This reflects partly the derelict land and industrial obsolescence resulting from the decline of older extractive and manufacturing industry such as coalmining, oil-shale mining, steel, and heavy engineering, and partly an unimaginative approach to the planning of many new housing areas, in an understandable but ultimately ill-conceived effort to build the maximum number of new houses as quickly as possible in response to intolerable housing conditions. The image, and unfortunately in some areas the reality, of environmental degradation can be a deterrent to the attraction of new industry, and to the chances of an area generating new job opportunities from within the existing community as many of the more skilled and enterprising groups move to more attractive surroundings such as the New Towns. There are some encouraging signs that progress is now being made through area initiatives co-ordinated by the Scottish Development Agency, tree planting and the cleaning of the stonework of buildings, and a more sensitive approach to housing improvements. There tends to be a time-lag between improvements taking place and a more favourable image becoming established, particularly in the minds of industrialists and others outside the area concerned. Even here, however, there are some hopeful signs, as illustrated by the at least partial success of recent publicity campaigns to promote a new image of Glasgow by emphasizing its considerable attractions.

The policy framework

Distinctive administrative arrangements for regional planning at both the Scottish and intra-Scotland level have evolved in response to Scotland's political history and separate legal system, and a perceived need within Scotland, which is of long standing and commands widespread consensus, to give priority to economic development objectives. Underpinning the system is the position of the Secretary of State for Scotland as a Cabinet Minister, and his extensive range of interests and responsibilities exercised through five Departments based in Edinburgh and collectively known as the Scottish Office. The direct powers of the Secretary of State have increased over time and now extend to agriculture and fisheries, education, health, local government, housing, physical planning, road and sea transport, electricity, tourism, and responsibility for agencies such as the Highlands and Islands Development Board (HIDB) and the Scottish Development Agency (SDA). The Secretary of State also has responsibilities for manpower policy in Scotland (since 1977) and administration of Regional Selective Assistance (since 1975) and Regional Development Grants (since 1984)—although it should be emphasized that the main instruments of economic policy remain with UK Departments. This unique range of responsibilities has allowed a number of different priorities and approaches to be adopted in relation to Scotland, for example over the allocation of public expenditure, policy towards New Towns, and the geographical extent and powers of local authorities in Scotland. The nature of the Scottish Office is also well suited to the co-ordination of policies at a regional scale and there was early emphasis in Scotland on the integration of economic and physical planning, as exemplified by the 1963 and 1966 White Papers and a series of advisory regional planning studies carried out in the succeeding ten years, culminating in the West Central Scotland Plan (1974).

During the 1970s two key developments were the reorganization of local government and the establishment of the SDA (both 1975). To a greater extent than in England, some of the top-tier authorities in Scotland cover functional city regions, most significantly in the case of Strathclyde Regional Council, which (uniquely for a major British conurbation) extends to a very large region beyond the built-up area of Clydeside. Most observers feel that the Council has been reasonably successful in taking advantage of the scope which its geographical remit and range of powers allow to plan its infrastructure provision and other policies in a co-ordinated way; there are no proposals analogous to those in England to abolish the Metropolitan Councils. With only nine top-tier authorities in Scotland (twelve if the Island Councils are included), the Scottish Office's task of overseeing local government and identifying priorities is a more manageable one than in England.

The SDA was set up with powers to build and manage factories, to undertake environmental improvement and other infrastructure projects, and to assist industry though equity and loan finance (including the attraction of inward investment to Scotland in association with government departments). Its expenditure in 1982–3 was some £100 million, and its resources and flexibility make it an important instrument for regional economic development in Scotland. The SDA (as is also the case with the longer established HIDB, which has a wider range of powers appropriate to the special problems of the Highlands) decides its priorities in consultation with the Scottish Office. Over the first five years of the Agency's life, the great majority of its expenditure was devoted to its factory provision and environmental roles, with only some £25 million out of £266 million being devoted to direct assistance in industry (McCrone and Randall 1985). The initial target for rates of return on its investments in industry was not achieved, and the financial duty was revised in 1980 with the aim of ensuring that funds provided by the Agency for this purpose do not involve a net subsidy. In recent years particular attention has been given to small businesses and high technology industries such as electronics, biotechnology, health care, and offshore technology—sectors which it is believed have long-run growth potential, are suited to the strengths which Scotland has, and can further the restructuring of the Scottish economy. Environmental improvement, factory building, and urban renewal expenditure has become increasingly concentrated in a number of area initiatives which the SDA is undertaking in conjunction with local authorities and the private sector in areas such as the East End of Glasgow, Clydebank, the Garnock Valley, Dundee, Motherwell, and Leith. The SDA plans to spend some £200 million in these areas alone from its own resources over the lifetime of the projects (some of which extend to 1987), and total spending from all sources will be much greater. In selecting area priorities, account is taken of government regional and urban policy priorities as well as a view of future potential. In the 1980s there has been a move away from the building of standard factories towards more innovative forms of property development, with special schemes for urban areas and rural areas. More generally, the emphasis of the SDA's work is increasingly on generating complementary investment from the private sector.

The structure which has evolved in Scotland clearly has a number of advantages: for example, the position of the Secretary of State as a Cabinet Minister; the functional coherence of some of the local government regions; and the flexible response to problems which the main agencies allow. But there remain important constraints on the extent to which policy in Scotland can depart significantly from that in other parts of the UK, or can in practice bring about a major divergence in trends from those in the rest of the country. First, the centralized nature of national economic policy, and the close links between the Scottish economy and the rest of the UK, mean that economic trends in Scotland are inevitably strongly conditioned by developments in the wider UK economy. Where aspects of economic policy are administered in Scotland (for example, selective financial assistance to industry), there are national guidelines to ensure a uniformity of approach in different areas of the UK. Secondly, there are strong social and political pressures in favour of consistency and uniformity of policy in different regions; this tends to constrain the extent to which, for example, the allocation of public expenditure between different programmes can vary markedly. Finally, it should be borne in mind that the impact of administrative arrangements on the solution of problems can easily be exaggerated unless they lead to the availability of additional resources. Even if this were the case in relation to the Secretary of State's position in Cabinet and the role of the SDA, there are clearly limits to the extent to which any such advantages could be replicated for all regions simply by setting up similar systems.

The strengths of the Scottish arrangements which may be more capable of replication elsewhere stem from the framework they provide for the more effective co-ordination of policies, for example regional and urban policies, and the ability to take more account of different regional circumstances. For example, a rather different and arguably more consistent approach has been pursued in Scotland in relation to New Towns and local authorities over many years. The emphasis placed by the SDA on high-technology industries is a further indication of a long-term perspective. The Scottish system also offers a mechanism for integrating recent initiatives such as Enterprise Zones and Freeports into a view of spatial priorities seen at regional level. These features (for example, the broadening of the base of the Scottish electronics industry to which the SDA has contributed) may have a favourable impact on the scope for economic development in the long run, while gains through better administration and co-ordination of policies are valuable in their own right. But their direct contribution to economic performance in the short term should not be exaggerated. It seems unlikely that the new Regional Councils played more than a minor part in Scotland's broadly favourable record during the 1970s, compared with more fundamental forces such as the country's changing industrial structure, the impact of regional policy, and North Sea oil. The setting up of the SDA was an important development, but again, its main impact is likely to be in the longer term.

Conclusion

During the 1970s the Scottish economy made considerable progress in improving its performance relative to that of the UK. This reflected a combination of favourable circumstances, with the boost from North Sea oil reinforcing the more gradual effects of an improved industrial structure helped by regional policy and other public expenditure programmes over a much longer period. While the effects of North Sea oil were the most dramatic, it seems reasonable to attribute a significant part of the credit for this advance to underlying shifts in the capacity for growth of the Scottish economy brought about by the fairly consistent application of regional development policies over the postwar period. The gains of the 1970s conceal a big deterioration in absolute unemployment levels, as in other parts of the UK, and also increasing inequality, particularly between much of West Central Scotland and to some extent Dundee on the one hand, and the more prosperous areas of Scotland such as Aberdeen and Edinburgh on the other.

There is a need for caution in assessing prospects, since some of the factors which have sustained the Scottish economy in the past may not operate as strongly in the future, and some of the underlying problems associated with a peripheral location and a limited capacity for self-sustaining growth may become more evident. Severe problems of environmental dereliction and an unfavourable image also persist in some older urban areas. While the regional policy changes announced in 1984 are likely to lead to a reduction in expenditure in Scotland of around £90 million per annum by 1987–8 (a similar proportionate reduction to that expected for regional policy expenditure in Great Britain as a whole), regional policy will continue to be a favourable factor. The SDA also represents a strength partly through its resources (although to an increasing extent these are matched in other parts of Great Britain, for example through the growth of expenditure on inner-city policy in England), and also through the longer-term potential of an administrative framework which enables better co-ordination of urban and regional policies in the promotion of economic change.

Overall, the experience of the 1970s is an encouraging one which gives grounds for some optimism. Psychologically the rapid growth in some areas, particularly associated with North Sea oil, may have led to a wider self-confidence and to a climate more encouraging to new enterprise. If the industrial revolution gave a legacy of an unfavourable industrial structure which has taken decades to transform, the depression of the 1930s produced social attitudes often antagonistic to economic change which now also show signs of becoming less fixed. New industries, such as North Sea oil and electronics, and new settlements, such as the New Towns, are playing their part in this fundamental change. The impact of the Scottish administrative system on economic performance should not be exaggerated; but it has some strengths which provide a useful framework within which to encourage further changes. The objectives of economic development are not easy to attain. They require consistency of approach and an ability to identify and give emphasis to a longer-term perspective. While the relative improvement in Scotland's performance in the 1970s partly reflects special factors such as North Sea oil, the important contribution made by postwar regional development policies, which have been more gradual in their impact, should not be overlooked.

Note

The views expressed in this chapter are personal, and do not necessarily reflect those of the Industry Department for Scotland.

References

Carter, C. (1986), *The Scottish New Towns: Their Contribution to Post-War Growth and Urban Development in Central Scotland*, Duncan of Jordanstone College of Art.

Department of Trade and Industry (1983), *Regional Industrial Policy: Some Economic Issues*, London, HMSO.

—— (1984), *British Business*, 10 February 1984.

Firn, J. (1975), 'External Control and Regional Development: The Case of Scotland', *Environment and Planning A* 7, 393–414.

Forsyth, D. (1972), *US Investment in Scotland*, New York, Praeger.

Henderson, R. A. (1980), *The Location of Immigrant Industry Within a UK Assisted Area: The Scottish Experience*, Oxford, Pergamon.

Hood, N., and Young, S. (1980), *European Development Strategies of US Owned Manufacturing Companies Located in Scotland*, Edinburgh, HMSO.

House of Commons (1977), *Official Report (Hansard)*, 18 March 1977 (WA 347–348), London, HMSO.

—— (1983), *Official Report (Hansard)*, 1 February 1983 (WA 83–84), London, HMSO.

—— (1984), *Official Report (Hansard)*, 2 July 1984, London, HMSO.

Johnston, T., Buxton, N., and Mair, D. (1971), *Structure and Growth of the Scottish Economy*, London, Collins.

McCrone, G. (1969), *Scotland's Future*, Oxford, Blackwell.

——, and Randall, J. N. (1985), 'The Scottish Development Agency', in R. Saville, ed., *The Economic History of Modern Scotland 1950–80*, St Andrews.

McDermott, P. (1976), 'Ownership, Organisation and Regional Dependence in the Scottish Electronics Industry', *Regional Studies* 10, 319–35.

McDowall, S., and Begg, H. (1981), *Industrial Performance and Prospects in Areas Affected by Oil Development*, Edinburgh, Scottish Economic Planning Department.

Moore, B., and Rhodes, J. (1974), 'Regional Policy and the Scottish Economy', *Scottish Journal of Political Economy* 21, 215–35.

Oakey, R. (1984), *High Technology and Small Firms: Regional Development in Britain and the US*, London, Frances Pinter.

PEIDA (1985), *Transport Costs in Peripheral Areas*, Edinburgh, Industry Department for Scotland.

Randall, J. N. (1982), 'The Comparative Birth Rate of Enterprises New to Manufacturing in Scotland and the UK', *Scottish Economic Bulletin No. 24*, Edinburgh, HMSO.

—— (1985), 'New Industries and New Towns', in R. Saville, ed., *The Economic History of Modern Scotland 1950–80*, St Andrews.

Scottish Office (1980), *Scottish Economic Bulletin No. 20*, Edinburgh, HMSO.

—— (1981), *Scottish Economic Bulletin no. 22*, Edinburgh, HMSO.

—— (1984), *Scottish Abstract of Statistics No 13*, Edinburgh, HMSO.

Scrimgeour, P. A. A. (1984), 'Employment in Industrial Research and Development in Scotland and the UK', *Scottish Economic Bulletin no. 29*, Edinburgh, HMSO.

Storey, D. (1983), Memorandum to Select Committee on Welsh Affairs Inquiry on The Impact of Regional Industrial Policy on Wales', House of Commons, 1983–4.

Toothill Committee (1961), *Inquiry into the Scottish Economy*, Edinburgh, Scottish Council (Development and Industry).

CHAPTER 11
Northern Ireland

P. J. Bull and M. Hart

Of all the UK planning regions, Northern Ireland (see Figure 11.1) is without question the most severely handicapped. On the one hand, its manufacturing sector is crippled by a sectoral concentration in declining industries, relative inaccessibility to British and especially European markets, and the increasing importance—at least during the 1960s and 1970s—of relatively large, externally owned branch plants. On the other, both its economy and society suffer from the severe paraplegia of religious intolerance and civil unrest. Indeed, throughout the post-Second World War period Northern Ireland consistently recorded the most unfavourable results in the UK on virtually all the standard indicators of regional economic health, whether in terms of rates of unemployment or infant mortality, income per head or the level of emigration (Isles and Cuthbert 1957; Murie *et al.* 1969; Busteed 1974; Harvey and Rea 1982; O'Dowd *et al.* 1980; Rowthorn 1981; Hoare 1982; 1983). Table 11.1, for example, provides selected indicators for the late 1970s. Furthermore, during the last forty years there have been both persistent and consistent spatial variations of well-being within the province, with the east tending to be the most favoured (Hoare 1982; Bull 1984*a*).

Figure 11.2 shows that unemployment rates in Northern Ireland in March 1985 were lowest in the east, with the Belfast and Ballymena travel-to-work areas recording rates of less than 20 per cent. The highest rates were in the south and west, where Cookstown and Strabane recorded rates of more than 35 per cent. However, it must be remembered that the south and west are the most rural parts of the province and have relatively few inhabitants (Hoare 1982). The majority of the people of Northern Ireland and over 60 per cent of the employment opportunities are concentrated in the Belfast travel-to-work area. Since the early 1960s a number of attempts have been made to limit the growth of the city of Belfast, and to slow down rural depopulation by diverting new investment to other towns in the province. These attempts have included the designation of growth centres, district and expanded town schemes, the improvement of the province's road network, and increasing development grants with distance from Belfast (Caldwell and Greer 1984; Hoare 1981). However, although some investment has been diverted to the south and west, the majority has taken place in the east, and especially in the Belfast travel-to-work area. Indeed, this was to be expected given that this area possesses the largest and most diverse labour market in the province, the only international airport, and, more importantly, the two main ports of Belfast and Larne.

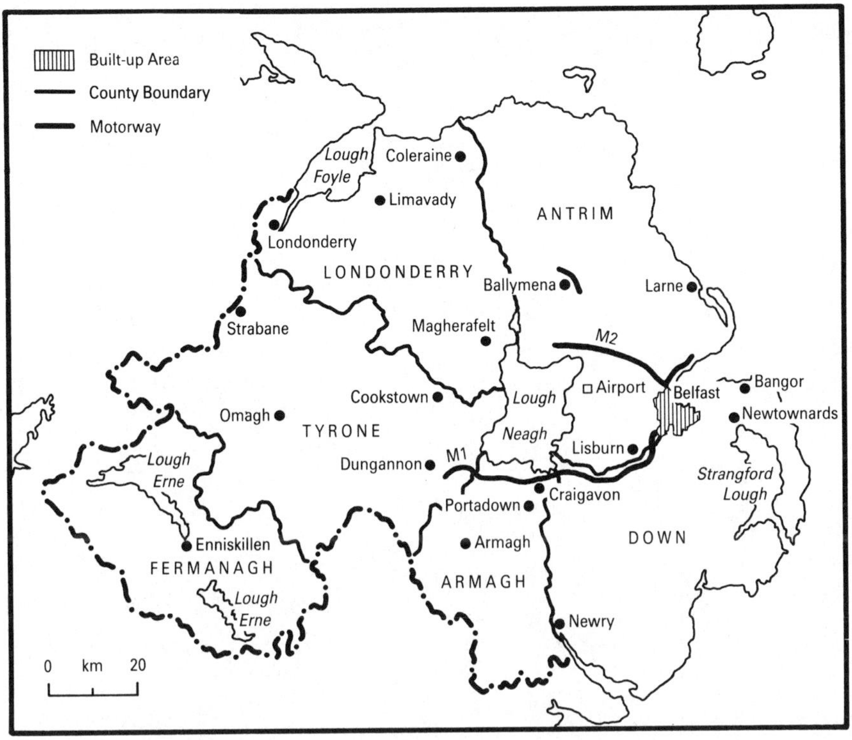

Figure 11.1. Northern Ireland

Furthermore, as Hoare (1982) has pointed out, attempts to overcome Northern Ireland's internal regional problem have been compounded by its wider economic problems. The province has been so desperate for investment that it has been unable to jeopardize the chances of obtaining new companies by insisting that they go to the most deserving places.

In recognition of its severe economic and social problems, a great deal of public money has been spent in the province. For example, in 1981–2 public expenditure in Northern Ireland was £3,218 million, representing 75.6 per cent of the province's gross domestic product (Northern Ireland Economic Council (NIEC), 1984*a*). Clearly, if parity of opportunity, welfare, and service provision across the regions of the UK is to guide public expenditure, then Northern Ireland's socioeconomic disabilities justify a level of expenditure per head above the national average. In Table 11.2 it can be seen that, in terms of this form of expenditure, Northern Ireland was in fact somewhat unfavourably placed before 1968. During the 1970s, however, expenditure in the province increased rapidly relative to other regions, to the point where, in 1977–8 Northern Ireland received 41 per cent more public expenditure per head than England and Wales, and 13 per cent more than Scotland. However, the aim of this chapter is not to assess whether the level of public expenditure in Northern Ireland can be

Table 11.1 Selected economic and social indicators: Northern Ireland and other UK regions

Indicator	Great Britain				UK average
	Northern Ireland	South East	North	Scotland	
Unemployment (% average 1981, n.s.a.)	18.4	10.0	15.3	13.8	11.4
Average weekly earnings, £, April 1981					
male	129.7	152.4	134.7	140.0	140.5†
female	88.5	99.6	88.0	87.1	91.5
Activity rates, 1979*					
male	75.1	77.8	77.4	78.0	77.4†
female	44.9	46.9	46.1	49.3	47.0
Net emigration (No. per 1000 population, av. 1975–8)	−5.2	−1.4	−2.4	−2.0	
Infant mortality (Infant deaths 1 yr per 1,000 live births)	13.4	11.6	12.4	12.1	12.1
Supplementary benefits, 1977–80, £ per head of population	62.4	36.5	46.5	42.1	40.3
Family Income Supplement, 1978–79, £ per head of population	2.08	0.30	0.39	0.56	0.42†
% heads of households in professional and technical posts, 1979–80	5.4	9.9	6.3	7.9	7.5
% heads of households in administrative and management posts, 1979–80	2.3	11.8	5.6	7.2	8.5
Per capita GDP, 1980 as % UK	74.9	115.1	92.7	96.0	100.0

Source: Harrison 1983.
* Civilian labour force as a percentage of those aged 15 and over.
† Great Britain average only.

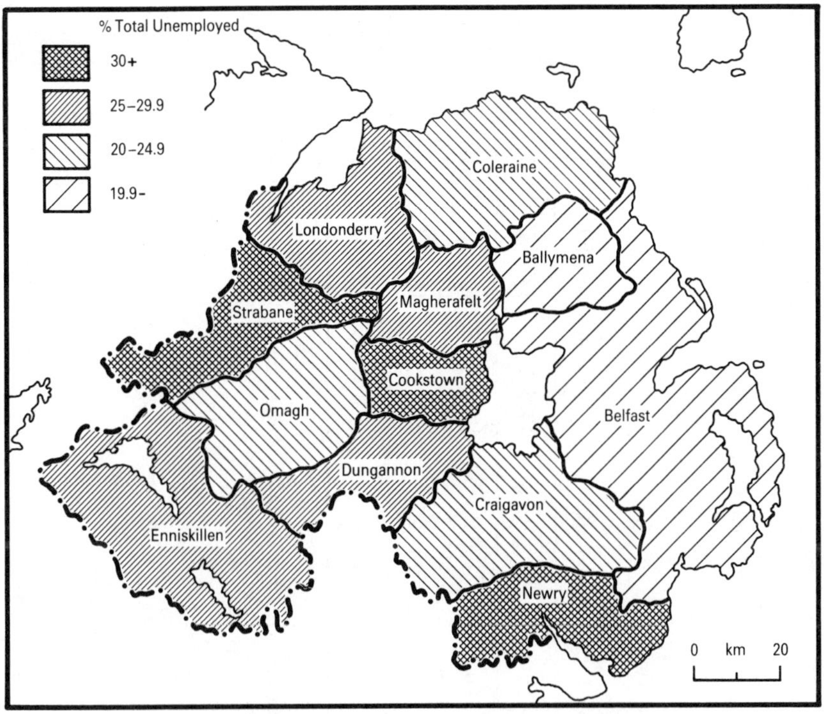

Figure 11.2. Unemployment in Northern Ireland (March, 1985)

justified, but simply to review the ways in which public money has been spent in the province, with particular attention being focused on the support given to industrial development (ID). This task has been greatly assisted by the recent publication by the NIEC of a series of reports on the priorities of government spending in Northern Ireland and the ID programmes of the province (NIEC 1983*a*; 1983*b*; 1984*a*). To provide a context for this discussion, this chapter begins with a review of recent economic trends in the province.

Recent economic trends

After the Second World War, the economic health of Northern Ireland in terms of gross domestic product (GDP) per head of population improved most significantly relative to the UK between 1958 and 1968. During this period, GDP per head rose annually on average by 3.5 per cent compared with 2.8 per cent for the nation as a whole (NIEC 1983*a*). Nevertheless, even at the end of this period of very favourable regional growth, GDP per head in Northern Ireland was only 75.0 per cent of the equivalent figure for the UK (Harrison 1982). After this point, growth in GDP per head tended to follow the national trend until 1979, when the province began to decline at a much faster rate than

Table 11.2. Identifiable* public expenditure per head, Northern Ireland and other UK countries, 1959–78

Region	1959–60	1962–3	1965–6	1968–9	1971–2	1974–5	1976–7	1977–8
England	100	100	100	100	100	100	100	100
Scotland	105	118	111	134	125	118	123	128
Wales	95	99	94	101	104	97	101	100
Northern Ireland	88	92	97	103	111	112	136	141

Source: Northern Ireland Economic Council 1984*a*.

*Relates to six main programmes—Health and Personal Social Services, Education (excluding universities), Housing, Other Environmental Services, Transport (excluding railways), and Law and Order (excluding police).

the nation. Between 1979 and 1981 the annual rate of change in GDP per head was −2.6 per cent in the UK compared with −5.0 per cent in Northern Ireland (NIEC 1983*a*).

Employment trends in the province tended to follow the above variations in per capita GDP. From 1961 to 1979 employment grew from 540,000 to almost 600,000, followed by employment contraction in the early 1980s. Over this twenty-year period, however, marked changes took place in the sectoral balance of employment (Bull 1984*b*). Figure 11.3 shows the distribution of employees in employment by industrial sector in Northern Ireland in 1960, 1970, and 1980. It is clear that the most profound change in the employment structure of the province was the growth of the service sector, which was particularly dramatic in professional and scientific services (SIC Order 25). Employment in this industry, which totalled almost 42,000 in 1960, grew by 63 per cent in the 1960s and by 58 per cent in the following decade. One of the most important components of the expansion of service jobs during the last two decades has been growth in the public sector. Indeed, at its peak in September 1982, 213,500, or 45.1 per cent of the province's workforce, were employed in the public sector (NIEC 1983*c*).

Since the Second World War the number of manufacturing jobs in Northern Ireland has followed a downward course, which accelerated rapidly during the 1970s. Even during the economically relatively successful years of the 1960s the province lost approximately 4,000 manufacturing jobs. This trend disguises the fact that some of the more traditional industries in the province, such as textiles, clothing and especially shipbuilding, shed very large numbers of jobs during this decade. Shipbuilding alone, for example, lost 14,000 jobs during the 1960s. However, at the same time job expansions in new establishments in electrical, instrument and mechanical engineering, metal goods, food and drink processing, and within textiles itself in man-made fibres, helped to offset the severe decline of the established manufacturing industries. Unfortunately, during the 1970s not only did the traditional manufacturing industries in the province continue to shed labour, but many of the new growth industries of the 1960s also began to lose jobs, resulting in a 28 per cent decline of manufacturing employment during this decade. The service sector continued to expand, and as a consequence the percentage share of employment in manufacturing declined from 32 per cent in 1970 to 25 per cent in 1980.

As in most other regions of the UK, therefore, Northern Ireland in the 1970s and early 1980s witnessed a marked shift in the balance of employment opportunities in favour of the service industries, with many jobs in manufacturing, and indeed in agriculture, being lost from the economy (Lloyd and Reeve 1982). Many of the new service-sector jobs, along with a substantial proportion of the smaller numbers of new jobs in manufacturing, were occupied by women. Thus, between 1971 and 1978 the female activity rate in the province increased from 35.4 to 43.4 per cent (Harvey and Rea 1982). Employment problems in Northern Ireland, especially for men, have been compounded by an expansion of the population of working age, which is expected to grow by 8,000 a year between 1984 and 1988 and to continue to grow well into the next century

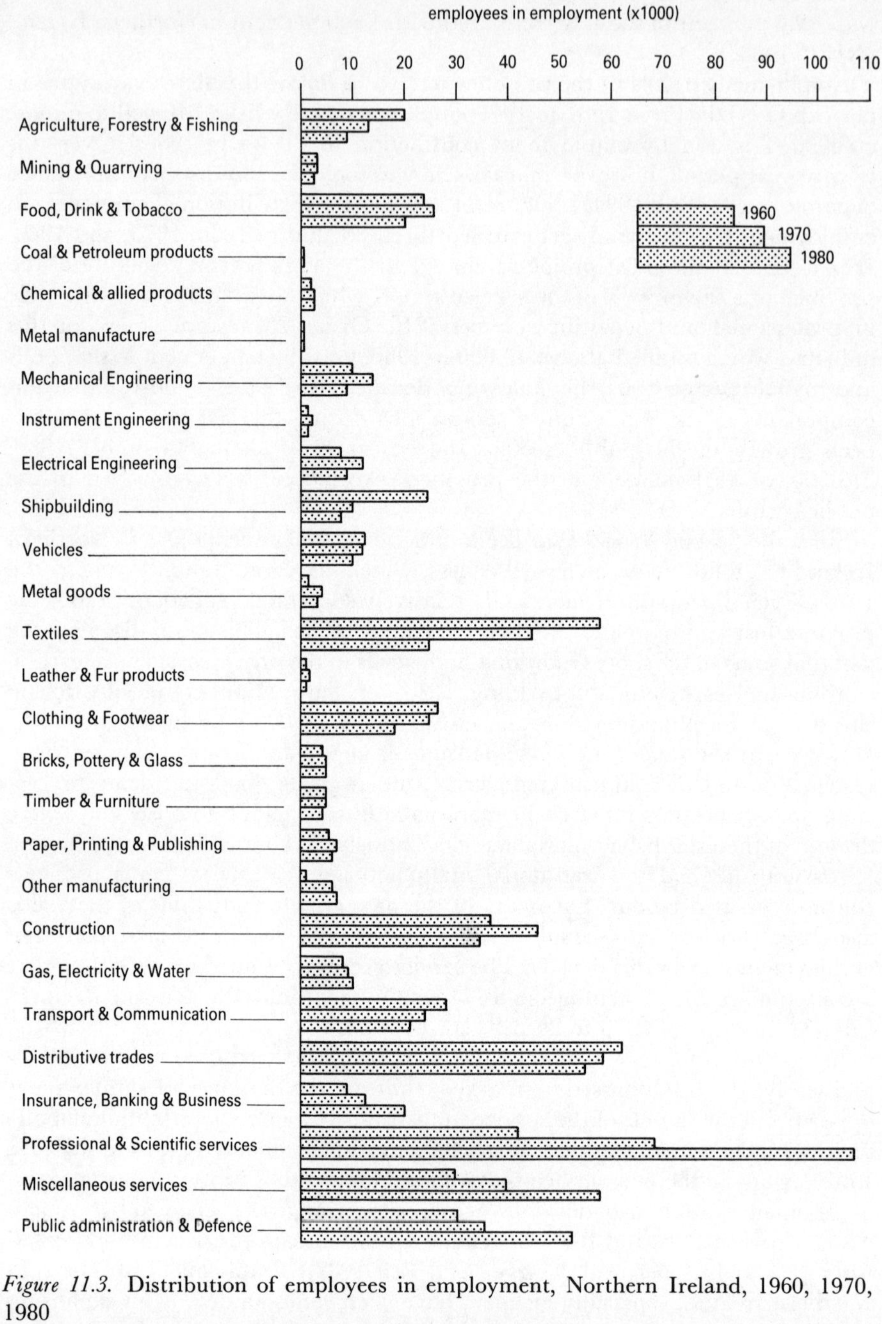

Figure 11.3. Distribution of employees in employment, Northern Ireland, 1960, 1970, 1980

(NIEC 1984*b*). Thus, unless the number of people emigrating from the province increases substantially from the present 5,000–6,000 per annum, the employment problems of the province will tend to get worse rather than better.

From the late 1940s, unemployment rates in Northern Ireland fluctuated at between three and four times the national level until the mid-1960s, when their relative position began to improve to about twice the national figure by the early 1970s. However, throughout this twenty-year period, unemployment rates in Northern Ireland remained in single figures. Since then the position has changed dramatically. On the one hand, the relative position of the province has tended to improve. For example, in September 1984 Northern Ireland's rate of unemployment was only 1.6 times the national figure. On the other hand, both rates have risen alarmingly (Harrison 1982). In September 1984, Northern Ireland's rate of unemployment was 21.9 per cent, 8.3 percentage points higher than in the UK as a whole (*Belfast Telegraph*, 4 October 1984).

Recent trends in public expenditure

As has already been shown, expenditure per head of population in Northern Ireland by central government did not begin to exceed average UK levels until the early 1970s. However, by the end of this decade the province had achieved substantial relative gains. In real terms, public expenditure in the province also increased substantially, for example by 35 per cent between 1973–4 and 1984–5. Some of this increase was, of course, the direct result of population increase, but most represented a real increase in the standard of provision (NIEC 1984*a*). Changes in public expenditure during this period by sub-programme are given in Table 11.3. Given the sharp rise in unemployment, a large increase in expenditure on the social security programme was to be expected. Similarly, the increasing complexity of combating Northern Ireland's problems of civil unrest and terrorism necessitated an increase in spending on law and order. However, a critical review of expenditure on the other sub-programmes reveals some unfortunate and unexpected results.

One possible measure of the success of a public expenditure programme in a problem region such as Northern Ireland would be the degree to which parity with national standards had been achieved. Of the other sub-programmes, the largest increase in expenditure between 1973–4 and 1984–5 occurred in housing. However, given Northern Ireland's, and especially Belfast's, notorious housing problems, the increase was in no way sufficient to bring the province's housing provision into line with national standards (Singleton 1983). On the other hand, by the mid-1970s Northern Ireland had achieved effective parity with the UK in three other important sub-programmes: transport, education, and health. Transport's parity was largely due to extensive infrastructural projects undertaken after the designation of the province's growth centres and the new city of Craigavon in the mid-1960s (Caldwell and Greer 1984). By the beginning of the 1980s these projects were drawing to a close, and therefore public expenditure on transport tended to be much lower in the 1980s than during the previous decade (Table 11.3). However, while expenditure on the

Table 11.3. Changes in public expenditure by sub-programme in Northern Ireland, 1973–4 to 1984–5

Sub-programme	Percentage of total		Change (1975 prices)	
	1973–4	1984–5	£ m.	%
Agriculture	2.2	2.2	+8	+32
Industry, energy, employment	18.4	10.2	−50	−25
Transport	5.4	2.9	−17	−28
Housing	6.6	8.4	+53	+73
Other environmental	4.8	4.0	+7	+13
Law and order*	9.0	10.3	+54	+54
Education	15.7	14.6	+44	+25
Health	13.4	16.4	+97	+65
Social security	21.4	29.3	+202	+85
Other public/common services	3.1	1.7	−9	−26
Total	100.0	100.0	+389	+35

Source: Northern Ireland Economic Council 1984*a*.
*Excludes costs of the British Army.

transport programme declined, expenditure on education, and especially on health, continued to rise. Indeed, health provision progressed from a position of relative inadequacy in the early 1960s to one of relative excess by the end of the 1970s, especially in terms of hospital beds per head of population. Yet, perhaps surprisingly, health expenditure has been planned for expansion in real terms until 1988 (NIEC 1984*a*).

What is unfortunate in these patterns is that spending on the industry, energy, and employment programme, in part designed to overcome unemployment, the characteristic on which Northern Ireland is most clearly disadvantaged relative to the UK, was reduced by 25 per cent. It is also worth noting that, although expenditure on health and education provides a service to the community and not simply employment, the jobs that were generated in these two programmes were relatively expensive. For example, in 1983 the cost per job-year was £11,000 in the health service and £9,900 in education. By contrast, the cost per job-year in the industry and employment programme was £5,570 in government training centres, up to £3,300 in job release schemes, £2,188 for the support of large manufacturing projects, and only £562 for the Local Enterprise Development Unit (NIEC 1984*a*). Surely a much greater priority should have been given to expenditure on industry and employment during the last decade.

Industrial development assistance

Within the general area of industry, energy and employment policy there have been many recent decisions by government which have had a major impact on the economic development and labour market characteristics of Northern Ireland. For example, over the last decade a great deal of public money has been used for job-maintenance, counter-redundancy, and training schemes especially for the young unemployed. Indeed, 16,350 people were engaged in such schemes in August 1983 (NIEC 1983*c*). Government decisions in 1984 and 1985 in the energy sector, however, will lead to job losses. In particular, over 1,000 jobs are expected to be lost as a result of the run-down of the town gas industry in the province, due to lack of financial support and the refusal to allow Kinsale natural gas from the Republic of Ireland to be piped north. Admittedly, an unknown number of new jobs will be generated from the exploitation of the lignite deposit on the eastern shore of Lough Neagh, but these are unlikely to compensate for those lost in the province's gas industry. This section, however, is principally concerned with government assistance to private manufacturing because, until the 1980s, this was the only sector to benefit directly from ID assistance.

Since 1921 Northern Ireland has enjoyed a large degree of autonomy over its industrial development programme. Although constrained by general financial guidelines set by Whitehall, local politicians, until the imposition of direct rule in 1972, formulated their own ID grant structure and intraregional location policies to meet their own perceived needs (Hoare 1981). These policies were adminstered initially by the Ministry (latterly the Department) of Commerce, aided from the early 1970s by the Northern Ireland Development Agency (NIDA) and the Local Enterprise Development Unit (LEDU). However, following a review of ID assistance in the province in 1979–80 it was decided that all ID functions—curiously, excepting LEDU—should be brought together in one new organization to be known as the Industrial Development Board.

The regional policy incentives in Northern Ireland are different from those in Britain in two important respects. First, selective financial assistance is offered as an alternative to Standard Capital Grants (equivalent to Regional Development Grants in Britain) rather than as an additional layer of assistance. Second, unlike in Britain, the selective package of individually negotiable capital and employment grants is of far greater importance than the automatic assistance. For example, of planned ID expenditure in Northern Ireland in 1983–4, 65 per cent was for selective assistance and only 35 per cent for automatic grants, whereas the equivalent figures for Britain were 20 per cent and 80 per cent respectively (NIEC 1984*c*). One of the principal recommendations of the White Paper on Regional Industrial Development (1983), which does not encompass Northern Ireland, was a shift from automatic to selective forms of assitance, as already exists in Northern Ireland.

Since 1932, financial assistance for industrial development in Northern Ireland has been offered with the direct aim of attempting to overcome the province's unemployment problem. From the 1960s until the mid-1970s, however, economic reports such as the Wilson Report (1965), the 1970 Northern Ireland Development Programme for 1970–5, and the Quigley Report in 1976 advocated ID assistance not only to attract firms to the area to provide jobs

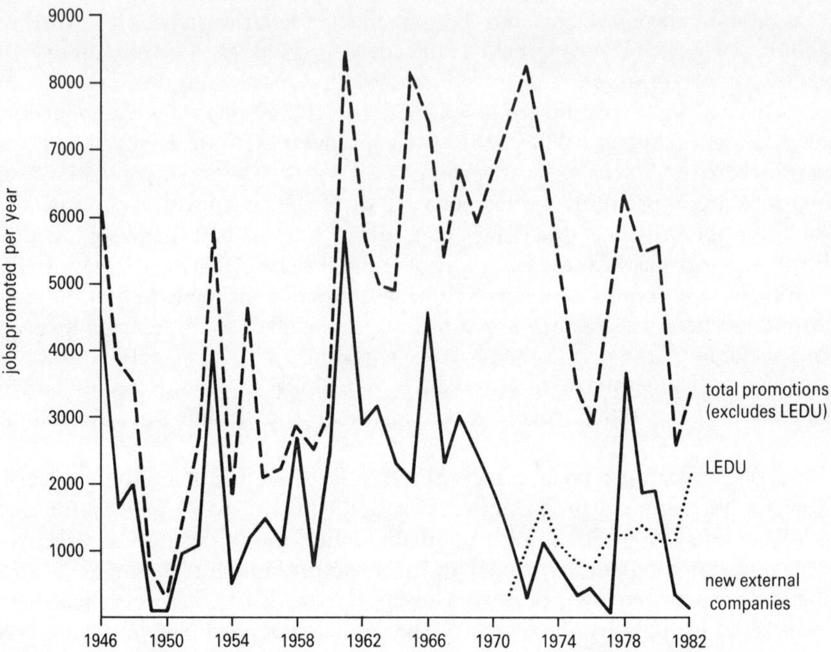

Figure 11.4. Industrial Development job promotions in Northern Ireland 1946–82

but also to stimulate regional self-generating economic growth. The Quigley Report advocated the attraction of big firms to the province in fast-growing sectors to act as the propulsive force for local economic expansion.

Industrial development legislation helped to promote 170,000 jobs in Northern Ireland between 1946 and 1982, which accounted for over 1.4 million man-years of employment (NIEC 1983*b*). Figure 11.4 details the temporal trend in ID-promoted jobs in two separate series: the total number of ID-promoted jobs from all sources of investment, and those provided by externally owned companies investing in Northern Ireland for the first time. The former category therefore includes the latter. However, it is important to realize that, once new companies are established in the province, any additional jobs they provide are not included in the new external companies series. After the initial postwar surge of reconstruction, ID-promoted jobs reached their lowest annual total in 1950. Indeed, with the exceptions of 1953, when GEC and Norton Abrasives established branches, and 1955, when new investment principally in the existing clothing sector took place, the 1950s were typified by relatively low numbers of ID-assisted jobs. By contrast, there was a marked growth in jobs promoted in the 1960s, as a consequence of the national intensification of regional policies during this decade. The greatest annual number of jobs promoted was achieved in 1961, largely as a consequence of almost 6,000 generated by investment from outside the province. ID-promoted jobs continued at this relatively high level until 1972, from which point an irregular decline to 2,500 in 1981 took place. Of particular interest here is the fall-off of new external projects after 1970, an important factor in the decline in the total number of jobs promoted. The beginning of the De Lorean affair in 1978 represents an exception to this trend. Yet, although there was little external investment to be acquired at this time, encouragement to branches of large firms to locate in Northern Ireland was still forcefully advocated by economic reports on the province and actively pursued by the development agencies.

The total number of ID-assisted jobs in the province expanded throughout the 1960s to compensate in part for the many jobs lost from existing manufacturing activity. This expansion continued until 1974, reaching a peak of 71,500. Since then the total number of ID-assisted jobs has declined, but at a slower rate than in the non-assisted sector, resulting in an increase in their relative importance in the province. For example, in 1980, ID-assisted employment represented 45 per cent of all manufacturing employment in Northern Ireland (Harrison 1982). Nevertheless, the fact that the latter half of the 1970s, and indeed the first four years of the 1980s, have been characterized by a persistent absolute decline in the number of ID-assisted jobs is an extremely worrying feature for the development of the Northern Ireland economy (Black 1981; NIEC 1983*a*; Bull 1984*b*; Simpson 1984). Clearly the optimism of the 1960s, when it was believed that from the ID-assisted activity self-sustaining regional economic and employment growth would develop, was not fulfilled in the 1970s and 1980s.

From an analysis of 477 ID-assisted projects between 1951 and 1980s, Simpson (1984) has shown that on average, assisted projects reached an employment peak after only six years, from which point their employment levels began to decline. From a similar analysis of all ID-assisted projects from 1945 to June 1982, the NIEC (1983*b*) demonstrated that employment contraction began on average 8.1 years after opening for those still in existence in 1982, and after 6.8 years for those which had closed during the study period. In addition, it was shown that job loss came more from closure than *in situ* shrinkage, the most striking example of which is found in the man-made fibres industry in the province. In 1974 over 9,000 people—7 per cent of the total manufacturing workforce—were employed in this industry. By 1982 this total had fallen to 1,337, 78 per cent of the jobs being lost as a result of the closure decisions of three companies which had received ID assistance for their projects: ICI, Courtaulds, and British Enkalon (NIEC 1983*b*).

Up to the end of 1979, 325 *entirely new* manufacturing projects had been established in Northern Ireland with ID assistance, of which 144, 43 per cent, had closed. Of these closures the majority occurred after 1970, with forty taking place between 1975 and 1979 (Bull *et al.* 1982). Furthermore, according to Black (1981), between January 1979 and the last quarter of 1981, 110 substantial assisted and non-assisted manufacturing plants closed in the province, accounting for 13,500 redundancies. This process has continued unabated.

Explanation of the high closure rate of ID-assisted industry in Northern Ireland and the resultant loss of employment is difficult. Recent slumps in

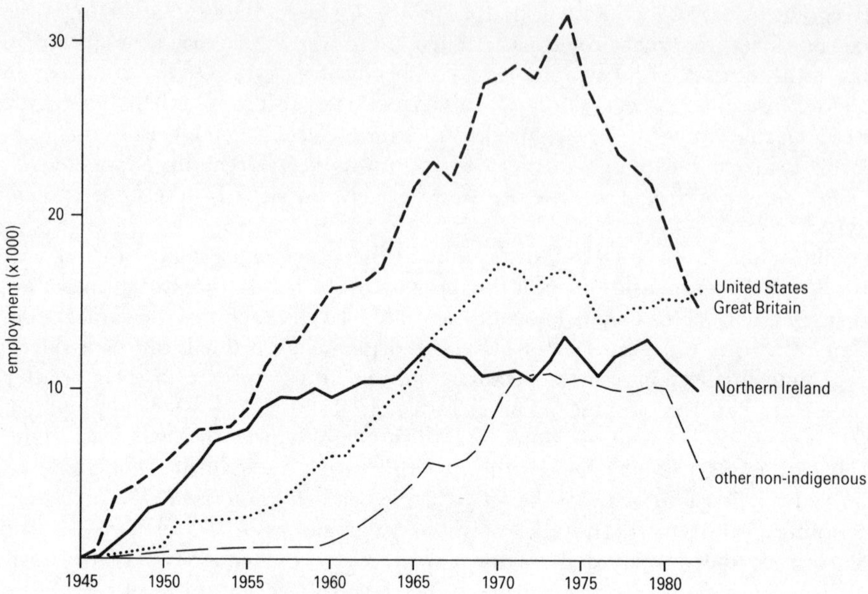

Figure 11.5. Industrial Development employment in Northern Ireland, 1945–82, by nationality of ownership

world demand for manufactured products must have had a major impact. But as Simpson (1984) has pointed out, although the majority of losses of ID-assisted projects and employment have occurred over the last ten years, the rates of contraction have been too severe to be accounted for simply by recession. There is some evidence to suggest that nationality of ownership may be an important explanatory variable. In Figure 11.5, for example, it would appear that projects owned by firms with their headquarters in Great Britain lost jobs at a much faster rate after 1973 than those from Northern Ireland or the United States. Furthermore, in terms of the closure of assisted projects, Bull *et al*. (1982) have shown that GB projects not only recorded the greatest number of project closures among the principal national ownership groups (see Figure 11.6), but also recorded the greatest rate of closure. Compared with a closure rate for all new ID-assisted projects by the end of 1979 of 42.5 per cent, British-owned projects recorded a rate of 53 per cent, Northern Ireland projects 33 per cent, and North American projects only 22 per cent. Perhaps a substantial proportion of new British assisted projects represented marginal capacity set up principally in the 1960s to benefit from generous regional aid when demand was buoyant and future prospects relatively favourable. Such capacity would then have been surplus to requirements when the demand for manufactured goods fell in the post-1970 period, and would therefore have been closed. By contrast, North American investment, which from its inception may have been planned to supply a relatively large market such as the EEC, rather than

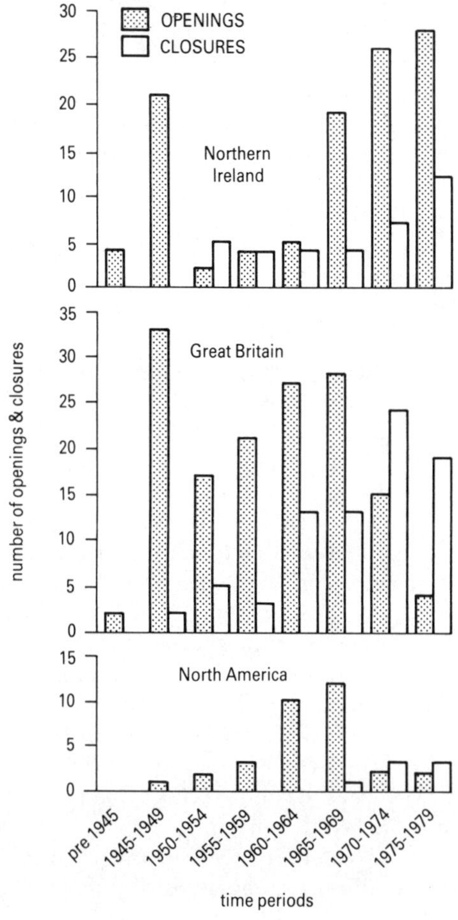

Figure 11.6. Government-assisted manufacturing projects in Northern Ireland: openings and closures by time period and area of origin

simply additional capacity for existing markets as in the case of British projects, may have had a much better chance of survival. Against this, however, the NIEC (1983*b*) econometric analysis of the duration of employment in all ID-assisted projects between 1945 and 1982 did not find nationality of ownership a significant factor. Instead, employment durability was found to be positively related to project size and project type, that is, to entirely new projects rather than to local expansions. But, of course, employment durability and project-closure rates are two very different characteristics of ID-assisted industry. Therefore, given its major impact on the economic well-being of the province, the high rate of ID-assisted industry closure after 1970 still necessitates detailed and urgent research.

It is clear from the previous discussion that in recent years ID-assisted industry has failed either to promote sustained employment growth or even aggregate employment stability in the province. However, assisted industry has helped to create a modest degree of industrial diversification. After the Second World War the manufacturing base of the province was dominated by textiles, clothing, food and drink, and shipbuilding. By 1980 the importance of shipbuilding persisted more in the minds of the people of Ulster than in the reality of the numbers employed. Textiles, clothing, and food and drink, however, were still of major importance in the manufacturing sector. Regional policy had encouraged the development of new industries such as consumer electronics, automotive components, rubber products, and man-made fibres along with the introduction of new processes and products in existing industries; but two sets of actors militated against these developments having any major impact on the employment structure of the province.

First, it must be remembered that Northern Ireland's only locational asset, in addition to generous levels of regional aid, is the availability of relatively cheap labour. The province has few economically viable natural resources, with the recent lignite find on the eastern shore of Lough Neagh being one of the few exceptions, and is relatively inaccessible to mainland European markets (Keeble *et al*. 1982). Thus, it is not surprising to discover that, although all seventeen manufacturing orders of the 1968 Standard Industrial Classification were represented in the ID-assisted openings after 1945, the majority were in industries such as textiles, food and drink, and clothing which are relatively labour-intensive, and industries on which Northern Ireland was already dependent. Indeed, 22 per cent of all new ID project openings between 1945 and 1979 were in textiles (Bull 1984*b*). Secondly, many of the projects encouraged on diversification grounds, such as Grundig, ICI, Goodyear, and Rolls Royce, have been closed during the last fifteen years.

From Figure 11.6 it can be seen that only new projects from Northern Ireland were established in any significant numbers during the 1970s. However, their employment creation record in absolute terms was of a modest nature, due to their much smaller size compared to projects from outside the province. For example, in March 1980 the average number of people employed in projects from Northern Ireland, Britain, and North America was 88, 197, and 441 respectively. Nevertheless, with the relative paucity of jobs promoted during the 1970s and 1980s, especially in new projects from outside the province (see Figure 11.5), the importance of these indigenous projects must not be overlooked. In addition these figures do not include the employment promotional activities of LEDU, which as Figure 11.5 shows, have been one of the few successful features of the Northern Ireland economy since 1971 (Busteed 1976; Cooley 1976; Hart 1983; 1984).

LEDU was established in 1971 with the following objectives:

(*a*) to promote employment in existing small businesses
(*b*) to encourage the setting up of new enterprises
(*c*) to foster craft industry

The Unit's acitivities were originally intended to be confined solely to manufacturing firms with less than fifty employees in the rural west of the province. In 1980, however, LEDU's remit was widened substantially to include service industries and problem inner-city areas such as Belfast, to safeguard employment in 'viable companies', and to seek out mobile small industry from the UK mainland.

Between 1971 and 1983, LEDU was involved in the promotion of 15,334 jobs in 1,544 projects (LEDU 1983). Although the absolute levels of employment generated by LEDU have been small (see Figure 11.5), the jobs have been created extremely cheaply. For example, at 1983 prices, recent average cost per job-year figures from NIEC (1984*a*) were £562 for LEDU-assisted projects and between £718 and £2,188 for projects assisted by the Industrial Development Board or its predecessor, the Department of Commerce. Probably as a consequence of their indigenous origins, few LEDU-assisted projects have contributed to the industrial diversification of the province (Hart 1983). Nevertheless, it is clear from this evidence that there are many local people in Northern Ireland willing to try to become successfully self-employed. This of course may be the direct result of rising unemployment, with redundant workers attempting to pursue one of the few routes to gainful employment open to them (Harrison and Hart 1983). Unfortunately, the origins of new small firms in Northern Ireland have not yet been satisfactorily researched, and the number of potential self-employed businessmen and women is unknown.

Recent work on the modelling of regional entrepreneurship in the UK has indicated that Northern Ireland possesses low levels of entrepreneurship (Storey 1982; Whittington 1984). The explanation according to Storey (1982) is primarily related to the region's low proportion of workers employed in manufacturing plants with less than ten employees, whereas Whittington (1984) suggests that 'social factors', particularly a low proportion of home ownership and a high proportion of manual workers, may be more important. These are important issues which, for the future well-being of the Northern Ireland economy need to be investigated in detail. However, for the foreseeable future it is clear that the performance of the regional economy will be dictated by the behaviour of the larger firms (Black 1981; Hart 1983; 1984). Table 11.4 illustrates this point by presenting data on employment change by size of manufacturing establishment in the province over the period 1971–81. Whilst the small establishment category of less than fifty employees was the only one to experience net employment growth, this gain was overshadowed by employment losses in the other size bands, and especially in plants with more than 500 employees. However, rather than pointing to a positive growth in the small manufacturing firm sector, the expansion of employment in small establishments may also reflect the contraction of larger establishments and the planned disintegration of large companies into small units in the face of recession and declining demand (Hart 1983; Shutt and Whittington 1984). This important aspect of small-firm development has hitherto been unexplored, but is clearly relevant in the context of the future activities of small-firm development agencies such as LEDU.

Table 11.4. Employment by size range of manufacturing establishment in Northern Ireland, 1971–81 (SIC Orders 3–19)

Size range	1971		1981		% change 1971–81
	No.	%	No.	%	
1–49	21,381	12.5	22,932	19.6	+0.9
50–99	15,698	9.2	12,646	10.8	−1.8
100–199	23,195	13.5	18,115	15.5	−3.0
200–499	42,053	24.5	26,385	22.6	−9.1
500–999	20,441	11.9	11,360	9.7	−5.3
1,000+	48,762	28.4	25,520	21.8	−3.5
Total	171,530	100.0	116,958	100.0	−31.8

Source: Annual Census of Employment, Department of Economic Development.

Economic impact of civil unrest

In a discussion of Northern Ireland's recent economic development, we cannot avoid a consideration of the extent to which civil unrest and terrorism in the post-1968 era have been a contributory factor in the region's poor performance. Several authors have attempted to answer this question in terms of the number of jobs foregone as a consequence of the 'troubles' (Moore *et al*. 1978; Rowthorn 1981; Fothergill and Gudgin 1982). Moore *et al*. (1978) suggest that Northern Ireland might have acquired an additional 20,000 manufacturing jobs between 1969 and 1976 but for the 'troubles'. Fothergill and Gudgin (1982) estimate that by 1979 between 20,000 and 25,000 manufacturing jobs had been 'lost' from the province in this way. For the whole decade of the 1970s, Rowthorn's (1981) estimate of job loss in the manufacturing sector is 25,000. The similarity of these three results, derived using somewhat different estimating procedures, may suggest that they offer a realistic estimate of the impact of civil unrest on manufacturing employment in the province. This may be the case, but such shift-share-based estimates are fraught with problems, not least that of estimating what would have happened to employment without civil unrest by extrapolating from past trends. This is very difficult, given the unusually high employment growth-rates in certain manufacturing industries in the province in the 1960s as a result of high rates of corporate expansion and reorganization in the UK and a very active regional policy. It is likely that employment in manufacturing would in any case have declined in the 1970s owing to the world recession and a reduction in interregional mobile investment. Nevertheless, it seems intuitively reasonable to suggest that the 'troubles' also caused a substantial loss of manufacturing jobs.

This loss would have resulted only to a minor degree from the actual bombing of premises (Davies and McGurnaghan 1975) and far more from the cancellation, and perhaps diversion to other areas, of projects which under more normal circumstances would have located in the province. These cancellations may have included establishments which would have been entirely new to the province and expansions of those already in existence. The 'troubles' therefore must be seen as severely damaging the image of the province to the point where, despite a very generous ID package of financial incentives, it became almost impossible to attract any new investment from outside (Black 1981; Hoare 1981; Harrison 1982). This was particularly true with respect to new investment from North America, as can be seen from Figure 11.6. After 1969 a dramatic fall of new American openings took place in Northern Ireland, while investment from this area continued to form a major element of industrial development in the Republic of Ireland (Bull *et al*. 1982).

As a direct consequence of a reduction of new industrial investment in Northern Ireland in the 1970s, the construction industry generated fewer jobs than might otherwise have been expected. In addition, despite repair work on bomb-damaged property, the social upheavals associated with the civil unrest severely restricted the house-building programme in the public sector, which also resulted in fewer jobs in the construction trades. However, the industry to suffer most from the very negative image of the province in the 1970s was tourism. Employment in the hotel and catering industry in Northern Ireland fell by 27 per cent between 1968 and 1974, compared with an increase of 28 per cent in Great Britain (Davies *et al*. 1977). Compensating in part for many of the jobs lost in the secondary and tertiary sectors of the province, civil unrest resulted in the creation of up to 12,000 new jobs in the security industry during the 1970s, as well as approximately 3,000 jobs in various public agencies dealing with the social and economic consequences of the conflict (Rowthorn 1981). When all sectors of the Northern Ireland economy are taken into account, Rowthorn estimated that the 'troubles' resulted in a net loss of approximately 23,750 jobs in the province during the 1970s. If these jobs had indeed come into existence then, all other things being equal, the number unemployed in Northern Ireland in 1980 would have been reduced by over 25 per cent. Thus one most conclude that the 'troubles' have had a substantial negative impact on the development of the Northern Ireland economy.

Conclusion

Using a series of different indicators of regional economic success, this chapter began by demonstrating the extremely disadvantaged nature of Northern Ireland within the UK. To some degree in recognition of this situation, public expenditure per capita in the province increased substantially, in both absolute and relative terms, during the 1970s and early 1980s. During the period 1974–84 large increases in public financial support took place in social security, housing, health, education, and the police. However, over the same period, expenditure on industry, energy, and employment fell by 25 per cent. Given Northern Ireland's chronic unemployment problem, such a reduction in this area of government expenditure is extremely worrying. It could be argued that such a reduction represented a realistic assessment of the likelihood of securing investment from outside the province at this time. However, given the low annual cost per job of ID-promoted jobs compared with other forms of publicly funded employment, it should have been possible to switch resources more towards local businesses of all sizes, and perhaps even to the service trades. It may well be that Northern Ireland has traditionally possessed very low levels of entrepreneurship, but there is no evidence to suggest that the local potential for new-business generation has been exhausted. In the view of the NIEC (1984*a*:30), between 1974 and 1984 industrial development in Northern Ireland was not 'effectively prosecuted', at a time when industrial development in the province's nearest neighbour, the Republic of Ireland, was given top priority, and when Northern Ireland was suffering the additional disadvantage of civil unrest.

Throughout the 1950s and especially during the 1960s, Northern Ireland benefited substantially from new ID-assisted manufacturing capacity, which helped to a large degree to offset employment losses in many of the traditional industries of the area such as clothing, textiles, and shipbuilding. Unfortunately, throughout the 1970s and early 1980s the province struggled, unsuccessfully in many cases, to keep the ID-assisted industry generated in earlier years, and to attract new investment to the area. Most certainly there was no sign of the self-sustaining regional economic growth that a number of regional economic reports had earlier suggested might be stimulated by such external investment. Part of the loss of ID-assisted capacity and employment may be accounted for by the recessions of the last fifteen years. However, as Simpson (1984) has intimated, the loss has been too great to permit such a straightforward explanation. It appears that there has been almost a systematic preference on the part of businesses since 1970 to close capacity in Northern Ireland as part of corporate rationalization and restructuring. The negative image of the province generated by the 'troubles' may also be part of the explanation. A further cause may be that much of the ID-assisted capacity established in the 1960s was truly marginal to many corporate needs and was therefore closed very rapidly in the international economic crises of the 1970s, resulting in a greater than expected employment contraction in the province. In the 1970s and 1980s, therefore, many of the ID-assisted businesses established in earlier years have added to the problem they were initially supposed to help overcome.

Although the number of employees in employment continues to fall, the rate of loss in 1984 and 1985 became much slower than in the early 1980s. In addition, there are currently some positive signs in the regional economy, including growth in manufacturing output, and a number of manufacturing industries, including even shipbuilding, reporting relatively favourable future prospects and growing order-books. However, because of the supply-side conditions in the labour market, these developments will make no impact on the growing number of unemployed people in the province. An end to the 'troubles' would of course begin to encourage new investment in Northern Ireland, especially from outside the province. However, even if this did occur, the restoration of the image and attractiveness of Northern Ireland to its immediate pre-1968 status would take many years. In the shorter term, therefore, unless there is a marked change in the apparent low priority given to employment generation and the stimulation of economic activity—and there has been no evidence of such a change in recent financial statements for the province—the dole queue in Northern Ireland will get longer and the level of socioeconomic ill health will become progressively worse.

References

Black, W. (1981), 'The Effects of the Recession on the Economy of Northern Ireland', *The Irish Banking Review*, December issue, 16–23.

Bull, P. J. (1984*a*), 'Employment Location Trends in Northern Ireland, 1959–1978, with Particular Reference to Rural Areas. In P. M. Jess, J. V. Greer, R. H. Buchanan, and W. J. Armstrong, eds., *Planning and Development in Rural Areas*, Belfast, Queen's University.

—— (1984*b*), 'The Impact of Government Policy on Industrial Diversification: The Northern Ireland Case', in B. M. Barr and N. M. Waters, eds., *Regional Diversification and Structural Change*, Vancouver, Tantalus Research.

——, Harrison, R. T., and Hart, M. (1982), 'Government Assisted Manufacturing Activity in a Peripheral Area of the UK: Northern Ireland', in L. Collins, ed., *Industrial Decline and Regeneration*, Edinburgh, University of Edinburgh

Busteed, M. A. (1974), *Northern Ireland*. Oxford, Oxford University Press.

—— (1976), 'Small-scale Economic Development in Northern Ireland', *Scottish Geographical Magazine* 3, 172–181.

Caldwell, J. and Greer, J. (1984), 'Physical Planning for Rural Areas in Northern Ireland', in P. M. Jess, J. V. Greer, R. H. Buchanan, and W. J. Armstrong, eds., *Planning and Development in Rural Areas*, Belfast, Queen's University.

Cooley, A. (1976), 'Approaches to Encouraging Small Indigenous Industrial Development' in R. Clubley, ed., *Indigenous Industrial Development*, Aycliffe and Peterlee Development Corporation.

Davies, R. and McGurnaghan, M. A. (1975), 'Northern Ireland: The Economics of Adversity', *National Westminster Bank Quarterly Review*, May issue, 56–68.

——, ——, and Sams, K. I. (1977), 'The Northern Ireland Economy: Progress (1968–75) and Prospects', *Regional Studies* 11, 297–307.

Fothergill, S. and Gudgin, G. (1982), *Unequal Growth*, London, Heinemann.

Harrison, R. T. (1982), 'Assisted Industry, Employment Stability and Industrial Decline: Some Evidence from Northern Ireland', *Regional Studies* 16, 267–85.

—— (1983), 'Industrial Development Policy and the Restructuring of the Northern Ireland Economy', paper presented at the Anglo-Canadian symposium in industrial geography in Calgary, Canada. Mimeo,

—— (1986), 'Industrial Development Policy and the Restructuring of the Northern Ireland Economy', *Environment and Planning C; Government and Policy* 4, 53–70.

—— and Hart, M. (1983), 'Factors Influencing New Business Formation: A Case Study of Northern Ireland', *Environment and Planning A* 15, 1395–412.

Hart, M. (1983), 'The Small Firm Entrepreneur: An Analysis of his Role in the Belfast Urban Economy', paper presented to the SSRC Urban and Regional Economics Seminar Group, Belfast.

—— (1984), 'Local Agencies and Small Firm Formation: The Case of Northern Ireland,

1971–1981'. In B. M. Barr and N. M. Waters, eds., *Regional Diversification and Structural Change*, Vancouver, Tantalus Research.

Harvey, S. and Rea, D. (1982), *The Northern Ireland economy with particular reference to industrial development*, Newtownabbey, Ulster Polytechnic Innovation and Resource Centre.

Hoare, A. G. (1981), 'Why They Go Where They Go: The Political Imagery of Industrial Location', *Transactions of the Institute of British Geographers*, n.s. 6, 152–75.

—— (1982), 'Problem Region and Regional Problem', In F. W. Boal and J. N. Douglas, eds., *Integration and Division: Geographical Perspectives on the Northern Ireland Problem*, London, Academic Press.

—— (1983), *The Location of Industry in Britain*, Cambridge, Cambridge University Press.

Isles, K. S. and Cuthbert, N. (1957), *An Economic Survey of Northern Ireland*, Belfast, HMSO.

Keeble, D., Owens, P. L., and Thompson, C. (1982), 'Regional Accessibility and Economic Potential in the European Community', *Regional Studies* 16, 419–31.

Lloyd, P. E. and Reeve, D. E. (1982), 'Recession, Restructuring and Location: A Study of Employment Trends in North West England 1971–1977', *North West Industry Research Unit Working Paper* no. 11, Manchester, School of Geography, University of Manchester.

Local Enterprise Development Unit (1983), *Annual Report*, Belfast, LEDU.

Moore, B., Rhodes, J., and Tarling, R. (1978), 'Industrial Policy and Economic Development: The Experience of Northern Ireland and the Republic of Ireland', *Cambridge Journal of Economics* 2, 99–114

Murie, A. S., Birrell, W. D., Roche, D. J. D., and Hillyard, P. A. R. (1969), 'Regional Planning and the Attraction of Manufacturing Industry in Northern Ireland', *Research Paper no. 4*, London, Centre for Environmental Studies.

Northern Ireland Development Programme, 1970–75 (1970), Belfast, HMSO.

Northern Ireland Economic Council (1983*a*), 'Economic Strategy: Historical Growth Performance', *Report* no. 38, Belfast.

—— (1983*b*), 'The Duration of Industrial Development Assisted Employment', *Report* no. 40, Belfast.

—— (1983*c*), *Annual Report 1982–83*, *Report* no. 39, Belfast.

—— (1984*a*), 'Public Expenditure Priorities: Overall Review', *Report* no. 42, Belfast.

—— (1984*b*) *Annual Report 1983–84*, *Report* no. 44, Belfast.

—— (1984*c*), 'Submission to the Government Review of Standard Capital Grants', *Paper* no. 7, Belfast.

O'Dowd, L., Rolston, B., and Tomlinson, M. (1980), *Northern Ireland: Between Civil Rights and Civil War*, London, CSE Books.

Quigley Report (1976), *Economic and Industrial Strategy for Northern Ireland: Report of a Review Team*, Belfast, HMSO.

Rowthorn, R. E. (1981), Northern Ireland: An Economy in Crisis', *Cambridge Journal of Economics* 5, 1–31.

Shutt, J. and Whittington, R. C. (1984), 'Large Firm Strategies and the Rise of Small Units: The Illusion of Small Firm Job Generation'. *North West Industry Research Unit Working Paper* no. 15, Manchester, School of Geography, University of Manchester.

Simpson, J. V. (1984), 'An Investigation into the Employment Generated by New Industry Locating in Northern Ireland, 1951–80', paper presented to the Statistical and Social Enquiry Society of Ireland, Belfast. Mimeo.

Singleton, D. ed. (1983), 'Aspects of Housing Policy and Practice in Northern Ireland',

Occasional Paper in Planning 3, Belfast, Department of Town and Country Planning, Queen's University.

Storey, D. (1982), *Entrepreneurship and the New Firm*, Beckenham, Croom Helm.

Whittington, R. C. (1984), 'Regional Bias in New Firm Formation in the UK', *Regional Studies* 18, 253–6.

Wilson Report (1965), *Economic Development in Northern Ireland*, Cmnd. 479, Belfast, HMSO.

CHAPTER 12

Public Policy for Regional Development: Restoration or Reformation?

P. J. Damesick and P. A. Wood

In October '36
They took a trip,
The men who made the ships,
Searching for some kind of salvation. (. . .)

March on, Marshall Riley's army,
Marching for your rights, you've surely earned them.
March on, Marshall Riley's army,
The lessons that you taught us, who has learned them?

Song 'Marshall Riley's Army', Alan Hull (1978),
from the Lindisfarne album, 'Back and Fourth'

During the 1970s both support for the established form of regional policy and its practical scope were undermined by the widespread impact of manufacturing decline and rising unemployment, and the dwindling supply of mobile investment. Two factors, however, favoured retention of regional policy in some form. The first was continuing party political pressure to be seen to be responding to the sense of grievance and the social needs associated with regional economic disparities. The second was the fact that the UK had to maintain a system of Assisted Areas in order to draw on EEC funds for regional development. In the changes of 1976–7, 1979, and 1984, therefore, Labour and Conservative governments eschewed formal abandonment of regional policy, concentrating instead on reducing the cost of such a policy and, in the 1984 revision, attempting to make it more cost-effective by linking a lower level of expenditure more closely to job generation.

For the present, therefore, regional industrial policy lives on in a muted version of its former self. The broader conception of regional economic planning, on the lines of the 1960s model or as advocated in some regional plans of the 1970s, no longer has a place in the management of change in the UK space economy. Interventions in regional and local economic development have nonetheless proliferated, moving away from centrally administered regional policy into other channels, often with a more localized focus and a greater degree of decentralized initiative. This shift is reflected in the continued support for regional-level agencies in Scotland, Wales, and Northern Ireland, in the administration of the urban programme, and, most prominently, in local authority economic initiatives.

Earlier chapters have shown that the reasons for disillusionment with traditional regional policy have differed between central government and regional and local levels. Central government cut spending on regional policy after 1979 to serve its overriding aim of reducing public expenditure, but also because the existing policy was inefficient in terms of the cost per job created, and the economic case for trying to reduce regional disparities had been weakened, it was thought, by high unemployment generally. Government found, however, that as fast as the map of regional assistance was rolled back, pressures grew to find new ways of responding to economic problems and emergencies in particular localities. Hence, a whole string of new agencies and initiatives came to be added to the spatial policy armoury—Urban Development Corporations, expansion of the urban programme through Urban Development Grants, the designation of a second batch of Enterprise Zones only twelve months after the first 'experimental' eleven, the Merseyside Task Force, NCB (Enterprise) Ltd to help coal closure areas, Freeports, and City Action Teams.

At the regional and local levels, there was also concern over the effectiveness of regional policy, but here the most powerful criticisms centred on the apparent insensitivity of blanket aid programmes to the needs and problems of particular areas. These programmes were also poorly co-ordinated with other policies on industry, public spending, and local government that were undermining regional employment. Thus, for example, as earlier chapters have documented, in regions like Wales, the North, and Yorkshire and Humberside, regional aid was seen as wholly inadequate to counterbalance the impact of contraction in nationalized industries. In the conurbations the squeeze on local-authority spending negated gains from the urban programme. In the North, there was also evident frustration at central government's refusal to follow the advice offered in the 1977 Regional Strategy that regional development policy should embrace a wide range of regionally relevant public expenditure. Likewise, in the West Midlands, it is argued that regional representations to central government about the underlying problems of the area's economy in the 1970s and early 1980s fell on deaf ears, until too late.

While regional perceptions of the inadequacies and contradictions of spatial policy are stressed by several of our contributors, a rather more positive note on the role of regional policy is sounded in the chapter on Scotland. Although serious economic problems persist in Scotland, there is evidence that regional policy has less obviously failed in this region than in some others; indeed, the development of a Scottish electronics industry ranks among the more notable successes. The lesson from the Scottish case appears to be that regional policy can only achieve this measure of success when applied consistently and vigorously over the long term, and when it is supported by other favourable circumstances. The special case of Northern Ireland is a salutary reminder of the limited effectiveness of even a very intensive policy effort in inherently unfavourable circumstances. In Scotland, the impact of North Sea oil must of course be taken into account, but equally, it possessed an administrative structure which may have been conducive to a more coherent approach to regional problems than in certain English regions. Moreover, the office of the Scottish Secretary of State has provided an influential channel for communicating the region's needs to central government.

The presence of a regional development agency is another feature of the Scottish (and Welsh) policy framework that has attracted considerable attention in some English regions. It seems widely accepted that the SDA and the WDA are valuable vehicles for promoting economic regeneration in their respective regions. However, it is worth asking what functions these agencies perform that could not be handled by local authorities, equipped with similar powers and resources. Cameron (1985) has attempted to assess the relative merits of local authorities and regional development agencies in this respect, concluding that the advantage lies with regional agencies principally for major-firm rescue operations, the retention of local ownership in key companies, and promoting the growth of new sectors. Cameron considers that, in these cases, an agency approach allows an appropriate level of resources and expertise to be deployed, and avoids the dangers of duplication of effort and competitive subsidization. Even here, however, the merits of an agency solution might be less if the requisite powers and resources were vested in large strategic authorities. Cameron's view still leaves a substantial range of development agency activity—the SDA's role in urban renewal and in its area initiatives, for example—which could be carried out by local authorities if the necessary resources were put at their disposal. Indeed, most of the SDA's resources are devoted to activities on which there has recently been a large increase in expenditure in England through the urban programme.

Existing regional development agencies are the creatures of central government, reflecting its reluctance to put resources directly in the hands of local authorities. Through their semblance of devolved initiative, the agencies allow the centre to influence spatial policy priorities at arm's length. This mode of intervention has been deployed and sustained in Scotland and Wales essentially because of its advantages, from central government's viewpoint, as a way of responding to well-articulated regional interests there, rather than because it is intrinsically superior to alternative arrangements. Where government has not felt the need to allow a greater degree of decentralization to regional or local levels of decision-making, it has shown no compunction in imposing its own policy solutions on particular areas over the heads of local authorities, as in the establishment of Urban Development Corporations in London and Liverpool.

This is not to deny that, as things stand, the development agencies in Scotland and Wales provide a valuable capacity for policy initiatives to be tailored to the particular problems and opportunities of those regions, and 'for the creative investment of public funds in ways which are less obvious within "normal" government departments' (Cameron 1985: 11). Conversely, local efforts to develop such a capacity in the English conurbations were undermined by the decision, largely on political grounds, to abolish the metropolitan authorities. The crucial mistake in spatial economic policy in the early to mid-1980s may come to be seen, not in the reduction in regional aid itself, but in the failure of central government to support regional and local economic initiatives consistently on a wider scale.

The loss of the metropolitan counties will be a major blow to the regions involved on several counts, both technical and political. For example, some of the most significant innovations in local economic development policy and procedure may disappear with their parent authorities after 1986. Several English regions will certainly lose a major component of their political voice, and hence the ability, as it has developed since 1974, to make effective representations to central government; their capacity to utilize EEC funds may also be impaired. Local authorities' efforts to develop region-wide forums for consideration of strategic planning issues, to fill the gap left by abolition of the Economic Planning Councils and central government's withdrawal from regional planning, will also be severely hampered by removal of the metropolitan authorities.

A major reason for the failure during the 1980s to develop a convincing framework of policy responses to regional and local economic problems was the increasingly uneasy relationship between central and local government. The willingness of local authorities across the country to increase their involvement in the economic development of their areas has largely been met with indifference or hostility from central government. The 1983 White Paper on regional industrial development simply did not consider whether certain local initiatives could be beneficially supported by, or perhaps integrated with, regional policy measures. Yet, in proposing a greater emphasis on selective rather than automatic assistance, and in advocating the promotion of indigenous development and new and small businesses, the White Paper charted a direction for regional policy which logically should have involved more decentralized initiatives and greater responsiveness to local conditions. The detailed local intelligence and practical experience developed within many local authorities and their agencies could be invaluable to such a regional policy. Instead, the White Paper seemed to assume that 'remote control' from Whitehall, perhaps with a slightly expanded role for the DTI's regional offices, would be adequate to the task.

There are two principal reasons why central government chose not to build more upon the efforts of local authorities in the spatial policy revisions after 1979. One is that it did not regard local authorities as suitable agencies for economic regeneration. Obviously, authorities vary in their competence in this field, and many smaller authorities have the expertise and resources for only limited intervention. The removal of the most powerful local authorities from the English conurbations is thus all the more regrettable. This, however, points to the second reason; where local authorities were in fact able to undertake more ambitious forms of economic intervention, this frequently conflicted with the Conservative Government's own economic philosophy, with its emphasis on market-led adjustment and recovery. Indeed, local economic initiatives undertaken by Labour-controlled authorities in, for example, Greater London, the West Midlands, and Sheffield were explicitly intended to demonstrate that there was an alternative to central government's approach. Even sympathetic observers of these types of initiatives, aimed at 'restructuring for labour rather than capital', have admitted that they could have only a very limited impact in terms of job creation or preservation, given the resources available for them. Their real importance lies in the ideological sphere, in that with each success, however small (and most have been), they served as exemplars of the type of policy that could be applied to much greater effect on a larger, including a national, scale (Duncan and Goodwin 1985).

However, it is not only Labour-controlled authorities in declining urban areas which have found cause to challenge the Government's preference for market-based solutions. In the South East outside London, this preference has run into direct conflict with pressures from its own supporters for firm adherence to Green Belt and other policies of planning restraint. The Government's desire to see planning policies become more accommodating to the demands of private house-builders and industrial and commercial developers is thus not shared at the local level in many areas of the South East, where the primary interest is in preserving the existing environment. A philosophy of 'letting the market decide' can be as politically unacceptable in relatively prosperous areas of the country as in the more obviously disadvantaged regions.

The case of South East England emphasizes the need for regional planning to reconcile the demands of the economy and the environment. In a wider context, also, it demonstrates that the issue of regional disparities involves the longer-term national economic interest. Over-concentration of growth and development pressures within the South East would not only create problems within the region in the long term, but would also have adverse effects on less favoured areas. The further concentration of the nation's qualified manpower, together with the more advanced and innovative sectors of the economy, in southern England would reduce the capacity for indigenous development and successful adjustment in other regions. A failure to counter trends towards growing regional imbalance could mean that, over the longer term, national economic success becomes precariously dependent on the continued dynamism of the 'core' region of the South East, while other regions are increasingly 'peripheralized', being relegated to competition with lower-wage countries for routine production.

It is likely that spatial policy, and the related issues of devolution and the structure of subnational government, will be on the political agenda again in the late 1980s. Evidence assembled in earlier chapters points to the pressures for change in the UK policy framework for tackling 'regional problems', in the widest sense of that term. Despite the diversity of regional situations and experience analysed by our contributors, and their differences of approach, there appears to be a degree of convergence on the minimum requirements for such a policy framework.

The first of these requirements is to break with traditionally compartmentalized views of the role of the state in regional and urban development. The 1983 White Paper on regional policy rightly stated that regional and local economic development is affected by a wide range of central and local government policies, but it failed to follow through the implications of this fact. The Inner

City Partnerships were of course intended to overcome problems in urban renewal created by the horizontal and vertical divisions in responsibility and resource allocation within central and local government. Their limited success reflected a failure to overcome organizational inertia in mainstream resource allocation, and to counterbalance the overall priority given to reducing public spending. Similarly, regional industrial policy and any revived form of regional planning cannot achieve their objectives if they do not work in concert with, or are vitiated by, other, often ostensibly non-spatial, policies.

Second, policy responses to problems of regional and local economic development need to be set within a framework of regional strategic thinking and planning. Examples to support the case for a regional-scale perspective range from the need to develop a coherent planning response to the development pressures associated with the M25 in the South East to the futility of treating the problems of declining inner cities in isolation from the larger urban regions of which they are an integral part. There is, of course, the thorny issue of how to arrive at an effective administrative or organizational basis for regional planning. The removal of the metropolitan counties from the administrative map seems likely to create both the need and the opportunity to look again at the planning arrangements in the largest urban regions in England. Local authorities in several regions have already sought to enhance their capacity for region-wide monitoring/consultative exercises, through 'standing conferences' or other arrangements. For the present, these form the obvious basis on which to build attempts to co-ordinate planning policies, and to promote common regional interests in employment and economic development.

This points to the third requirement—that regions should be able to press their claims forcefully upon central government. The co-ordinated campaign by the Northern consortium of local authorities during the Stansted Inquiry obviously failed in its main objective, but it did succeed in broadening the debate over airports policy into one where regional needs had to be considered alongside the siting of expanded facilities for London. Other national policy debates similarly need to be opened up to include explicit attention to the regional dimension. The initiative for this must lie with the regions, since past experience shows that the centre takes note of regional interests only when it has to. The element of advantage of the three 'national' regions in this respect, with a Minister to speak on their behalf, should not be over-stressed, but the evidence suggests that advice and representations from the English regions need to find more effective channels of communication to Whitehall and Westminster.

The fourth requirement is a more decentralized approach to policy implementation, building, where appropriate, 'from the bottom up' and allowing greater scope for a selective targeting of assistance which is sensitive to the particular circumstances, problems, and opportunities of different areas and of different groups within areas. This applies not only to economic development measures as such, but also to policies to deal with the social consequences of economic restructuring and high unemployment that some areas will have to cope with well into the foreseeable future. While adequate national systems of welfare support are obviously crucial, it is perhaps only through more local initiative and involvement in various forms of social 'self-help' strategies that some communities will find ways of coming to terms with a persistent shortage of full-time, well-paid, and secure jobs.

These then are four basic requirements which, our review suggests, need to be incorporated in arrangements for the management of regional growth and decline in the UK: abandonment of narrow conceptions of government's role in regional development; a framework of regional strategic thinking and planning; more effective channels of communication between regions and central government; and greater scope and support for devolved initiatives. There is nothing particularly new or radical in these ideas; much informed opinion has pointed in similar directions over recent years. Equally, there are no panaceas here to the large, enduring, and complex problems which beset many areas of the UK. There is only one message that, if policy-makers were to take seriously the lessons of past experience, there is clearly room for improvement. This is not simply a call for reviving, in some more vigorous and consistent form, regional planning and policy approaches that have been tried in the past. Our review of the experience of the last twenty years points to basic principles which were inadequately reflected in earlier policy approaches. These remain valid, but they now need to be adapted in practice to fit the changed economic conditions of the late 1980s and 1990s. The presently enfeebled state of regional planning and policy provides both motive and opportunity for a fresh start, with new initiatives appropriate to these changed conditions.

References

Cameron, G. (1985), 'Regional Economic Planning—The End of the Line?', *Planning Outlook* 28, 8–13.

Duncan, S. S., and Goodwin, M. (1985), 'The Local State and Local Economic Policy: Why the Fuss?', *Policy and Politics* 13, 227–53.

INDEX